SPORT COMMUNICATION

Sport is a global business. Now more than ever, sport communication professionals need to understand sport's global reach in order to develop their full potential. This is the first textbook to introduce the fundamental principles and practice of sport communication from an international perspective. Combining business strategies with insights into social issues such as gender, disability, and national identity, this is an accessible, practical, and engaging guide to the essentials of sport communication.

Aimed to enhance learning at both undergraduate and postgraduate levels, each chapter contains special features tailored to meet the needs of students and instructors. These include learning objectives, chapter summaries, activities, reflections, discussion questions, recommended resource lists, and original cross-cultural case studies that demonstrate sport communication theories put into practice. Its twenty chapters explore communication in sport across all levels, from interpersonal communication and team building to strategic communications, and in all forms of media, from print and broadcast to social media.

Sport Communication: An International Approach is an essential text for any course on sport communication, sport business or sport management.

Chuka Onwumechili is Professor of Strategic, Legal and Management Communication at Howard University in Washington, D.C., USA. Alongside his role as Department Chair, he is Editor-in-Chief of *The Howard Journal of Communications*, a position he assumed in September 2014. He has authored, co-authored, and co-edited ten books, including most recently *Identity and Nation in African Football: Fans, Community and Clubs*. He has also published in several peer-reviewed academic journals. His research interests currently focus on football and communication, particularly as it intersects with the African continent.

SPORT COMMUNICATION

AN INTERNATIONAL APPROACH

CHUKA ONWUMECHILI

LONDON AND NEW YORK

First published 2018
by Routledge
2 Park Square, Milton Park, Abingdon, Oxon OX14 4RN

and by Routledge
711 Third Avenue, New York, NY 10017

Routledge is an imprint of the Taylor & Francis Group, an informa business

© 2018 Chuka Onwumechili

The right of Chuka Onwumechili to be identified as author of this work has been asserted by him in accordance with sections 77 and 78 of the Copyright, Designs and Patents Act 1988.

All rights reserved. No part of this book may be reprinted or reproduced or utilised in any form or by any electronic, mechanical, or other means, now known or hereafter invented, including photocopying and recording, or in any information storage or retrieval system, without permission in writing from the publishers.

Trademark notice: Product or corporate names may be trademarks or registered trademarks, and are used only for identification and explanation without intent to infringe.

British Library Cataloguing-in-Publication Data
A catalogue record for this book is available from the British Library

Library of Congress Cataloging-in-Publication Data
Names: Onwumechili, Chuka, author.
Title: Sport communication : an international
    approach / Chuka Onwumechili.
Description: Abingdon, Oxon ; New York, NY : Routledge, [2018] |
    Includes bibliographical references and index.
Identifiers: LCCN 2017013926 | ISBN 9781138281868 (hbk) |
    ISBN 9781138281875 (pbk) | ISBN 9781315270920 (ebk)
Subjects: LCSH: Communication in sports. | Mass media and sports.
Classification: LCC GV567.5 .O69 2018 | DDC 070.4/49796—dc23
LC record available at https://lccn.loc.gov/2017013926

ISBN: 978-1-138-28186-8 (hbk)
ISBN: 978-1-138-28187-5 (pbk)
ISBN: 978-1-315-27092-0 (ebk)

Typeset in Melior
by Apex CoVantage, LLC

Printed and bound by CPI Group (UK) Ltd, Croydon, CR0 4YY

I dedicate this book to my parents, Professor Cyril Onwumechili and Mrs. Cecilia Onwumechili, along with my wife, Adora, and children, Chiamaka, Kamso, and Kaodinna, who all encouraged me as I worked on this book for months. I love them and wish the best for each one of them.

CONTENTS

Preface	xiii
Acknowledgments	xvii

1 Studying communication and sport	**1**
Learning objectives	1
Understanding sport	2
Communication	3
Communication and sport: an international approach	4
Why study communication and sport?	5
Case: grassroots sport and facing up to culture	8
Careers in sport communication	9
Part I Communicating sport	**17**
2 Interpersonal communication and sport	**19**
Learning objectives	19
Defining interpersonal communication	20
Goals of interpersonal communication	21
Culture's impact	22
The self and its presentation	22
The other and perception	24
Interpersonal situations in communication and sport	26
3 Communicating leadership in sport teams and organizations	**37**
Learning objectives	37
Leadership communication	37
Leadership approaches and styles	40
Case: leading in a tough and demotivating environment	46

Climate and culture: leadership impact	48
Power and leadership in sport	50
How successful sport personalities communicate leadership	51
Developing leadership	52

4 Strategic communication in sport — 57
- Learning objectives — 57
- Issues of persuasion — 58
- Building a sport organizational image and brand — 62
- Cultivating strong media relations — 63
- Community relations — 67
- Managing athlete communication — 67
- Case: facing a challenge to image and brand — 68
- A template for strategic sport communication — 70

5 Traditional media — 75
- Learning objectives — 75
- Defining traditional media — 75
- Interdependence between professional sport and traditional media — 76
- Newspapers — 78
- Magazines — 80
- Radio — 81
- Television — 83
- Growth and impact of transnational media — 84
- Case: transnational television confronts tradition — 86
- Sport media and communication strategies — 88

6 New media — 93
- Learning objectives — 93
- Characteristics of new media — 95
- Types of new media — 97
- Functions of new media — 100
- New media and change in sport consumption — 102
- Case: new media and Chinese swimmer broach taboo subject — 103

Part II Audience and diversity — 109

7 The fan — 111
- Learning objectives — 111
- Who is a fan? — 111
- Types of sport fans — 112
- Ways in which sport fans are motivated — 113
- Methods fans use to consume sport communication — 116

	How fans demonstrate identity and practice rituals	116
	Case: Serena makes her day	120
	How sporting organizations cultivate fan groups	122
	Dysfunctional and violent behavior among fans	125
8	**Disability and sport**	**129**
	Learning objectives	129
	Defining disability in sport	129
	The issue of ableism	131
	Media coverage	132
	What wheelchair athletes think about media coverage	134
	Case: ableism in sport faces challenge	135
	Using new media	137
	The Paralympics	139
	Oscar Pistorius, media communication, and sport	140
	The Norwegian example	140
9	**Gender, race, and ethnicity**	**144**
	Learning objectives	144
	Gender and sport communication	145
	Race and sport communication	149
	Case: an American university faces budget cuts	151
	Ethnicity and sport communication	153
	Policy regulations	155
10	**Nationalism, culture, and identity**	**160**
	Learning objectives	160
	Nationalism	161
	Case: nationalism reigns as Pakistan meets India in cricket	165
	Issues of identity in sport	168
	Impact of culture on sport and communication	171
Part III	**Markets and sport as commodity**	**179**
11	**Sport promotion and economics**	**181**
	Learning objectives	181
	Economics of sport promotion	182
	Sport and marketing	186
	Sport promotion	187
	Promotion through advertising	188
	Sport sponsorships and challenges	191
	Branding issues	195
	Case: sponsoring a sporting event in the community	196

12	**The sporting mega event**	**201**
	Learning objectives	201
	Why have mega events grown?	202
	Communication: rationalizing public support for mega events	204
	Increasing resistance	205
	Mega events as media spectacle and globalization	206
	Case: conflict escalates for and against hosting	210
	The IAAF world championship	212
13	**Image and crisis communication**	**216**
	Learning objectives	216
	Sport crisis communication	216
	Preparing for crisis with communication	219
	Confronting crisis	222
	Communication: apologia and prior reputation	226
	Case: cyclist Landis struggles to repair image	227
Part IV	**Special issues in sport communication**	**233**
14	**Sport heroes and celebrities**	**235**
	Learning objectives	235
	The sporting hero	236
	The sporting celebrity: factors and celebrity types	237
	Sport celebrity as product endorser	239
	Case: the celebrity athlete and choices in the future	243
	Examples of sport celebrities	244
15	**Health, sport, and communication**	**252**
	Learning objectives	252
	Health issues in sport	252
	Sport organizations and communicating athlete health	253
	Communicating concussions in sport	256
	Case: American gridiron football and the case of concussion	259
	Media and drug abuse in sport	261
	Epidemics and sport communication	262
16	**Sport fiction, fantasy, and video games**	**268**
	Learning objectives	268
	Introduction	268
	Fantasy sport	269
	Fantasy sport as competitive fandom	270
	Motivation to participate	271
	Fantasy sport communities	272

Case: fantasy, fandom, and sport competition	273
Sport video games (SVGs)	275
Motivation to play SVGs	278
Video game community: FIFA	280
Fantasy sport and SVGs: social impact	281

17 Legal and ethical issues in sport communication — 285

Learning objectives	285
The rights of media in sport	286
The limits of media	287
Public vs. private figures	288
Rights of sport organizers	288
Athletes and rights	290
Copyright and trademark issues	291
Ethical issues	294
Case: Nadal and defamation	294

Part V   Measurement and research in sport — 301

18 Sport analytics — 303

Learning objectives	303
Introduction	303
Attributes of organizations focused on analytics	304
Benefits of analytics	307
Importance of analytics in sport management communications	308
Case: preparing for the championship	309
Importance in media communications	311
Importance in secondary industries	312
Analytics in action	313

19 Theorizing in communication and sport — 318

Learning objectives	318
Introduction to theory	318
Communication theories that apply to sport communication	320

20 Scholarly research — 332

Learning objectives	332
Introduction	332
Qualitative and quantitative research methods in sport	333

Glossary	347
Index	350

PREFACE

Sport communication is a relatively new field of academic study indicated by the fact that few books are available to students who are interested in the field. However, there is little doubt that interest in studying sport communication is on the rise, with many students undertaking study in the area, several higher education institutions introducing degrees and courses on the subject, and an increasing number of academic journals being established to serve scholars in the field who investigate several aspects of sport communication.

Despite demonstrated interests in the subject, books from an international approach are rare. *Sport Communication: An International Approach* is a textbook designed to provide this important approach in an increasingly globalized world. The text is also designed for cross use by both undergraduate and graduate students. It is essentially an introductory text that surveys much of the field covering sport communication in today's world. In addition, it includes theoretical and research applications that are of interest to students at the graduate level. Importantly, it is truly an international text, as it draws principles and practices from across the world.

ORGANIZATION OF THE TEXT

The text has 20 chapters that address diverse issues in international sport communication. Fundamentally, the text is divided into five major parts. The first includes chapters that address basic communication contexts and channels in the field of sport, and the second part pays attention to consumers or audience for sport communication. The third part has chapters that address issues of sport as commodity and related issues. The fourth part combines several issues, varied at times, but pertinent to sport communication in today's world. The final part is in three chapters addressing research and measurement of sport communication.

The introductory chapter exists outside of the five parts of the text. It focuses on making a case for the study of sport and communication from an international perspective. It does this by first providing a clear understanding of key terms and concepts before presenting reasons why studying the field has become increasingly important. This introductory chapter closes by identifying a variety of careers in the field in order to support students who may wish to practice.

Part 1 of the text, which addresses basic communication contexts and channels in sport, includes five chapters. The opening chapter, Chapter 2, is on interpersonal communication and sport. It begins by identifying interpersonal communication goals of different individuals and how culture impacts those goals and differentiates goals between or amongst different persons. Key sections of this chapter also describe both sides of interpersonal communication (i.e. the self and the other).

Chapter 3 is on leadership communication, providing detailed discussions of leadership styles and approaches. Importantly, the chapter answers questions on how climate, culture, and power associate with leadership. The next chapter looks at how sport communication messages may be designed for strategic effect. This important chapter identifies ways to design persuasive messages, how sporting organizations build image and brand, and how such organizations create strong and effective relations with the media and community while managing athletes' communication. The final two chapters of Part 1 address types of communication media used in reaching consumers. The first is traditional media, which constitute legacy print media like newspapers and magazines, and broadcast media like radio and television. Additionally, it also notes that other traditional media are used in places like Africa. Each medium is discussed in terms of how it may be used to communicate sport to consumers. One of the sections in this chapter notes the increasing presence of media transnationalism. The final chapter on new media notes how these types of media differ from traditional ones and their impact on consumers. Several new media are also described at length.

Part 2 on sport communication consumers consists of four chapters. The first, Chapter 7, is on fans, which are differentiated from spectators. This chapter provides descriptions of fans and what they do, how they are motivated, and methods they use to consume sport communication. Next is a chapter on persons experiencing disabilities. Persons with able bodies often assume their superiority in sport skills over those who are experiencing disabilities. However, this chapter demonstrates that this ableist view could be incorrect. Nevertheless, ableist views permeate and influence communication of sport for those experiencing disabilities. Chapter 9 is on gender, race, and ethnicity. It is a chapter that exposes biases in communicating sport. These biases include gender, race, and ethnicity and cover a large area of how sport is communicated to consumers. The final chapter in Part 2, Chapter 10, is on nationalism, culture, and identity. It follows the lead of the previous chapter by examining issues that divide consumers of sport. In this case, it demonstrates the existence and projection of separate nationalism in sport and shows how culture impacts sport communication and various types of identities in sport.

Part 3 of the text views sport communication from the perspective of sport as a commodity, and it has three chapters. Chapter 11 focuses on issues of marketing promotion and economics. This chapter analyzes different ways that sport has been turned into a commodity and the building of close relationships between sport and the business world. The next chapter, Chapter 12, on sporting mega events, touches on similar issues but from the lens of events that bring sporting consumers together from all over the world. The chapter stresses the importance of global media in making mega sporting events notable and the economics that make it possible. The final chapter in Part 3, Chapter 13, is on image and crisis communication. At first glance, this chapter may appear out of place in Part 3, but on close examination, it shows that concern about image and crisis are intricately linked to the significance of revenue in sport and the adverse effects that can come from the loss of image. The chapter points to how organizations prepare for such adverse crisis and how to counter them when they occur.

Special issues in sport communication form Part 4 of the text and include four chapters, from Chapters 14 to 17. Chapters in Part 4 are topically potpourri, yet each one is essential, focusing on an issue that is significant in today's sport communication. The first one, Chapter 14, is on sporting heroes and celebrities. This chapter notes how sport heroes and celebrities are created and/or accentuated by the media. Importantly, it notes how media use sports celebrities to sell products. The chapter on health, sport, and communication, Chapter 15, looks at recent health issues in sport broken into three types and how athletes and sporting organizations communicate those health issues. Chapter 16 focuses on sport fiction, discussing fantasy sport and sport video games, which are increasingly important in the world of sport and are increasingly discussed in sport media. The last chapter, Chapter 17, is on legal and ethical issues in the field, including defamation, trademark, and copyright issues, among other issues.

Part 5 of the text is on measurement and research in sport communication. The first chapter, Chapter 18, is on an issue that is rarely addressed in sport communication texts: sport analytics. Sport analytics has become a key aspect of sport communication for consumers as well as other stakeholders in the field. Beyond sport analytics, Chapter 19 touches on sport communication theories. The chapter on theories describes selected communication theories that are applicable to sport communication. The final chapter, Chapter 20, addresses scholarly research in the field. Similar to the chapter on theories, this chapter selects research methods – some are qualitative and others quantitative – and briefly discusses each of them with application examples.

FEATURES OF THE TEXT

The text has several features that help an instructor make his/her class exciting for students. Each feature is designed to heighten interest and to ease learning of the

material for students. The features include discussion questions, activities, brief reflections, cases, photographs, and video/web resources.

Discussion questions appear immediately after each chapter, and they are designed to evaluate how much learning the student has done. Therefore, the questions cover principles discussed in each section of the chapter. The activities that follow are outside the classroom assignments that enhance learning of the chapter material. Some of the activities are to be completed by student groups.

Brief reflections assume that most sport communication activities occur in each student's social life. Therefore, reflection narratives are designed to get the student to think about those activities and how they relate to content of the completed chapter. In essence, by reflecting, the student strengthens his/her ability to apply what is learned from the chapter. The cases, which are mostly two pages long, feature application of chapter material to a scenario that may be fictional or non-fictional. Each case is followed by a list of questions encouraging the student to think about real-world problem solving.

Photographs are included throughout the text to present visual examples of principles discussed in various chapters. This approach is based on the knowledge that student learning is significantly helped by visuals. Finally, at the end of each chapter are recommendations of video resources that also enhance learning of chapter materials. A significant number of the video resources can be accessed free of charge by the student through YouTube. Additionally, web resources recommendations enhance learning. The web resources include text materials that provide additional details to chapter contents.

ACKNOWLEDGMENTS

I acknowledge several individuals whose assistance has been critical to completion of this textbook. Chief among these are Dr. Roxane Coche, who is Assistant Professor of Broadcast and Sports Journalism in the Department of Journalism and Strategic Media at the University of Memphis in the United States. Roxane provided a significant number of photographs used in this text. Also, Mauricio Jordan Souza Coelho provided a photograph used for the text. I deeply appreciate their help in easing completion of this text and making it richer than it would have been without their assistance.

Additionally, I appreciate the assistance of my home institution, Howard University, which provided the time required to complete most of this book. The university approved a sabbatical leave in the Fall of 2016 that helped tremendously in data collection and most of the writing for this text. Thank you.

Chuka Onwumechili

CHAPTER 1

STUDYING COMMUNICATION AND SPORT

LEARNING OBJECTIVES

After reading this chapter, you should be able to do the following:

- Understand the meaning of sport and be able to differentiate it from game.
- Understand the meaning of communication and various types and levels of communication.
- Understand the relationship between communication and sport.
- Appreciate the meaning of an international approach to communication and sport.
- Understand how different cultures impact communication and sport.
- Become aware of and appreciate reasons for the study of communication and sport from an international perspective.

Sport has become big business in recent times. Figures show that global sport generated $145.34 billion in 2015 (Statista.com). It has become an activity that affects the lives of so many people, whether they are in Bangkok, Berlin, Rio de Janeiro, Kingston, or Yaounde. People may be directly involved by playing a sport or having a family member who plays a sport. However, the most prevalent way in which most people become involved in sport is through communication media. A good example of this occurred in 2010, when an estimated 3.2 billion people watched at least one minute of the 2010 World Cup. This is an amazing number when one considers that the estimated population of the world was 6.9 billion at the time. In essence, one of every two persons in the world, at the time, watched the World Cup! It is difficult to imagine another event that attracts that type of attention across the world. This chapter focuses on sport and communication and how those two intersect from an international perspective. It further makes a case for studying sport communication and discusses several career options in the field.

UNDERSTANDING SPORT

In certain parts of the world, **sports** is used instead of **sport**. However, throughout this text sport refers to a single kind of sport and sports is used to refer to multiple kinds of sport. While we often recognize what a sport means, we often use the word interchangeably with the word **game**. However, there is a difference between those two activities. **Game** is a rule-bound activity for entertainment, recreation, or amusement purposes. These rules are often unnatural and are created specifically for the conduct of a particular game. For instance, games include boxing, card playing, party games, lawn tennis, hide and seek, *Jeopardy* on American television, or the *Raid the Cage* game shown on Israeli television. A game requires the use of a person's intellectual capacity.

Generally, **sport** is a type of game that involves physical exertion and skill and is usually undertaken for competition. For instance, lawn tennis is a sport but card playing is not; boxing is but *Raid the Cage* is not. Those who participate in sport are known as athletes because they are physically able and skilled to participate in

Photo 1.1 An athletic stadium, which could host sport events communicated to the rest of the world.

Source: Dreamstime.com, reprinted with permission

a particular sport. Participating in a non-sport game does not require one to be an athlete. Thus, while a game is not necessarily a sport, a sport is always a game.

Furthermore, it is important to realize other ways in which the word *game* may be used. For instance, a game may refer to a specific sport contest. A lacrosse game may refer to a single lacrosse contest that involves two teams. It is from this perspective that one should view the concept *Olympic Games*, which refers to several sport games that take place during a particular Olympics.

COMMUNICATION

Communication is defined in several ways. Some of the definitions are quite broad and others are narrow. One of the broadest definitions of communication is the definition by Osmo Antero Wiio (2009) that one *cannot NOT communicate*. Wiio, a Finnish professor, outlined what can be described as four laws of human communication, particularly at the interpersonal level. One of those laws is that we cannot not communicate, which means that whether we intend to or not, there is always communication. In essence, communication occurs just by our mere presence. This is an overly broad way of describing communication that does not leave us a way to discriminate between what is and what is not communication.

Weaver and Shannon (1963) provide us with a model from which to define communication. This definition is much more narrow and discriminatory than Wiio's idea of communication. The model provides a visual outline of communication between a sender and receiver and constitutes key concepts such as message, disruptive noise, and feedback. It shows us that communication takes place when both the sender and receiver have a shared understanding or meaning of the message that is designed to produce a certain effect. The process of reaching this shared meaning or understanding is the communication process.

There are various contexts for communication that include intrapersonal, interpersonal, small group, organizational, mass, and multidimensional. As we shall learn, in communication and sport, each of these contexts matter. For instance, **intrapersonal communication** takes place when an athlete or a fan communicates with the self about a sport activity. A male, for instance, may self-identify as a field hockey fan in Germany by watching the triumph of German male teams in field hockey competitions at various Olympics. This individual may adopt the sport and build his game in the mold of Florian Fuch, who is a field hockey star in Germany. **Interpersonal communication** may take place during interaction between a female volleyball player and her coach. This type of communication takes place between two people. **Small group communication** usually involves at least three persons and as many as 20 persons who work as a group. In such groups, communication may be both relational and task-focused. Most sport teams work within the context of small group communication. These contexts may involve tactical discussions or team training for an upcoming game. **Organizational communication** refers to communication that takes place in an organizational context. These types of communication can be either formal or informal and are used to inform, persuade, and promote goodwill among members as well as the organization's publics. Sport organizations may consist of large teams (including backroom staff and administration), associations, and institutions organized in hierarchical structures that work towards a shared goal. **Mass communication** refers to delivering messages through a mass medium to a large number of persons who are widely dispersed. Newspapers, magazines, radio, television, and Internet platforms can each serve as a mass medium for delivery of such messages. Major sporting events like the Olympics, Wimbledon Tennis Championships, and the Rugby World Cup are brought to a large audience through mass media. **Multidimensional communication** may be delivered through a platform that allows various contexts of communication to take place. These contexts of communication could include interpersonal, small group, organizational, and mass communication. All of those contexts are delivered via the same platform. This frequently occurs via an Internet or Web platform termed *social media* such as Facebook, Twitter, Instagram, and so on. Such media environments allow both interaction with a large number of people at the same time or a dyadic (i.e. two-person) interaction.

COMMUNICATION AND SPORT: AN INTERNATIONAL APPROACH

We have already defined both sport and communication. This book is concerned with how those two concepts interact (i.e. how does communication take place *in* sport and *about* sport). We already should get the idea that human interaction always is centered on communication. It is impossible to have interaction without communication. Sport involves a significant amount of human interaction and, thus, communication is a central aspect of sport. It does not matter whether that sporting moment is one in which a coach is deeply thinking (intrapersonal) about what tactical maneuver she should apply to ensure her team's victory in a badminton contest or a star athlete is tweeting about her opponent's roughhouse tackles during a soccer game. Each of those events constitutes sport communication, which is part of this book's focus.

Importantly, the approach of this text is to study communication and sport from an international perspective. You are probably wondering what this means. It means that this textbook is focused on the intersection of communication and sport in multiple countries. Thus, instead of solely focusing on studying communication and sport in the United States, France, or Britain, the focus is on communication and sport in various countries of the world with examples on various types of sport, communication contexts, and countries such as India, Germany, France, Britain, Nigeria, Brazil, and so on.

An international approach recognizes that cultures differ from region to region, country to country, and even within countries. These differences ultimately affect communication and sport. **Culture** refers to shared beliefs, values, and norms among a defined group of people. For instance, one culture may differ from another because one believes that the life process is a cycle that includes birth, living, death, and re-birth (reincarnation), while another believes that the life process is linear and involves birth, living, and death. Values may differ as well. The United States, for example, values individual effort and achievement, whereas in China the group or collective effort and achievement is considered more valuable. Norms or practices may also differ. In the United States, males and females sit together as spectators to watch sport, whereas in some Muslim countries, women cannot participate in a mixed sporting environment. Essentially, culture is a fundamental aspect of the identity of athletes and sporting audiences in different parts of the world and, therefore, studying the communication of sport from an international approach has to consider culture and its deep impact.

REFLECTION

Plan a one-day journal on sport communication. On that day, record all that you encounter which you believe should be considered sport communication. Then examine the data. How many times do you watch sport communicated over a medium such as on television, radio, Twitter, Facebook, or Instagram, among others? Also, how many times did your friends bring it up in a day, and what did they talk about? How many of your encounters would you label international sport communication? Why? Think about the definition of the jobs held by those who bring to you information on sport. Reflect on all of that.

WHY STUDY COMMUNICATION AND SPORT?

The communication of sport for the benefit of a mass audience goes back a few centuries to the 1790s when the first sport magazines appeared in Britain (McChesney, 1989). That idea was later to spread to other parts of the world, including the United States, where the first mass communication of sport also occurred through magazines such as *Spirit of the Times* in the 1820s. Today, sport is communicated to the public through various mass media platforms. Sport is widely consumed and is regarded as essential in today's world. However, that was not always the case. Initially, sport was considered vulgar and frowned upon by societies that defined "proper" behavior as respect for each other, friendliness, cordiality, and civility. Thus, public competition involving a sport like boxing was widely frowned upon, at least publicly, and seen as an example of social decadence that was only practiced by the rough dregs of society. No respectable publication was expected to indulge in reporting such events and behavior.

McChesney (1989) points out that early reports of sport in magazines were by writers who used pseudonyms to protect their identity. Such writers did not want to be publicly associated with participating in events that were considered decadent. They also chose the sport they covered with extreme care. Thus, the early focus was on horse racing and not human contests. It was much later that sport magazines began to cover cricket and boxing after they realized that increasing numbers of persons were purchasing and consuming sport magazines. McChesney points out that *Spirit of the Times* reached a circulation of 100,000 by the 1850s.

Of course, with comfort in the knowledge that the public liked sporting contests, the first full-fledged sport reporters began to emerge, and they began to use their real names in sport reports. Among the first was Henry Chadwick of the *New York Clipper* (Stevens, 1987) in the 1850s, who went ahead to popularize baseball in America. Newspapers and other mass media followed by dedicating space and time to sport coverage.

The study of sport communication as an academic field could be said to have taken the same trajectory. The study of sport communication was initially considered unserious and recreational and did not become accepted until the last few decades when academic degrees began to be awarded in the field and several academic journals began to emerge.

There are several reasons for studying communication and sport. These reasons stem from personal interest, the rise in the importance of sport, understanding human behavior, learning about emerging research in the field, understanding how culture intersects with sport communication, the fact that sporting events have become mega global events, and learning about careers in the field. We elaborate on each of those reasons in subsequent paragraphs.

People have **personal interest** in sport for various reasons and, thus, it may attract them to study sport or to read about it. Sport obviously provides entertainment in our lives and serves as a discussion topic for social engagement. For instance, the Fédération Internationale de Football Association (FIFA) World Cup generates conversation at home, among friends in school, and at the workplace. Sport also provides us with an element of danger that we crave. As spectators, we know we will not die from it, but we pray and are supremely engaged during competition as we will our team to win. A positive result brings to us a high state of excitement and joy while defeat creates sadness and grief for us. Human nature is essentially competitive, and we want to come out successful in things that we participate in. That nature and primal urge pushes us to seek victory. As spectators, we seek vicariously to win by urging our team on. These interests often lead some of us to develop an interest in studying sport communication.

Moreover, the **importance of sport** in our world has been increasing for years. The spectatorship has risen tremendously, particularly among those who watch the game via a mass medium. Statista.com projected that 350 million people watched the 2014 World Cup that took place in Brazil; 170 million people watched the

Union of European Football Associations (UEFA) Champions League Final of 2014; 140 million watched the Winter Olympics opening ceremony; and 125 million people watched the American Super Bowl. In the most populated country in the world, China, close to 70% of television viewers watched the 2012 Olympics! (Watanabe, Nie, & Yan, 2013). But beyond the large numbers of spectatorship, revenues have also risen widely across the world. Several mass media companies pay millions of dollars to secure rights to broadcast sporting events, and other companies pay hugely to sponsor sport leagues or become associated with them. PricewaterhouseCoopers (PwC) projected a close to $35 billion global sport media rights market for 2015. The sport market, as projected by PwC (2011), has China increasing by 3.3% to $3.4 billion, Brazil to $4.2 billion (5.3%), and Russia to $871 million (4.6%) by 2015. This rise in sport profile has increased the importance of sport communication as an area for academic study.

Studying sport communication also provides opportunities to learn about **human behavior** and communication. Sport is a human social event where participants exhibit different types of human behavior. These behaviors may include competing for a resource, communicating in small groups, praying, laughing, and demonstrating sadness and happiness. The entire gamut of human behavior is exhibited in sport communication. By studying sport communication, we learn about these human behaviors.

We also have opportunities to learn about **research areas** in sport communication by learning about the field. Students have opportunities to learn about research in sport communication via studying the field. Sport communication is a relatively new area of academic study with several emerging research areas, and there are opportunities not just to learn about emerging research areas but also to discover and understand relationships between communication and sport.

An international approach to the study of sport communication is rooted in understanding how **culture impacts sport communication**. Sport communication is increasingly crossing cultural borders in many ways. For instance, transnational transmission of sport, such as the English Premier League and the Spanish La Liga, which are shown practically all over the world, brings to global homes some knowledge of foreign culture. Twitter and other social media platforms provide perspectives from all over the world on different types of sport and sporting events. These events reach us with accompanying cultural baggage, and we learn about the intersection of culture and sport communication. For instance, at the Olympics we may see women in Islamic hijab and see Senegalese athletes in African *Buba* during the opening ceremony.

By studying sport communication, we learn about **mega sporting events** that are watched by millions of people all over the world. These sporting events allow us to understand both international and intercultural relations that inform other areas of cultural studies such as intercultural communication or cross-cultural studies. Importantly, few events in the world are truly mega and attract millions of media communication consumers. Most of those are sports.

Finally, we learn about several existing and **emerging careers** associated with sport communication. As mentioned earlier, the communication and sport field is emerging and growing. In recent years, several academic fields related to sport have developed, there are increasing students in the field, and several academic journals have emerged. This means also that new careers are being created within the field. We can learn about all of those developments by studying communication and sport.

GRASSROOTS SPORT AND FACING UP TO CULTURE

"We have millions of children who can become major international stars in a few years," Pankaj claims. He had watched the recent Olympics where India performed poorly, but yet he is claiming that it can change in a few years. His country is one of the most populated in the world, and yet at the Olympics it barely won a few medals while much smaller countries took a haul of medals. Anushri disagrees: "Look, many parents do not care about sport in this country. They want their children to be doctors, engineers, computer scientists, and so on." Pankaj, however, insists that he and others can change that. Pankaj is full of ideas. After all, he built a very successful national engineering company, and he believes that he has the ability to build sport into a success, despite the culture mentioned by Anushri. There are millions of children who play sport in the streets at a young age, but they end up abandoning sport for school or a trade. Sport, for years, has been considered an endeavor for the never-do-wells.

Pankaj has already met with several other CEOs to begin preliminary discussions on how to make his dreams come true. He is pushing on even though his trusted partner, Anushri, is not fully on board. Pankaj realizes that not all of his CEO friends agree with him. Many of them have voiced similar concerns reflected in Anushri's views. The country has not always supported sport development, despite the large number of nationals. Sporting facilities are poor, and parents and children are focused more on classroom education than on sport. In fact, in a recent focus group discussion conducted by Pankaj's team, several parents did not understand why a child should focus on sport. They want their children to become wealthy and live comfortably in a traditional family structure. One parent said at the focus group: "Sports men and women end up being poor and they panhandle in the streets of our cities. Why would I want my child to join them?"

Pankaj, however, is resolute. He has the support of a key CEO friend, Gajrup, who has the clout to get others to invest in Pankaj's scheme. Both meet frequently to discuss details of the plan. Pankaj already launched the proposed sport organization as Hope of a Nation (HON), and many school districts have agreed, in principle, to outsource their sport curriculum to HON. HON would bear the costs while the schools provide facilities when available. Pankaj's vision is not only to develop sport at the school level but also to set up sport academies outside of schools, providing elite facilities for those with talent to perform at elite levels. HON has begun to receive the investment funds needed to equip its academies. Gajrup has received commitments from two major national companies and is working on several others. However, a number of them are skeptical of HON's plans, pointing to cultural issues and wondering how profitable such a venture could be.

In any case, HON has also made preliminary contact with some parents to gauge how much they may be able to afford if they have children in HON's academies. These meetings have been in small groups, but in some cases Gajrup or Pankaj has each met with single families. HON has worked out the figures and believes that the venture is profitable at a certain scale and subscription. However, all of these are plans. Anushri does not believe that the numbers needed to become profitable can be met in a few years, and yet the investment funds needed are significant. She has been fully in charge of the background research and setting up focus group meetings with coaches, parents, and business persons.

Pankaj believes that the increasing importance of sport will help convince parents that their children may live a comfortable life after sport, and they could also become wealthy and well known. After all, there are examples of successful sport men and women that can be used for testimonies. While he acknowledges the difficulties in overcoming culture, Pankaj believes that setting up a good communication plan would be helpful. But how should he go about accomplishing these plans?

Discussion questions

1. Identify various sport communication contexts found in the case. Provide examples to support each context.
2. What cultural norms of this country are demonstrated in various conversations in the case? Do you believe that such norms can be overcome by HON? Why?
3. Which sport communication position(s) should HON hire and why?
4. At the end of the case, Pankaj has ideas, but how would you help him in accomplishing his plans for HON?

CAREERS IN SPORT COMMUNICATION

We mentioned a reason for studying sport communication is to learn about careers in the field. Numerous sport communication jobs are available globally in a variety of categories. In this section, sport communication jobs are divided into four categories, but it is important to note that there are more jobs in the field than are captured in this section. The four categories are jobs with sporting organizations, mass media organizations, specific athletes, and independent jobs.

Sporting organizations

Here a sporting organization refers to a sport team, an institution such as a school, and a sporting association, among other types of organizations. These organizations, depending on their size, would have a **Director of Information**. A Director of Information is usually the top information and communication manager in a sporting organization. This individual is responsible for overall communication strategy of the organization and supervises several other employees. A higher education degree is required for this position, along with years of experience in managing within a sport organization.

A **Media Relations Officer** is responsible for being a liaison with different types of sport media. He or she may also be responsible for ensuring that the media receive important information about the organization. He or she arranges for press releases and organizes press conferences. He or she may also be responsible for ensuring that athletes and technical managers for athletes are available to mass media representatives. A higher education degree is required for this position, and someone who likes to network and build positive relationships is a plus. Importantly, an individual in such a position must enjoy writing.

A **Public/Community Relations Officer** is responsible for building and maintaining organizational goodwill with the organization's publics and the community. The individual organizes community events to bring representatives of the organization closer to people in the community. For example, the individual may arrange for community service events by athletes, which may involve visiting the sick, school visits, speaking engagements, and other types of events. This position requires someone who is active and willing to spend hours outside of the office. The position also requires a higher education degree, preferably in public relations or sport management.

Sport Marketer is a position that is responsible for marketing the organization through various means. A sport marketer is involved in seeking sponsorships or partnerships for the organization's operations and projects. This individual may also help with selling event tickets to special groups and strategizing on how best to promote the organization. The individual may also purchase advertising spots or space in different media. This position requires someone who enjoys sales and is able to build and maintain relationships with various businesses.

Social Media Specialist is a position that is specialized in many organizations. However, as more people in the working population become adept at social media, it is unlikely that this position will continue to be a specialization. The position requires someone who is adept at different types of social media communication, including websites, Facebook, Twitter, Instagram, Snapchat, and similar platforms. These individuals are expected to represent the face of the organization on social media platforms visited by large numbers of the organization's publics. Presently, recent higher education graduates are employed to fill this position. The position is also available through mass media organizations.

The positions described here are just a few prominent sport communication positions in sporting organizations. However, as sporting organizations grow, newer positions also become available. For instance, several sporting organizations have begun to expand into owning media outlets. Association Football teams, such as Benfica Football Club of Lisbon in Portugal and Chelsea Football Club of London in England, now own television stations. In such cases, these organizations employ people to fill positions that are associated with mass media units.

Mass media organizations

Mass media organizations include traditional media such as newspapers, magazines, radio, and television. As mentioned earlier, these organizations bring sporting events to people's attention, no matter how dispersed they are from each other. To do this successfully, they employ a number of people to ensure that messages delivered to the public are efficient and effective. Ultimately, this means that they have a large number of sport communication jobs. Following are some of the sport communication jobs available in such organizations:

A **Reporter/Writer** is responsible for covering a sporting event for a news organization and writing a report of such event. A reporter/writer may be assigned to a particular beat. For instance, a reporter/writer may be assigned to an important and popular local team for the season. In such a position, the reporter/writer is responsible for covering the team and breaking news stories about the team. Also, this person, along with an assigned photographer, often covers a sporting event for a big media organization. In smaller organizations, the same individual may be the photographer and writer. The position requires a very good writer who often has a journalism degree.

A **Sideline Reporter** is responsible for providing "inside" information on a team from the sideline or from a position very close to the team on the field or court of play. These positions are often filled by "attractive females" according to Billings, Butterworth, and Turman (2012), but increasingly men are also hired for this position. Sideline reporters are widely used to cover sport in the United States and some South American countries. In 2011, a major story broke about an attractive sideline reporter, Ines Sainz, of Mexico's TV Azteca, who was sexually harassed by a coach and players of the New York Jets in the United States. A sideline reporter does on-the-spot interviews of team officials, players, and fans during a game, practices, or events. Often these are very brief interviews that attempt to bring the audience closer to ongoing issues at the location.

A **Sport Editor** is usually a former reporter or writer who has risen from the ranks. The editor helps write and edit sport stories. He or she ensures the accuracy of sport reports and makes decisions on what appears in the mass medium that he or she edits. This requires being abreast of information in the sporting world and developing sources for stories. Editors assign responsibilities for covering events and stories and they set periodic agenda for such coverage. This position requires excellent writing skills and a good eye for proofing written material. A higher education degree is necessary for this position, usually in journalism or sport communication.

A broadcaster serves in a visible position, if on television, and is required to be on camera. Of course, this is not the case if it is on radio. However, these days you may have someone who appears on both television and radio because of ongoing media convergence. On television, two persons are usually paired for live sporting events where there is a **Play-by-Play Announcer/Commentator** and an **Analyst/Color Analyst**. The term color analyst is a North American term, which is referred to elsewhere as "analyst" or "summariser." The announcer or commentator describes the live event as it occurs so that the audience is able to follow the action. The analyst spices up the announcement by providing interesting background on the team, the athletes, and other related events in a conversational manner with the announcer. Both positions require individuals who are able to speak clearly and fluidly. These individuals must be deeply knowledgeable about the sport they are working on.

A **Sport Producer** is responsible for a broadcast sport program. A producer is behind the scenes but must have deep knowledge of production on radio or television. He or she has responsibility for conceiving programs and managing those programs. This task includes recruiting those who participate in the program, and it may involve directing the live program. A producer position may be categorized further into different types from Segment Producer to Executive Producer. The position requires higher education and a deep knowledge of sport.

A **Columnist** is an experienced writer hired to maintain a column in a print publication. Increasingly, these individuals are freelancers, which means they are not full-time employees of a media organization. A sport columnist may write generally on several sports or specialize on a particular type of sport. The columnist is deeply knowledgeable about sport and is an excellent writer, often with a higher education degree.

A **Sport Analyst** is a position that involves the ability to deeply analyze a sport. Though former athletes and coaches are usually hired for this position, analysts can also be those with deep interest in the sport. Depth of knowledge in the sport is usually the criterion for hiring for this position.

A **Sport Show Anchor** works in a studio and must be knowledgeable about sport topics and speak fluidly. Anchors introduce the topics and control participation of other contributors to the show. A higher education degree is required and experience in the media is necessary.

A **Sport Talk Show Host** is deeply knowledgeable about sport and familiar with current sport topics. The person is interactive and should like to debate and seek out controversial and popular topics in order to generate public participation in the show and drive high audience ratings.

Jobs with athletes

There are jobs available with specific athletes, particularly popular athletes who are highly compensated. Some of these positions involve sport communication. Following is a position that athletes may fill after hiring a sport agent:

Publicists are hired by athletes who are considered celebrities. The hiring athlete is widely popular among sport fans. Publicists promote the athlete's image and are responsible for scheduling community events for the athlete.

Independent positions

Independent positions are those where the person is self-employed but makes income from a type of sport communication work. These types of positions are increasing all over the world as new digital communication technologies provide communication access that is unparalleled in history. Following are a few of such sport communication jobs:

A **Blogger** is a person who maintains his or her own online sport journal for public consumption. Numerous sport blogs communicate all kinds of information on sport. Some focus on statistics, others may include interviews, others break major news, and so on. Bloggers may develop large public followings by sharing views that are controversial and/or popular. Successful bloggers are able to earn a living through advertising on their blog sites and may attract employment at bigger and more traditional media organizations.

Fanzines are popular in Europe, where sport fans create unofficial sport publications on their favorite teams. Some fan-created fanzines become popular. For instance, a popular football fanzine is *When Saturday Comes*, which became critical about how football is administered in England. Fans establish such publications and distribute them among fellow fans, and some fanzines, like blogs, become popular and attract interest from mainstream media.

A **Film/Documentary Maker** may be an individual who chooses to make video stories of sporting teams or activities and then pitches them to larger media organizations. This type of work requires expertise in video scripting, producing, and editing.

A **Sport Researcher** does not have to be self-employed. However, we have chosen to describe one that is self-employed. This position requires someone with the skill to research sport and analyze relevant data, which is then made available to media organizations for use in sport stories.

A **Freelance Writer/Journalist** does the same thing as a reporter/writer described earlier. The only difference is that the freelancer is self-employed but pitches stories and reports to larger media organizations for a fee.

A **Video Game Designer** requires creative video game skills and some knowledge of computer programming. A person in this position is more likely to be employed by sport video gaming companies. They have to have knowledge of sport.

The positions described above are not exhaustive, but they provide an idea of careers available in the sport communication field. As sport communicators become experienced, they are likely to transition into managerial and/or executive positions like vice president or president positions where they manage a large number of staff involved in sport communication.

CHAPTER SUMMARY

This chapter introduces sport communication by defining and describing both sport and then communication. For sport, it differentiates *sport* from *game*. For communication, it elaborates on various contexts of communication. It then shows how both sport and communication interact, particularly from an international perspective where one must be mindful of cultural effects. The chapter also makes a case for the study of sport communication by citing the increasing importance of sport and noting its several benefits. The final section of the chapter provides examples of careers in sport communication. These careers can be found in sporting organizations, mass media organizations, with specific athletes, and also as an independent service provider.

DISCUSSION QUESTIONS

1. What is the difference between a sport and a game? How would you classify *Scrabble*?
2. Small group and organizational communication appear to be similar communication contexts. Are there any differences between the two? Can we use the number of people involved in communication to accurately classify communication as group or organizational?
3. What makes a sport communication activity international? Please elaborate with examples.
4. Why should someone become interested in the study of sport communication?
5. Think of how culture impacts international sport communication. Provide at least three examples of how culture may do this.
6. There are numerous examples of careers in sport communication. Which of the careers interest you the most and why?
7. If you had to develop an independent sport communication company, which one is it likely to be? Please explain and justify why that would be the preferred one.

ACTIVITIES

1. Review sport communication job advertisements in your local newspaper or online. Report on the jobs, making sure that you identify the most prominent job positions and the requirements for those. Indicate steps that you may take in order to be eligible to apply for one of the positions that you identified.
2. Visit a sporting organization or a sport media organization located near your institution. Interview a manager in that organization to fully understand the job description for that individual and his or her daily and frequent activities. Find out how long they have been on the job and what they like and do not like about their job.
3. Speak to a top manager of the Athletic Department at your institution. Find out how the department publicizes its athletic teams. How does the department facilitate interpersonal meetings with individual athletes or group meetings with athletic teams? What are the benefits of those meetings?

VIDEO RESOURCES

The Business of Sports. This YouTube video shows how sport has become big business in the United States. The event is hosted by the Millken Institute and can be accessed via www.youtube.com/watch?v=iS5UNbpsHsw.

What Is Sport Management? Source: www.youtube.com/watch?v=pMkddGWE1lI

How Media Relations Job Shapes Sports Career – Jen Duberstein. Source: www.youtube.com/watch?v=E5SYsg4nTpk

RECOMMENDED WEB RESOURCES

Careers in sports management webcast by American Public University. This can be found through this link: www.youtube.com/watch?v=mM_zsAQavwQ

Indeed.com job advertisement website: www.indeed.com/jobs?q=sports+communications

Importance of Communication in Sports by Bo Hanson. This can be found via www.athleteassessments.com/importance-of-communication-in-sports/

REFERENCES

Billings, A., Butterworth, M., & Turman, P. (2012). *Communication and sport: Surveying the field*. Thousand Oaks, CA: Sage Publications.

McChesney, R. (1989). Media made sport: A history of sports coverage in the United States. In Wenner, L. (Ed.), *Media, sports, and society* (pp. 49–69). Newbury Park, CA: Sage Publications.

PwC (2011, December). Changing the game: Outlook for the global sports market to 2015. www.pwc.com/gx/en/hospitality-leisure/pdf/changing-the-game-outlook-for-the-global-sports-market-to-2015.pdf.

Statista.com (n.d.). www.statista.com/statistics/.

Stevens, J. (1987, Fall). The rise of the sports page. *Gannett Center Journal*, 1: 1–11.

Watanabe, N., Nie, T., & Yan, G. (2013). Evolution of sport broadcast commentary: The case of China. *International Journal of Sport Communication*, 6: 288–311.
Weaver, W., & Shannon, C. (1963). *The mathematical theory of communication.* Champaign, IL: University of Illinois Press.
Wiio, O. (2009). *Communication usually fails – except by accident: Wiio laws and the future of communications.* Espoo, Finland: Delta Books.

PART I

COMMUNICATING SPORT

Source: Roxane Coche, reprinted with permission

CHAPTER 2

INTERPERSONAL COMMUNICATION AND SPORT

> **LEARNING OBJECTIVES**
>
> After reading this chapter, you should be able to do the following:
>
> - Understand the meaning and goals of interpersonal communication.
> - Identify the impact of cultural differences on interpersonal relationships.
> - Recognize how presentation of self may affect interpersonal communication outcomes.
> - Recognize how your perception of others may affect interpersonal communication outcomes.
> - Recognize and become familiar with interpersonal communication contexts in communication and sport.
> - Become aware of the nature of emotion and how its management impacts interpersonal relationships in communication and sport.
> - Differentiate between types of listening and understand their process and importance in building positive relationships.

Interpersonal communication is a fundamental type of communication in sport. It is what connects an athlete to another, a coach to an athlete, and so on. For example, a star athlete is preparing to lead her team in the final of a tournament. She is having doubts about her ability to do this because she has a headache and one of her teammates is unable to play because of an injury. The coach steps in and invites the athlete for a private talk. They talk about how they have overcome odds in a difficult tournament to get to the final. The coach reminds the athlete that this is only one game but a very important one and that the team needs her for this one game. The coach motivates the athlete to give her best for this final game.

This scenario is what may be described as interpersonal communication. It is a conversation between two persons. It is what helps to build lasting relationships and success. Unfortunately, poor management of interpersonal communication can do exactly the opposite (i.e. destroy relationships). Therefore, its importance cannot be overstated.

DEFINING INTERPERSONAL COMMUNICATION

McCornack (2013) defines interpersonal communication as "a dynamic form of communication between two people in which the messages exchanged significantly influence their thoughts, emotions, behaviors, and relationships" (p. 11). This definition points to the fact that interpersonal communication is not static. It changes as the exchange of information takes place. The topic may switch from one issue to the next, and new information may lead to a shift in focus. It also notes that this type of communication involves two persons, a dyad. Finally, the definition notes that the messages exchanged during the process of communication have an effect on both participants. This effect may be just on their thoughts or it could be much more, including an effect on their relationship.

The communication that is exchanged during interpersonal communication does not only speak about the content of the messages that are exchanged. Instead, interpersonal communication often provides information on the relationship between the participants. This type of information is often embedded in the nonverbal communication that accompanies messages. Embedding does not mean that such nonverbal communication cannot be observed. How a word is said, the eye contact, the volume of the message, and the posture of the receiver are all ways that expose the relationship between parties in an interpersonal communication.

Furthermore, interpersonal communication in sporting situations may be affected by emotions. The extreme joy expressed by an athlete to a teammate after a point has been scored demonstrates a common emotion communicated during a sporting encounter. **Emotion** involves an intense and expressed reaction that symbolizes a physiological reaction to an event. It can be expressed by language, nonverbal communication, and/or other sudden behavior. Our primary emotions include anger, disgust, fear, happiness, sadness, and surprise. At times, emotions can be blended. For instance, remorse is a blended emotion that includes disgust and anger.

Because some emotions may be detrimental to relationships, persons involved in interpersonal communication must develop **emotional intelligence**, which is the ability to manage their own emotions and use them to solve interpersonal sport communication problems. For instance, a coach may call an athlete aside to speak about the athlete's poor play during the interval of a competition. The athlete feels anger because he feels that the error in the play was due to another teammate's fault. If he expresses this anger, conflict with the coach may spiral uncontrollably. The athlete must **listen actively** to the coach. This means focusing on understanding what the coach is saying and evaluating the facts and details provided by the coach while withholding the urge to rush into a response. The athlete then thinks about how best to respond in competent ways to establish commonalities by not ignoring points made by the coach. This way, emotion is managed competently for a more positive interpersonal communication result.

Listening actively involves taking into consideration various types of listening styles, which are action-oriented, time-oriented, people-oriented, and content-oriented, according to Bodie and Worthington (2010). The **action-oriented** listener looks forward to brief and precise messages while discouraging elaboration; **time-oriented** listeners also listen for brief and precise messages but often focus on having only a certain amount of time to listen; **people-oriented** listeners seek commonalities from the messages being delivered; and **content-oriented** listeners focus on evaluating the message and detail presented in the message.

GOALS OF INTERPERSONAL COMMUNICATION

People who participate in interpersonal communication have goals that they seek to fulfill. In a coach/athlete interpersonal communication, for instance, each party seeks to accomplish multiple goals. It is rare for a party to seek to achieve a singular goal. Each party often seeks to achieve a multiplicity of goals. These goals can be some of the following: instrumental, self-presentation, and relationship.

An **instrumental goal** is designed to serve as a means towards other achievement. A party is often aware of this goal and has intentionally set out to achieve it through an interpersonal communication act. The goal may be directly revealed to the other party, if the source of the message wishes to do so. For instance, at the beginning of this chapter, we mentioned a conversation that a coach may have with a star athlete about required effort to win a final game. In such a case, the instrumental goal for that interpersonal communication is to convince the athlete to play her best so that the team may win the final game.

A **self-presentation** goal may take place during the interpersonal communication between the coach and the athlete. The coach may want to present himself as a motivator while the athlete may want to present herself as a brave athlete who plays her best during important games. While these goals of self-presentation are rarely explicitly revealed, they impact how each person participates in the communication.

A third type is a **relationship goal**. In interpersonal communication, a participant may intend to end, build, or maintain relationship. Relationship is a key goal of the human needs hierarchy developed by Abraham Maslow in 1970. In Maslow's hierarchy of needs, he wrote about physical and safety needs, which are fundamental needs that each of us seek to fulfill before any other thing. However, when those physical/safety needs are met, we switch attention to meeting higher-order needs such as socialization (i.e. to be accepted by others and to form a social bond with others). Relationship goals serve those needs.

CULTURE'S IMPACT

Though there is a tendency for each of us to assume that most interpersonal communication encounters take place between acquaintances, it is important to realize that a significant number of encounters involve people from different cultural backgrounds. As we already know from the Weaver and Shannon model (1963) of communication, when people from different cultural backgrounds engage in communication, there is a high chance of miscommunication.

There are multiple reasons why miscommunication could occur in such intercultural communication. Of course, one is the language used in conversation. Language may hinder the ability for full expression and understanding because each party may not be versed in the language used by the other for communication. Importantly, nonverbal symbols may be very difficult to interpret since nonverbal communication is associated with specific cultures. Then there are issues of differences in beliefs, values, norms, and artifacts between persons from different cultural backgrounds. Each of those elements may introduce miscommunication.

The chance of miscommunication and the complexity of communication between people from different cultural backgrounds point to the impact of culture on interpersonal communication.

THE SELF AND ITS PRESENTATION

A very important factor in interpersonal communication is the *self*. It is from self that all interpersonal communication actions are derived. Therefore, understanding components of *self* is key to understanding interpersonal communication in sport. **Self** is defined as the culmination of self-awareness, self-concept, and self-esteem, where self is the evolving character of the individual. The self is ever evolving because ongoing activity that surrounds the individual continually impacts the individual. It is never ending.

Self-concept is how one sees herself or himself. It is influenced by a host of factors that include culture, social institutions such as religion and school, as well as family, friends, and gender. These influences lead the individual to develop certain beliefs about who they are. For instance, they may lead an individual to believe that he or she is "a strong athlete." After all, he or she has been told so in conversations with friends and others. He or she has observed what the school describes as "strong athletes" and he or she shares the same traits with those who have been observed as "strong athletes." In certain parts of the world, people believe that ethnic traits determine whether an athlete would have certain characteristics or not. For instance, among Igbos of Nigeria, the belief is that Igbo males are naturally and physically strong. This, then, may influence the self-concept of an Igbo athlete.

Factors mentioned above also influence things that persons hold as important to them or what they value. For instance, an individual may be guided by the principle that "fairness is the right thing in sport." Of course, this may come from what the individual had been taught at home, in school, and/or in the church. The individual may use that value to judge others' actions. Finally, self-concept is also based on attitudes that an individual develops over time. Attitudes reflect evaluative appraisals about who one is. For instance, "I *like the fact* that I express fairness to others" or "I am *comfortable* with being a strong athlete."

Self-awareness refers to an individual's ability to observe and evaluate herself or himself. In essence, the individual is able to "step out of their body or person" and observe self in action. The individual is aware of this ability and this action and is then able to reflect on it. By being self-aware, the individual is also able to compare self against actions of others and assign meanings to actions of others. Self-awareness enables us to recognize "our fairness" after we have acted or behaved in a way that is socially described as fair.

Self-esteem is the evaluation outcome that we assign to our self. This evaluation ranges from positive to negative. One has a low self-esteem when his or her overall evaluation of self tends towards the negative end of the range. He or she has high self-esteem when the overall evaluation outcome inclines to the positive end of the range. This evaluation of self impacts interpersonal communication outcome during sport communication. For instance, think back to the brief scenario described earlier in this chapter between the coach and a star athlete. In that scenario, the outcome would be quite different depending on whether the star athlete, for example, has high or low self-esteem. If she has high self-esteem, then she would develop the confidence to see her team through the final of the tournament. The team may win or lose, but that is not the point. The point is that with high self-esteem she will do all within her power to play her best and encourage her teammates to do the same. If she has low self-esteem, her doubt about her abilities will become heightened. This will most likely dampen her ability to play her best in the final game, and she will be of little help to her teammates in the quest for the team to succeed.

The self described so far is called the private self. Often, that self is similar to the self that we also present to the public. However, on certain occasions this will not be the case. At times, the individual may present to the public a different self. This occurs when an individual may feel that he or she may not be accepted if they were to present their private self to the public.

The Johari Window (see Table 2.1) is a visual model for the relational self. Scholars Joseph Luft and Harry Ingham (1955) developed the model, which describes four areas of self. These areas are the Public, Secret, Hidden, and Unknown. The Public includes things about us that we choose to disclose to others. The Secret includes things that we know about ourselves that we do not want to disclose. The Hidden includes things about us that others know but that we do not realize about

Table 2.1 A graphic representation of the Johari Window.

PUBLIC
SECRET
HIDDEN
UNKNOWN

Source: Adapted from Luft and Ingham (1955)

ourselves. The Unknown are things that we and others do not know about us. They are exhibited from time to time during relationships in an unconscious way, and we do not realize it and the public has no previous clue of its existence. During stages of interpersonal communication, we choose how much of the self can be made public to the other participant in interpersonal communication or how much we should keep secret. As the table shows, we control the two top rows but not the bottom two.

The blank or white top row shows that the public self of an individual is known to both the individual and others. The light grey second row indicates that secrets of the individual may be shared with others. The darker grey third row shows an individual's hidden part, which is unknown to the individual but known by others. The darkest row (bottom) shows that large characteristics of an individual are unknown to both the individual and others. The hidden part is unknown to the individual but known by others.

Generally, presenting the *self* during interpersonal communication can be strategic. During early stages of relational development, we may choose to limit both the depth and the breadth of *self* that we disclose to the other person. By breadth, we refer to different parts of ourselves that we share, and by depth, we refer to how detailed we are in sharing a part of our selves. As our comfort level with the other person increases during interpersonal communication, we may choose to increasingly expose more and more parts of our self and more details of each of those parts.

THE OTHER AND PERCEPTION

Interpersonal communication is not only influenced by the self. It is also influenced by our perception of the other party and the context. **Perception** refers to how we make sense of the world around us. This involves how we select certain things to focus on, how we organize those things in our minds, and how we interpret situations. This entire process is culture bound and, thus, may be different from one culture to the other or from one country to the other.

In Nigeria, for instance, an individual's homeland is considered very important. In fact, when individuals meet for the first time, one of the expected question is "Where are you from?" This question is meant to establish someone's hometown or homeland and their ethnic background. This information is critical because perception is influenced by this knowledge because belonging to an "in-group" is weighed more heavily than being an "out-group" member. The selection phase of perception is influenced by the determination of whether the person is an in-group or out-group member. Certain aspects of the individual's behavior are then unconsciously selected as they confirm the status of in-group or out-group. The selected aspect of behavior is used to organize events occurring during the exchange of interpersonal communication. This process helps interpretation of an interpersonal communication event. Parties are then able to explain or make attributions on why certain things occur. In the Nigerian case, the individual's behavior is attributed to that person's homeland or ethnic background. This leads to what Heider (1958) refers to as a **fundamental attribution error**, which occurs when a party attributes the other person's actions to an internal cause (e.g. the person's character or personality) rather than attributing those actions to the effect of external causes (e.g. conditions that the person faces or the context that they encounter).

While we have given a Nigerian example to show how culture may influence perception during interpersonal communication encounters, the key elements that each participant in an interpersonal communication event selects may differ not just based on culture but also based on gender and personality. The basis of gender as a point of difference in how people perceive things is not well established in research. Some studies have found differences between gender and others have found little or no difference. Personality is measured by five traits: degree of openness, conscientiousness, extraversion, agreeableness, and neuroticism. Personality has a strong influence on how we perceive actions by others. Essentially, we project our personality onto our expectations of others, expecting them to be like us and to act as we would act.

Perceptions of the other person can lead to an overall negative perception or positive perception of that person. This is what is referred to as the **Gestalt effect**. A positive Gestalt has an impact on how we predict future communication with that person. In such a case, it leads to a **halo effect** where we continue to perceive the person's actions as positive and often dismiss signs that question such a perception. If the person unexpectedly performs a negative action that is contrary to our perception, then we are quick to attribute it to an external reason over which the person had no control. On the other hand, instead of a halo effect we may have a negative Gestalt about an individual, and this leads to a **horn effect**. This effect is where we perceive the person's future action negatively, so even when they do something positive, we attribute that action to an external impact on them and not something that they had internal control over. Whereas if they carried out a negative action, it confirms our perception and we attribute it to their internal control (i.e. they had done it as part of their character).

We also develop stereotypes about groups of people, and a person from such a group is believed to undertake the group's characteristics and have no individual personalities of themselves. **Stereotypes**, therefore, refer to simplistic impressions of other people where we attribute perceived group characteristics to all members of such a group and ignore whatever individual variation of characteristics that each member may have. Let us look back at the Nigerian case. For instance, if an Igbo Nigerian perceives Yoruba Nigerians as untrustworthy, then an Igbo coach may immediately distrust a Yoruba athlete, even though this athlete may have shown very reliable traits. In such a case, the coach has stereotyped that athlete.

INTERPERSONAL SITUATIONS IN COMMUNICATION AND SPORT

As you may imagine, there are numerous interpersonal communication situations in sport. They occur in all types of sport, whether it is an individual-based sport like tennis or a team-based sport like hockey. There are also numerous studies on these types of sport communication. This section discusses what takes place in sport interpersonal communication and its impact. It also points out under which context certain types of interpersonal communication are likely to take place. Three contexts are discussed as coach/athlete, coach/parent, and parent/athlete.

Coach/athlete

This context is important because the interpersonal relationship between a coach and athlete is believed to be a significant reason for an athlete's success. Studies such as Bloom (1996), Nakamura (1996), and Spink (1991) confirm the link between such relationship and athletic success. In fact, Orlick and Partington (1986) claimed that "almost all of the athletes who performed to potential at the Olympic Games had a very close personal bond with their coaches" (p. 4). Jowett and Cockerill (2002) named successful coach/athlete relationships as Ron Rodden and Linford Christie (100m Olympic gold medal), Frank Dick and Daley Thompson (Decathlon Olympic gold), and Peter Coe and Sebastian Coe (1500m Olympic gold). Jowett (2003) identifies **trust**, **respect**, **commitment**, and **understanding** as critical elements in an effective interpersonal relationship between a coach and an athlete.

However, what constitutes an effective interpersonal communication relationship between a coach and athlete may differ from place to place. For instance, studies in places like France (d'Arripe-Longueville, Fournier, & Dubois, 1998) and some Asian countries have found authoritative coaches to be effective because they meet the athlete's expectation. Athletes in those countries see the coach as parent-like. In essence, they expect the coach to be authoritative, knowledgeable, and to supervise him or her (for success). They do not expect the coach to be a "friend." Nangalia and Nangalia (2010) stated this about coaching in Asia:

> The coach in Asia is not seen as an equal. He or she is seen as a respected elder or teacher. This status is ascribed from the social hierarchy present in Asian society.
>
> (p. 56)

Photo 2.1 A coach teaching a child tennis. Such a relationship involves much interpersonal communication.

Source: Dreamstime.com, reprinted with permission

Nevertheless, this expectation differs from expectations elsewhere. Culver and Trudel (2000) studied an elite alpine skiing team in Canada, examining teenage female athletes' interpersonal communication with their coaches. Unlike the Asian example mentioned earlier, the athletes expected interactive interpersonal relationships with their coaches as they moved from pre-teen to more adult status.

Skiing is an important sport in Canada, where the sport has featured a national competition for more than half a century. Canada's culture shares a close relationship with the American culture of openness in a democratic rather than autocratic system. In this environment, therefore, the expectation of an interactive interpersonal relationship is not surprising, and athletes feel that it is critical to their success because it motivates them, increases their confidence, teaches them more, enhances their self-esteem, and provides psychological support. It shows, also, that this open interactive communication is important at all points and in most contexts. In times of crisis, the athlete needs reassurance from the coach's feedback and support. However, the study found that interpersonal communication is available on technical and tactical issues but rarely on psychological issues, which is increasingly critical at elite levels.

> **REFLECTION**
>
> Perhaps you played organized sport during your younger years or maybe you have a family member who did. Think about your experience or those of a family member during your childhood. What kind of relationship did you or the family member have with a parent or with a coach? Was the relationship positive or negative and why? How was communication between you/family member and the other person (parent or coach)? Are there things you would have liked to change in that communication? If yes, what are those things? If not, why not? Reflect on your answers to those questions and think about sections of this chapter that you read.

Coach/parent

Coach/parent interpersonal communication can be rare in some countries but is an important sport communication issue in several Western countries. Why is this? In Western countries, parents are significant participants in the choice of sport by their children, and they remain involved until their children grow into adulthood. However, in other places such as Africa, parental involvement is rare. In such places, the child often decides to play a sport, and the parent may never watch the child play the sport. The few instances of parental involvement usually is the parent discouraging the child from a focus on sport.

In the West where parental involvement is significant, it means that interpersonal communication with coaches becomes an issue in the athlete's success. Unlike in Africa, most parents in the West encourage their child's participation in sport for several reasons, including socialization, recreational activity, educational scholarships, and other economic reasons that accrue from the child graduating to professional sport.

McLean (2008) reported that most studies of coach/parent interpersonal relationship focus on disturbing aspects of such relationships, including the parents' disruptive and abusive behaviors. In places like Australia, youth sport organizations have devised a code of conduct for parents in order to prevent negative behaviors. Of course, when those behaviors go unchecked, they adversely affect the child's performance. Instead, parental support, rather than pressure, helps the athlete.

Hellstedt (1987) describes three types of parents and recommends strategies for interpersonal communication with each with the goal of helping the youth athlete develop. **Parental** types are the underinvolved, the moderately involved, and the overinvolved. Hellstedt points out that interpersonal communication with each type of parent is important and must involve sharing realistic expectations about the child's potential and providing feedback. Overall, Hellstedt's recommendation focuses on creating an open communication environment while delineating the boundaries that parents should not cross and sharing information on how parents may effectively support their child's development in the sport. The underinvolved and overinvolved parents are especially a handful. For the underinvolved, the child athlete feels abandoned and may begin to see the coach as a surrogate parent. In such cases, coaches must encourage parental involvement in their child's development. The opposite is the case with the overinvolved parent. There is tremendous pressure on the child to develop, perform, and win, leading to frequent parental interference in coaching activities. In such a case, the coach must keep channels of interpersonal communication open but work with the athlete to achieve a certain level of independence while avoiding open conflict with the parent. The coach must help the parent realize what is realistic for their child and establish clear roles for the parent while providing frequent feedback.

Parent/athlete

Parent/athlete interpersonal communication can be one of the most difficult in sport communication. Of course, there are successful parent/athlete relationships, including those that led to great careers for the Williams sisters, Maria Sharapova, and Martina Hingis in tennis. However, hundreds of athletes fail because of poor interpersonal communication with parents. In fact, Delforge (2006) concludes that "oftentimes at a local, regional and junior level, parental behavior is a hindrance rather than a help to the child's progress" (p. 5).

Delforge points to several factors as determinants of how conducive interpersonal communication between the parent and athlete would be. These determinants are age and personality of both player and parent, family type, and social background of the parents. Often, highly involved parents attempt to live vicariously through their child. In essence, they will pressure the child to achieve far more than may be possible considering the child's abilities. This can become a difficult situation for the child.

Here, I narrate a case in youth soccer (association football) that I witnessed. The player in this case was a first-generation American, born to Greek parents. The player had average ability, but it did not stop the father from pressuring the child at practices and in games. The father was a fan of the sport and followed Greek football religiously, even though he was now resident in America. It was clear in my conversations with him that he wanted his child to play professional football, perhaps for Greece, but the child was 14 years old at this time. The father would correct the player incessantly and publicly in front of the player's peers. He would run commentary on the player's performance during games. Although these commentaries were in Greek and not understandable to the rest of the parents, one could make out a few words. The commentaries were loud, and the player's mother tried unsuccessfully to get her husband to calm down. The player was unraveled by his father's running commentaries and would frequently wave him off as the game went on. One can only imagine what was going on in the child's mind. The child did not make the grade in the sport and moved down from the academy level to the lower club travel level.

Studies also affirm the importance of parent/athlete interpersonal relationships. A study by Babkes and Weiss (1999) shows that athletes who perceived parental interaction to be supportive had "higher perceptions of competence, intrinsic motivation, and sport enjoyment" (p. 57). It seems that certain factors are very important in interpersonal sport communication between parents and athletes. Delforge labels those factors as "favorable behaviors," and they include support and encouragement, motivating and demanding, playing down the importance of competition and defeat, attentiveness to the child's need, allowing the child to participate in decisions, and maintaining positive overall communication.

CHAPTER SUMMARY

This chapter focuses on interpersonal communication and sport. It begins with a definition of interpersonal communication and also identifies the goals of such communication between two persons. These goals are usually instrumental, self-presentation, and relationship.

Photo 2.2 Children playing youth soccer where the only spectators may be parents who communicate with them interpersonally.

Source: Author

COACHING YOUTH SPORT AND COMMUNICATING WITH PARENTS

Lisa Smith has coached youth basketball for five years and experienced few negative interpersonal communications with parents. Yet, she has been a hard-nosed coach who drives her girls to the best athletic performance that each of them can produce. Usually, this leads to several local and statewide championships, and several of her girls continue on to excellent college athletic careers. But this year is different.

She is now coaching U-16 girls, and her team is classified as elite, with several of her girls likely headed to top colleges in the next two years. One of her players is Anna Belcher, a thinly built 6-foot-tall girl who plays forward with decent shooting range but below-average defensive skill because her foot speed is slow, leading to foul calls. Anna was a leading athlete on her previous teams until Smith began to coach her in the U-16 Rough Riders.

Lately, Coach Smith has Anna playing as a reserve. Anna's father, Brendan, is unhappy. "How can you possibly bench Anna?" he asked Coach Smith. The coach is surprised by the question. "I know what I am doing," she responds. "I have been coaching youth sport, and I assure you that before Anna's career on my team is over, she will improve in several areas and become a good college player." Anna's father was unimpressed by Coach Smith's explanation. "I played the game, and I know that Anna is better than some of the girls that start on this team. I do not know what she has done that has led to this punishment. It is just unfair. Everyone can see that Anna is a superior player and her not starting is not helping the team. If you cannot see that, then I am not sure how good your coaching skills are!" That was it for Coach Smith. She walked off. She has promised herself that when a parent begins to question her ability as coach, then it is time to ignore them.

Coach Smith can see improvement in Anna's play, but it has not been at a level where she deserves to start ahead of any starter on her team. Besides that, Anna has played enough minutes in each game to be noticed by several college scouts watching the team play in tournament showcases.

Unfortunately, Anna has increasingly become moody. She is not happy that she is not starting. At home, her father has made it a habit to correct every part of her play, and he has spoken harshly about her skill and screamed at her on occasions: "Why can't you show aggression? You just let people go past you as if you do not exist. You need to be quicker. I am not spending money paying for you to be on the Rough Riders if the only thing you do is feel comfortable sitting on the bench."

Anna feels that she is perhaps no longer as good as she used to be. She is no longer confident about her ability when talking with her father. But what she is unsure about is why her coach keeps telling her that she is improving. She realizes that she has been working hard, and her coach has pointed to areas in which she has improved. She has also heard positive comments from her teammates but not from her father. She just does not understand what her father is asking her to do, and she dreads his attendance at games. At times, when she is alone, she wonders whether playing basketball is worth it. She thinks *all the effort that I am putting on improving has not made me a starter on my team, and my father does not even acknowledge my efforts.*

At a recent showcase with some of the best basketball players in the country, Anna averages 20 minutes on the court as a substitute. It represents the most minutes played by a non-starter. Anna plays reasonably well, scoring 10 points, but her inability to match up well with a speedy opponent allows the other team to beat the Rough Riders by three points late in one game. The coach speaks to the team and congratulates Anna on her play but points out a few things that she needs to work on. Anna is encouraged and is looking forward to telling her father immediately after the team meeting.

But as she comes out to meet her father for the journey back home, she notices that her father is visibly upset. She does not know why. A few seconds later, he explodes: "What exactly were you doing in the last few seconds to let that player get past you? You are just not improving, Anna. What is so difficult in defending other players?" Anna breaks down sobbing. She is emotionally distraught. She has given her all in this game, and her coach has acknowledged it, but *why not my father* she thinks. Her father is silent, but he believes that it may be time to stop Anna from playing basketball.

The next day at practice, Anna shares her story with one of Coach Smith's assistants. The assistant speaks to Coach Smith, who is unhappy about the situation. She now plans to call Anna's father and have a meeting with him about the need to change his communication style with his daughter. Coach Smith thinks about her previous communication with Mr. Belcher and is not too sure what the outcome of this one would be. However, she does not want to lose Anna.

Discussion questions

1. What type(s) of interpersonal communication goals should Coach Smith seek to achieve when communicating with Mr. Belcher? How does she make sure that Anna does not quit basketball?
2. How would you analyze Anna's *self* and her presentation of self in her interpersonal communication with her coach and then with her father?
3. Plot Anna's *self* using a Johari Window. You may fill up gaps that the case may have been silent on by making assumptions about Anna's personality.
4. Is there *fundamental attribution error* on the part of Mr. Belcher when analyzing his daughter's performance? If so, why?

The chapter points to a preponderance of interpersonal communication during activities that symbolize sport communication. Importantly, because the focus of the text is international sport communication, the chapter notes miscommunication that results from cultural effects on interpersonal communication between persons from different cultural backgrounds.

An important aspect of interpersonal communication is presentation of self during communication. This recognizes the importance of self-concept, self-awareness, and self-esteem during such a context. While self-presentation is important during interpersonal communication, the chapter notes that the perception of the other during such context may be riddled with inaccuracies that lead to attribution errors, halo effect, horn effect, and stereotyping, among others.

The final section of the chapter provides three examples of interpersonal communication situations in sport. The examples are coach/athlete communication, coach/parent communication, and parent/athlete communication.

DISCUSSION QUESTIONS

1 In which ways is the relationship between two parties exposed during interpersonal communication?
2 Which cultural reasons explain miscommunication during interpersonal sport communication between persons from different cultural backgrounds?
3 What is *self*? Please provide a definition and describe various attributes of self.
4 Describe the Johari Window and how it is used in understanding *self* in interpersonal communication.
5 What is *fundamental attribution error*? Provide example of how this occurs in an interpersonal sport communication situation.

ACTIVITIES

1 Visit a youth sport team practice or game in your neighborhood. Observe how a parent may relate to his or her child athlete. Introduce yourself to the parent and ask for his or her feeling about the child's participation in sport. Then write a report about your visit, making sure that you focus on interpersonal communication between the parent and his or her child athlete.
2 Watch a film on sport. During the film, carefully pay attention to interpersonal relationships demonstrated in the film. There would be several such relationships but focus attention on a key one. Make sure that you make copious notes of what you observed and then write a three- to four-page report on your observations, analyzing them based on principles discussed in this chapter.
3 Set up an interview with a college athlete. During the interview, find out from the athlete how he or she communicates with the coach. Does the athlete consider communication with the coach positive or negative, or both? Why? Make sure the athlete provides examples. Use the interview information to write a report on the athlete's interpersonal communication with the coach.
4 Visit a nearby sporting venue where immigrant populations play sport. Talk to some of the immigrants who participate in the sport, asking them questions about their sport and whether they communicate with athletes from a different country about sport. What were difficulties in that communication and why? Take notes and then write a report on what you found.

VIDEO RESOURCES

Touching the Void (Documentary/106 mins.). This is a documentary on two climbers and their challenging journey up the Andes Mountains in 1985.
Hoop Dreams (Documentary/170 mins.). This documentary follows the lives of two inner-city Chicago athletes who struggle to play college basketball with hope of making it to the elite professional basketball league in America.

So This Is College (Film). In this film, college teammates Biff and Eddie compete for the love of Babs Baxter.
Youngstown Boys (Film). This is a story of the relationship between a college gridiron football coach and his star player.
Champions: A Love Story (Film). This film is about two teen athletes who fall in love while training for figure skating.
Wimbledon (Film). Two players pursue a love relationship during a Wimbledon tennis tournament.

RECOMMENDED WEB RESOURCES

Communication skills training for interactive sports: http://the-coach-athlete-relationship.wikispaces.com/file/view/Communication+Skills+Training+for+Interactive+Sports.pdf
Effective communication: A key to effective officiating: www.ausport.gov.au/sportsofficialmag/
Guidelines for interpersonal communication: http://sportsconflict.org/resource/

REFERENCES

Babkes, M., & Weiss, M. (1999). Parental influence on children's cognitive and affective responses to competitive soccer participation. *Pediatric Exercise Science*, 11: 44–62.
Bloom, G. (1996). Life at the top. In Salmela, J. (Ed.), *Great job coach!* (pp. 139–178). Ottawa, ON: Potentium.
Bodie, G., & Worthington, D. (2010). Revisiting the listening styles profile (LSP – 16): A confirmatory factor analytic approach to scale validation and reliability estimation. *International Journal of Listening*, 14 (2): 69–88.
Culver, D., & Trudel, P. (2000). Coach-athlete communication within an elite alpine ski team. *Journal of Excellence*, 3: 28–54.
D'Arripe-Longueville, F., Fournier, J., & Dubois, A. (1998). The perceived effectiveness of interactions between expert French judo coaches and elite female athletes. *The Sport Psychologist*, 12: 317–332.
Delforge, C. (2006). Analysis of parent-player relationships and the role of the coach. *Coaching & Sport Science Review*, 38: 5–6.
Heider, F. (1958). *The psychology of interpersonal relations*. New York: John Wiley & Sons.
Hellstedt, J. (1987). The coach/parent/athlete relationship. *The Sport Psychologist*, 1: 151–160.
Jowett, S. (2003). When the 'Honeymoon' is over: A case study of a coach-athlete dyad in crisis. *The Sport Psychologist*, 17: 444–460.
Jowett, S., & Cockerill, I. (2002). Incompatibility in the coach-athlete relationship. In Cockerill, J. (Ed.), *Solution in sport psychology* (pp. 16–31). London: Thompson Learning.
Luft, J., & Ingham, H. (1955). *The Johari window: A graphic model of interpersonal awareness* (Proceedings of the western training laboratory in group development). Los Angeles, CA: University of California.
Maslow, A. (1970). (2nd ed.). *Motivation and personality*. New York: Harper & Row.
McCornack, S. (2013). *Reflect & relate: An introduction to interpersonal communication*. Boston, MA: Bedford/St. Martin's.
McLean, K. (2008). Dealing with parents: Promoting dialogue. *Sports Coach: An Online Magazine for Coaches*, 30(1): 1–3.

Nakamura, R. (1996). *The power of positive coaching.* Boston, MA: Jones and Bartlett.

Nangalia, L., & Nangalia, A. (2010). The coach in Asian society: Impact of social hierarchy on the coaching relationship. *International Journal of Evidence Based Coaching and Mentoring,* 8(1): 51–66.

Orlick, T., & Partington, J. (1986). *Psyched.* Ottawa, ON: Coaching Association of Canada.

Spink, K. (1991). The psychology of coaching. *New Studies in Athletics,* 6(4): 37–41.

Weaver, W., & Shannon, C. (1963). *The mathematical theory of communication.* Champaign, IL: University of Illinois Press.

CHAPTER 3

COMMUNICATING LEADERSHIP IN SPORT TEAMS AND ORGANIZATIONS

> **LEARNING OBJECTIVES**
>
> After reading this chapter, you should be able to do the following:
>
> - Understand team leadership communication in sport teams.
> - Recognize the difference between communication and management in teams and in sport organizations.
> - Recognize application of various leadership styles in sport at various levels and contexts.
> - Understand leadership styles of various great leaders in sport and how their communication styles help with accomplishments.
> - Identify climate and culture in sport organizations and leadership impact.
> - Identify power and leadership in sport organizations.

LEADERSHIP COMMUNICATION

Communicating leadership in sport is essential to the success of teams and organizations in sport. Sport is a field where leadership has been studied for a long period, and every day consumption of sport features discussions about great coaches and players who lead teams to success in competitions or in some type of innovation or the other. Thus, the intersection of sport and leadership is nothing new. However, this chapter narrows its focus on an aspect of leadership, which is essential to success. That aspect is leadership communication, or how leaders communicate to their followers in order to achieve success. Leadership communication may be within a small group/team or within organizations. Small groups usually number 3 to 20 persons and are often close knit with a flat hierarchy of leadership, whereas organizations are much larger with tall hierarchies. Players of Guandong Evergrande Volleyball Club, who play in the Chinese professional women's volleyball league, will be regarded as a small group, but the club's larger organization would, in addition, include a backroom administrative team and other staff. Communication, involving the team, is regarded as small group/team communication, whereas communication involving the entire organization refers to organizational communication.

The chapter discussion begins with defining a few key terms clarifying concepts that are important to a discussion of how leadership is communicated in sport. These concepts are leadership and leadership communication. In addition, the chapter will differentiate between the concepts of leadership and management.

Leadership is the ability to influence others in the direction of achieving a vision and goals that form that vision. Leadership exists in all aspects of human activity, and it is vital for success in sport. In sport, a leader is someone who has the ability to influence others in order to achieve a vision. This definition makes it clear that a leader starts with a vision. For instance, a sport leader may have the vision that his or her team will become the national champion, and there may be several goals towards achieving that vision. Such goals may include playing with passion, developing a great team defense, and avoiding major conflicts within the team. The leader persuades members of his or her team to believe and become committed to the vision and goals.

For instance, South Africa's Francois Pienaar is reputed to have led the South African rugby team "The Springboks" to a World Cup victory in 1995 after the team failed to compete in the previous two World Cups because of the country's practice of apartheid. No one expected South Africa to win the World Cup, but they did it in front of their fans and gingered by Pienaar. Pienaar's qualities as a leader led to his appointment as captain on his first test, and he remained captain until his last test. Prior to the 1995 World Cup, South Africa was seeded ninth, and no one gave them a chance, but Pienaar showed leadership in making his teammates believe that victory was possible. Remarkably, in the final game against New Zealand, Pienaar developed a calf sprain, but he refused to leave, and he completed the game to show solidarity with his team. It was likely that while Pienaar's vision was to win the 1995 World Rugby Cup, he had several goals for how to get there. For instance, he wanted his teammates to be committed to playing well and overcoming adversities. Furthermore, it is obvious that he wanted the entire nation to back the team on the way to winning the World Cup. But getting the support of the nation was not easy because Springboks was supported by Whites, and Blacks loathed the team. To overcome this, Pienaar took the team to Robben Island to visit Nelson Mandela in prison. This was a move to get Black South African support. At the end, after the team won the World Cup, Pienaar made it clear in his speech that victory was not just for the team but for all South Africans.

Pienaar's leadership was beyond just the field of play. After the team won the 1995 World Cup, the South African Rugby Football Union (SARFU) offered an apartheid-like contract to the only Black member of the Springboks, Chester Williams. Williams was arguably the team's second most important player, but his contract offer did not reflect that. Pienaar led a stand-off against SARFU and convinced his teammates to sign for the World Rugby Corporation and not SARFU. Eventually, SARFU was able to stave off the stand-off. Pienaar's leadership was widely acknowledged, and a film called *Invictus* was made about him and President Mandela to show their remarkable leadership during that historic event.

President Mandela, despite misgivings by Black South Africans, gave his full support to the Springboks, calling the team a symbol of the new rainbow nation of South Africa. The Springboks, during apartheid, was the sport symbol for racism and apartheid, as it was largely restricted to only White players. President Mandela made an astute political decision to support the team and attend its games among a largely White South African audience. In the final game, President Mandela wore the Springboks' shirt, underlining his support. These actions went a long way in softening Black South Africa's stance against the team in a mood of reconciliation.

The examples of leadership provided above give us an idea of how leadership is communicated to followers. However, it is important to provide a definition as well. **Communicating leadership** involves communicating in such a way that delivered messages modify "attitudes and behaviors of others in order to meet shared group goals and needs" (Hackman & Johnson, 2009, p. 11). Leaders are great communicators and storytellers. They use communication to effectively manage the emotions of followers, build a productive climate, and keep followers focused on the vision.

Hackman and Johnson (2009) point to how leaders use dramatic elements to create a sustaining story that makes an impression on followers. These elements include framing, scripting, staging, and performing. **Framing** refers to structuring an overarching message to help followers interpret the vision. For instance, the leader of a team that has lost multiple times in championship games may create a frame of winning the championship as being within reach this time. This frame is supported with the talent of the team and the leader's message that the city expects it and that the team has to take the responsibility for bringing the championship to the city. **Scripting** refers to providing guidelines and directions for making the vision achievable. In this case, the leader may define these guidelines as attending practices without excuse, supporting teammates, playing harder than ever, and everyone committing to team tactics. **Staging** refers to creating the public image of the team's commitment to winning the championship. This may involve the leader placing motivating posters around team facilities, delivering motivating messages during press conferences, and referring to team commitment, among other supporting themes and props. Finally, **performing** refers to practicing behaviors that are recommended in the script. The leader leads in this regard by ensuring that he or she is always at practices, is first to support teammates, plays hard, and follows team tactics. The leader also reminds others and encourages them.

Photo 3.1 Coach talking to players of his team. This type of communication requires a demonstration of leadership.

Source: Dreamstime.com, reprinted with permission

Though *leadership* and *management* are often used interchangeably, they are different concepts. A leader is focused on the vision or overall direction of the team, group, or organization, whereas a manager ensures that current tasks are accomplished effectively and efficiently. This differentiation based on delineating functions presents the subtle difference between the two concepts. In reality, Hackman and Johnson (2009) argue: "Managers may act as leaders" (p. 11). Crust and Lawrence (2006) point out that the role of association football manager merges the traditional roles of both manager and leader. Thus, rather than expecting every sport manager to be restricted to manager functions, it is instructive that the title of the position does not always define exactly the functions of the individual who bears such titles. What is important is to fully understand the functions of the individual in order to understand whether those functions symbolize those of a manager or those of a leader.

LEADERSHIP APPROACHES AND STYLES

Scholars approach the study of leadership from several standpoints about what characterizes leadership or what kinds of things influence application or demonstration of leadership. These approaches are traits, functions (behavioral), situations, relationships, and the idea of transformation. Each approach is described as follows:

Trait approach

The **trait** approach to leadership assumes that personal characteristics determine leadership. However, Stodgill (1974) found that more than 100 traits are associated with leadership, which tend to confound and confuse the knowledge on leadership. Some of the traits are confirmed by research, including traits related to intelligence, altruism, and honesty. In a study of the big five personality factors, four of them, including extraversion, conscientiousness, neuroticism, and openness, are associated with leadership, but agreeableness is not. However, the idea that leaders are born and not groomed is not supported by research.

Some personality traits also lead to **leadership styles**, such as autocratic, democratic, or laissez-faire. Style refers to a pattern of communication that is largely enduring and that a leader uses when communicating with followers. In essence, a leader uses a style, which reflects the leader's personality, while interacting with followers over time. A sport leader who uses an *autocratic style* dictates to followers what needs to be done and does not actively listen to the opinions of followers. These leaders believe that they have all the answers, and followers are there to listen and act accordingly. Freeman's (2015) description of the Philadelphia Eagles' coach describes one such leader. Freeman wrote: "You understand that he doesn't want to be challenged, so don't f – king challenge him. It's pretty simple. I get it. Some guys don't." Freeman was citing one of the players in a tumultuous season with Coach Chip Kelly of the Eagles, which is a gridiron football team in the United States. However, this leadership style may be preferred in some cultures and is effective because followers yearn for such a leader.

Leaders who use a *democratic style* are those who are high in openness. They support follower communication and encourage information sharing. Sport leaders who exhibit this type of leadership consult followers before making a decision. In some cultures, this style is preferred. Kajtna and Baric (2009), in a study of Slovene coaches, found that successful ones are those who use a democratic style with reduced directivity and increased attention to an athlete's feelings and needs.

The *laissez-faire style* is without strong direct leadership. Instead, followers are left to make their own decisions, and the "leader" generally delegates responsibility. This style is effective if followers are highly self-motivated, experienced, and skilled. If not, the result may be chaos. Pederson, Miloch, and Laucella (2007) cite the leadership of an American baseball team by Pete Rose in the 1980s as an example of this type of leadership. The team environment became chaotic and the coach was dismissed.

Functional (behavioral) approach

This approach does not assume that leaders are born with certain personalities that make them leaders. Instead, it focuses on learned behaviors of persons. A person is then perceived as a leader if his or her adopted and cumulated behaviors are those that are identified as leader behaviors. These behaviors are categorized into two of three general roles that persons play within groups or organizations. The roles that support leadership are task-related and group building/maintenance.

Task-related roles define activities that lead a group or organization in accomplishing a specified task. For instance, a player who speaks to others about how to operationalize an on-field tactical maneuver or speaks to others about how to help the team close the margin of points against an opponent. All those examples are specific to the team task of winning a game or championship.

Group building/maintenance roles do not focus on a task, but yet they act indirectly to support accomplishment of a task. Hackman and Johnson (2009) identify these roles as encourager, harmonizer/compromiser, gatekeeper, and standard-setter. Ultimately, the person acts to bring team members together and to create a positive communication climate that supports task accomplishment.

Individual roles do not support leadership. These activities do not support either task or group building and maintenance. Instead, the activities may be disruptive to group effectiveness. Examples of such roles are domineering behaviors that disparage the views of others, an intense focus on personal recognition, or demonstrating cynicism and/or an uncaring disposition.

Situational approach

This approach developed as several questions arose to challenge claims of both trait and behavioral approaches to leadership. For instance, it became clear that no single trait determines leadership and, in certain cases, traits associated with leadership appear to conflict with each other. Similar issues confront the behavioral approach. In response, scholars began to believe that leadership is situational. This means that leadership varies according to the situation.

Several situational leadership models exist, including Fiedler's Contingency Model, the Path-Goal theory, the decision-making model of leadership, Cognitive Resource theory, Strategic Contingencies theory, and Hersey and Blanchard's Situational Leadership theory.

In Hersey and Blanchard's **Situational Leadership theory**, a leader considers various elements before adopting a leadership style. A leader must first determine his or her followers' readiness level based on followers' abilities and motivation to complete a task (see Table 3.1). A leader uses a certain relationship level and a task orientation towards followers based on level of readiness. Readiness level 1, which reflects followers with low motivation and low ability, requires ensuring task accomplishment through high task-directing and low relationship communication.

Table 3.1 Leadership styles, included as cell narratives, are based on the ability and motivation of followers.

FOLLOWER READINESS		MOTIVATION	
		HIGH	LOW
ABILITY	HIGH	**READINESS 4** **Delegate:** Use low relationship with low task direction	**READINESS 3** **Encourage:** High relationship building and low task direction
	LOW	**READINESS 2** **Selling:** Build high relationship and use high task directing to guide	**READINESS 1** **Ensure:** Use low relationship with high task directing

Source: Adapted from Hersey and Blanchard (1969)

Readiness level 2 reflects followers with low ability but high motivation. For this group, the recommended leadership type is selling, which includes building high relationship and using high task-directing. For Readiness level 3, which has followers with high ability but low motivation, the leader focuses on low task direction but high relationship to encourage participation. Finally, Readiness level 4, which is followers with high ability and high motivation, requires delegating via low task direction and maintaining low relationship.

A situational leadership model such as Hersey and Blanchard's requires a highly agile sport leader with the ability to adapt to varying situations. For instance, a coach who is highly task-focused when working with a team of young professionals may require being hands off when working with veteran players. It is difficult to find this characteristic in a single individual and, thus, you often read that a team with young athletes prefers a certain coach because the coach has a track record of working successfully with a young team. Unfortunately, while CEOs of companies have years to fix a company, a sport coach often has no such leisure, particularly in a high-visibility sport. Crust and Lawrence (2006) report that a professional coach in association football averages below two years on the job, which is "seldom conducive to the successful management of a complex business" (p. 28). Thus, time to adapt to changing situations may not be quite adequate, and new situations may force a change in leadership.

Relationship approach

Unlike other approaches, the relationship approach focuses on development of mutually beneficial relationships between followers and leader. However, it is important to note that this relationship is not between all followers and a leader. Instead, a leader develops an in-group and an out-group from followers.

The Leader-Member Exchange (LMX) theory by Graen and Uhl-Bien (1998) exemplifies an approach to leadership based on relationships. In-group members feel an obligation and sense of responsibility because of their relationship with the leader, and this leads to trust, mutual influence, and more and wider responsibility and latitude on task issues. Of course, such members become highly satisfied, more productive, more likely to provide honest feedback, and more committed. Characteristics of these members include similarity with the leader. Out-group members experience the opposite. Though they can move into the in-group, as long as they remain in the out-group they are often not trusted, and they lack support from the leader. Leader communication to out-group members is characterized by authoritarian and task-oriented messages. Out-group members become susceptible to higher turnover and have general dissatisfaction with work and the leader.

There are examples of LMX in sport teams. Yildiz (2011) confirms the existence of LMX in a study of 107 players of six professional football teams in Turkey, where results show that high LMX inversely influences burnout of professional players. Case (1998) tested the basic principles of the LMX theory between coaches and 178 players in a female basketball summer camp. The study found support for LMX where starters on the basketball teams scored significantly higher on the leadership scale compared to other players.

However, there are aspects of LMX that do not describe effectively what happens in some professional sports. For instance, Graen and Uhl-Bien's (1998) use of LMX to examine sport teams shows exceptions to building in-group membership. They describe a three-phase model for leadership-making that moves from stranger to acquaintanceship to partnership, but the model is not always accurate in the development of in-group membership. For instance, they found that coaches usually include the top athlete of their team as part of the in-group. These athletes skip the three phases. For the coaches, inclusion of the top athlete is a way to accomplish a winning vision and to sustain the coach's position in the team. This athlete and the coach may not necessarily pass through a stranger phase, particularly if the athlete has already achieved superstar reputation and is traded or transferred to the team. In such a case, there is a drive to achieve partner status right away.

Transformational approach

This approach focuses on leadership that results in high productivity among followers. Essentially, the leader uses his or her charisma to inspire followers to a high level of self-motivation, empowerment, and belongingness. Followers take the initiative to accomplish the leader's vision. This approach is different from other leadership approaches because instead of focusing on satisfying basic physiological (food, water, among others) and safety (security, order, among others) needs of followers, it goes into satisfying higher follower needs, such as belongingness, self-esteem, and self-actualization.

Transformational leaders exhibit five key characteristics: they are passionate, visionary, interactive, creative, and empowering. These leaders are not sticklers for rules. Instead, they regard rules as flexible and may change according to norms of the group as long as the vision of the group or organization is accomplished. Hoption, Phelan, and Barling (2007) describe ice hockey great, Wayne Gretzky, as a transformational leader. They show through others' perception of Gretzky and narration of encounters with him that Gretzky inspires his teammates to go above and beyond to achieve for a greater goal than each of them have. They noted Gretzky's exceptional communication ability in bringing people together and how he works towards accomplishment of goals.

Other sport-related leadership approaches

Though we have shown how each leadership approach applies to sport communication, there are lingering doubts about the effective application of some of the approaches. Crust and Lawrence (2006) argue that early sport-specific research provides little support to existing leadership approaches and that sport teams have unique characteristics that make application difficult.

Invariably, sport-specific leadership approaches emerged because of those difficulties. Sport-specific approaches include Grusky's group structure model, Chelladurai's multidimensional model of leadership, and the shared mental model of leadership.

Grusky (1963) introduced the **group structure model**, which suggests a leadership approach based on an athlete's position on the sport field. In essence, the model proposes that players who occupy more central positions in team sport are more likely to develop leadership qualities than are colleagues who play in peripheral positions. The logic is that a central position – or what is sometimes described as a spine position – means that the player's tasks are dependent on others and, thus, players in those positions have to coordinate the on-field activities of others to be successful. By doing so, they are more vocal and develop other leadership skills. Grusky's initial proposal is supported by baseball data, which show that players who play in central positions like catcher and shortstop end up becoming managers more often compared to players who play in other positions. The proposition is also supported by other studies, such as Lee, Coburn, and Partridge (1983) on association football in England and by Melnick and Loy's (1996) study of rugby players in New Zealand. Notwithstanding the results of those studies, scholars believe that far more studies of other sports are needed to confirm the proposition.

Chelladurai developed the **multidimensional model of leadership**, which is widely used to study leadership in sport (Chelladurai & Riemer, 1998). The model proposes that leadership effectiveness depends on management of interactions among three critical elements of the leader, group members, and situational constraints. In essence, positive results such as effective performance and satisfaction are achieved when critical elements are aligned. For instance, the leader's behavior matches expectations of group members and the situation faced by the group or team. However, when there is failure in alignment, then the leader must be adaptable in order to be successful. This adaptability might mean the leader changing his or her leadership style to fit the situation, persuading team members to adapt if that is the problem area, or removing the problem, which may be a group member or members. Chelladurai's work proposes that an autocratic style is appropriate for large teams like in gridiron football, in interactive team sports such as volleyball and basketball, and for more complex situations. A democratic style is preferred for co-acting sports such as swimming, tennis, badminton, or bowling.

LEADING IN A TOUGH AND DEMOTIVATING ENVIRONMENT

The Nigerian national football team overcame high odds to win a medal in men's soccer at the 2016 Olympic Games. However, the journey to victory was marked with several challenges, and it took the leadership of the team captain to keep the team focused on the prize when it seemed difficult to do so.

The team's captain, Mikel Obi, is an unassuming, strong, and considerate leader. He was made both captain of Nigeria's Olympic football team and captain of Nigeria's entire athletic contingent to the Games. It was the first time a football player assumed such a mantle for Nigeria. His leadership characteristics were notable even when he was on the Nigerian youth teams. He was made captain of the country's U20 team to the World Youth Cup in 2005, where he led the country to a second-place finish. Since then, he has remained influential in the country's senior national team for a long period, becoming one of four players that unofficially provide leadership to the rest of the team. At the 2013 Cup for African Nations and the 2014 World Cup, the national team coach made Mikel his primary confidant, even though Mikel was neither captain nor assistant captain at the time.

For the 2016 Olympic Games in Rio, Mikel was one of two over-age players selected to a team of U23 players. FIFA allows each country to select no more than three over-age players to participate in Olympic football during the Games.

Mikel's public personality is quiet, but within the team he is highly respected and fondly referred to as *Odogwu* by players who follow his lead. *Odogwu*, in Igbo language, refers to conqueror or leader. It is a testament to his leadership skills, which are evident behind the scenes, and the Rio Olympics brought that to the fore.

Mikel left his professional club – Chelsea FC of England – to join Nigeria's Olympic camp in Atlanta, United States. About the same time, it appeared that the Nigerian government abandoned the team, claiming in the media that the team had not received approval to leave the country to train in the United

States. Nigeria's Minister of Sport, Solomon Dalung, claimed: "They (Olympic team) didn't tell us what they were there (Atlanta) for and who took them there. . . . Because they are (the Olympic team), they went to the US and they are having problems, does that become our business?" The players did not receive promised daily camp allowances, and the team had little or no funds to pay for its accommodation in Atlanta. Mikel arrived and met the coach and players and set about helping to rectify problems. Mikel's meetings are usually on a one-and-one basis, and he is friendly even to younger and newer players, who are usually ignored by senior players in a culture based on high power distances. Mikel says that: "We (he and the coach) tried to calm the players, make them see the bigger picture and not let external things influence us."

Eventually, Mikel paid for parts of the team's accommodation and feeding costs. The team, however, had no funds to travel to the Games in Brazil and began to pressure the government to meet its responsibilities to take teams to the Olympics. Eventually, the government provided a 25-seat aircraft for the long flight to Brazil a few days before the team's opening match. However, Mikel led players to reject the aircraft, pointing out that the aircraft's flight range was not good enough for the trip, as it would have to refuel a few times in order to get to Brazil, and there were safety concerns on such a small aircraft. He dug in his heels until the government found a bigger airplane.

The team arrived in Brazil just a few hours before its first match against Japan. Mikel had to speak with the players, informing them to remain focused on the big prize, which was winning the gold medal. The team, without rest, went on to beat Japan 5–4, conceding two late goals because of fatigue. But the team's travails in Brazil had only begun. Mikel had to pay close to $5,000 to take care of hotel bills and then led a protest ensuring that players received three weeks of camp allowances that were left unpaid.

While Mikel worked tirelessly behind the scenes, there were government officials unhappy about his leadership. If they could delay paying athletes, they would have more funds available to take care of their own needs during the trip. They, however, could do very little about Mikel since the latter had full support of the team, and players saw him as one who could fight for player rights and protect players. In fact, a Nigerian journalist wrote: "None of the other players would have had the gravitas to pull off such a demand (for a change of aircraft). Mikel was also at the forefront of a training boycott to press home their demands for unpaid allowances to be settled." Though Mikel's work ensured that players were compensated, it also increased conflict between team and sport officials, as well as the government. How far would such uneasiness with Mikel's leadership take Nigeria on its quest to become a football power?

Discussion questions

1. What approach to leadership do you think Mikel Obi took and why?
2. How did Mikel Obi communicate leadership to his teammates?
3. The last sentence in the case mentions uneasiness with Mikel's leadership among the sporting leaders and government. Do you think Mikel's leadership will be effective in helping Nigeria to reach its potential in world football? Why?
4. The Minister of Sport cited his non-approval of the team's Atlanta camping as reason for not funding the team. Do you think that is a good reason? Why?
5. How may one apply Chelladurai's multidimensional model of leadership to Mikel Obi's leadership style? Indicate how that model may be used to analyze Obi's leadership of the team at the Olympic Games.

The concept of a **shared mental model of leadership** is based on the logic that a sport team's effectiveness requires a critical mass of influential players sharing the same values of performance as the leader. In essence, the team leader, who may be the coach, would work to identify key team players who share the same performance vision and values as the leader. The coach disseminates his or her ideas through this group of influential players. Crust and Lawrence (2006) cite a BBC program, which documented how the England national team coach for association football, Sven-Goran Ericksson, works with team psychologist, Dave Collins, to identify three influential players on the team who bought into the ideas of Ericksson and helped disseminate and persuade others to achieve the coach's vision.

REFLECTION

Think of a sport film or documentary that you watched and that demonstrates strong leadership personalities or leadership styles that attract followers. What are the key elements of the leadership style that you observed? Why did they seem to work effectively? Why do followers commit to follow such leaders? Do you think that other elements of leadership are not portrayed in sport films and documentaries? If yes, which ones? Reflect on answers that readily emerge as you review the questions.

CLIMATE AND CULTURE: LEADERSHIP IMPACT

Organizations usually have a culture that differentiates one organization from the other and identifies the way things are done in the organization over a period of time.

Within such organizations also exist climates that are more immediate and often reflect a working environment influenced by current leadership.

Organizational culture is the assumptions, values, and symbols shared by an organization and its members over a period of time. Those three elements are enduring. The organizational culture is reflected in predominant language used in describing what the organization is and is shared in organizational stories. Furthermore, culture is reflected in the organization's rituals and its heroes. The organization's assumptions are beliefs about relationships and tasks within the organization, whereas values are those things that the organization feels are important. Symbols are artifacts of the organization, which may include myths, frequently used language, written materials, metaphors, heroes, technologies, and buildings, among others.

Sport teams cultivate particular cultures that they seek to maintain over time. Real Madrid Football Club in Spain has developed a culture of sport excellence and achievement. Jerome (2008) briefly captures this culture in these words:

> Maybe the greatest in the world of football. Nevertheless, any number (of things) can explain what Real Madrid really means. It's not a matter of titles, it's not a matter of players. It's all about excellence, tradition, and pride. These three words are part of Real culture.
>
> (para. 1–3)

Real Madrid's culture of excellence has been built over so many decades that it goes back to the era of Santiago Bernabeu as Club President in the 1940s. Bernabeu began a policy of signing the best players in the world in the 1950s and developing facilities. This led to numerous titles in Spain, Europe, and the world. Importantly, the culture drives the team to seek the best in whatever it does. It seeks the best coaches in association football and the best players. At one time, it signed several of the world's best players in the 1990s and became known as "The Galacticos" (a galaxy of stars). Recently, it marketed itself worldwide and became the second most valuable sport team in the Forbes World's Most Valuable Sport Team list at $3.65 billion, behind gridiron football team Dallas Cowboys (Trehan, 2016).

Organizational climate refers to "the type of social and emotional atmosphere leaders create for followers" (Hackman & Johnson, 2009, p. 258). Often, organizational climate is confused with organizational culture when that does not need to be the case. Culture is more enduring, whereas climate is deeply affected by a particular leadership style. Thus, using the Real Madrid example, while the culture has been relatively stable for a long number of years, the climate has changed from time to time. For instance, a certain type of manager may lead to an open and supportive climate because the leadership style is democratic and based on building and maintaining relationships. Under a more autocratic manager, the climate would change. Real Madrid has gone through an autocratic manager in Fabio Capello to a more democratic one in Jose Mourinho. Yet, despite these differences in climate under Capello and Mourinho, the culture of excellence remains relatively stable in Real Madrid because whether the climate is autocratic or democratic, the entire club maintains the value of excellence, continues to use stories of its past heroes such as Bernabeu and Alfredo Di Stefano, and continues to recruit the best players in the world, among other symbols of its excellence.

POWER AND LEADERSHIP IN SPORT

Power and leadership go hand in hand. **Power** refers to the ability to influence others and requires others to be willing to accept that power. In essence, exercising power is only possible because of the relationship or interaction between persons. It is important to realize, however, that all acts of influence do not mean leadership. For instance, a player who disrupts training and forces the event to come to an abrupt end may have exercised influence, but that does not define leadership by such a player.

Leaders exercise power in order to achieve a group or organizational goal. That is what essentially links power to leadership. Leaders may or may not use various sources of power, including rewards, coercion, expertise, and legitimacy.

Reward power simply means that the person who exercises such power has the ability to provide something valuable to those who need it. For instance, the president of a swimming club may exercise reward power because he may design coaches' bonuses based on the accomplishments of their swimming teams. This power motivates each coach to work extra hard with their respective teams, knowing that he or she cannot get bonuses if the team fails at competitions.

Coercive power focuses on the ability to punish. It is based on fear. In essence, a leader uses it to get subordinates to achieve a particular goal. Sport teams in Nigeria use coercive power by threatening and sometimes reducing salaries or bonuses of athletes after poor on-field results. In some cases, teams demote coaches because of such poor results.

Expert power is based on a person using his or her knowledge to influence others. Frequently, sport media focus on expert power by citing a preponderance of experienced veterans on winning teams. Buffa (2016) wrote that the experience of veteran players in the Denver Broncos was one of five reasons why the Broncos would beat the Carolina Panthers to win Super Bowl 50. His prediction was correct, but we have not done any data-based research to confirm that experience is responsible for the Broncos' victory! However, Buffa's claim is not unusual in sport media. Such claims are based on the belief that veteran experience is vital and that veterans lead younger teammates by informing them on how to prepare and about subtleties of play at that level.

Legitimate power is based on the official position occupied by a leader. In essence, position grants the leader written authority over others. For instance, the position of a sport coach and/or team captain grants authority to persons in those positions. For instance, the coach has the authority to determine which player starts for a handball team.

HOW SUCCESSFUL SPORT PERSONALITIES COMMUNICATE LEADERSHIP

You have learned about different types of approaches to leadership and studied organizational culture and climate. Furthermore, you have learned about the relationship between leadership and power. In this section, we briefly describe characteristics of sport's revered leaders and how they communicate leadership. These individuals are acknowledged for their ability to lead others.

Vince Lombardi (NFL/USA) was a famous gridiron football coach in America. He went through his entire professional career without a losing season. He also took over poor teams and made them winners in his first season with each one. Today, his statue is erected in front of the Green Bay Packers' home stadium in Green Bay, Wisconsin, and the championship trophy of the entire league is named after him. Lombardi's leadership style was effective, and he adapted his style to the needs of the team. When he took over poor-performing teams in New York and Green Bay, he was a task-directed leader who worked the players hard because his players lacked ability. He also created high relationships with his players, and they all wanted to do whatever he wanted in order to accomplish goals. He was also innovative and is credited with introducing zone blocking in the league when other coaches frowned at such a strategy. He is reputed to be a great communicator who delivered his ideas in clear terms.

José Pékerman (Soccer/Argentina) is an Argentine association football coach who has won several youth championships at the continental and global levels. He then coached Colombia's national team to great heights including the 2014 World Cup. He is a leader who is confident about his abilities and remains focused on his vision, resisting criticisms. One of his long-time assistants, Hugo Tocalli, is quoted as describing Pékerman as a "strong personality" (Wilson, 2016b). His players, however, accept his leadership because he believes that each one of them is capable of contributing when they buy into his system and they develop self-belief. This led to Arango (2014) describing Pékerman as: "(ingraining) a state of mind in the Colombian player and (creating) a winning culture" (para. 12). He also is willing to experiment with tactics and personnel.

Martin Johnson (Rugby/England) is the antithesis of what most people recognize as a leader. He led his Rugby club, the Leicester Tigers, to several cup victories. He became idolized following England's World Cup win of 2003 under his captainship. He is believed to be one of the greatest lock forwards in rugby. Johnson is a huge man but taciturn and an unlikely person to be named captain. As leader, he preferred to empower others around him to have self-belief and to lead in such a way that power and responsibility is devolved away from a central point. Caulkin (2004) wrote that Johnson's style of leadership is a "kind of inclusive leadership (that) increases the organisation's agility and power to act at the same time. . . . Leadership isn't authority; it's everyone taking responsibility for making decision as robust as it can be, by contest if necessary" (para. 11).

Clare Connor (head women's cricket, ECB/England) was captain of England's cricket team for six years. She became captain when the team was poor. Her leadership helped inspire the team to successes during her tenure. Connor's retirement saw her take her leadership off the field. She became director of England Women's Cricket and was in the forefront of establishing a cricket league for women in the country. Clare is known as being persistent in pushing the interest of those she leads and developing positive relationships with each of them. Among those interests was convincing England Cricket to sign female players to contracts. This type of representation led to player willingness to listen to her and fight to support her vision.

Stephen Keshi (Soccer/Nigeria) was a Nigerian professional football player who was credited with leading the migration of top Nigerian footballers, along with footballers from other West African countries, to Europe to play professionally. He was made captain at all stages of his career, including club and the Nigerian national team. After his playing career, he became a successful coach leading a lowly regarded Togolese national team to an improbable World Cup qualification and winning the Africa Cup with Nigeria, as well as taking Nigeria to the final 16 of the 2014 World Cup. Keshi, named "Big Boss" by colleagues, is reputed for fighting for the interest of followers even to the detriment of his position. Wilson (2016a) described him as both a brawler and the most successful African coach. In addition, Keshi's style was to build close relationships with team members and other publics. Many of the players he coached point to his clear communication and motivational skill.

DEVELOPING LEADERSHIP

Developing people for leadership positions in sport is studied by several scholars, and patterns of this development is understood in the field, particularly in the Western world. Generally, leadership in sport within a group of athletes requires providing effective communication, serving as a liaison between several groups and publics, assisting in preparations, participating in the disciplinary planning and process, and serving as a role model for other athletes. Not all athletes are capable of playing these roles. Therefore, it is important to find out how those who assume those roles and perform well in them prepare themselves prior to serving in such roles.

Most scholars agree that sport leaders usually demonstrate two abilities: (1) the ability to perform tasks (i.e. highly skilled in the sport) and (2) the ability to express or communicate with others. There are few exceptions. In a study by Wright and Côté (2003) of Canadian athletes, they found that in addition to development of sport-specific skill and ability to relate to others, a strong work ethic and cognitive knowledge of the sport is also necessary.

High skill development is possible through early involvement in the sport for the athlete and usually requires parental assistance. Opportunities for skill development are provided through playing with older kids. That encourages the athlete to develop much faster than his or her peers because more skill and speed is required to cope against older children during pre-teen years.

Relational aspects involve taking leadership among peers during pre-teen years, for instance. Coaches assign highly skilled players to lead others in response to particular problems during training at a young age. However, beyond these opportunities to interact with others, players who end up becoming leaders in later years are those who play linking roles with teammates. They do not confine themselves to a limited clique of a few teammates but are open to interacting with most of their teammates.

Work ethic is associated with being highly skilled. Players with a very good ethic practice their sport during organized training and outside of it. They are passionate about the sport. These additional hours of play provide them with a skill edge over their contemporaries. Importantly, that ethic, passion, and high skill level make them role models for peers.

Finally, they also are more cognitively advanced in their knowledge of the game compared to peers. Their passion for the game leads them to watch professional games on television and, in certain cases, read widely about the sport. These activities provide them cognitive advantages and also provide opportunities to discuss knowledgeably with coaches at an early age, which creates relationships that lead to leadership positions.

CHAPTER SUMMARY

Leadership is defined in this chapter, and effective sport leadership in a difficult circumstance is demonstrated, with the example of Francois Pienaar's leadership of the South African Springboks to win the 1995 World Rugby Cup. The chapter also points to how good leaders lead followers, citing four communication factors including framing, scripting, staging, and performing.

A major section of the chapter focuses on identifying various leadership approaches and styles appropriate for understanding leadership in sport. The different approaches include trait, functional (behavioral), situational, relationship, and transformational. Importantly, the section identifies three approaches that are developed specifically for leadership in sport (e.g. the group structure model by Grusky, Chelladurai's multidimensional model of leadership, and the shared mental model of leadership).

Other sections of the chapter include one on climate and culture, where both concepts are defined and differentiated. The differentiation is important considering the difficulty of separating both concepts. Another section of the chapter focuses on power and leadership in sport, which includes a listing and discussion of sources of power. This section provides examples of effective leadership in sport. Five sport personalities are described in a later section to demonstrate successful sport leadership. The last section identifies how leadership may be developed in athletes.

DISCUSSION QUESTIONS

1. What are key differences among three leadership approaches developed for sport leadership?
2. Are trait approaches to leadership appropriate in today's description of leadership in sport?
3. Describe how a sport leader, such as a volleyball coach, may apply leadership communication using elements of framing, scripting, staging, and performing.
4. What are differences between concepts of organizational communication climate and organizational culture?
5. Considering various sources of power, which one would you think is most effective in sport communication? Why? Provide an example of how that source of power is applied in sport leadership.
6. Outline how you may go about developing sport leadership among children who participate in youth sport.

ACTIVITIES

1. Identify a major team sport coach. Describe how he or she demonstrates leadership and what has made such leadership application successful. Write a report describing your finding.
2. Identify a leader of an international sporting organization and provide a leadership profile for the identified person, making sure that you provide at least three examples of his or her demonstrated leadership. What type of leadership does the individual demonstrate? Write a report on your finding.
3. Work as a small group to study the current communication climate in the athletic department of your institution. Also identify the sustained culture of the same department. Then compare both the climate and culture before submitting a group report of what you find.
4. Visit a youth sport league in your neighborhood. Observe how the youth athletes interact with peers and coaches. Be sure to identify those that you consider leaders and why. Present this information to your classmates and instructor.

VIDEO RESOURCES

I Believe in Miracles (Documentary/1h 44min) is a story of Nottingham Forest's back-to-back European championships under the outstanding coaching leadership of Brian Clough and his assistant.
Inning by Inning: A Portrait of a Coach (Documentary/1h 46min) is a profile on the winningest coach in American college baseball history.
China Heavyweight (Documentary/1h 34min) is on rural Chinese teenagers who were recruited to prepare for the Olympics under the leadership of Coach Qi Moxiang.
The Diplomat (Documentary/50 min.) is a story on Katarina Witt, one of East Germany's most famous athletes and her leadership and struggles.
From the Rough (Drama/1h 37 min.) is a story of the first woman to lead an African American college golf team. It demonstrates her leadership and struggles.

RECOMMENDED WEB RESOURCES

The role of power in effective leadership (A Research White Paper). www.ccl.org/wp-content/
The art and science of leadership. www.nwlink.com/~donclark/leader/leader.html
Workplace Culture vs. Climate – why most focus on climate and may suffer for it. www.cultureuniversity.com/

REFERENCES

Arango, J. (2014, June 24). World Cup 2014: Jose Pekerman the 'overpriced Argentine' gives under-achieving Colombia winning habit. *The Telegraph.* www.telegraph.co.uk/
Buffa, D. (2016, February). Super Bowl 50: Five reasons the Denver Broncos can win. https://fansided.com/2016/01/26/super-bowl-50-five-reasons-denver-broncos-can-win/
Case, R. (1998). Leader member exchange theory and sport: Possible applications. *Journal of Sport Behavior*, 21(4): 387–395.
Caulkin, S. (2004, January 24). The pitch-perfect leader. *The Guardian* www.theguardian.com/business/2004/jan/25/madeleinebunting.theobserver
Chelladurai, P., & Riemer, H. (1998). Measurement of leadership in sport. In Duda, J. (Ed.), *Advances in sport and exercise psychology* (pp. 227–253). Morgantown, WV: Fitness Information Technology.
Crust, L., & Lawrence, I. (2006). A review of leadership in sport: Implications for football management. *Athletic Insight* (The Online Journal of Sport Psychology), 8(4): 28–48.
Freeman, M. (2015, August 10). Eagles players say Chip Kelly's dictatorial style is the issue, not racism. http://bleacherreport.com/articles/2538528-eagles-players-say-chip-kellys-dictatorial-style-is-the-issue-not-racism
Graen, G., & Uhl-Bien, M. (1998). Relationship-based approach to leadership. Development of leader-member exchange (LMX) theory of leadership over 25 years: Applying a multi-level multi-domain perspective. In Dansereau, F., & Yammarino, F. (Eds.), *Leadership: The multi-level approaches* (pp. 103–158). Stamford, CT: JAI Press.
Grusky, O. (1963). The effects of formal structure on managerial recruitment: A study of baseball organization. *Sociometry*, 26: 345–353.
Hackman, M., & Johnson, C. (2009). (5th ed.). *Leadership: A communication perspective.* Long Grove, IL: Waveland Press, Inc.

Hersey, P., & Blanchard, K. (1969). *Management of organizational behavior – Utilizing human resources*. New Jersey: Prentice Hall.

Hoption, C., Phelan, J., & Barling, J. (2007). Transformational leadership in sport. In Beauchamp, M., & Eys, M. (Eds.), *Group dynamics in exercise and sport psychology: Contemporary themes* (pp. 45–62). New York: Routledge.

Jerome, N. (2008, July 7). Real Madrid: Where excellence happens. http://bleacherreport.com/articles/35588-real-madrid-where-excellence-happens

Kajtna, T., & Baric, R. (2009). Psychological characteristics of coaches of successful and less successful athletes in team and individual sports. *Review of Psychology*, 16(1): 47–56.

Lee, M., Coburn, T., & Partridge, R. (1983). The influence of team structure in determining leadership function in association football. *Journal of Sport Behavior*, 6(2): 59.

Melnick, M., & Loy, J. (1996). The effects of formal structure on leadership recruitment: An analysis of team captaincy among New Zealand provincial rugby teams. *International Review of Sociology and Sport*, 31: 91–108.

Pederson, P., Miloch, K., & Lucella, P. (2007). *Strategic sport communication*. Champaign, IL: Human Kinetics.

Stodgill, R. (1974). *Handbook of leadership*. New York: The Free Press.

Trehan, D. (2016, July 13). Real Madrid, Barcelona and Manchester United make top 10 on Forbes List. www.skysports.com/football/news/11835/10500344/real-madrid-barcelona-and-manchester-united-make-top-10-on-forbes-list

Wilson, J. (2016a, June 8). Stephen Keshi: Brawler, talker and most successful black African coach of all time. *The Guardian*. www.theguardian.com/football/2016/jun/08/stephen-keshi-brawler-talker-most-successful-black-african-coach

Wilson, J. (2016b, June 22). Colombia v Chile: A compelling clash of theories as Argentina coaches do battle. *The Guardian*. www.theguardian.com/football/2016/jun/22/colombia-chile-copa-america-argentina

Wright, A., & Côté, J. (2003). A retrospective analysis of leadership development through sport. *The Sport Psychologist*, 17: 268–291.

Yildiz, S. (2011). Relationship between leader-member exchange and burnout in professional footballers. *Journal of Sports Sciences*, 29(14): 1493–1502. DOI: 10-1080/02640414.2011.605165

CHAPTER 4

STRATEGIC COMMUNICATION IN SPORT

LEARNING OBJECTIVES

After reading this chapter, you should be able to do the following:

- Define and give examples of strategic sport communication.
- Identify critical elements of persuasion central to the success of strategic sport communication.
- Explain how to build a sport organizational image and brand.
- Identify important aspects of building and maintaining strong media relations.
- Recognize key factors of hosting community events.
- Describe how to effectively manage athlete communication.
- Recognize and develop elements of a strategic communication plan.

Earlier chapters discussed the growing importance of sport in the world and different ways in which sport communication takes place. Many of those ways are uncoordinated, which means that a single organization may communicate to its publics with multiple voices and, sometimes, with conflicting messages. Such a situation is sub-optimal for a sporting organization. Danger occurs because communication is not always effective and it can also become adversarial, leading to losses in various areas including financial and relationships. Thus, sporting organizations and others involved in sport must learn how to manage communication for positive outcomes. One way to do this is by implementing what is known as strategic sport communication.

Generally, **strategic communication** refers to developing a strategic or a master plan for crafting and delivering positive messages, through appropriate communication channels, to identified publics with the goal of building lasting goodwill and value. For effectiveness, the impact of strategic communication must be measured against well-thought goals.

Sport teams all over the world develop and implement a strategic communication plan. An example is a recent plan developed and announced by the Athletic Director of the University of North Carolina (Goheels.com, 2013). The plan was announced at the beginning of 2013 and is scheduled to last for four years. The university's plan represents a strong strategic plan developed by internal staff after consultation with external publics of the university's sport teams. Involving these external publics is often crucial as their buy-in helps make implementation successful. Goheels.com (2013) describes a strategic plan as setting the stage

> for moving an organization forward to a new, positive direction. A strategy speaks to the employees, and also speaks to the external constituents about whom we are and where we're going. The goal is to have the decision-making of everyone in the organization to be particularly aligned with the mission, values, vision and priorities of that organization.
>
> (para. 7)

ISSUES OF PERSUASION

Persuasion is the process of modifying and/or changing a person's beliefs, values, attitudes, or behaviors related to an idea or object, by using communication symbols. According to Larson (2013), our knowledge about persuasion goes back to ancient Greek when Aristotle came up with what is believed to be among the first systematic thinking about persuasion. Aristotle pointed out that effective persuasion depends on presenting a type of proof or appeal. He noted also that one could present three types of appeals in order to persuade a person. These types of proofs are ethos or credibility, pathos or emotions, and logos or logic.

Ethos, or credibility, is an appeal that presents the source of a persuasive message as credible. In essence, the receiver of the message perceives the message source to be believable. For instance, a message on what is needed to win the sprints at the Olympics is more believable when delivered by the world 100-meter champion, Usain Bolt, than when delivered by the captain of a volleyball team.

Pathos, or emotional appeal, refers to persuasive messages that appeal to our innermost fears, guilt, anger, pride, or happiness. The television advertisement for the United Nations' World Food Programme featuring one of the world's best football players, Zlatan Ibrahimovic, is an emotional appeal. In the advertisement titled "805 Million Names," Zlatan is bent over in deep thinking, and he talks about millions of people in the world facing hunger and his wishes that he could have space on his body to tattoo all their names but there is not enough space. He then reminds viewers that whenever they see him score and take off his shirt or hear his name they should remember the 805 million people. It is an appeal of guilt. It is an appeal that makes us uncomfortable that while we enjoy the talent of Zlatan, we must remember that many of us are unfortunate. This persuades us to do something about it. Give whatever little we have to help.

Logos, or logic, relies on a process of reason to persuade the message receiver. Statistics, analogies, or historical precedence may be used as evidence to support this appeal. A sport team that plans to position itself as the pride of the nation may use logic as evidence to support this positioning. In such a case, the team may use statistics to show its previous successful representation of the nation, its development of local young talent, and its recruitment from within the nation, among other types of evidence to support the claim that it is the pride of the nation.

Ultimately, for strategic sport communication to be successful, it must use persuasion appropriately in order to achieve its goals. This section will focus attention on detailed descriptions of various aspects of persuasion. These include discussing four key premises that persuasive messages often depend on and the types of evidence included in such messages.

Key premises of persuasive messages

Effective persuasive messages are based on accumulated premises and knowledge about humans. Larson (2013) argues that four kinds of premises justify persuasive messages. Larson describes each of those premises as an appeal. The premises, or appeals, are listed as follows:

1   Appeals to deeply held human needs
2   Appeals to human emotions
3   Appeals to attitudes
4   Appeals to human cognitive consonance or dissonance

Deeply held **human needs** must be considered when designing persuasive messages. Abraham Maslow developed a hierarchy of needs well over half a century ago. Despite how old Maslow's work is, it remains relevant today. He categorized human needs into a hierarchy of five levels with lower-level needs more critical than upper-level needs. Maslow's hierarchy of needs, presented from lower to higher needs, include basic physiological needs (shelter, food, water, and basic needs to sustain life), security needs, affiliation and belongingness, love and self-esteem, and self-actualization. Maslow argues that lower-level needs must be satisfied before a person becomes conscious of higher-level needs. In essence, persuasion must be appropriate to a target audience. If you appeal to a higher-level need when your audience is yet to satisfy lower-level needs, then persuasion would fail. Importantly, by appealing to the appropriate need for a specific audience, the persuader will be successful in motivating the receiver to act in a certain way. For instance, if an audience demonstrates a need for safety and security, an appeal to those needs and an offer to satisfy them will motivate the audience to act in a way the persuader wishes.

The second premise is **human emotions**. This was briefly mentioned in the discussion of Aristotle's pathos. Humans make significant decisions based on emotional state and, thus, persuasive messages attempt to rouse emotional states in order to deliver beneficial messages. As mentioned earlier, emotions can be aroused through fear, guilt, anger, pride or patriotism, and happiness or joy.

Fear reflects a threat of harm that creates a feeling of helplessness. The persuader often offers a solution. The solution, however, must be adequate and convincing or else the receiver may ignore the message.

Guilt arises because the persuader points to a violation, which is designed to make us uncomfortable, but then offers a way to atone for the violation. An example of guilt is demonstrated during the previous discussion of pathos.

Anger arises when things do not work out the way we hope and we feel hurt and become frustrated or may even wish to strike out at a defined target. It is an appeal that can be used to rally fans around their team. In 2011, the American professional basketball team Cleveland Cavaliers lost its star player, LeBron James, to the Miami Heat. The owner of the Cavaliers, Dan Gilbert, generated anger among fans of the Cavaliers by writing an open letter to the fans in the media to rally them around the club and in anger against James. He wrote as follows:

> As you know, our former hero, who grew up in the very region that he deserted this evening, is no longer a Cleveland Cavalier. . . . The good news is that the ownership team and the rest of the hardworking, loyal, and driven staff over here at your hometown Cavaliers have not betrayed you nor NEVER will betray you. . . . I personally guarantee that the Cleveland Cavaliers will win an NBA Championship before the self-titled former "King" wins one.
>
> (Kanalley, 2011, para. 5, 7, and 11)

Pride is also another example of human emotion. This appeal celebrates accomplishment and persuades the audience to accept the accomplishment as something important to their lives. A team, for example, may take out an advertisement thanking its fans for their support during a championship run. The message could focus on what the team achieved and how fans played a significant role in that accomplishment.

Finally, an appeal to happiness and joy focuses on an attempt to convince the audience that a certain action will bring them happiness or joy. Frequently, humor and testimonials may be used to drive home this point. Sport teams may use this appeal to attract fans to attend games with a promise that attending leads to enjoyment and happiness.

There are also appeals to **attitudes**. An attitude refers to someone's predisposition to act towards an idea or object. Studies show that media messages are capable of creating a favorable image towards an idea or product. This leads to the audience developing positive attitudes towards that idea or product. Thus, persuasive messages may not get the target audience to act immediately in ways that the persuader may want, but at least it may get the audience to develop a predisposition to act in that way. In essence, persuasion creates an intention within the receiver to carry out a behavior in the direction that the persuader intends. Of course, it is not as simple as stated so far. Other critical variables motivate the receiver to act, including whether the message is associated with the receiver's pre-existing values, among other essential variables.

Finally, there is also appeal to **cognitive consonance or dissonance**. Consonance exists when two types of information are aligned or in agreement and, therefore, are mutually reinforcing. Dissonance is the opposite. In dissonance, the two types of information conflict and arouse discomfort within the person who receives the information. Because of this psychological situation, a persuader can provide us with consonant information in order to persuade us to adopt an idea or product. In addition, if the information the persuader delivers is dissonant, then the persuader does so with intention to change our position. They then offer a way to return to consonance. For example, a sport team that is seeking the city's support for building a sporting facility may send out information to residents pointing out that the team that they hope would win a championship cannot do so with the current substandard facility available. This type of message is intended to create dissonance in the minds of residents. Then persuasion can take place by pointing out that good facilities are associated with winning teams.

Evidence to support persuasive messages

Different types of evidence are frequently used to support persuasive messages. These include direct experience, vicarious experience, and rationalization. The most compelling is **direct experience**. Unfortunately, direct experience is not easy to provide to a large number of people who may be the target audience for a sport team. However, in cases where it is possible to do this, it provides the most compelling evidence. For instance, if a team intends to attract spectators frequently to its home games, it provides the most compelling evidence to achieve this goal by providing a positive outcome for those who are currently attending home games. Essentially, those spectators become repeat customers because of their direct experience in the games that they have attended. **Vicarious experience** requires hearing about the experience from a third party. Thus, a sport team may use testimonials from other fans or a video of fans at a home game in an attempt to convince its audience to attend home games. A third type of evidence is **rationalization**. Here, a team may use data, polls, or logical reasoning to convince its target audience to attend home games.

BUILDING A SPORT ORGANIZATIONAL IMAGE AND BRAND

Fortunato (2008) points out that "principles of branding are increasingly being applied to the management of sports organizations" (p. 361). **Branding** refers to a communication process where the goal is to place, in the consumer's mind, an image of an idea or product. It requires a strategic plan and campaign, with a consistent theme, that helps to create an image that attracts and retains consumers. Many sporting organizations are involved in the process of branding as part of marketing to the public (Mullin, Hardy, & Sutton, 2014).

The process of branding involves four key steps: creating brand awareness, building brand image, developing brand equity, and maintaining brand loyalty. Each of those steps requires in-depth planning and takes time. It all begins by planning a strategy for creating the brand. This requires full understanding and agreement on what the sporting organization's vision and goals are and designing a consistent theme. Without having a consistent theme, a brand image is impossible to develop. Instead, the lack of consistency creates confusion in the mind of the target audience. The audience is unable to have a single image of the product and may not even have the product as part of an *evoked set* of products in their mind.

It is after developing a branding theme for the product that the organization begins to move towards creating a **brand awareness** using multiple communication channels. These channels create adequate exposure for the brand. The brand message would include different promotional items such as a logo, slogans, advertisements, and other promotional materials and events. Each of those must reflect a consistent theme. It is also important for officials of the sporting organization to make public appearances to help create brand awareness. In fact, Richelieu and Desbordes (2009) point out that teams such as FC Barcelona, which have created international brands, undertake international tours and recruit players internationally to support international merchandising and develop an international fan base.

The **brand image** is built after the public becomes aware of the brand. The image is a set of beliefs that the target audience has about the product. This image is derived from a consistent message theme delivered through various communication channels and across different products where the brand may be extended. Fortunato (2008) provides examples of these extensions when he cites the National Football League (NFL) in the United States as not only communicating about its game but also developing extensions such as NFL Films, NFL Properties, and NFL Charities, which are part of the NFL's brand communication. A sporting organization reflects a positive image in the content of its messages concerning the brand. The previous section on how to develop persuasive messages is important here as those concepts are applicable in creating a positive brand image among the target audience.

Fortunato (2008) notes that **brand equity** is built when the target audience begins to make strong positive associations with the brand's image. In essence, the audience begins to link their own value to the perceived product image. This is a very strong phase for the product because when audience values are associated with a product's image, it reflects a potentially successful product branding.

The ultimate goal of branding is to reach the phase of **brand loyalty**. This is the phase where the target audience adopts the brand. The goal of the sporting organization is not just product adoption by the audience but also that the brand continues to retain this audience. Brand loyalty provides several benefits to the organization, including tangible benefits such as revenue from merchandising and intangible benefits such as "emotions fans experience at the stadium and the sense of belonging to the team" (Richelieu & Desbordes, 2009, p. 11).

> **REFLECTION**
>
> You probably have a favorite sport team that you watch on television or cable. Think about that team and the image the team brings to mind. It is likely a positive image. Think about how you would describe that image to a friend. How do you think others would describe the image? What may have symbolized that image for you and others? Your answers reflect the enduring image of the team.

CULTIVATING STRONG MEDIA RELATIONS

Mass media reports are important to sporting organizations. Sporting organizations can always buy space and time in the media to communicate to stakeholders, but that is only a small fraction of how a sporting organization communicates to large audiences. The most critical communication comes from reports that appear in pages and spaces of the sport media for which the organization does not pay, and yet those reports make or mar sporting organizations. To impact some of those reports, sporting organizations develop effective media relations as part of strategic communication.

Media relations strategy is designed to create a good and positive working relationship with the sport media. This relationship, when good, is beneficial for both sport media and the sporting organization. This relationship creates a good atmosphere whenever either party initiates contact. Usually, the organization may initiate contact when it wants a particular type of news to be disseminated by the media, and the media initiate contact when seeking background to particular news, confirming aspects of a particular story, reacting to events, or seeking other types of information.

Preparing for media contacts

Media contacts can be anticipated by a sporting organization, but they require ongoing work by the organization to be effective in anticipating contacts. One major way of anticipating and preparing for media contacts is constant monitoring of the environment. For instance, a sporting organization must keep up with related sporting news and events on a daily basis in order to anticipate whether the media may initiate contact or whether the sporting organization should do so. What is important is that if the organization anticipates that the media may develop a story, then the organization must be prepared. This may mean doing additional research in order to be prepared to answer questions that the media may ask.

Preparation could include making a top executive or executives in the organization aware of the story and the research generated in response to the story. The executive or executives must practice how best to respond to the media. This includes being prepared to answer anticipated media questions, speaking authoritatively but in a friendly manner, demonstrating credibility, avoiding negative nonverbal communication, and avoiding speculation. This type of preparation is important as a poor interview could hurt the organization.

Initiating and maintaining media contact

In many cases, the organization does not wait for the media to initiate contact. Instead, the organization initiates contact in order to achieve different communication goals. The organization has several tools at its disposal for initiating media contacts. These tools include media releases, media conferences, interviews, media kits, and fact sheets.

Media releases are important ways for contacting the media, and all sporting organizations must use this option because they are effective in disseminating news to the public. However, media releases should only be used when an organization has important news to share with the public. It should not be used in a frivolous manner. Among important news requiring a press release are major appointments, retirements, signing a major player, signing a major sponsorship, suspension of a key player, and other major stories that are newsworthy.

Media releases should be written in a professional format, which means using the Associated Press (AP) Style and in an inverted pyramid. It should be written for immediate release to the public and include a headline that the media may choose to use. The media release should be brief and usually in one but no more than two pages. It should include quotes from key people. At the end of a media release, the organization adds information about the organization that is unrelated to the news. The release should include contact information of multiple people in the organization in case the media wishes to obtain additional information. Finally, the media release should either be sent via email or fax because immediate dissemination is vital. The Federation of International Basketball Associations (FIBA), for example, announced its 3x3 World Tour via a press release (FIBA.com, 2016).

Media conferences are used when media releases are inadequate for information that the organization wishes to disseminate to the public. However, for a media conference the media must receive advance invitation and time must be provided for question-and-answer session for the media. A top executive is usually the one to speak at such a conference, along with others who may be closely associated with the event. For instance, if it is news about signing a major player, not only is the organization's executive present but the player and coach should also be present and scheduled to speak. Most media conferences last for no more than 30 minutes, including the question and answer session. In most professional leagues, teams are scheduled to participate in a brief media conference right after each game.

Interviews may be scheduled following a request from the media or a request by the sporting organization. This requires a great deal of preparation on the part of the organization in order to prepare the staff member or athlete who will be interviewed. The preparation should include practice sessions that involve questions that the organization anticipates from the media, and answers are also practiced. Media interviews require that the interviewee is confident, knowledgeable, and credible.

Media kits are usually distributed to the media during media conferences, but they should be ready at all times to be used when necessary. These kits showcase the sporting organization and, therefore, they should be glossy and include action photographs that are attractive. They include information that the media can use to fill up their stories and provide background. The kit should include fact sheets, media releases, and biographies of key staff and athletes.

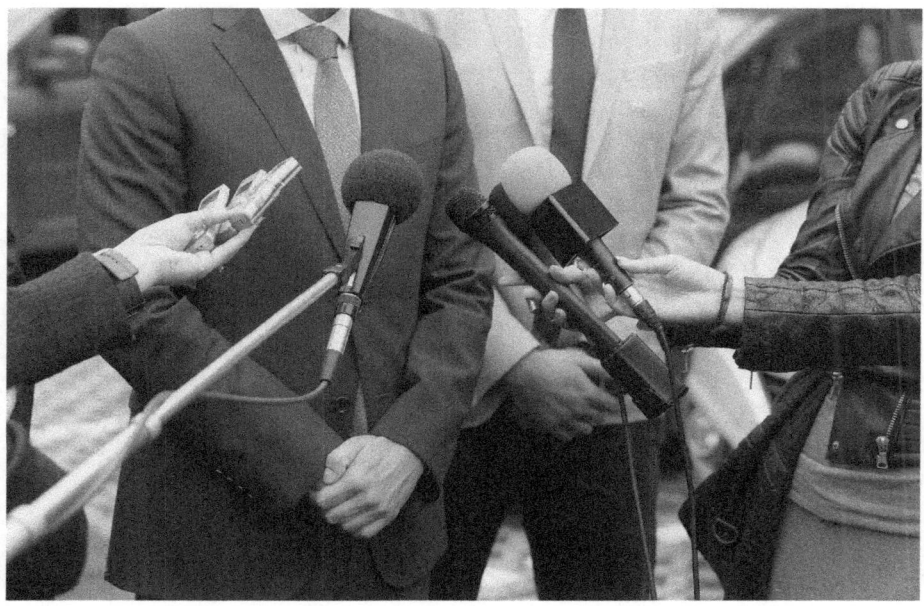

Photo 4.1 Interviews may involve representatives of multiple media units.
Source: Dreamstime.com, reprinted with permission

Photo 4.2 An official speaking at a media conference. Communication is fed through several microphones provided by media representatives.

Source: Dreamstime.com, reprinted with permission

A **fact sheet** is usually included as part of a media kit. However, it is discussed separately here because of its importance. It provides highlights on a single page and can be designed to be general or specific to a topic. A general fact sheet focuses on the organization and includes a brief history as well as key information for the season. A specific fact sheet focuses on news topics for which it was designed and it highlights background and key points pertaining to the topic.

COMMUNITY RELATIONS

Sporting organizations build substantial community goodwill through programs that cater to community relations. These programs may involve players visiting communities to sign autographs and presenting team gifts to children. It also includes visits to hospitals, shelters, and schools, and could involve food drives. There are examples of such programs. For instance, during the Super 8 stage of the 2007 ICC Cricket World Cup in Guyana, the South African team visited the Dorothy Bailey Health Centre in Georgetown, Guyana (Sutton-Jones, 2007). During the visit, the team talked about HIV and AIDS with students who were at the center representing *Children Unite against AIDS*. The team made pledges and went outside and played cricket with the children.

It is difficult, sometimes, for people to see how this type of relationship building helps a sporting organization. However, it does not only help, but it is critical. For instance, the visit by the South African cricket team led to a media conference, which was helpful to the team and the health center. Both received publicity. Moreover, publicizing the visit would likely earn the South African team some local Guyanese fans and support at the World Cup in Guyana. Importantly, such community activity enhances the image of the sporting organization and creates positive public perception of the organization. Publicity likely increased public awareness of the health center.

MANAGING ATHLETE COMMUNICATION

Athletes can be managed just as a sporting organization is managed. Athletes need similar goodwill and seek to build a positive brand image. In that regard, several issues discussed in this chapter apply to athletes. There are several organizations, all over the world, that are set up to manage athlete communication as well as manage athletes in other areas. For instance, Global Sports Communication is based in Nijmegen, The Netherlands, and it manages top athletes from all over the world. Listed among its 150 clients are world-class athletes such as Haile Gebrselassie, Kenenisa Bekele, Florence Kiplagat, Eliud Kipchoge, and Caterine Ibarguen. Gebrselassie is a two-time Olympic champion and four-time world champion in long-distance running. Ibarguen is a Colombian who holds the South American record for triple jump. The organization markets its athletes and provides professional advice.

FACING A CHALLENGE TO IMAGE AND BRAND

Team Desire is an athletic organization based in the Atlantic Islands. It has accomplished a lot with international athletics in the last three decades. The current General Manager of *Team Desire*, Isaiah Bedeau, recently recruited excellent athletes from regionals it organized. However, one of those athletes, Lawrence Boldon, became injured during preparation for an international meet.

Mr. Bedeau is stunned and alarmed that a fan has already tweeted about the injury. The information on Twitter is not accurate. Mr. Bedeau places a call to his staff in charge of *Team Desire's* social media communication: "Kate, did you see the tweet that came through just a few minutes ago?"

"Yes, I did," Kate responded.

"You know we do not want to alarm our supporters about Boldon's injury. They expect us to win the upcoming meet as we always do, and we have always claimed that we are the leading athletic team," Mr. Bedeau stated.

"Well, is Boldon going to be ready? You know our success rests on his shoulders," Kate said.

"Boldon is going in for a medical check tomorrow, but we do have others who are capable if he is out," Mr. Bedeau noted.

"Well, what should I do?" she asked. "We just can't let that tweet go without a response."

"Go ahead and respond, but we are calling an official conference tomorrow."

Kate proceeded to respond to the tweet informing *Team Desire's* followers that Boldon's injury is being examined and a conference will occur tomorrow with an update. She cautioned about inaccurate reports. Well, the initial tweet that was placed from a non-company person was already being retweeted widely. Worse, it suddenly hit talk radio with sport analysts speculating about *Team Desire's* chances at the upcoming meet. Many analysts predicted that the team would fail and that it was already in decline as it no longer has promising talents. Mr. Bedeau is concerned. In the last few decades, *Team Desire* has spent a huge amount of funds building an image of excellence in athletics and as leader and pace setter, but now some doubt is beginning to crop up from the media. He thinks, *we need to ensure that our image is maintained.*

Media conference

Mr. Bedeau and the club coach, Ms. Alexander, both brief the media about the team. Bedeau speaks on recent efforts to recruit top talent and the team's confidence that it remains an exemplary athletic club. He notes many top talents continue to join *Team Desire*, and the club continues to host top class events and leads in innovation. Coach Alexander focuses on the upcoming international meet and announces that Boldon suffered a minor injury during a recent practice, but the diagnosis is good with Boldon expected to be ready for the meet. She also notes that Boldon has already started treatment and is responding well so far. Coach Alexander informs the media that there are several superior athletic talents in the club, and many of them would become notable based on expected performances at the upcoming meet. Both Mr. Bedeau and Coach Alexander answer some questions, and Boldon also appears at the conference and is made available to some media representatives. Boldon shares optimism as he answers questions:

> "I feel okay and should be 100% by the time of the meet. Right now, I am working with the physio and doing all that she has asked of me," he said.
>
> In a response to another question, he says, "Yes, there was a lot of pain when I sustained the injury, but the doctors took care of that. Right now, the pains have gone down considerably and I am focused on getting ready."

Several media report the press conference the next day with quotes from Mr. Bedeau, Ms. Alexander, and Boldon. Some of the media expand their stories by writing deep articles based on the interview with Boldon. Other media use media kits provided by *Team Desire* that mention talented recruits and initiatives of the club. Mr. Bedeau's spirit is high, and he believes the image and brand of *Team Desire* is sustained. But with some callers into radio talk shows raising a few doubts, is Mr. Bedeau correct?

Discussion questions

1. Did Mr. Bedeau and *Team Desire* take the right steps to meet their goal of image and brand maintenance? Why?
2. Was it necessary for *Team Desire* to delay responding to the initial tweet on Boldon's injury? Why?
3. What could be key items in *Team Desire*'s strategic sport communication plan? If you had to design such a plan, what steps would you take?
4. Do you feel that the organization's supporters believe *Team Desire*'s messaging from the media conference? Why?
5. Is Mr. Bedeau accurate in his conclusion that the organization's image and brand is sustained? Is there any danger from radio callers expressing doubt about *Team Desire*'s messages?

A TEMPLATE FOR STRATEGIC SPORT COMMUNICATION

At the beginning of this chapter, I mentioned that strategic communication refers to a "master plan for crafting and delivering positive messages, through appropriate communication channels, to identified publics with the goal of building lasting goodwill and value." This section identifies various parts of that master plan and discusses and applies each to a situation in a sport organization. The organization is pseudo-named Athletic Club (Aztecs) in an urban city. The club has a vision to become the premier athletic club in the nation.

Key parts of a strategic communications plan

Each strategic communication plan is unique, but effective plans share the similar parts. The shared parts are critical, and all plans must have them. Essential parts of a plan are listed as follows:

- Goals
- Audience Profile
- Communication Messages
- Selected Communication Channels
- Activities and Materials
- Partnerships
- Implementation
- Evaluations and Adjustments

To design effective **Goals** requires examining an organization's vision, values, and beliefs and monitoring the environment to determine appropriate goals that help advance the organization towards fulfilling its vision. Environmental monitoring requires a SWOT analysis (Strengths, Weaknesses, Opportunities, and Threats that pertain to the organization).

A SWOT analysis of the Aztecs may yield the following information: great coaches and recruiters (Strength), current funding ranked number 30 in the nation (Weakness), several emerging top athletic talents in various regions in the country (Opportunity), and two aggressive competitors are ranked in top 10 of funding in the nation and planning to recruit in the Aztecs' region (Threat). These are brief examples. In an actual analysis, there would be multiple factors identified in each part of a SWOT analysis.

Based on this analysis, the Aztecs may develop the following goals: (1) to make the Aztecs a top club choice of athletes' families in the next two years; (2) increase awareness of the Aztecs Club among communities within one year; and (3) increase its funding base by 50% in two years.

Audience Profile is the next step in a strategic communication plan. The audiences identified in the previous section on goals should each be addressed here.

Although this section specifically focuses on developing a profile for each of those audience segments, it is also important to point to secondary audiences that may exist. A secondary audience is audience groups that may be affected if a goal becomes successful. The audience profile includes characteristics of the audience related to the product or idea communicated. The profile should point to obstacles that may prevent the audience from fully participating and then benefits that accrue if they choose to participate.

Based on goals identified in the previous section, the Aztecs would draw up profiles of three primary audience segments. The segments would be the athlete and athlete's family, the national audience for the sport, and funders (i.e. businesses that are likely interested in funding athletes). Philanthropists could be a sub-section of funders. Characteristics of each segment should be thoroughly analyzed using the principles provided previously.

Messages are the heart of strategic communication and are designed bearing in mind how effective they would be when delivered to selected audience groups. They are also designed for a specific audience using the type of information presented in the discussion of persuasive messages earlier in the chapter. Above all, messages should be clear, consistent, and credible.

Of course, there would be a different message for each audience segment. These messages must be appropriate, using persuasive elements such as ethos, pathos, and logos mentioned earlier in the chapter. For funders, it is particularly important to use logical appeals because they would want to be convinced, with logic, that funding the Aztecs is of great benefit to them. Of course, the Aztecs must also establish credibility and the ability to achieve its vision.

The next step is to identify **communication channels** through which messages will be sent. Channels include television, social media, radio, newspapers, magazines, websites, community centers, and street festivals, among others. There are numerous communication channels, but not all of them are effective in reaching a particular audience. Therefore, a channel must be carefully selected to ensure that it is appropriate and effective for reaching a particular audience.

For the athlete and athlete's family, it is important to identify the type of media channels they prefer. For instance, because of their relatively young age, athletes may use mostly social media. However, the Aztecs may also use face-to-face events for this segment. The Aztecs may use personalized communication, such as e-mail invite, for parents. For funders, personal face-to-face meetings and telephone calls may be used. For a national audience, social media and mass media audiences may be preferred.

Choosing **materials and activities** that go into the communication channels constitutes the next element. Of course, materials and/or activities must match the communication channel. Activities include media conferences, talk shows, meetings, and event staging, among others. Materials include fliers, brochures, letters, posters, public service announcements (PSAs), videos, advertisements, documentaries, and promotional items, among others.

Based on selection of communication channels, the Aztecs may then choose activities like staging events where face-to-face meetings would take place or arranging for visits. Materials may include promotional materials and giveaways, posters, advertising copy, and letters.

Partnerships require identifying potential partners that meet the needs of the organization. These partners are groups, organizations, and businesses that share mutual interests with the sporting organization.

Partners for the Aztecs may include sporting gear companies and companies that produce athletic beverages. These partners may not provide help to increase the funding rank of the Aztecs, but they provide support in kind, such as sport uniforms and beverages to Aztec players and at events hosted by Aztecs. In return, those partners build consumers for the future.

Then it is time to **implement** the strategic communication plan. Implementation is critical and requires managing time, budget, and staff towards the goal of putting into action all plans discussed. Thus, budget must be agreed on at this point, and staff members responsible for certain activities are clearly identified and a timeline for various accomplishments are set.

The Aztecs would draw up activities over a two-year period and attach costs to each of those activities in order to generate a budget. Importantly, the Aztecs would also draw up timelines to accomplish several activities, leading to eventual goal achievement within the duration mentioned in the earlier part of the strategic communication plan.

The next step is **evaluation**. On paper, this is seen as the last stage of the process, but in actuality it may not be. It can be ongoing. At specified periods, the Aztecs should evaluate its activities and plans to determine what is working and what is not. If it is not working, adjustments are made and implemented before re-evaluation takes place.

Evaluation may involve a variety of measurement methods. For example, a click analysis on social media platforms may indicate awareness levels as required in goal number 2. Telephone survey questions may also address the level of awareness among survey participants. These surveys should be distributed to a nationwide sample. The same survey may also inquire if a household has an athlete in the sport of interest to the Aztecs. If the answer is yes, then the Aztecs may find out if the Aztecs club is considered a top choice for the athlete. For funding, an appropriate measure would be the level of funds raised after a period of two years compared to the level of funding at this time. These measures identified here would also be taken mid-course in order to determine how well the Aztecs is doing with its goal implementation and assist in making early adjustments to help goal achievement.

CHAPTER SUMMARY

Strategic communication is central to sport communication and/or sport management communication. This chapter focused on key aspects of strategic communication in sport. Not only does it explain what it means, but it also establishes why such a master plan is essential.

The chapter is broken into a few important sections that help with effective strategic communications. For instance, one of the opening sections is on persuasive messaging or communication. This section describes what persuasion is and its main elements using Aristotle's concept. Importantly, it reminds us that persuasion appeals to human needs, emotions, attitudes, and cognitive consonance or dissonance. There is also need for evidence to support persuasive messages, and the type of evidence may be based on direct experience of the source or a vicarious experience learned from another person's encounter. The third type of evidence is a rational one, which is based on things like data or agreed-upon facts.

An additional section focuses on image and branding, two concepts that sporting organizations increasingly crave. In the field, several terms associated with branding can be confusing, but the section identifies some of the most common, such as building a brand, image, equity, and loyalty. Each of those terms is described and differentiated from the others.

The chapter also describes relationships that a sporting organization or an athlete may build. One is media relations and the other is community relations. Each is described with expanded discussion on media relations and how organizations develop several tactics to initiate and maintain contact with the media.

The final section presents a template that organizations may use for strategic sport communication. This template provides brief descriptions of key parts of a strategic communication plan.

DISCUSSION QUESTIONS

1. What do you think are benefits of a good strategic communication plan?
2. Demonstrate the difference between a persuasive appeal to a person's emotions and an appeal to the person's attitudes.
3. How would you describe brand equity as opposed to brand image? Use examples from a sporting product or service to support differences between brand equity and image.
4. Are there different goals that an organization may want to achieve when it decides to use a media conference instead of interviews? Please elaborate to demonstrate differences.
5. What is the difference between a media kit and a media fact sheet?

ACTIVITIES

1. Assume that you and members of your group are in charge of developing a strategic sport communication plan for a new elite club in town seeking to develop

a fan base. Use the template in this chapter to design a strategic communication plan for the team.
2 Attend a press/media conference of a sporting organization in your community. Listen to the club's message and the question-and-answer session that follows. Afterwards, write a story based on communication presented by the organization at the conference.
3 Identify an elite sporting team in the country and study recent media messages pertaining to this team. Analyze those messages, seeking to identify the brand that the team hopes to build and the brand image of the team. Present the result of your analysis in a three- to four-page written report.

VIDEO RESOURCES

Michigan State Women's Basketball Media Day 2016: Suzy Merchant (YouTube video/17.04 min.).
Sports Media: Get in the Game (TV Talk-show Media City aired September 30, 2007/1h). Explains the skills needed to work in sports media.

RECOMMENDED WEB RESOURCES

Ozanian, M., & Schwartz, P. (2007, September 27). The world's top sports brands. *Forbes*. www.forbes.com /2007/09/26/ sports-brands-teams-biz-sports_cz_mo_0927sportsbrands.html
The New Yorker media kit. www.condenast.com/brands/new-yorker/media-kit/?src=tny-footer
Clapp, B. (2015, November 23). Starting a career in sports media relations. *WorkinSports.com*. www.workinsports.com/blog/starting-a-career-in-sports-media-relations/

REFERENCES

Federation of International Basketball Associations (FIBA.com). (2016, July 15). Mexico City ready on eve of 2016 FIBA 3x3 world tour season. www.fiba.com/3x3worldtour/2016/mexico/news/mexico-city-ready-on-eve-of-2016-fiba-3x3-world-tour-season
Fortunato, J. (2008). Pete Rozelle: Developing and communicating the sports brand. *International Journal of Sport Communication*, 1: 361–377.
Goheels.com. (2013, January 9). Tar Heels announces strategic plan. www.goheels.com/ViewArticle.dbml?ATCLID=205865095
Kanalley, C. (2011, May 25). Dan Gilbert letter: LeBron James 'Narcissistic,' 'Deserted' Cleveland, says Cavs majority owner (Text). *The Huffington Post*. www.huffingtonpost.com/2010/07/08/dan-gilbert-letter-lebron_n_640318.html
Larson, C. (2013). (13th ed.). *Persuasion: Reception and responsibility*. Boston, MA: Wadsworth.
Mullin, B., Hardy, S., & Sutton, W. (2014). (4th ed.). *Sport marketing*. Champaign, IL: Human Kinetics.
Richelieu, A., & Desbordes, M. (2009). Football teams going international: The strategic leverage of branding. *Journal of Sponsorship*, 3(1): 10–22.
Sutton-Jones, S. (2007, April 2). South African cricket team visits community health centre in Guyana. www.unicef.org/sports/index_39276.html

CHAPTER 5

TRADITIONAL MEDIA

> **LEARNING OBJECTIVES**
>
> After reading this chapter, you should be able to do the following:
>
> - Understand what traditional media are and their various types.
> - Describe unique traditional media that are not well known globally.
> - Learn about mutual benefits in the relationship between traditional media and sport.
> - Learn about the impact of transnational media in consumption of sport.

Although a large part of sport communication takes place without the benefit of traditional media, traditional media provide opportunities to reach a large number of viewers simultaneously for any sport. What makes the relationship between traditional media and sport significant is that while media provide a vehicle for reaching large numbers of people, sport provides access to great number of viewers and revenue to the media. Thus, there is mutual benefit to the relationship between traditional media and sport.

DEFINING TRADITIONAL MEDIA

By traditional media one refers to a number of mediums consumed by a large number of people, often regarded as a "mass" of people. This allows delivery of a message from a source or multiple sources to a large number of people. Therefore, the name "mass media" is appropriate in describing this group of mediums. What makes them traditional is that they existed before the development of digital technologies.

There are key components from the definition that we should pay attention to. The first is the medium. A medium is an intervening platform through which a message may be sent from one person to another. In this case, this medium must have the capability of reaching a large number of people and do this at roughly the same time. The "mass" of people refers to a large number of people that share relatively few things in common and may inhabit geographic points distant from each other.

Types of traditional media

There are numerous types of traditional media. These media include dance theaters, magazines, newspapers, books, radio, television, and film. There may be other mass media specific to some cultures that are not listed. Dance theater may be a surprise to you, because it is rarely identified as a mass medium. Therefore, you may wonder why it is on the list. However, it is an example of a mass medium that is not universally known as a medium for mass communication, but it is effective in the areas where it has been popularly used for that purpose. Ugboajah (1986) described **dance theater** as a mass medium prevalently used in rural Africa. In rural African communities, traditional dancers are employed to visit places where a mass of people congregate. For instance, such troupes may visit a packed marketplace and then commence dancing. This attracts a large number of people who watch the dance and give gifts, usually monetary, to dancers acknowledging their dancing skills. At an appropriate time during the dance, dancers stop and perform a skit for the benefit of the audience. This skit (equivalent to an advertisement scene) is designed to sell a product or introduce an idea. The troupe, using the entire act, hopes to persuade spectators to adopt whatever message is conveyed in the act. This is what Ugboajah identifies as *oramedia*, coining the term from a combination of the words "oral" and "media." Dance theaters may be used to promote upcoming wrestling matches between two notable males or a wrestling competition between villages. Dance theaters are effective means of promotion because messages such as announcing upcoming wrestling matches reach a large number of people simultaneously, and these individuals disseminate the news through a network of friends who are absent on that market day.

As mentioned above, there are several types of traditional media. There is not enough space to discuss all of them. Therefore, only four notable ones are discussed subsequently: newspapers, magazines, radio, and television. We will discuss each of those after presenting the interdependence of media and sport.

INTERDEPENDENCE BETWEEN PROFESSIONAL SPORT AND TRADITIONAL MEDIA

Traditional media such as newspapers, magazines, radio, and television are intricately linked to sport in a mutually beneficial relationship. Bernstein and Blain

(2002) argue that: "it is often difficult to discuss sport in modern society without acknowledging its relationship with the media" (p. 3). Sport depends on media to extend its mass appeal and expand its revenue source. On the other hand, media depend on sport to attract large numbers of consumers in order to expand media revenue and fill out programming space with popular programs. Now, let us look into each of those claims.

In 2014, 350 million people were projected to have watched the FIFA World Cup final match, 170 million for the UEFA Champions League Final, 140 million for the Winter Olympics opening ceremony, and 125 million for the American Super Bowl. These astronomical figures are possible because of mass-mediated communication. Using the 2014 World Cup final as an example, only 74,738 persons were at the stadium to watch the final out of the 350 million who viewed the game simultaneously over a mass medium. This affirms the first claim about media extending the game to a mass number of people.

Revenue from the sale of media rights, specifically television broadcasting rights, has rapidly increased over the years and in most parts of the world. In the United States, it is predicted that 2018 revenue from media rights will outstrip revenue from gates for the first time (Bond, 2015). In 2014, gate receipts were $17.7 billion while media rights brought in $14.6 billion. By 2018, gate revenues are expected at $19.72 billion compared to $19.95 billion predicted from media rights. Already, media rights constitute the largest revenue sector in South America, accounting for 38.3% of the total (PwC.com, 2011). In Europe, television rights for five top football leagues in England, Germany, Spain, Italy, and France rose by a staggering 25% in 2013 (Panja, 2013). Six of Europe's top football clubs each earned more than 100 million euros from television income in 2013. These revenues help sporting organizations to afford the astronomical salaries paid to athletes and coaches.

On the part of the media, access to large numbers of viewers is the bargaining chip needed to demand high fees from businesses for advertising space. In the United States alone, annual company spending on sport advertising is $34.9 billion (Plunkettresearch.com). For the 2016 Olympics, NBCUniversal estimates at least $1 billion for its sale of 30-second advertising spots on television. This is the equivalent of just less than $100,000 for a 30-second spot (Steinberg, 2015; Pomerantz, 2014). An NBCUniversal spokesperson is quoted as stating that the number of expected viewers would be staggering. Sport programming outstrips other types of programming in attracting viewership. PwC.com (2011) notes the following: "With an average US audience of 111 million viewers, the 2011 Super Bowl became the most-watched programme of any kind in the history of American television" (p. 6). In other countries, the story is similar. Whenever the national football team of a country is playing a competitive game on television, it becomes the most watched program in that country for that day. In essence, there is hardly a non-sport program that outstrips a major sport program in traditional media viewership.

Ultimately, the interdependent relationship between media and sport has helped bring in unprecedented finances to the sport industry. Research from plunkettresearch.com (2015) reports that the estimated size of the global sport industry is $1.5 trillion.

NEWSPAPERS

Newspapers were the first modern mass medium to reach millions of people. Very early in the twentieth century, newspapers in Japan became involved in building relationship with sport. This involved covering various sports, sponsoring events, ownership of sporting organizations, and building sporting facilities. Horne (2005) argues that the need to build markets for newspapers and products led to Japanese newspapers using sport. Sport attracts thousands of consumers, and advertisers seek how best to consistently reach consumer markets. Newspapers in Japan provided a conduit to these markets through coverage of sport, including baseball. However, sport coverage was limited to general newspapers. Nevertheless, newspapers specializing in sport, such as *Nikkan Supotsu*, began to emerge in Japan by the 1940s. According to Horne, "by 1964 it (*Nikkan Supotsu*) had a circulation of one-and-a-half million daily, as well as six new rivals" (p. 419). Horne adds that several sport newspapers have circulations over one million daily.

Beyond covering sport on the pages of newspapers, newspapers became involved in sponsoring athletic events. Horne writes that sponsorship included a five-mile swimming competition in 1901 and five years later the first Japanese marathon. The *Osaka Mainichi* sponsored both events. Each of the events increased reader interest in the newspaper. Most importantly, organizing such events, which were unusual types of athletic events in those times, generated public discussions not only about the events but also about the newspaper. The reports led to a rise in newspaper readerships.

Newspapers also go beyond sponsoring sport events to owning sporting organizations. Fitts (2005) reports that *Yomiuri Shimbun* established the oldest Japanese baseball team, among current professional baseball teams, in 1934 as a team of All Stars to play against touring American All-Star teams. However, two years later it became one of the teams to play in a newly formed Japanese Baseball League and was then known as Tokyo Kyojin. *Yomiuri Shimbun* is owned by media conglomerate Yomiuri Group. *Yomiuri Shimbun* is the largest circulated newspaper in the world, with about 13 million readers. The newspaper widely publicizes the team, now known as the Yomiuri Giants, and the media organization uses its deep pockets to recruit the country's best players, leading to record championships and becoming the country's most popular team.

In Japan, newspapers are also involved in building sporting facilities, according to Horne. Horne's work mentions how newspapers such as *Asahi* and *Osaka Mainichi Shimbun* worked with the Hansin Railway Company to fund construction of

Photo 5.1 Newspapers represent a type of traditional communication media.
Source: Dreamstime.com, reprinted with permission

Koshen Stadium in Nishinomiya in 1924. The newspapers were involved because of community support and interest in secondary school baseball for which the stadium was built. By participating, the newspapers wanted to demonstrate community interest and to generate goodwill and support from the community.

In Nigeria, the first newspaper business intimately linked with sport was the *West African Pilot* established by one of the country's top politicians, Dr. Nnamdi Azikiwe, in 1937. Though the newspaper was established as the first indigenous press to take an anti-colonial stance, its popularity was not only due to its political angle but also due to its extensive coverage of sport. However, the relationship between this newspaper and sport did not end in basic reporting of sporting events. Instead, the newspaper promoted the Zik's Athletic Club (ZAC), which was also established by Azikiwe. ZAC clubs included track and field, boxing, cricket, football, swimming, and tennis teams. They were established all over the country and helped build goodwill for the newspaper and the owner's political career.

Newspaper organizations' link to sport is prevalent in many parts of the world and should not be considered unusual. Newspapers find sport to be beneficial just like any other business considers sport. Therefore, the relationship between newspaper businesses and sport must be seen as a business decision on either side.

Beyond general newspapers with a section dedicated to sport coverage, some newspapers specialize on reporting sport. Some of these include *La Gazzetta dello Sport* (Italy), *Corriere dello Sport* (Italy), *Tuttosport* (Italy), *Marca* (Spain), *L'Equipe* (France), *Record* (Portugal), *Fanatik* (Turkey), *Olé* (Argentina), and *Sporski žurnal* (Serbia). *Marca* is the leading sport newspaper in Spain, and at times its readership outstrips that of the country's top newspaper, *el Pais*. These specialized sport newspapers may focus either on various sports or on a single sport, providing reports of on-the-field activities like general newspapers or on rumors, background, and social activities that may not be available in general newspapers. There are some that focus on traditional tabloid-type reporting of gossip and sensationalization.

In recent years, hardcopy newspaper circulations have declined. This trend is attributed to several factors, including change in reading habits from paper to digital, availability of newspaper editions online, and the rise in price of hardcopy newspapers. Smith (2016) reports that the decline in newspaper circulation and newspaper jobs has been sharp over the last two decades. He notes that Britain's *Independent* newspaper ended its print edition by 2016, and newspaper decline is sharp in places like Australia, America, and Europe. Asia is the only place, Smith argues, that circulation has held on reasonably. Bucking the decline trend are newspapers in China, India, and Japan (Le, 2012), where increases in circulation were as large as 16% by 2012; those three countries are responsible for over half the world's newspaper circulation. Doctor (2015) places the problem, largely, on the increasing cost of single newspapers as the industry attempts to maintain revenue levels in the midst of circulation decline.

MAGAZINES

Since the mid-1600s when the first magazine – *Erbauliche Monaths Unterredungren* – was published in Germany, print magazines have existed, with some of them focusing on general interest and others specializing in various areas, including sport. Magazines appear periodically and are lighter in content compared to newspapers (the exception is news magazines). General interest magazines publish articles on glossy paper with colored photographs. The content of magazines, along with their paper and photo quality, differentiates them from regular newspapers and leads to subscribers saving copies of magazines in contrast to a newspaper publication, which is quickly disposed after it is read.

There are a variety of sport magazines all over the world, with some dedicated to coverage of sport in general. Examples are *Sports Illustrated*, *ESPN*, *Sport & Fitness*, *Sky Sports Magazine*, and *Sport Life*. Others such as *College Sports*, *SI Latino*, *School Sport*, and *Women in Sport* cover a specific demographic, while some others including *Golf Digest*, *Cycle Sport*, *World Soccer*, *Surfing Life*, *Runner's World*, *All Out Cricket*, *Boxing Monthly*, *Slam*, and *Motosport* cover a specific sport. Furthermore, some sporting organizations have their own magazines, such as *Benfica* and *Arsenal*.

Emergence of digital-based media has adversely impacted print magazines. However, it must be acknowledged that this adverse effect has not only come from the new digital media but also come from other traditional media. Horne (1992) argues that magazines face competition from both television and newspapers that encroach on what was previously the preserve of print magazines, particularly as it pertains to sport coverage. He claims:

> as television has developed it has preempted much of the traditional editorial role of newspapers (news reports), which in turn has hastened the latter's shift toward 'much of the traditional editorial preserves of magazines – analysis, entertainment, instruction, light relaxation. . . . Newspapers have tended to drop news in favor of celebrity features, gossip, entertainment, and sport since 1945.
> (p. 180)

Though Horne's focus is on the demise of *Sportsweek* in Britain, his statements are true of competition that sport magazines face elsewhere in the world.

The emergence of digital sport news and programs adversely affects magazines as it does newspapers. Stynes (2014) reports that magazine circulation, calculated through subscriptions and newsstands sales, fell about 2% in the first half of 2014. This continues a slide that has been going on for years. The world's largest circulating sport magazine, *Sports Illustrated*, lost numbers for several years from its height of 3 million. Travis (2013) claims that magazines have declined in newsstand sales by 56% since 2007! General interest magazines, as well as sporting magazines, began to turn to digital platforms by offering digital publications in response to consumers switching in droves to digital platforms.

Despite these pressures on sport magazines, they are considered important in relation to sport, particularly for the involved sport fan. Their in-depth sport stories and relaxed writing may not exist in print as much as they did in the past, but such writing has shifted somewhat to digital platforms, which is discussed in the next chapter.

RADIO

Radio remains an important traditional medium for sport communication, but in some parts of the world the role of radio has changed over time. In the Western world there is an ongoing shift to digital platforms, but radio remains the medium of choice when people are in automobiles and driving. In that part of the world, radio is rarely considered the medium of choice at home. In the developing world, particularly in remote villages, radio is the medium of choice for all types of mass communication regardless of context. There are several reasons for this positioning of radio in the developing world. One major reason is that radio remains, in several countries, the only broadcasting medium that covers the entire country, because television usually covers only urban areas. Second, the lack of access to electric power in the remotest areas and illiteracy limit access to newspapers, which requires a literate readership, and also limits access to television, which depends on electrical power. The lack of power also limits access to digital platforms.

With radio's resilience, therefore, it serves as an important medium for sport communication in various parts of the world. Of course, it provides quicker sport news and events compared to both newspapers and magazines. Also, events can be reported live. This advantage of broadcasting media means that they are used for live communication of sporting activities and events such as important games. However, because radio broadcasting is only based on audio communication without video, the broadcasters must create the picture of the sporting action in the listener's mind. This requires someone with the ability to create imagery and mimic the fast pace of a sporting event, enabling the audience to feel present at the scene of the event.

In many countries, very good radio sport commentators become celebrities because they have that ability. Michael Abrahamson, for example, is well known in South Africa for his radio commentaries at various sporting events, including the 2010 FIFA World Cup on Radio 2000 of South Africa and English commentaries of various sports at the Athens Olympics in 2004. He has also done radio commentaries on a variety of sports such as cricket, athletics, rugby, and volleyball. Des Scahill's commentary in the horse racing of 1986 when Dawn Run won the Cheltenham Gold Cup is considered one of the most famous commentaries in Irish sporting history.

However, sport communication in radio does not only involve commentaries on live events. Over the years, radio has become more specialized, moving from general radio programming to specialty radio programming, including sport. Thus, sport radio stations have developed, particularly in the United States and in other parts of the world such as Brazil (Bradesco Esportes FM), ESPN Radio (USA), Five Live Sports Extra (Britain), Beijing Tiyu Guangbo (China), Radio Sport (New Zealand), DZSR Sports Radio (Philippines), and 88.9 Brila-FM (Nigeria). These stations are dedicated to sport programming.

Sport talk

Sport radio, in addition to sport commentaries on live events, includes sport discussion programs and call-in sport programming known as sport talk radio. Sport talk is believed to have started in the United States in March 1964 under Bill Mazer on New York's WNBC (AM). Sport talk shows often tend towards discussion of controversial topics and include outrageous comments and boisterous debates involving callers. The more conflict involved, the better the talk show and the more involved the audience becomes. This type of radio programming attracts a loyal but narrow core audience of young men with disposable income.

Radio stations, like newspapers and magazines, have also developed an online presence. This is a way of keeping up with the times and competing with digital radio stations that are only found on the Internet without a presence over the air.

TELEVISION

A large number of the sport audience watch games over the air through broadcast television or through cable television and satellite. The conduit through which the video gets to the audience does not matter as long as the audience receives the videos through a television set, though increasingly a number of the audience access sporting videos through their telephones, tablets, and laptops.

Television frequently pays the largest amount to secure rights to sporting events. In 2013, the BT Group paid 900 million pounds (about $1.33 billion) for exclusive three-year British rights for the European Champions League and Europa League (Panja, 2013). This was an incredible amount, doubling the amount paid by British Sky Broadcasting Group and ITV for rights to those sporting leagues. Why did BT offer so much? Because those competitions are premier soccer competitions in Europe that attract the largest audiences and the biggest advertisers that pay to BT Group a premium for advertisement spots in programs pertaining to those leagues.

As noted elsewhere, money from such rights increasingly serve as the largest piece of revenue for sporting organizations. Media organizations, like the BT Group, extract benefits from selling space at huge sums to advertisers and by reselling rights to small stations, selling exclusive footage to other media organizations, and attracting huge audiences that positively affect program ratings of a specific sporting program and other programs. In essence, obtaining rights to major sporting events is good business for both the television station as well as the sporting entity.

Television has many advantages that make it the preferred platform for watching sporting events. Like radio, it can bring sport information instantaneously, which newspapers or magazines cannot. Furthermore, it has both audio and video and, thus, the audience benefits from watching the sporting event in real time and having an expert explain to them what they are watching. Over the years, television has employed former sport persons to participate in analysis and comment on the sport that they played. This provides a credible expert view of the game. Importantly, television coverage increasingly includes behind-the-scenes coverage that takes the camera to the training ground, locker room, and other locations where the audience hitherto had no access.

Cable television in the 1980s brought to the audience specialized channels, including those that are dedicated to sport. Essentially, such channels are equivalent to sport radio discussed in the previous section. The Entertainment Sports Programming Network (ESPN) has multiple channels focusing on different types of sport programming. Sport is now covered from a wide range of angles and deeply analyzed. One of the new forms of analysis is discussion of team tactics, a topic rarely dealt with just a few decades ago. Now, coaches are brought in to discuss tactics and use advanced technologies to explain to the audience what possible team strategies and tactics are employed. In some sports, these technologies have included heat maps to indicate areas on the field that a player has concentrated efforts.

Television also has its own sport talk shows that mirror radio sport talk shows. The same formula used in radio sport talk shows works well in television, using a combative host who attracts attention. One of the most controversial episodes occurred on an ESPN2 talk show hosted by Jim Rome in 1994. Jim Rome is a very popular but combative host who prides himself as a hard-hitting host who does not spare his guests. On that day, he had quarterback Jim Everett as a guest and derided Everett several times by calling him "Chris Evert" (i.e. the female tennis player) because Everett had ducked and gone to the ground in an American gridiron football game to avoid a sack when no pressure existed. Well, Everett warned Jim Rome not to call him "Chris" on the ESPN2 show. Jim Rome, sensing a big story, called Everett "Chris" on the show. Everett threw Jim Rome to the ground, and the live show was immediately blacked out. The next day, it was a big story all over American media that brought new viewers to Jim Rome's show seeking additional thrills.

Television, like other traditional media, is also available online, through digital streaming of sporting events or through streaming systems such as Roku.

REFLECTION

Identify your favorite sport and think about how it is covered by a general interest publication (newspaper or magazine) or a broadcasting station (radio or television). Then think about how that same sport is covered in a specialized sporting publication or specialized sport broadcasting program (sport radio talk show or sport program). Think about how coverage compares in the two contexts by examining coverage extent, depth, and quality, among other factors.

GROWTH AND IMPACT OF TRANSNATIONAL MEDIA

A growing area is transnational sport service. Transnational service refers to services across international borders. Growth, in this area, has primarily been through television.

Before the late 1980s, television in most places was restricted to service within national borders. There were few exceptions. Examples of exceptions were France and Britain, providing limited broadcasting via radio and television to their colonial territories. The United States, through the Voice of America (VOA), largely provided radio broadcasting to several territories across the world. These exceptions were few and far between. In the main, media were largely confined within national borders.

The environment for the growth of transnational television service depended on two developments. First was a worldwide domino-like liberalization of the broadcast environment in several countries. Many countries, where the national government controlled broadcasting, began to liberalize the media industry. Africa and Asia were particularly affected by this after the collapse of the Soviet Union and introduction of free capitalist principles in previously socialist-leaning countries. Liberalization allowed competition and private entry into the new broadcast environment. Some of the private entrants were companies from outside of the country. Second, technological development, particularly satellite television, proved to be a major driver in the new environment. In many cases, satellite television service spread much quicker than government attempts to liberalize markets. For instance, in several African countries governments lost control over the broadcast markets when their citizens began to access foreign programming via satellite dishes at their houses. Ultimately, satellite transmission of television programming made it much easier for programs to be delivered to great distances without building expensive repeater or retransmission stations.

New regulations allowing entry into markets by private providers meant that customers no longer required expensive satellite dishes to download television programming from other countries. Instead, the new television programming providers sell less-expensive encrypted television packages to customers that include smaller satellite dishes. Providers also provide less-expensive cable television programming to customers' homes. Akindes (2011), Chalaby (2005), and Alegi (2010) all note that sport filled up a large percentage of programming in Africa by new providers. In fact, Chalaby claims that 25% of Canal Horizon's programs is sport. In Africa, Canal Horizon from France dominated the sport broadcasting provided to Francophone African countries, and South Africa's Supersport TV began to provide continent-wide sport programming through multiple television channels. America's ESPN provides worldwide sport programming across several countries and continents.

The emergence of transnational media has impacted sport communication in various ways, including increasing and decreasing revenue for different geo-located sporting organizations, creating global brands, changing sporting cultures, changing the way sport is consumed, and impacting local media sport coverage.

Teams and leagues, shown across the world, profit from transnational television broadcasting. Most of the teams and leagues are based in Europe, and they have been able to generate increasing media rights revenue mentioned earlier in this chapter. Additionally, they generate revenue from merchandising across borders and earning sponsorship money. However, local sporting organizations have lost significant revenue. Akindes (2011) wrote that:

> local games are not attended as much as before. An administrator at ASEC Abidjan (a large club in Côte d'Ivoire) remarked that stadiums are empty and that even the matches of ASEC-Africa (the long-time rivals of Côte d'Ivoire) are not sold out anymore.
>
> (p. 2183)

Transnationalization also means that brands of major sporting organizations and athletes are extended across borders. In the past, an athlete was relatively unknown until a mega world event. That is no longer accurate. As long as that athlete's performance and activities are frequently present in transnational media, then the athlete's brand is probably going to be on the rise.

The result is that local sporting cultures are changing. For instance, all over Africa, spectators watch games wearing shirts of their favorite teams. In the past, team colors were not worn to games in several African countries. This is a phenomenon that was largely adopted from watching transnational television. On the sporting field, local teams celebrate the way their idols celebrate on transnational television. In essence, behaviors are learned through watching transnational transmission of games. For instance, the longstanding culture of football matches on Saturday evenings in Nigeria has been affected. In 2016, Nigeria moved prominent league games to Friday nights to avoid conflicting with transnational televising of European league games (Ngobua, 2015).

The way sport is consumed has also changed in local areas. A key change is where games are consumed. In places like Africa and Asia, football games were mostly consumed by going to the stadium to watch a match. Today, a large percentage of football games watched by fans are no longer in stadiums. Instead, they are consumed in what Akindes (2011) and Onwumechili (2009) describe as "viewing centers" and/or "bars." Akindes stresses as follows: "One Burkinabe journalist found that 'there are more than 50 video clubs in Ouagadougou (the capital of Burkina Faso) where you can watch all European league games'" (p. 2181).

Finally, local media coverage of sport has been affected. Onwumechili (2009) found that local Nigerian newspapers dedicate a large percentage of sport coverage to European football while ignoring local games. In essence, these newspapers mirror sport transmission of transnational media.

TRANSNATIONAL TELEVISION CONFRONTS TRADITION

Mr. Luiz Rodriguez is worried. "We have to find a way to get people to watch our games," he said to Carlos Ramirez, his assistant at the Federation. Carlos is browsing a recent report of average league attendances in the local premier league, and the numbers are shocking. In the last five years alone, the average shrunk, from 20,000 to 8,000. With the decline in attendance numbers come declines in sponsorship, broadcasting rights money, and local newspaper coverage. More worrying, there are reports that clubs may have to sell top-salaried player contracts to avoid steep debts. It is indeed, "dangerous times," according to Carlos. The local football federation is deeply concerned.

Mr. Rodriguez is aware that most football fans have moved on to watching football on television. However, they are not watching local football. Instead, they are engrossed in watching foreign football televised from Europe. Worse still, local football stars are leaving the country to play in Europe as they seek big payouts. Local teams are forced to use less-talented veterans or young emerging players. The local government television ABS-TV continues to maintain rights to the local premier league, but they pay a small fee that is dropping. The fees had never been significant in the first place because government insists that local football is of public interest and that a national price control commission has to set the price based on revenue generated from its coverage and a 15% revenue commission to the federation. Of course, advertising and sponsorship revenues are declining, and so is commission due to the federation.

Mr. Rodriguez wants the government to allow the federation freedom to negotiate a deal, but government officials continue to insist on tradition. Meanwhile, a sport television station – *Deporte Mundial TV* – from a neighboring country entered the market following recent market liberalization. It is making huge revenues by broadcasting live European football games and spectators are subscribing in droves to watch those games.

"Where have the advertisers gone?" asked Mr. Rodriguez's friend, Ariana Ramos. Mr. Rodriguez knows. Many of them have moved on to *Deporte Mundial TV*. They have simply followed consumers to European football league games via *Deporte Mundial TV*. They are paying more to sponsor sport programs or to advertise in sport programs at *Deporte Mundial*, but they are happy. They are reaching more people than ever before, "not just in our country but in many other countries in the region," Mr. Rodriguez says.

Carlos informs Mr. Rodriguez that he has a plan that may help the federation and local football. He says that his plans are A and B. "Plan A is to inform government that local football is no longer a public interest, and we can show this with the most recent data indicating that most people now watch foreign football leagues," Carlos argues. "So what does that do for local football and us?" Mr. Rodriguez queries. "Well, either it takes us off the hook to negotiate our own deals, or it may get government to curb media coverage of foreign football.

Either way, we are getting help," Mr. Ramirez states. Mr. Rodriguez thinks about it and concludes that he wants something more positive. "So what is Plan B?" he asks. "Plan B is to ask government to subsidize the league or else clubs will go away and public interest dies. Furthermore, have government force *Deporte Mundial* to cover our league since it is in the public interest," Carlos adds. "Is there a Plan C, genius?" Mr. Rodriguez quips.

Mr. Rodriguez believes there is a way around this problem. He knows that he has a responsibility to build up the local league. It is his burden. How does he go about this? That is the question to which he isn't yet ready with an answer.

Discussion questions

1. Is there another possible plan out there that you may have? Your Plan C?
2. What are the impacts of transnational television such as *Deporte Mundial TV*? Are those impacts positive or negative? Or both? Please explain.
3. If the federation is successful at convincing the government not to designate elite football as a public interest, do you think that the federation broadcasting local games on another television station can win back sponsors and advertisers in competition against *Deporte Mundial TV*, which reaches across national borders? Please provide support for your thinking.
4. What actions, if any, do you think local football clubs could take to cultivate sponsors and advertisers?
5. If you had to choose between Plan A and B put forward by Mr. Carlos Ramirez, which would you prefer? Provide details of which one you prefer and why.

SPORT MEDIA AND COMMUNICATION STRATEGIES

Sport communication relies on basic principles for determining what should be given prominence and what should not. The sporting media make choices, and these choices are based on certain considerations. Journalists who report on news in general have developed a list of how to determine what to report. Principles used for such evaluations are referred to as news values. However, these values differ from one journalism culture to the next. There are six to twelve such values that are widely used in decision making on what to report. Most of those values also apply in sport communication.

Twelve news values are listed as follows:

1. Is it impactful or consequent?
2. How immediate or timely is it to report?

3   Does it involve a prominent personality?
4   How close to our local interest is it?
5   Does it involve controversy?
6   Is it a bizarre occurrence?
7   How trendy is it or how current is interest in it?
8   How big a story is this?
9   Does it have human interest?
10 Is it entertaining?
11 How helpful is it for our audience to know?
12 Is it a necessity for the public?

Affirmative responses to the questions determine the newsworthiness of an event or activity. The more a particular event provides affirmative responses to each question, the more it will be given prominence by the news media. Sport media use similar criteria for evaluating a sporting event.

A study by Gee and Leberman (2011) finds slightly different results in France. Gee and Leberman wanted to find out what informs media decision makers in selecting stories to cover and whether such criteria differ in media coverage of both male and female athletes and teams in France. They found that decision makers use three key criteria, which were newsworthiness, nationalism, and notoriety.

Newsworthiness reflects the use of the criteria mentioned earlier. That is a much easier decision, but decisions are not solely based on news values. Instead, decision makers apply additional criteria, such as nationalism or what can be referred to as proximity. In this case, it means that the athlete's nation matters. For instance, a French athlete's performance receives far more prominence in French media compared to an athlete from a different nationality. Notoriety refers to some combination of human interest and prominence centered on the athlete, sport, or particular event. Most decision makers cite someone like rugby scrum-half Sebastien Chabal. Chabal was not an exceptional player and was frequently used as a substitute. Yet, when he retired, there was a mass reaction in social media that was never seen before concerning a recent French rugby player. French media created Chabal's popularity. Mortimer (2014) writes that French marketing companies selected Chabal to be the face of France hosting the 2007 Rugby World Cup because Sebastien looked like a "caveman" with his unkempt beard. The media promotion and publicity surrounding Chabal exploded and swept through France, and

> This manliness was soon making him (Chabal) money, lots of it, what with the launch of his clothing range, wine label, a hotel-restaurant and even a Chabal cuddly toy. As early as January he was dressing up as a fairy in a bizarre TV advert for a currency exchange company.
>
> (para. 11)

For women's sport, Gee and Leberman (2011) find that media employ slightly different criteria in addition to those already mentioned. For instance, they did not simply require good but exceptional performance for women's sport to receive prominence in the media. The media also require the athlete to be good looking. Lastly, they largely focus coverage on women who excel in sport that the media do not perceive as a male preserve. In essence, women participating in sport such as rugby, football, and boxing are less likely to be covered in French sporting media.

CHAPTER SUMMARY

Traditional media, or what is referred to as legacy media, remain important in sport communication despite the rise in social media. By traditional media, this chapter refers to television, radio, newspaper, magazine, film, and books. In certain cultures and countries, traditional media include what is called *oramedia*, a word coined from the English words "oral media." These media are used for communicating sport to a large number of consumers.

The chapter delves into a deep discussion of the interdependence between professional sport and traditional media. Professional sport benefits from the relationship through exposure to a great number of people who may be widely dispersed and unable to attend a live sporting event. Additionally, a large part of sporting revenue comes from the media. On the other hand, traditional media's largest audiences are those who consume sporting communication, and traditional media make a significant part of their revenue from selling advertisement on sport programs and space. Thus, the interdependent relationship is symbiotic. The section also reviews specialized sport media publications and programs, including those owned and produced by sporting organizations.

The chapter notes that increasing media globalization has come from transnationalism of media communication. In essence, some traditional media reach consumers that cut across national borders, and they impact how people consume sport.

A final section of the chapter focuses on sport media and communication strategies. These strategies expose values that the media use in determining which sporting news to cover and how to cover it. The section points out that criteria for sport media coverage may also depend on the gender of the athletes.

DISCUSSION QUESTIONS

1 What is traditional media? Do you think traditional media coverage of sport is consumed by a great number of people today? Provide support for your answer.
2 Why is *oramedia* considered mass media? Why do you think dance theater is powerful in the culture where it exists?
3 The relationship between professional sport and traditional media is considered strong. Can one of them survive without the other? Why?

4 What created the environment that led to the phenomenal growth of transnational media? Do you think that transnational media are good for the world? Provide support for your answer.
5 Are values for covering sport different from one country to another? Provide examples to support your answer.
6 Do you think that traditional media will remain strong as sources for sport communication to consumers?

ACTIVITIES

1 In a week, watch two sporting events on television. One should be a program on an event played in another country and the other an event taking place in your home country. How do the two events impact your attitude towards the teams that you watch? Are you emotionally attached to the teams? Write a report on your views after watching the televised sporting events.
2 After reading the chapter section on communication strategies of sport media, apply what you have read to analysis of a sport news report in your local newspaper and then to a national newspaper report (this paper must be published in a city different from where you live) of a sporting event. Then write a report comparing the strategies of both newspapers.
3 Listen to your favorite sport radio talk show. Make sure to identify all announced sponsors and advertisements during the show. How may each of those (sponsors and advertisers) benefit listeners of the show? Do you think the show is interesting? Why? Write a report on your observation.

VIDEO RESOURCES

Play by Play: A History of Sports Television (Documentary). On YouTube.
Mind Control: Television, Sports, News Media Are Used to Manipulate & Control You! (YouTube video/ 11 min.).
Inside the Control Room: Turning NFL Football Into Primetime Television (YouTube/12.24 min.)
Sports Television Panel at the Paley Media Council (YouTube/50.43 min.).
Unleashing the Live Experience: How Sports Television Engages Today's Fans (YouTube/ 1:00:18).

RECOMMENDED WEB RESOURCES

Malone, T. (2012, April 25). History of sports media. https://sportsandpr1. wordpress.com/2012/04/25/history-of-sports-media/
Canal+ launches new sports channels for Africa. www.digitaltveurope.net/400391/canal-launches-new-sports-channels-for-africa/
Association for International Broadcasting (AIB). http://nabanet.com/nabaweb/ news/articles/58_files/delegate_book_final_170215.pdf

REFERENCES

Akindes, G. (2011). Football bars: Urban sub-Saharan Africa's trans-local 'stadiums.' *The International Journal of the History of Sport*, 28(15): 2176–2190.

Alegi, P. (2010). *African soccerscapes: How a continent changed the world's game*. Athens, OH: Ohio University Press.

Bernstein, A., & Blain, N. (2002). Sport and the media: The emergence of a major research field. *Culture, Sport, Society*, 5(3): 1–30.

Bond, P. (2015, October 19). Sports industry study: Media rights to overtake gate revenue in 2018. *The Hollywood Reporter*. http://www.HollywoodReporter.webarchive

Chalaby, J. (2005). *Transnational television worldwide: Towards a new media order*. London: I. B. Tauris.

Doctor, K. (2015, March 13). Newsonomics: Single-copy newspaper sales are collapsing, and it's largely a self-inflicted wound. *NiemanLab*. www.niemanlab.org/

Fitts, R. (2005). *Remembering Japanese baseball: An oral history of the game*. Carbondale, IL: Southern Illinois University Press.

Gee, B., & Leberman, S. (2011). Sports media decision making in France: How they choose what we get to see and read. *International Journal of Sport Communication*, 4: 321–343.

Horne, J. (1992). General sports magazines and "Cap'n Bob": The rise and fall of *Sportsweek*. *Sociology of Sport Journal*, 9: 179–191.

Horne, J. (2005). Sport and the mass media in Japan. *Sociology of Sport Journal*, 22: 415–432.

Le, E. (2012, April 17). Newspaper boom in Asia defies trends in West. www.ibtimes.com / newspaper-boom-asia-defies-trends-west-438358

Mortimer, G. (2014, May 7). Sebastien Chabal: Legend or myth? www.rugbyworld.com/

Ngobua, D. (2015, July 24). Nigeria: LMC to introduce night matches. www.dailytrust.com.ng

Onwumechili, C. (2009). Nigeria, football, and the return of Lord Lugard. *International Journal of Sport Communication*, 2(4): 451–465.

Panja, T. (2013, November 10). Top soccer leagues get 25% rise in TV rights sales, report says. www.bloomberg.com/

Plunkettresearch.com (2015). Sports industry statistics and market size overview. www.plunkettresearch.com/statistics/sports-industry/

Pomerantz, D. (2014, February 4). Get ready for more Olympics coverage (and more Ads) than ever before. *Forbes Business*. www.forbes.com/

PwC (2011, December). Changing the game: Outlook for the global sports market to 2015. www.pwc.com/gx/en/hospitality-leisure/pdf/changing-the-game-outlook-for-the-global-sports-market-to-2015.pdf.

Smith, G. (2016, April 19). The fading newspaper. www.bloomberg.com/

Steinberg, B. (2015, August 4). NBCU expects more than $1 billion in advertising for 2016 Rio Olympics. http://variety.com/

Stynes, T. (2014, Aug. 7). Print magazine sales decline in 1st half of 2014. *The Wall Street Journal*. www.wsj.com/

Travis, C. (2013, March 7). What's the future of Sports Illustrated? www.outkickthecoverage.com/

Ugboajah, F. (1986). Communication as technology in African rural development. *Africa Media Review*, 1(1): 1–19.

CHAPTER 6

NEW MEDIA

> **LEARNING OBJECTIVES**
>
> After reading this chapter, you should be able to do the following:
>
> - Understand different types of new media for communicating sport.
> - Become acquainted with why new media impacts sport communication.
> - Become aware of different functions of new media in communicating sport.
> - Describe how new media changes the way sport is consumed globally.

The previous chapter discusses traditional media and points to a decline in usage of traditional media by a growing number of people. Though traditional media are not expected to go away any time soon, it is clear that while their usage is declining, the usage of new media is on an incline and, in many cases, the incline is rapid. At this point, it is necessary to define exactly what new media refer to. The definition is not an easy one, as several scholars offer varying definitions of new media. Here, we define **new media** as information media that offer content on demand via digital devices that allow user-to-user interactivity and are not limited by geographic locations. Most new media are accessed via the world wide web. Examples of new media include social media sites, blogs, online news sites, Twitter, and discussion forums, among others. It is important to note, however, that while we describe old media as newspapers, magazines, books, radio, and television, the attempt to provide a strict differentiation between traditional and new media is not that simple. For instance, traditional media can be offered through a digital platform, which means that such offerings immediately turn the content into new media.

The rise in new media platforms is demonstrated in startling April 2016 statistics provided by Chaffey (2016). It shows that Facebook has 1,590 million active users,

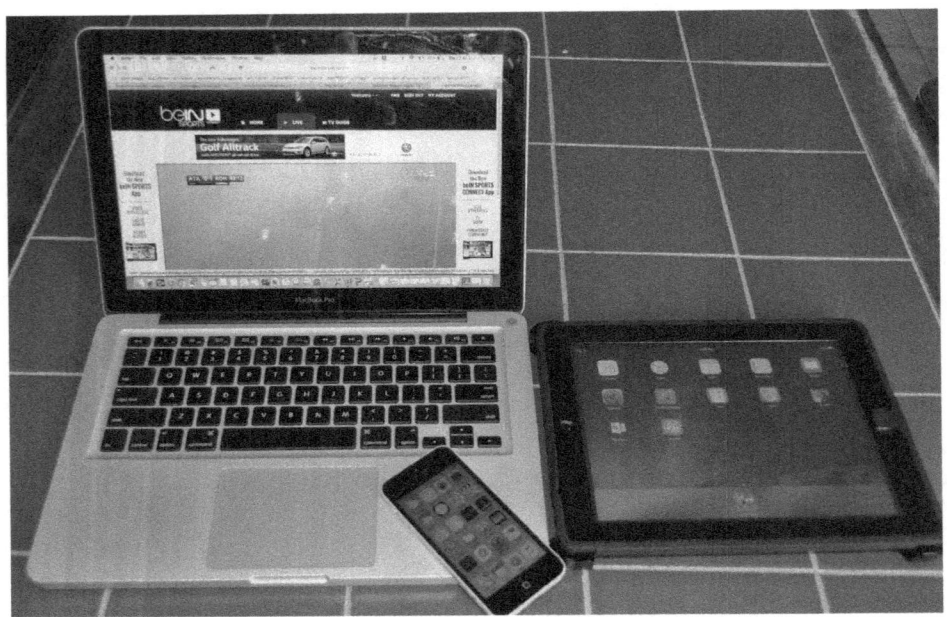

Photo 6.1 New digital media platforms for sport communication. Here a laptop, a tablet, and a telephone are shown.

Source: Author

followed by WhatsApp at 1,000 million. Popular social media sites widely used in Asia-Pacific regions, such as QQ (853 million), WeChat (697 million), and QZone (640 million), are all ahead of the popular ones such as Tumblr (555 million), Instagram (400 million), and Twitter (320 million) used in the West. Chaffey also shows that Twitter and WhatsApp are the fastest-growing new media. Chaffey's summary also shows that in terms of annual growth, the number of active mobile social media users is at 17%. The largest Internet use is in East Asia with 867 million persons, but the largest penetration is in West Europe and North America, which are both over 80% compared to East Asia's 54%. In terms of percentage of users visiting a social media site in the most recent month, the Philippines, Mexico, and Turkey lead with over 90% each on Facebook; and Indonesia, Turkey, and Saudi Arabia lead with over 60% each on Twitter.

Data related to sport communication are not dramatically different. Statista.com's February 2014 data shows that Facebook is the most popular new media for accessing sport all over the world. However, there are differences in some countries. For instance, the data show that people in Indonesia, Japan, and Russia prefer watching sport on YouTube. In the United Arab Emirates (UAE), YouTube is a close second to Facebook. In Japan, Twitter, although second to YouTube, is more popular than Facebook for following sport.

In essence, the media environment for sport communication is undergoing a major transition with a tilt towards use of new media. What this means is that those who study sport communication or are presently making a career in the industry cannot afford to ignore new media. In the sections that follow, we delve into the details of new media and sport communication.

CHARACTERISTICS OF NEW MEDIA

Though new media are defined earlier in this chapter, the definition is general, and it is difficult to identify specific media that are classified under the term new media. One way to make this much easier is to identify and describe characteristics of new media. These characteristics, as we shall see, will help us differentiate new media from traditional media, particularly in reference to sport communication.

Eight characteristics of new media will be described subsequently: absence of gatekeepers, multimedia content, loads of information, instantaneous information, connectivity, interactivity, user-generated content, and the creation of a sense of immediacy.

A major difference between new media and traditional media is the **absence of a gatekeeper** or gatekeepers in new media. In traditional media, there is usually a professional who determines the final communication message we receive from the source. For instance, a producer determines what type of information the audience receives from a television sport program. An example might be *SportsCenter*, which is a popular day-long sport news program produced on ESPN. The producer makes choices about which sport news the audience will consume from a plethora of sport events and activities that happen all over the world on a daily basis. The producer who makes this decision is a gatekeeper who determines which sport news is allowed to go through the "gate." A similar gatekeeper would be an editor in a newspaper or a magazine. There is also a producer for sport radio programs. These are gatekeepers. This gatekeeper is largely absent in new media, or at best the gatekeeper is far more dispersed (i.e. there are so many of them). A good example is sport messaging on Twitter. Each entity on Twitter (sport organization, athlete, fan, among others) has the ability to post information on Twitter without going through an editor or producer for approval. This democratizes the information shared in new media because the decision makers are dispersed, compared to decision makers in traditional media. While this lack of gatekeeper democratizes sport news and removes restrictions to what the audience receives, it is also a double-edged sword. The lack of a gatekeeper means that some of the shared information can be inaccurate.

While traditional media are restricted to certain forms of message delivery, new media are not. What does this mean? A magazine (traditional) may restrict consumers to sport content in print and photographs, but television may offer more by adding video and audio. New media have the ability to add all of those (i.e. print, still photographs, audio, and video). Only television, among the traditional media, is able to match the multimedia content possibility offered by new media.

However, new media offer far more than television's multimedia content. New media provide access to **loads of sporting information** and from several sources as discussion on gatekeeping already demonstrated. The Internet browser, for instance, provides a gateway to accessing all types of sporting information in various forms and from a variety of sources. For instance, by using a browser, a consumer may access sporting information from an event that occurred decades ago, and this information may be in the form of text, audio, or video – or all those forms in an integrated shape.

Importantly, the load of information found in new media is accessed **instantaneously**. In essence, a consumer can access information whenever he or she wishes to do so. Though traditional media like radio and television provide instantaneous information, the consumer does not control the time of access. Thus, the big difference is that on new media, the consumer has the power to access what he or she wants to consume and at what time to do so, whereas in traditional media the source of the message makes those types of decisions.

New media also offer **connectivity**. Essentially, new media connect consumers to each other. This is something that traditional media are unable to accomplish. Consumers of traditional media are only connected to the medium that they consume but not to other consumers of the same medium. The ability for consumers to connect with each other allows creation of vibrant communities through new media and provides opportunities for members of these communities to develop relationships within this digital community or outside digital communities.

Communities created through connectivity of new media demonstrate an additional characteristic of new media, which is **interactivity**. This refers to consumers' ability to communicate with each other or communicate with the source of sport information just consumed. Traditional media, on the other hand, are largely designed to provide one-way communication from source to consumers of information. There is hardly adequate room for meaningful feedback. In new media such as Facebook, for instance, there is abundant room for feedback. Consumers respond to any sporting information provided to them and, in several cases, this ability generates longwinded conversations about the sporting information.

Another characteristic is that new media include substantive **user-generated content** and communication, whereas this is relatively absent in traditional media. Facebook, WhatsApp, and Twitter, for example, consist of user-generated content. Users or consumers create much of the information. A more vivid example is analysis of an athlete moving from one sporting organization to another. In traditional media, such as a magazine, a resident writer employed by the magazine authors a lengthy analysis of this athlete's movement from one club to the other. In contrast, the same event analyzed on Facebook involves fans making comments about the move and providing analysis on how they think the player may fare in the new club and how the move affects the athlete's previous club.

Finally, new media have the characteristic of **immediacy**. By immediacy, we do not refer to timeliness. Instead, the term refers to making something appear important or exciting or interesting in such a way that it provides us with a sense of exciting human familiarity and closeness. This is a subtle difference that we feel with new media compared to most of traditional media. Contrastingly, traditional media give us a sense of distance from those communicating with us because they talk to us, they provide information, and we simply consume without having a sense of closeness with those that provide such information. For new media, the consumer's ability to interact with others, including the information provider, creates a sense of closeness because the consumer is able to hold a conversation, argue with, debate, comment, and receive a response from the other.

TYPES OF NEW MEDIA

A variety of new media participate in sport communication. While each exhibits the characteristics of new media discussed in the previous section, they differ from one another in various ways because of the platform used in reaching consumers of their sport messages. Few of these media are discussed in this section, focusing on online news media, fan discussion forums, blogs, social media networking sites, Twitter, YouTube, and WeChat.

Online news media are websites for news. These may be traditional media that have developed digital platforms to complement traditional platforms or news media developed solely on a digital platform. Importantly, these media provide sport communication with interactive features for consumers online. For example, the *Chicago Tribune* newspaper, which is also available online, allows consumers to respond to each sport news article. For instance, in an American gridiron football story, Wiederer and Campbell (2016) reported that a key player of the Chicago Bears was out for the season following an injury to his knee. Of course, the hard copy of the story provided no opportunities for consumers to instantly respond to the story. The digital copy, however, provided such opportunities. Comments like the following then came from consumers:

> The guy (athlete) was way too light to play center. Looked like he was on ice skates. So then he bulks up 20 pounds or so and apparently that extra weight was not something his legs were ready to handle re the strenuousness of football. When you're rebuilding a team from the ground up, you can't afford to take on "projects". Maybe he'll turn out great eventually, but right now you can only conclude the pick was a mistake. He wasn't ready to play NFL center – so Pace (General Manager) should have passed.

Fan discussion forum is also a new type of medium for sport communication. These are created online for fan participation in discussing all matters concerning their team. A discussion board is a message board available on the web where users, with similar interests, visit virtually to leave a message or respond to messages posted by others. Messages are organized into threads of topics. Usually, each message board is dedicated to a particular sport or team and is created by fans. However, there are cases where a sporting organization creates a discussion forum for its fans. A good example is the Pittsburgh Penguins website. The Penguins club is a member of the National Hockey League (NHL) in the United States, and the club's website hosts a message board for its fans. This site is one of several created by the NHL for each of its member teams. There is a fan-created board for the Celtic Football Club of Scotland called *Kerrydale Street*, which has more than 17,000 members and 8 million posts in mid-2016. Board discussions are vibrant on anything Celtic, but there are rules on posting etiquette and other issues because discussions can degenerate to abuses and threats. There are also fan discussion boards that serve as aggregation sites for several related sub-boards. A major one is called *Big Soccer*, and it hosts a variety of sub-boards catering to national teams such as the USA, England, Netherlands, Bosnia, Mexico, China, Japan, Iraq, and Italy, among others. It also has sub-forums on women's soccer.

Blogs are journals or brief articles on a specific topic that appear regularly online. These articles are opinionated, and many of them offer opportunities for readers to make comments in the same way as online news media sites described earlier. There are numerous blogs that focus on sport. Initially, blogs were created by sport fans and hosted on independent online sites. However, this has changed. These days, sporting organizations and big media host blog sites or have acquired popular blog sites established by sport fans. Popular sport blog sites include *SB Nation* and *Bleacher Report* in the United States. Those two blog sites cover many teams from all sports as well as other sporting issues. *SB Nation*, for example, hosts 315 blog sites, many of which have Facebook, Instagram, and Twitter links, and they represent differing voices of fans. Managers for these blogs are paid, while regular contributors receive a stipend and write a few times each week.

Social media networking sites are also used for sport communication. The most popular of these is Facebook. This is a digital site that allows users to develop relationships with others of their choice by sharing stories, photographs, and video. Facebook allows members to build a page that is accessible to the public. This page may be used as a website. Athletes, sport fans, writers, and sporting organizations use Facebook pages to communicate sport. Millions of people are fans of athletes on Facebook. Fan Page List (n.d.) keeps social media statistics of brands, celebrities, and sports, among others, and reports that tennis star Maria Sharapova has over 15 million people as fans on her Facebook page, and she is not even among the top 15 athletes in terms of number of fans. Sport teams also maintain Facebook pages for disseminating information to those who have befriended the team. Among the top 10 sport team leaders in number of fans are eight football teams in Europe, with each of them logging over 24 million fans. However, even non-football sporting organizations like Ultimate Fighting Championship (UFC) has more than 19 million fans on Facebook. Then there are fans and avid sport communicators who use Facebook pages to blog about sport and share stories.

> **REFLECTION**
>
> Think about your favorite sport blog that is interactive. Which sport is it on and how often do you get to read the blog compared to other sources of sport communication? Why is the selected blog attractive to you? What makes the blog interactive? Does it get a lot of fan reactions, and when does it elicit these responses? Think about how you will characterize the language of responses on a scale of polite to impolite. This reflection and recollection will bring to mind the role blogs play in sport communication.

Besides the use of Facebook pages, a significant amount of sport communication occurs on **Twitter**. Twitter is a digital social platform that allows microbloggers to send messages limited to 140 characters to a list of followers. Still photographs and/or graphics interchange format (GIF) sometimes accompany messages called tweets. GIFs support animation of video for a brief period. Twitter also allows people to retweet (re-distribute) a message to their followers. Twitter has become a popular platform for breaking sport news and digital conversation, among other types of sport communication. Neely-Cohen (2016) claims that at least 70% of National Basketball Association (NBA) players in the United States are on Twitter. He added: "The NBA Twitter ecosystem includes professional gamblers, math geniuses, journalists, front office insiders, superfans, team PR reps, massive athletic apparel brands, cable news anchors, rappers, heads of states, and the very players being discussed" (para. 2). The NBA has more than 22 million followers on Twitter (Fan Page List, n.d.). Twitter allows athletes and teams to hold direct conversations with those who consume the sport. The popularity of Twitter for sport communication cannot be overstated. Here are a few statistics from Taylor (n.d.) that supports such a claim: there were 80,000 tweets per minute on Usain Bolt winning the 200 meters at the 2012 Olympics right after the event, and septuagenarian soccer player Pele had more than 100,000 followers a few hours after he debuted on Twitter.

YouTube is a website where users share or watch videos. Viewers of the videos may also make comments about the videos that they watch. Individuals or organizations may compile a list of certain sport video moments that present a particular

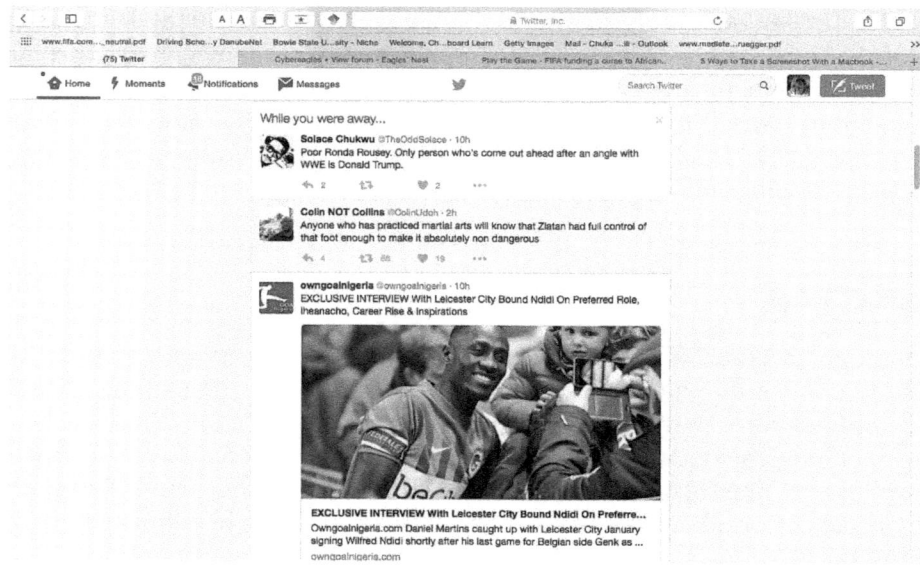

Photo 6.2 A Twitter page showing ongoing micro blogging.
Source: Author

goal. For instance, there is a 7-minute video on epic moments in track and field history, and there are also compilations of epic meltdowns by athletes in major competitions or in press conferences. In short, people may make any kind of video that they want and post it on YouTube. Others may record snippets or full game videos. These are publicly shared and viewed by thousands and millions of people. Increasingly, live sport events take place on YouTube.

WeChat, which is most popular in Asia, was originally developed in China by Tencent Guangzhou Research in 2011, but it now has more than 1 billion users worldwide with most consumers inside China. The app was initially developed for mobile telephone users, but it is used on other systems that use Windows and OS X. WeChat allows text and voice messaging, broadcast messaging, video, and sharing of photographs. It operates largely like WhatsApp, which was developed in the West. Sport media such as SuperSport, which dominates televised sport service in African countries, also provides sport communication to users of WeChat, but SuperSport is not the only sport media to do this; several others have as well, and users include sporting organizations, athletes, and sport consumers.

FUNCTIONS OF NEW MEDIA

The functions of new media are related to their characteristics. Here, the focus is on functions pertaining to sport communication. In essence, the question is how are new media used for sport communication? What values do they bring? Of course, there are exhaustive answers to these questions. However, answers lead to a few functions of new media in the field of sport communication that are addressed in subsequent paragraphs.

The new media have a major advantage over previous media types. They are **accessible** on the move. In essence, people no longer have to wait to get home to watch sport or buy a newspaper or magazine and then find a relaxing time to consume sport. Instead, they can consume sport wherever and whenever via a mobile communication gadget. Of the traditional media, only radio allows consumption while on the move and usually when driving in a car or when involved in a recreational activity such as jogging. Importantly, the ubiquity of new media and their tendency to offer a plethora of information on particular teams means that each fan has multiple options to access their favorite teams on the go.

Accessing sport, while mobile, provides opportunities for fans to participate in discussions involving their favorite teams. These opportunities are plentiful with each new media. Each of them provides **interactivity** with both the source of information and other consumers of sport communication. Importantly, interactivity brings sport consumers closer to athletes. Gutbrod (2012) writes that:

> Player tweets and linked pictures give fans the chance to experience the personal lives of their favorite players. Fans can learn about who the players are and how they interact. . . . Using Twitter in that way can help to humanize the players, bringing them down a few pegs from the pedestal that fans have placed them on.
> (para. 9–10)

Gutbrod (2012) points out that this interactivity can be positive and negative for athletes. Fans receive, from favorite athletes, feedback or responses to their comments. This makes the fan or consumer develop the feeling of being an insider. However, negative aspects include non-vetted communication from athletes that may be detrimental to the athlete as well as the sporting organization.

New media also serve to **democratize** sport communication. This is an important function that clearly differentiates new from the old media. Traditional media, which we refer to as old media, are top-down, which means that the source (designated a professional, i.e. the journalist) maintains control over what is communicated to a large segment of sport consumers. They serve as gatekeepers, selecting stories to pay attention to and those not to pay attention to. However, with new media all of that is not the case. Instead, everyone can become a source for sport communication. All you need is an account in one of the new media in order to develop an audience to whom you can communicate your opinions on sport. Communication is no longer top-down but revolves around many sources and many consumers. This new environment means that sporting organizations must work harder to maintain communication goodwill within their communities.

With interactive properties of new media, people are able to **communicate with more of those persons who share similar sporting characteristics and interests** as fans. For instance, online discussion forums allow like-minded persons to meet virtually to discuss topics of mutual interest. In the past, the opportunity to meet with like-minded consumers was restricted to the stadium on match days and at the local pub. Today, such meeting opportunities exist online and not only with those who live within proximity of each other but with others all over the world. It is a remarkable difference. This way, new media can create communities of like-minded sport people.

Sporting organizations take advantage of these created communities by collecting **relevant data** about them. Data generated through new media are dissected by a sporting organization to further segment consumers. Thus, new media are essentially a powerful tool for use by a sporting organization as well as media organizations.

New media have the ability to **segment** audiences because they use response mechanisms and digital tracking systems to collect a significant amount of data. On the other hand, sporting organizations analyze collated data from their medium or media. This creates efficiency in marketing to specific audiences. Furthermore, it allows organizations to reach specific segments with appropriate sport communication.

NEW MEDIA AND CHANGE IN SPORT CONSUMPTION

Already, statistics show that people increasingly consume sport using new media more than they do through traditional media. The change has been slow but steady over the years. The change is not just in consumer decision making but also in decisions taken by sporting organizations to put their products more in new media platforms. The trend, at varying rates, is occurring in different parts of the world and through different new media platforms.

Chaffey (2016) cites recent statistics from statista.com on social media that is revealing and confirms the transition from traditional media platforms to new media platforms for consumers. Particularly impressive is startling annual growth in usage of new media as of January 2016. Examples of significant growth within a period of one year is 17% in number of active mobile social users, 10% in growth of number of active Internet users, 10% in growth of number of active social media users, and 4% growth in number of unique mobile users. While Chaffey points out that most of the growth occurs in the Asia-Pacific region, it is important to note that growth is across other regions of the world as well but with lower rates. Think about this: in Africa there are 349 million users of the Internet, which is more than users in Western Europe, North America, Southeast Asia, and South America, when each of those is taken separately. Of course, the figure for Africa is barely 30% penetration of its total population, which signifies room for exponential growth in coming years. In regions where penetration is closer to population saturation, like North

America, Stadd (2013) provides data that show a transition from traditional to new media in terms of sport consumption platforms.

Stadd also shows that the percentage of sport fans who report consuming sport via traditional media declined from 2011 to 2013. For television, the decline was 96% to 94% and for print media from 53% to 52%. However, radio surprisingly increased from 42% to 44%. There were sharp increases for new media. Online (including YouTube) went from 56% to 63%, mobile went from 21% to 35%, and social networks (including Facebook and Twitter) went from 15% to 25%. The trends are expected to remain in years to come as more games, sport news, and analysis become available and proliferate.

NEW MEDIA AND CHINESE SWIMMER BROACH TABOO SUBJECT

Chinese swimmer Fu Yuanhui is beloved by many of her countrymen and women because she is known for what the *New York Times* describes as "over-the-top expressions," which include making fun of her "arms (being) too short" as an explanation for missing the silver medal at the 2016 Olympic Games in the 100-meter backstroke, which she finished one-hundredth of a second behind first place. Unlike several Chinese athletes known for their grim and unsmiling faces, Fu is full of excitement and boundless joy at competitions. This endears her to spectators across the world.

However, what really exploded on Twitter was comments she made after she narrowly missed winning a medal in the 4-by-100 meter medley relay at the Olympics. The media representatives noticed that she was crouching over during post-game interviews and asked if she had a stomachache. Her response stunned the world. She said: "It's because I just got my *period* yesterday, so I'm still a bit weak and really tired. . . . But this isn't an excuse for not swimming well." A period? That was shocking in itself for any athlete from anywhere to mention publicly to the media, let alone a Chinese athlete mentioning the word "period." After all, the subject is still taboo in many parts of the world and especially in China. Yet, here she was before millions of global viewers mentioning the word.

Fu Yuanhui's words went viral online. It was on YouTube, Twitter, and on Weibo. According to the *New York Times*: "Ms. Fu's candor immediately attracted a deluge of comments online. On Weibo, China's Twitter-like social media platform, the hashtag related to the subject was searched more than half a million times by the end of Sunday (next day), with many commentators expressing their support for Ms. Fu's openness."

According to the *New York Times*, comments like "Only those who have gotten their periods know how deathly painful it can be. . . . You are too awesome." There were male commentators who criticized Fu's decision to swim, claiming that it was unhealthy and unhygienic for other swimmers. However, the *New York Times* reported that other females responded to such comments and defended Fu by stating: "Don't talk to me about staining the pool red or taking medicine to stop one's period. . . . Haven't you heard of something called a tampon?"

While the online and new media comments raged and fans and sport consumers interacted not just with each other but also with other athletes, Fu's comments struck a chord. In China, public comments on a woman's period are taboo and rare. According to the *New York Times*, "Television ads for feminine hygiene products are banned during prime viewing times as inappropriate." The *New York Times* cites a Chinese feminist activist who claims that Fu Yuanhui's comments raised awareness in China where the topic is often approached with euphemisms.

Fu Yuanhui certainly touched a delicate issue, and the new media played a role of not just reporting whatever the media source wants to report or censor but allowed a significant number of sport communication consumers to participate in such an important discourse. However, although those who seek change in China hail the discourse, there are others who are stunned and would prefer the topic stay mute.

* Content for this case was derived from the *New York Times* story of August 16, 2016.

Discussion questions

1 Without new media and media transnationalism, would this sport story permeate China? What do you think?
2 In which ways do consumers benefit from this sport story emerging on new media platforms?
3 What do you think about a story like this that goes against the cultural norms of a society? Could it have been prevented, and should it have been prevented? Why?
4 Assume that you are a feminist sport activist. How would you go about taking advantage of sport communication like this?

How changes impact consumption experience

So how have changes in communication platforms affected how people consume sport? There are at least five changes that one can point to their impact. Each of them is discussed in subsequent paragraphs.

Jackson (2015) provides an example of a change with the following quote:

> Because of advances in technology, fans can check sports news and scores and watch live events virtually anytime and anywhere. . . . Social media's impact on sports, and how we consume sports, has grown exponentially. Fans no longer need to wait for ESPN's *SportsCenter* or the morning newspaper for the latest updates. Trades and signings are disseminated to the masses as soon as they happen.
>
> (para. 2 and 6)

In essence, what Jackson alludes to is transition to new media, which has changed consumption habits from one where there is a wait time or delay to get news of a sporting event to one where there is instant information on the event. Much of that instant information is obtained through new media platforms like Twitter.

There is also an increasing requirement to pay for mediated access to live sporting events. Previously, these sporting events were free over the air through television and radio. Several online media platforms now require subscription to access live sporting events. For instance, the Cup for African Nations (CAN), which takes place every two years and is the premier tournament for African soccer national teams, requires online subscription for those who wish to access the games from locations outside of Africa. However, a large number of live sporting events are still available for free through online sources.

One important impact of new media is the change in relationship between consumers and athletes. Prior to the prevalence of new media, most consumers rarely had access to athletes. Their contact with athletes was through watching them live at the stadium or through a communication medium or learning about them through a journalist. New media changed that. Today, consumers access athletes and hold conversations with them via media such as Twitter, Facebook, and Instagram. This has demystified athletes and made them more human in the eyes and thinking of sport consumers. Mango (2011) describes this as:

> both fans and opponents can now see these athletes as people and not just competitors. Before, an athlete was a number, position, weight class or event. Now, these athletes about whom we only knew what we read in the papers, are now much more accessible.
>
> (para. 4)

Having direct access to athletes has not only brought them closer to consumers but has also created another credible news source for consumers. Instead of relying on the accounts of journalists who interview athletes, consumers can now get direct news on injuries, team plans, an athlete's life decisions, and an athlete's preparation from the athlete. There are several examples of this. World champion heptathlete

Jessica Ennis of Britain announced her engagement via Twitter in January 2011. In February 2016, Nigeria's national soccer team manager, Sunday Oliseh, announced his resignation via Twitter.

However, new media have also elevated harsh discourse and abuses as part of sport communication. Consumers' access to sport communication with media, sporting organizations, and athletes has removed the decorum that previously existed in much of sport communication. In its place are trolls on social media websites. Trolls post inflammatory messages with the intent to provoke others into emotional responses. The harsh messages are directed at athletes, other sport personalities, and other consumers. During the 2016 Olympics, a Twitter fight broke out when Indian writer Shobhaa De tweeted "Goal of Team India at the Olympics: Rio jao. Selfioes lo. Khaali haat wapas aao. What a waste of money and opportunity." It was a harsh criticism of India's performance at the Olympics. De's comment met its match from Heena Sidhu, who is the first Indian to be ranked World No. 1 in pistol shooting. Sidhu responded with several tweets stating that the criticism was misplaced and asked why De does not sometimes write on sport to help develop sport better in the country. Other Indian athletes also tweeted to attack De's comments and to support Sidhu.

CHAPTER SUMMARY

This chapter discusses new media and their increasing importance in sport communication. In the previous chapter, the focus was on traditional media's decline in sport communication. The opposite interest is in play in this chapter, with statistics showing a rapid incline in new media and sport communication. These statistics show increasing use of platforms such as Facebook, Twitter, WhatsApp, blogs, and Instagram.

A major topic of discussion is the various characteristics of new media. These characteristics include the absence of a gatekeeper, an avalanche of sport information, and more user-generated content, among several other characteristics of new media. The chapter also provides brief descriptions of various types of new media generally used by sport fans and organizations. These include online news media, online discussion forums, Twitter, YouTube, and so on.

There are also brief descriptions of functions of new media such as accessibility and interactivity. Importantly, the new media environment is democratized compared to traditional media, which are controlled by an authoritative source. Instead of an authoritative source, new media allow those who participate in them to generate their own content and, thus, information is democratized.

The final section of the chapter describes how new media lead change in sport consumption. A major change is use of social media for sport communication. This also impacts the experience of sport consumers in various ways, such as the location where sport is consumed. Other changes occur in the rise of closer relationships between fans and athletes through platforms like Twitter and Facebook. The downside, however, is a rise in harsh speech, discourse, and memes surrounding sport in new media. This is helped by the fact that new media allow participants to be anonymous, which enables them to dismiss social etiquette.

DISCUSSION QUESTIONS

1. What are the major reasons for the rise of new media in sport communication?
2. What characteristics of the new media attract consumers and why? Do you think that the rise of social media would lead to phasing out of traditional media?
3. What reasons lead to elevated harsh discourse in new media?
4. How do new media help create communities of people who share similar characteristics? Is creating such new communities beneficial to sport communication?
5. Demonstrate how new media impact athlete/fan relationships.
6. Describe, in detail, how users generate sport content in a new media environment.

ACTIVITIES

1. As a group, identify a sporting event hashtag (#) occurring in the past six months. Search for various comments that use the hashtag and analyze the comments in order to make sense of them. Report your analysis in a group paper.
2. Identify YouTube videos about a recent media conference hosted by a major sporting organization. Compare the message in the video to a sporting news article in a traditional medium reporting on the same conference. Write a comparison report of at least three pages long and submit it.
3. Identify ten of your friends who also consume sport information. Ask each of them their preferred method for consuming sport information and why. Collate the information and then write a report.

VIDEO RESOURCES

Marcos Castro. *How to Build Your Social Media Strategy in Sports* (YouTube/50.45 mins.)
The Impact of Social Media on Sports and Entertainment (YouTube/ 55.45 mins.).
Social Media Issues in Sports (YouTube/39.12 mins.).
Doha goals 2014: Debate: Share Me – Social Media and Sport (YouTube/25.40 mins.)
Social Media's Impact on the Sports World (YouTube still photos/6.19 min.).

RECOMMENDED WEB RESOURCES

Laird, S. (2012, April 27). How social media is changing sports [INFOGRAPHIC]. http://mashable.com/2012/04/27/sports-social-media-2/#O27sI6A8OkqL

Cave, A., & Miller, A. (2015, June 23). The importance of social media in sport. *The Telegraph*. www.telegraph.co.uk/investing/business-of-sport/social-media-in-sport/

Peebles, M. (2015, April 28). It's good! How the NBA is winning at social media. www.complex.com/sports/2015/04/nba-social-media

REFERENCES

Chaffey, D. (2016, August 8). Global social media research summary 2016. *Smart Insights*. www.smartinsights.com/social-media-marketing/social-media-strategy/new-global-social-media-research/

Fan Page List (n.d.). Sports teams on Facebook. http://fanpagelist.com/

Gutbrod, E. (2012, Jun 11). The pros and cons of athletes being connected to fans on Twitter. http://bleacherreport.com/

Jackson, B. (2015, July 18). Sports media analysis: Social media brings instant updates, but there are drawbacks. *Miami Herald*. www.miamiherald.com/

Mango, K. (2011, August 15). How social media is changing the athlete's experience. www.chicagonow.com/

Neely-Cohen, M. (2016, January 8). NBA Twitter is changing the way we watch sports. *New Republic*. https://newrepublic.com/

Stadd, A. (2013, August 5). More sports fans turning to digital media over TV [STATS]. *Social Times*. www.adweek.com/socialtimes/

Statista.com (n.d.). Social media usage to follow sports according to Internet users in selected countries as of February 2014. www.statista.com/statistics/305655/social-media-usage-to-follow-sports/

Taylor, J. (n.d.). Great stats on sports and social media [Infographic]. http://oursocialtimes.com/

Wiederer, D., & Campbell, R. (2016, August 8). Bears' Hroniss Grasu out for season with torn ACL. *Chicago Tribune*. www.chicagotribune.com/

PART II

AUDIENCE AND DIVERSITY

Source: Author

CHAPTER 7

THE FAN

> **LEARNING OBJECTIVES**
>
> After reading this chapter, you should be able to do the following:
>
> - Become knowledgeable about different types of sport fans.
> - Understand the motivations of sport fans.
> - Identify methods fans use in consuming sport communication.
> - Describe how fans demonstrate identity and practice rituals.
> - Describe how sporting organizations cultivate fan groups.
> - Understand fan violence and dysfunctional fan behavior pertaining to sporting events.

WHO IS A FAN?

Sport will not be a success without the large number of people who consume it frequently. There are thousands of people who pay gate fees to attend popular team sports such as soccer, rugby, cricket, basketball, baseball, American gridiron football, top-flight track meets, and hockey, among other sports. There are millions of others who watch sport events through a mediated platform like television. Those individuals are the bedrock of sport popularity and its commercial success. Without them, companies will not pay millions and billions of money to advertise or market in the media to reach such huge audiences. This chapter is dedicated to understanding this audience described as sport fans.

But who is a **sport fan**? A sport fan is a person who is enthusiastic about sport. This individual is usually enthusiastic about one or more sports. He or she will go to any length to watch a favorite sport or to consume information on that sport or multiple sports. Additionally, the person will often enjoy conversations on their favorite sport. In essence, fans are involved participants in sport communication. The word "fan" comes from fanatic, which means someone who is unreasonably or excessively supportive of an endeavor. Fans have an uncritical devotion.

As you already know, not all of those who may consume a sport fit the above definition. Many people may attend a sporting event or a sporting activity without necessarily being fans. These are **spectators**. This simply refers to someone who looks at or observes a sport. Thus, while everyone who consumes a sport is a spectator by watching or observing it, not all of them meet the definition of a sport fanatic.

TYPES OF SPORT FANS

Fans of sport teams are not monolithic. There are different categories or types of sport fans. Billings, Butterworth, and Turman (2012) as well as Sutton, McDonald, Miline, and Cimperman (1997) describe three categories of fans. They use the degree of fan identification with a team or sport to determine the categorization of a sport fan. Identification with a particular sport and team is the prevalent way fans can be identified. Using such identification leads us to four categories of fans and not the three identified by scholars mentioned previously. These categories include the social fan, focused fan, and vested fan, which are also identified by previous scholars. The fourth category of fans is the ultra, or extreme, fan. Each of the four fan categories is described in subsequent paragraphs.

The **social fan** is less emotionally attached to a sport or team when compared to other types of fans. This type of fan goes along for social attachment that a sporting activity brings. He or she would enjoy going to a game and participate in spectator or crowd activity at the event but is not emotionally impacted by the game result. For them, it is attendance, being among friends, meeting people, and enjoying the atmosphere that highlights his or her participation. A social fan, for example, may attend a professional basketball game with friends but has not followed the performance of the teams and may not be familiar with the athletes participating in the game. At the game, he or she may support the home team and cheer just as loudly as others because he or she is having a good time and being entertained by the spectacle of the occasion. The social fan is not emotionally affected by the result of the game whether the home team loses or wins. This category of fan fits the spectator definition provided earlier, except that in this case the individual identifies with a team and is not merely observing the event. Yet, the individual is not strictly a fanatic as our previous definition claims.

A **focused fan** has moderate identification with the team and sport. Billings, Butterworth, and Turman (2012) describe the focused fan as someone who may have "a sense of civic engagement whereby they provide their general support to the city, town, or community sport teams" (p. 46). Essentially, this individual identifies with the team and would have an interest in the team's performance at games. He or she would attend some games. The focused fan's interest in the performance outcome of the team is what differentiates him or her from the social fan. However, a focused fan does not religiously check results of the team or become deeply emotionally invested in performance outcomes.

Sutton, McDonald, Miline, and Cimperman (1997) identify a third type of fan, labeled the **vested fan**. This type of fan is deeply invested in the sport and team. Performance outcomes affect this fan emotionally. This type of fan religiously follows events surrounding the team and may feel a deep sense of loss following his or her team's defeat. According to Billings, Butterworth, and Turman (2012): "Team outcomes are of critical import. . . . Not being able to work the day after the Cubs (American baseball team) are eliminated from the playoffs might be what you can expect from a vested fan" (p. 46).

The fourth type of fan, the **ultra**, is an extreme fan. This individual is not only as emotionally invested in the team as the vested fan, but this person considers him or herself as a soldier of the team. They find ways to officially work in support of their team. Dysfunctional fans can often be found in the ranks of ultras. These individuals may officially sign up to participate in the supporters' club of their team and attend games with the supporters' club and become involved in physical contests against opposing supporters or security personnel. The ultras can be found in support of professional soccer clubs all over Europe, but they are growing in other continents as well. Mullaney (2011) describes ultras as: "There's one thing that sets European football apart from sports in the US, or even football in the UK – the Ultras. Ultras are the fans who are inevitably the craziest, the most extreme, the most passionate and quite often, the most violent" (para. 1 & 2). These groups chant abuses of opponents and constitute security problems in many sporting arenas. They have spread to places outside of Europe, like in Egypt where the *White Knights* represent the Ultras of the Zamalek football club, and in the United States, the *District Ultras* was formed in 2010 in support of the DC United football club (districtultras.com, n.d.).

WAYS IN WHICH SPORT FANS ARE MOTIVATED

Thousands and millions of sport fans who make decisions to support a team or athlete are motivated to do so for a variety of reasons. Several reasons have been identified in research over the years. Reasons differ from one fan to the other, and a fan may have multiple reasons for their support. We list nine motivators as follows: (1) aesthetic beauty of the game, (2) a sense of accomplishment, (3) sensation from the game's drama, (4) escape from the drudge of daily living, (5) as a schedule filler, (6) for uninhibited expressionism, (7) to gain more knowledge, (8) as a way to connect with friends, and (9) because of physical attraction to athletes. Now, let us explore each of those motivators.

Billings, Butterworth, and Turman (2012) provide us with information on several motivators identified above. The first is **aesthetic beauty**. Fans are motivated to watch a sport or a particular team because they find the team and sport interesting or exciting. For instance, a fan may watch tennis because he or she finds the overhead smashes, serving of aces, and rallies to be of great interest. This perception by the fan constitutes what scholars describe as aesthetic beauty of the game in the eyes of that fan. Essentially, the sport provides quality entertainment for that fan.

> **REFLECTION**
>
> Think of your friends and family members. Not all of them support sport teams in the same way in terms of expressed emotional attachment to the sport or teams. What type of fan category will each of them fall into? What are the major characteristics of their behavior that leads you to categorize each person into a particular type of fan group instead of another group? Are you certain that others will agree on your categorization of each person?

Being a fan of a sport, team, or athlete produces a **sense of accomplishment**. Fans may support a team and vicariously benefit through the team's success, whereby the fan feels a sense of accomplishment, psychologically, when his or her favored team is victorious. The effect of this motivation is strong. For instance, extensive data show the link between a successful team and the rise of fan attendance at games and vice versa when the team is doing poorly. In essence, quite a number of fans are motivated by success, as it provides a positive feeling for them. You may also know that new fans, usually children, often support either a home team because of a family member or a highly successful team that may be outside of their community because of a sense of accomplishment that comes with such support. Billings, Butterworth, and Turman (2012) argue that a fan is also motivated by a sense of accomplishment when cheering their team and booing the other team ends with their team winning. They feel that they have contributed to their team's success.

A third motivator is **sensation from the drama** of a sporting event. The unpredictability of a sporting event provides a thrill tonic that excites. That sensation is a motivator for participating in sport and supporting a team. In many sports, rivalries between teams or athletes create a heightened sensation and expectation. For instance, in tennis, Novak Djokovic and Rafael Nadal have been rivals in several Grand Slams since 2006. Fans are motivated to watch those two play. In such a situation, the build-up, the drama from previous meetings between the two, and the unpredictability of the outcome creates a heightened sensation that motivates fans to observe the contest because they are unable to bear the helplessness and depressed feeling that they experience if they miss the match.

Other fans are motivated by a need **to escape** from the daily stress of living, according to Trail and James (2001). Fans use sport as an escape that offers entertainment and fun away from the drudge of work, family, and personal problems. These individuals may attend a sporting contest or stay at home to watch a sporting contest on television or through another medium of communication. By watching sport, they forget temporarily the problems that they are going through. Sport is a means of tension or stress release for such fans.

Similar to using sport as a means of escape, some fans use sport to **fill a schedule**. For these fans, they may have downtime where they have nothing scheduled to do. During such times, they flip through television channels and watch a sport program to have something to do for that period. For instance, a parent who is waiting for his or her child to get ready for school may sit in front of the television set and tune to a sport program while waiting for the child.

Sport also provides a context for **uninhibited emotional expression**. A sporting venue is one context where people are allowed to openly and widely express themselves without being considered "mad" or "wild." People may have their bodies painted and jump and scream before thousands of others to celebrate points scored by their team in a contest. This unbridled expression serves as a motivator for some fans to participate in sporting events.

Trail and James (2001) also cite **acquisition of knowledge** as another motivator for fans watching or participating in a sporting event. Billings, Butterworth, and Turman (2012) support this point made by Trail and James (2001), noting that fans may be motivated by "monitoring how the sport is performed (in order) to increase one's understanding for how it should be played" (p. 53). Media coverage of a sporting contest often involves slow-motion replays and expert analysis of plays and tactics enhancing a fan's knowledge of a sport. Thus, some fans are attracted to a particular sport and media sport program to become educated about a particular sport.

Trail and James (2001) also identify **social interaction** as motivation for watching sport. Sporting contests provide opportunities to be with friends and family to watch a sporting event. In essence, going to a game may be part of a family plan to spend time together. Also, staying home to watch the Olympics or the World Cup provides opportunities for friends and family to gather together to watch a sporting event. At these events or occasions, people have opportunities to build on their relationships. Therefore, some fans consider social interaction to be a strong motivator for watching or participating in a sporting event.

The final motivator is physical attraction. Trail and James (2001) identified **physical attraction** as an important motivator for sport fans. Izzo et al. (2011) investigated the motivations of Romanian soccer fans to watch the sport. They found that few females who are motivated to watch Romanian soccer attend the game because of several reasons, which included attraction to physical features of the athletes. Izzo et al. wrote as follows: "female spectators may not have as much technical interest in soccer team strategy (in this Romanian study), they focus on the more aesthetic elements of the game, which usually are the players, because they are seen as being physically appealing" (p. 7).

METHODS FANS USE TO CONSUME SPORT COMMUNICATION

Previous chapters identify media that sporting organizations use to provide sport communication to consumers. This section provides information on methods that consumers use in consuming sport information. As you can tell, the methods that consumers use are related to the media that sporting organizations use in providing sport communication to them. However, rather than go into detailed descriptions of these media, this section breaks consumer or fan methods into general categories and discusses how fans use such methods. It is this discussion, from the fan or consumer perspective, that is yet to be discussed. The general categories of consumption methods are direct consumption, interpersonal consumption, and mediated forms of consumption.

Fans consume sport **directly by observing** the sport in a location like a stadium or other sporting venue. This remains a significant method that fans use to consume sport. In fact, in youth or recreational sport, direct observation is by far the method that fans use in consuming sport. A recent such study of the United States by Project Partners (2014) shows that the percentage of fans consuming sport by directly attending a sporting event has held steady on an annual basis from 2011 to 2014 at slightly over 50%.

Fans may also consume sport through **interpersonal communication** with other consumers, who may be family members or friends. In this case, fans who are unable to attend an event to directly observe a sporting contest rely on communication from someone else about the event. Many sport fans consume a large amount of sport communication through this method as sporting myths, historical sporting events, and different types of sport communication are transmitted through interpersonal communication channels.

The third method used by sport fans for sport consumption is through **mediated communication**. By this, we mean the use of mass media and new forms of media discussed extensively in previous chapters. Project Partners (2014) report that the largest percentages of sport fans use this method in consumption of sport. The report notes that well over 90% of sport fans have used this method on an annual basis from 2011 to 2014. Other popular mediated methods include use of print (averaging over 50% of fans on an annual basis) and online, which has been rising from 56% in 2011 to 68% in 2014.

HOW FANS DEMONSTRATE IDENTITY AND PRACTICE RITUALS

In earlier description of various types of sport fans, it is noted that sport, team, and athlete identification play a key role in fanship. This section focuses on how fans demonstrate such identification and the rituals that they practice in the process.

Photo 7.1 Football fans at the stadium to directly observe a game. Others may choose to watch the game mediated through television or other forms of mass media.

Source: Author

Identification

Identity has been long studied by several scholars, and the results of studies provide much information that applies to identity in sport communication. Among early scholars in this area are Henri Tajfel and John Turner (1986), who note that people select groups that they feel strongly affiliated to and treat members of that group with some favoritism in comparison to members of other groups that he or she considers as out-group members. Members of the in-group are compatible and evaluated favorably. Sport fans, obviously, identify with a certain team or multiple teams.

In sport, fan identity with a team or athlete may be aspirational in the sense that the fan feels a strong identity with the subject because of the subject's positive performance, which matches the fan's aspiration to be successful. Invariably, the positive performance of an athlete or a team is considered as akin to a personal accomplishment or achievement of the fan.

Nevertheless, sport identity is not always based on strong performance of the team or athlete with whom the fan identifies. Instead, there are other reasons for fan identity in sport. These include community, ethnic, and nationalistic identity. A team, for instance, may be supported because the fan feels that the team represents the community and the fan feels a keen affiliation with the community. This perhaps explains why most sport teams draw their largest support base from their immediate community. Some sports and teams represent and attract most of their support from an ethnic group. In South Africa, for instance, the White population supports rugby while Blacks pitch their support for association football. Marc Fletcher describes this division in these words:

> Yet sport in the post-apartheid "Rainbow Nation" has also served to reinforce racial divisions. While the South African team competing at the 1996 Africa Cup of Nations was met with indifference by the white population, the rugby team was initially met with similar indifference from black South Africans in 1995.
>
> (p. 136)

Similar ethnic identities can be found elsewhere in Europe, Asia, and South America. There is also significant national identity with national sporting teams all over the world, as demonstrated amply during World Cups and Olympics.

Identity with a certain sport or sporting teams is not only communicated through support during games. In some cases, consumers express identity with sporting teams by serving on the boards of their favorite teams, and they have the right to vote on certain issues pertaining to the club.

Rituals

Identifying with a team is demonstrated in several ways. One of those ways is to participate in rituals. A **ritual** is defined as a series of actions or behaviors that an individual or members of a group perform regularly. Sport and teams have rituals. Football fans recognize rituals and participate in them as a demonstration of their identity. The following paragraphs describe rituals that include singing the national anthem, cheering, booing, doing the wave, singing songs, painting team colors, wearing certain sport shirts to games, and tailgating.

Playing the **national anthem** of a country is not reserved exclusively for state occasions but instead is used in international competition in sport. The playing of anthems whips up emotions among athletes and fans, who sing along, and some of them may wipe away tears of excitement and patriotism during the anthem. This activity is ritualized and takes place before the start of international competition. At the Olympics, the anthem of a gold-winning athlete is also played right after the award ceremonies.

Cheering and booing are also rituals that take place during a sporting contest. Cheering your favorite team or athlete may be as simple as hand clapping or may be a cultural type of cheer that varies from country to country or from one location to another. In Nigeria, for example, a favorite cheer in team sport occurs when a team is winning. The cheer for the leading team on such an occasion is "Aayyy" whenever a player of that team touches the ball and "OOOhh" when a player on the losing team touches the ball.

Doing the **wave** is believed to have started in football stadiums in Mexico, but it has now spread to other parts of the world and occurs in all types of sports. In Europe, the phenomenon is described as "la ola" or "Ola," which is the Spanish word for wave. The creation of the phenomenon is also attributed to Krazy George Henderson, who led a wave at an American baseball game in the early 1980s (Vecsey, 1984). In any case, the wave involves a synchronized rising of spectators from their seats to wave their arms over their heads from one section to the next until it goes around the stadium. Notably, the wave does not represent a cheer or demonstration of support for any of the contestants at the athletic event where it takes place. Instead, it represents an entertaining event for all spectators in attendance.

Singing is a ritual in sporting events in some parts of the world. In football, for instance, singing by spectators takes place for a large part of the game, particularly in England. Some of the songs are used to abuse and insult opposing teams or an opposing player while praising the team or player on the favorite team. In African countries, it is not unusual to have official supporter clubs that have their own bands, which play and sing praises of their favorite team during a contest. Walialula and Okong'o (2014) point to use of music and song to celebrate a popular Kenyan football club, Gor Mahia. They note that in the call and response that goes on, the songs recollect the great feat of the club and its connection to great achievements of the Luo ethnic group, which the club is perceived as representing. However, not all football song rituals are designed to support particular teams. Just like the wave, a song like "Ole, Ole, Ole" is a football anthem in stadiums, and it is designed to pump up the crowd and keep them excited. Kassing (2014) also describes the use of a noisy instrument, the vuvuzela, by South African football fans. Non-Africans attacked the use of the vuvuzela, seeking to ban the instrument from the 2010 World Cup, but South Africa argued successfully that the instrument is a cultural symbol. The fact is that the instrument has been used in South African stadiums for years before the World Cup, and it is a ritualized means of spectator participation at sporting events.

Body painting and wearing team uniforms are other rituals that fans use to communicate team identity. In essence, these color and team identifications clearly indicate where a person has anchored himself or herself and also easily identify who is part of the out-group. Of course, as we shall read in the next section, this provides sporting teams with opportunities to merchandise. Team identifications and exhibition of team artifacts do not occur only at sporting or team events, but on a daily basis. There are other team merchandises that fans display at their homes and in their cars.

A final ritual is **tailgating**. Tailgating refers to fans getting together outside the stadium to party before a sporting contest. This is popular in American sport, particularly American football, but it is also used during soccer games in America and elsewhere. Usually, fans set up a grill in the back of their automobile and then cook meat and other food, which they share while they play table games or a ball game

Photo 7.2 Fans of the Brazilian association football team are dressed for the part with painted faces, team colors, flags, and garlands matching national colors.

Source: Dreamstime.com, reprinted with permission

before going into the stadium to watch the sporting contest. Tailgating allows people not only to build relationships with family and friends but also to develop new ones with people that they meet at the stadium. It also provides time to communicate about sport with each other.

SERENA MAKES HER DAY

"I am amazed watching my parents get into it during Grand Slam tennis tournaments," Gordon Whitehead said while making a face. "Really, it is astonishing. I don't see them get emotionally attached when it is football, track, rugby, or other major sports. I just don't get what it is that gets them riled up for tennis," he added.

Gordon's friend, Lisa Terry, was surprised. "You guys are just a sporting family. Is tennis not a sport? You can imagine how I feel when I see you screaming at the television when a rugby game is on. It is crazy. How can a grown adult scream at a television screen because of sport? It does not make sense," she said.

"Lisa, rugby is the king of all sports. It is a man's game," Gordon responded.

"There you go again. A man's game? Really!" Lisa said.

"Yes, a man's game. Cut out all those pretentions, Lisa, how many ladies can compete in rugby?" Gordon stated.

"Well, ladies do. In any case, why do people really go crazy for sport?" she asked.

Lisa does not detest sport. After all, she attends games with Gordon, but for her sport is just another event to attend and meet other people. *Sometimes, Gordon just goes overboard*, she thinks. Earlier today, she saw for the first time Gordon's parents get animated watching Wimbledon tennis. In her mind, *this is exactly where Gordon gets all that passion. It is from his parents.* Gordon's mother, Angela, is particularly passionate. She pumps her fist like a teenager when Serena Williams hits a passing shot or gets an ace, and everything has to stop until there is a break in the televised game. She regales Lisa about Serena Williams' history, her championships, her injuries, and much more. Lisa pretends to take all the lessons in, but she is half listening. She really does not care that much about Serena or any of these tennis players for that matter. It just is not her thing, but she enjoys sitting with Gordon's parents and taking in the game while drinking wine.

Gordon's mother is really booing and cheering today, she thinks. So Lisa whispers to Gordon, "Why is your mother so involved in this game today?"

Gordon responds sarcastically: "Come on, Lisa, you didn't realize this is the final? Moreover, it is Serena against an arch rival."

Well, Lisa rolls her eyes at Gordon. "Hey, I just wanted to know. Am I not allowed to ask questions?"

Lisa decides to ask Gordon's mother why she invests so much emotional support in Serena. She waits till they make eye contact, and Lisa then asks: "Clearly, you like Serena so much? Why?"

Angela looks at Lisa as if in surprise. She then responds: "Of course, she is the best tennis player in the world. I have always liked her and her sister, Venus, since they were teenage stars. Serena is particularly good. Look at how smooth her game is. She is as strong as an ox. There is nothing to dislike." There is silence. Then Angela turns to Lisa: "How about you? Don't you like Serena?"

Lisa thought about it for a few seconds because she is unsure how best to respond. Then she said: "You know, I am not really into sport. I did not know much about Serena until you spoke about her today. I have learned a little about rugby, though, because of Gordon. Gordon seems so obsessed about rugby that sometimes I worry about his health when his team loses. But, honestly, I think tennis is a better sport. It is not as scary as rugby, surely."

Angela then said: "Wow, I did not know that. I thought you loved sport. Well, honey, you need to watch more tennis with me. I have told Gordon several times that rugby is a barbaric sport."

Gordon took one look at his mother and said: "Well, rugby is still the king. If it is so barbaric, how come much more people watch it than boring tennis?" His mother ignores his remarks and cheers Serena on.

At the end, Serena wins the tournament and Gordon's parents are ecstatic. They are very happy, and Gordon's mom is chatty over dinner. Serena's victory is hers as well. She talks up a storm about the game they had all watched. She seems to be replaying every point for everyone. Lisa wonders how Mrs. Whitehead's day would have been if Serena had lost the game. She could imagine how dreary it would be. Thankfully, she only witnessed her day after Serena won.

Discussion questions

1. What type of sport fan is Lisa Terry compared to Gordon and Gordon's parents?
2. Which of the methods for sport consumption is exemplified in this case and why?
3. Mrs. Angela Whitehead is certainly a fan of tennis star Serena Williams, but in which way is Mrs. Whitehead motivated as a fan?
4. Are there examples of fan rituals demonstrated in this case? If there are, cite examples and provide support for your examples.
5. There is insinuation of sporting rivalry in the case. Describe and explain how media may cultivate such rivalry.

HOW SPORTING ORGANIZATIONS CULTIVATE FAN GROUPS

Sporting organizations use abundant data on types of fans and fan behavior to design effective sport communication messages. These messages are designed to achieve a wide number of goals that include increasing and sustaining each organization's fan base as well as growing an organization's revenue through contact with the fan base. Therefore, this section discusses how sporting organizations cultivate fan groups. Sporting organizations use numerous strategies to cultivate these groups, and this section addresses a few of those, including providing fans with information on athletes and the team, providing fans with instruments in support of the team, building strong relationships with the community, and involving fans in aspects of team decision making.

An earlier chapter mentions that sporting organizations and/or athletes conduct media conferences to address several issues pertaining to the team and, at times, issues of community interest. These conferences **present information** that reflects the team or athlete's perspective. This is an important activity, particularly in situations of crisis and in non-crisis situations. Ensuring that the team presents a particular message helps stem the tide of rumors or team-damaging information. Another way of sharing information is providing glossy programs to fans attending games. These programs may be sold to fans at a low price, but the important thing is that the publication is designed to highlight achievements of the organization, its sporting milestones, and to celebrate the organization's athletes.

Teams may also present fans with tangible instruments at games or other activities encouraging them to support the team during contests. For example, teams present noisemakers, flags, and waving towels to fans for use to support the team during games. For example, basketball teams in the United States provide noisemaking items to their fans attending a playoff game in support of the team. Organizations also identify various fan groups in order to market merchandise to fans beyond game ticket sales. These merchandise include team apparel and other items in team colors. Increasingly, a significant part of a team's revenue comes from merchandise sales.

Teams also cultivate support of fans by building strong relationships with immediate communities. To do this, each team must be prepared to go beyond simply participating in sport-related activities. We already discussed some of the types of activities in Chapter 4. The bottom line with such community participation is that it builds goodwill within the community and helps cultivate political support from within the community as well as a positive perception of the team and its athletes among general members of the community.

Fans have also begun to earn positions on executive boards of sporting teams. This is, of course, mostly on sport teams that are publicly owned, and there are increasingly a number of such sport teams. For instance, a community-based corporation owns the Green Bay Packers, an American gridiron football team. SK Beveren of Belgium, Hajduk Split of Croatia, Jos Mighty Jets of Nigeria, Portimonense SC of Portugal, Athletico Bilbao of Spain, and Defensor SC of Uruguay are clubs owned by fans. There are others, not owned by fans, that elect to have a fan serve on the executive board. Fans serving on boards have opportunities to make or participate in making decisions that impact the club. Beyond being in significant decision-making positions such as on the board, the fans also have opportunities to communicate their preferences to the team. A good example is fan participation in naming a team. The re-naming of the Washington Bullets (a professional basketball team in America) to the Washington Wizards involved fan participation in the process.

Creation of myths

Myths, which refer to legendary stories of a remarkable feat or event that may not have a determinable basis of fact or a logical explanation, are abundant in sport and are often communicated and sustained by teams and consumers. This has always been an important aspect of sport communication.

The myths are important because they are communicated in order to establish heroes that should be emulated. In Nigeria, most children grow up learning about *Thunder*, the football player. He was real and there are records about him, and there are still those alive who saw him play from the 1940s until the 1950s. However, the myths surrounding him are simply mindboggling and hard to believe, and there are no independent records to authenticate some of the stories. The most incredible of the stories is that he once asked to take a penalty kick against his brother who was goalkeeping for the opposing team. Thunder struck the ball so hard that it "killed" his brother. Of course, this story has no basis in fact, but for children it is an exhilarating story that sends the message about how strong Thunder kicks the ball. Myths like those are multitude in several countries, and they are meant to create heroes.

The National Football League (NFL) in the United States, through its film and documentary unit, creates several myths about its players. These stories create a view that players are some type of superhumans. However, the stories help make the sport the most watched in the country. The NFL creates stories of giants against Lilliputians, the beasts against humans, and much more. There are myths as well in other American sports, including one about the *Miracle on Ice* when the American Olympic hockey team beat the Soviet Union at the 1980 Olympics. One such myth is that the victory was in the final game, and the other is that the American team had beaten everyone else before meeting the Soviet Union. Neither of those myths is actually true. The game was not the gold medal game, and the American team did not win all its games at the 1980 Olympics.

Creation of rivalry

Sport rivalries are a mainstay in sport, and they create entertainment, serve up storylines for the media and sport consumers, and create a major revenue source for the rival teams. Rivalries are marked by intense competition between competing athletes or teams. They exist in all sports and are cultivated by both athletes and sporting teams. Rivalries are fueled and sustained through communication, which occurs in the media or from athletes, administrators, and fans of teams. Rivalries are fostered by performance parity of teams, when teams share something in common like locality and the frequency of meeting in a sporting contest.

Major athlete rivalries include Greg LeMond versus Bernard Hinault in road cycling racing, Nancy Kerrigan and Tonya Harding in figure skating, Arnold Palmer and Jack Nicklaus in golf, Michael Schumacher and Mika Hakkinen in Formula One auto racing, Floyd Mayweather and Manny Pacquiao in boxing, and Steffi Graf and Martina Navratilova in tennis. Team rivalries include India and Pakistan in field hockey, Cuba and America in Olympics boxing, Brazil and Argentina in international soccer, and Australia and the West Indies in international cricket.

Palmer (2013) writes that sport rivalries bring in revenue. In his article, he points to a sharp rise in revenue when rivals meet, the importance accorded to rivalries by politicians, and how leagues, teams, and the media cultivate rivalries. All three are linked with the ultimate goal of increased sport communication and revenue seeking. Interested parties work very hard to create and sustain rivalries by developing stories around sporting events that create tension and a high level of expectation in sporting contests. Rivalries develop around critical occurrences highlighted in a storyline of such contests. These include city or regional pride, social class, and political issues that intersect with sport, among other things that may be used. For instance, teams may use their city location to develop a rivalry against a team from a city that is considered an economic rival; religion is also used in developing a rivalry between Celtic FC in Scotland (considered Irish migrants and Catholic) and Glasgow Rangers (considered Protestant) in Scotland; and social class is used in a rivalry between Zamalek FC in Egypt (considered a club of elites) and Al Ahly in Egypt (club of the people).

DYSFUNCTIONAL AND VIOLENT BEHAVIOR AMONG FANS

Rivalries and extreme fan identification with teams can lead to negative results. Such negative results are exhibited in dysfunctional activities such as event drunkenness, blasting officials and players, disorderliness, and public fighting. Wakefield and Wann (2006) examine what they term the dark side of sport supportership. Their findings attend to dysfunctional activities.

Gubar (2015) also studied violence perpetrated by some fans and argues that anonymity on the Internet and rising ticket prices create a feeling of entitlement among fans that fuel increasing dysfunction. Drunkenness at games contributes to negative behavior by many fans who either act alone or in a group. These acts start off with abuse directed at athletes or at fellow fans and quickly degenerate into public brawls.

The negative behavior also leads to other inexplicable acts like running into the field of play during a game to disrupt the game or acting in some other unexpected manner. There may also be cases where fans claim the existence of magical powers used by an opposing team. These claims do not necessarily require verification, but they lead to brawls or interference with ongoing sporting contests.

CHAPTER SUMMARY

Sport fans are central to the consumption of sport communication, but the meaning of fan and spectator is often confused. This chapter, therefore, defines both terms, ensuring that there is a distinctive difference in how those two terms are identified. Additionally, the chapter describes different types of sport fans, identifying four types: the social fan, focused fan, vested fan, and ultra fan. Those four types are differentiated on the basis of their emotional commitment to the sport and/or sporting organization.

The chapter also makes us aware of ways in which sport fans are motivated to participate in sport communication and consumption, such as using sport as an escape and using sport for emotional expression, for a sense of accomplishment, and for social interaction. Of course, the section mentions several other ways for fans to become motivated.

Fans also use direct observation, interpersonal communication, and mediated communication to consume sport. Direct observation could be where a fan watches the sporting event live; interpersonal communication is when two persons (fans) communicate about a sporting event; and mediated communication demonstrates fan consumption of sport via mass media.

Fans also identify with sport teams and practice rituals in support of their preferred team. These rituals include cheering and/or booing sporting teams, doing ritualized supporting practices such as the wave, singing, tailgating, and much more. All of those activities are rituals because they occur repeatedly as a pattern of fan activities associated with a sport event.

One of the final sections describes how sporting organizations cultivate fan groups. These processes include key communication during media conferences. Other means of cultivation include creation of myths surrounding a sporting team and creation of sporting rivalry with other teams. A final discussion topic in the chapter is a brief discourse on dysfunctional and violent behaviors among fans.

DISCUSSION QUESTIONS

1. Who is a fan? How do you differentiate a fan from a spectator?
2. Considering the way this chapter describes various types of sport fans, describe the difference between a social fan and a spectator.
3. How are sport fans motivated by emotional expression? How are they motivated through physical attraction?
4. Of the three methods that fans use to consume sport, which is the most used in recent years?
5. Name a fan ritual used during a sport event? How is it practiced?
6. Sporting organizations frequently cultivate fan groups through use of different types of activities. Explain how sporting organizations do this through creation of myths.
7. What types of fan dysfunctional and violent behaviors occur at sporting events?

ACTIVITIES

1. Make sure that you attend a few sporting events involving an athletic team of your school. At the events, be sure to observe the behavior of fans that support your school's athletic team. Identify rituals that such fans practice at the events. After the events, submit a written report of your observations.

2. As a group, visit an elite professional sport team in your city or nearby city. Speak to key staff of the organization to find out major teams that they consider rivals. Find out why they have named those teams, the history of the rivalries, and how the rivalries began. Make sure that you take copious notes to report to your class at a later date.
3. Speak to fans of an elite sport team in your neighborhood and ask them to narrate great moments in their favorite team's history. Make sure that you use probing questions to ensure that these fans provide a large amount of descriptive stories. Review the stories, identifying myths included in the stories. Make sure that you write a detailed report of your finding using this chapter's description of how to create a sporting mythology.

VIDEO RESOURCES

Big Fan (Film/1h 28 min.). This describes a fan of the New York Giants (American gridiron football) who is beaten up by his favorite athlete.
Football and Futbol Fans (YouTube/8.40 mins.).
Believeland (Documentary). This is an ESPN 30 for 30 series focusing on the struggles of sport teams in Cleveland, USA, and how struggles of the teams impact fans.
The Psychology Behind Sports Fans (YouTube/TEDx/12.57 mins.).

RECOMMENDED WEB RESOURCES

Whitbourne, S. (2011, December 30). The psychology of sports fans. *Psychology Today*. www.psychologytoday.com/blog/fulfillment-any-age/201112/the-psychology-sports-fans
Connors, J. (2016, March 24). Fantastic 'Believeland' digs deep into psyche of the Cleveland sports fan: CIFF 2016. www.cleveland.com/moviebuff/ index.ssf/2016/03/fantastic_believeland_digs_dee.html
Jones, J. (2015, June 17). As industry grows, percentage of U. S. sports fans steady. *Gallup*. www.gallup.com/poll/183689/industry-grows-percentage-sports-fans-steady.aspx

REFERENCES

Billings, A., Butterworth, M., & Turman, P. (2012). *Communication and sport: Surveying the field*. Thousand Oaks, CA: Sage Publications.
Districtultras.com. (n.d.). About. www.districtultras.com
Gubar, J. (2015). *Fanaticus: Mischief and madness in modern sports fan*. Mitchellville, MD: Rowman & Littlefield Publishers.
Izzo, M., Munteanu, C., Langford, B., Ceobanu, C., Dumitru, I., & Nichifor, F. (2011). Sport fans' motivations: An investigation of Romanian soccer spectators. *Journal of International Business and Cultural Studies*, 5: 96–107.
Kassing, J. (2014). Noisemaker or cultural symbol: The vuvuzela controversy and expressions of football fandom. In Chari, T., & Mhiripiri, N. (Eds.), *African football, identity politics and global media narratives: The legacy of the FIFA 2010 World Cup*. London: Palgrave Macmillan.

Mullaney, P. (2011, November 13). European football: The 10 craziest Ultras Groups. http://bleacherreport.com/

Palmer, B. (2013, August 2). How much is a sports rivalry worth? The economics of crosstown hatred. www.slate.com/

Project Partners. (2014). Know The Fan: The global sports media consumption Report 2014 (Commissioned by partners Sporting News Media, Kantar Media Sports, & SportBusiness Group). http://sportsvideo.org/

Sutton, W., McDonald, M., Miline, G., & Cimperman, J. (1997). Getting and fostering fan identification in professional sports. *Sports Marketing Quarterly*, 6: 15–22.

Tajfel, H., & Turner, J. (1986). The social identity theory of intergroup behavior. In Worchel, S., & Austin, W. (Eds.), *Psychology of intergroup relations* (pp. 7–24). IL: Nelson-Hall.

Trail, G., & James, J. (2001). The motivation scale for sport consumption: Assessment of the scale's psychometric properties. *Journal of Sport Behavior*, 24(1): 108–127.

Vecsey, G. (1984, October 6). Sports of the times: Permanent wave in Motown. *New York Times*, p. 121.

Wakefield, K., & Wann, D. (2006). An examination of dysfunctional sport fans: Method of classification and relationships with problem behaviors. *Journal of Leisure Research*, 38(2): 168–186.

Waliaula, S., & Okong'o, J. (2014). Performing Luo identity in Kenya: Songs of Gor Mahia. In Onwumechili, C., & Akindes, G. (Eds.), *Identity and nation in African football: Fans, community, and clubs*. London: Palgrave Macmillan.

CHAPTER 8

DISABILITY AND SPORT

LEARNING OBJECTIVES

After reading this chapter, you should be able to do the following:

- Define disability in sport.
- Understand ableism and how it affects disability in sport.
- Become aware of how the media communicate disability in sport.
- Understand how persons experiencing disability perceive their sport participation and sport communication.
- Understand critical issues pertaining to media coverage of the Paralympics.
- Become knowledgeable about athletes experiencing disability and their struggles for equality in a world of sport ableism.
- Understand measures taken by Norway in integrating participants experiencing disability into mainstream sport.

DEFINING DISABILITY IN SPORT

Sport and disability were rarely a point of discussion until a few years ago when scholarship interest increased as the issue of diversity in society, as well as sport, earned a position of primacy. Defining disability is a complex endeavor because disabilities occur in degrees, may be transitional, and there are many types. Despite these complexities, a person experiencing **disability** is someone who has either a sustained physical or mental impairment that prevents or limits the person's ability to participate in an activity. Note that this definition differs from the Americans with Disabilities Act's (ADA) definition, which does not require the person to have a "sustained" impairment. In the ADA definition, a person may experience disability temporarily.

Disabled-world.com claims that "currently around 10 percent of the total world's population, or roughly 650 million people, live with a disability" (para. 3), and the same organization cites "the World Bank estimate that 20 per cent of the world's poorest people have some kind of disability" (para. 4). Types of disabilities are numerous and make it difficult to categorize persons experiencing disability. This presents a problem of classification for those who conduct scholarship in the area. However, organized sport for people experiencing disabilities is split into three distinct groups: those experiencing hard of hearing, people experiencing physical disabilities, and people experiencing intellectual disabilities.

Deaflympics is the primary sport event for those experiencing hard of hearing, and it is sanctioned by the International Olympic Committee (IOC) for elite athletes who meet every four years since 1924. A winter Deaflympics was added in 1949. Athletes are eligible to compete at the games if they experience a hearing loss of at least 55 decibels in their better ear. The games disallow use of audio starting systems such as the bell or gun. Furthermore, athletes cannot use a hearing aid during the games.

Persons experiencing disability in hearing, along with other persons experiencing other types of disabilities, participate in several other sporting competitions at

Photo 8.1 Wheelchair athletes compete in archery.

Source: Dreamstime.com, reprinted with permission

local, national, and international levels. The most popular of the sporting events is the Paralympics, which takes place every four years and is held in the same venue and facilities where the Olympic Games take place. The International Paralympic Committee (IPC) organizes the Paralympic Games, which began in 1948.

THE ISSUE OF ABLEISM

Duncan (2001) describes **ableism** as a concept of the world tailored to serve the interests and abilities of able-bodied people, which makes it difficult for people experiencing disability to prosper. In essence, ableism assumes that sport demands the participant is able bodied in order to participate, and the best athletes are those who have a primed able body, not the typical able body. This ideal, therefore, marginalizes those bodies that are not able and leaves them with little or no opportunities to participate.

Ableism has a widespread impact on sport and how we consume sport. Three key impact areas are sport communication, public acceptance of sport participation by those experiencing disabilities, and the way rules impact sport.

Ableism sets a standard for what expectations of sport participation and performance is. Unconsciously, it says that sport is for those who are able bodied, and the benchmark for determining high-level performance is performance of elite athletes who are able bodied. Invariably, communicating sport is impacted by this belief about who can participate in sport and what high performance in sport means. Thus, media communication of sport frequently reflects ableist thinking.

Of course, media communication of sport from an ableist perspective has a deep and long-term effect on the consuming public. Numerous studies of mass media effects go back to almost a century of scholarship. Denis McQuail (2010) points out that consistent messages from mass media lead to adoption of those messages as reality by those who consume the messages. In essence, a consistent message disseminated by the media that able-bodied athletes produce the best sporting performances increases public acceptance of such a message. Consider sporting activities that are constantly presented to you via television and other media sources. They involve participants who are able bodied, whether it is the FIFA World Cup, Summer Olympics, or the International Association of Athletics Federations (IAAF) championship. This becomes the accepted idea of elite sport. It becomes difficult for sport consumers to accept those who experience disabilities as capable of elite sport performance.

Ableism also affects rulemaking in sport. Rules are made, specifically, to serve able-bodied athletes and marginalize those who experience disability. Rules are not neutral but, instead, create advantages for some athletes while disadvantaging others. Take the starting pistol that is fired to start track and field races or the bell rung to signal the start of the final lap in a long-distance race. Those sporting instruments assume participating athletes can hear and make it impossible for someone experiencing hard of hearing to participate without a supplemental prompt. Another example is the current rule in association football, which makes no room for a wheelchair-bound athlete to participate because players are only allowed to kick the ball with their feet. All of these rules are assumed and communicated to participants and consumers as neutral, but they are not. They are silent on how people experiencing certain types of disabilities may participate.

MEDIA COVERAGE

As mentioned previously, the media have a significant impact on how consumers of mediated messages and images view and perceive an object. Ferrara, Burns, and Mills (2015) studied people's attitudes towards sport performance by persons experiencing intellectual disabilities and acknowledged that: "Television in particular, given its reach and accessibility, has been found to influence attitudes toward people with disabilities" (p. 21). A series of studies of mass media effects confirm that media messages are a powerful influence over those who view media messages. Knowing this cause-and-effect relationship between mass media and consumer media message, it then follows that media coverage of sport performance of those experiencing disabilities is an important guide to how media consumers view sport performance of people experiencing disability. This section reviews how media communicate sport pertaining to persons experiencing disability.

A major complaint about media reports is that the media largely report the **events as social**. This means that the focus of the media is not on athletic achievement but mostly on relationships that occur in those events. In fact, earlier media coverage of sporting performance by those experiencing disability appeared in social sections of the media. However, such reports now appear in sport sections signifying, at least, some level of recognition by the media that such events are legitimate sporting events. An example of this framing of an athletic event as social is given by Hardin and Hardin (2003), who write that: "Marathoner Jean Driscoll's seventh win in the Boston Marathon's wheel chair division was framed as a 'social event' in a 1996 (event) in *Runner's World*" (p. 247).

A major criticism of sport communication, particularly by the mass media, regarding disabilities and sport is that **little or no media coverage** occurs. Newlands (2012) notes that American broadcaster NBC, which held the largest percentage of rights to cover the Olympics, failed to cover live the Paralympics that followed. Newlands adds that such a decision by NBC is not unique. Instead, major broadcasters in other countries also paid little attention. For instance, she adds:

> countries such as Taiwan also had no live media coverage of the 2004 Athens Paralympic Games. The Canadian Broadcast Company, and TV New Zealand showed four one hour specials of the 2000 Sydney Paralympic Games. . . . In the

UK, the British Broadcasting Corporation (BBC) . . . coverage of the 2010 Winter Paralympics was limited to one hour a night despite dedicating 160 broadcast hours to the Winter Olympics on BBC2.

(p. 216)

Hardin and Hardin (2003) confirm NBC's neglect of the Paralympic Games. Buysse and Borcherding (2010) argue that: "Although the numbers of athletes, sports, events, and participating countries have increased significantly since 1960, there has not been corresponding increase in media coverage of these elite athletes with disabilities" (p. 310).

The significantly low coverage of disability sport assigns persons experiencing disability the **status of outsiders** or "the other." Furthermore, such assignment gives the idea that the sport they participate in is not legitimate. In essence, the legitimate sport is the one that able-bodied athletes participate in. Legitimate sports are crowned by the mass media that cover them live and in quantity. The "illegitimate" ones, such as the Paralympics and other sports with persons experiencing disabilities, are defined by low media coverage or delayed broadcast. This subtle sport communication by the media is a vivid guide for the consumer on how to perceive various sports.

Hardin and Hardin (2003) point to the sport communication focus on **wheelchair athletes** and media use of such communication to symbolize athletes experiencing disabilities. They write that:

> Wheel chair users are already at the top of a media-constructed hierarchy of disability. They dominate modern images of disability, perhaps because the visual image is so strong that it allows the subject to be labeled as having disability without it being stated.

(p. 249)

This attention is also given to amputees, according to Buysse and Borcherding (2010), who find that the media feature the most coverage of disability and sport on wheelchair and amputee athletes. In fact, the authors find that China posted the most photographs on wheelchair athletes while South Africa showed mostly photographs of amputee athletes. It is likely that the choice of showing wheelchair and amputee athletes is made as the surest way to convey the notion that these athletes are those experiencing disability. However, by doing so, the focus is clearly on the medical condition of the athletes and not on their athletic achievements or feat. Moreover, this significant focus on athletes with physical disabilities ignores a large segment of athletes who experience other disabilities, such as those who experience intellectual disabilities and those who experience difficulty hearing. Furthermore, it stereotypes persons with disabilities who participate in sport as being in wheelchairs or amputated.

Perhaps the most significant complaints about media coverage of persons experiencing disabilities in sport are that coverage follows what is labeled **the *supercrip*** model (Newlands, 2012; Smith & Sparkes, 2012). This refers to media focus on the athlete's medical condition and/or how the athlete overcomes odds by achieving an athletic feat. It is a story that focuses on the individual courage of the athlete, but in many ways it is problematic. Newlands (2012) argues that "athletes defined by the 'supercrip' model promote ableism . . . where a higher value is put on 'normal' bodies that are part of the working majority" (p. 215). Newlands reaches this conclusion because a story about courage implies that athletes experiencing disabilities are not expected to achieve an athletic feat reserved for able-bodied athletes. In essence, the athletic achievement is unique.

Leavitt's (2009) work on advertising representations of athletes experiencing disabilities mirrors issues mentioned above. In fact, because **advertisements** are constrained by both time and space, their messages risk oversimplifying the complexities of life of athletes who experience disabilities. Leavitt studied several advertisements and found them promoting the supercrip model, and many significantly focus attention on athletes' medical conditions instead of athletic performance and achievement. The advertisements included those for Nike, Visa, BP Oil, Coca-Cola, and McDonald's. Leavitt also found the advertisements feature mostly athletes in wheelchairs and those that were amputees. Leavitt concluded, as other scholars have, that the supercrip model positions athletes experiencing disabilities as inferior to their able-bodied counterparts. Moreover, and at the very least, it sustains the binary between the able-bodied and disabled body.

REFLECTION

Have you ever spent time consuming media reports of sport performance by athletes experiencing disabilities? What did you think when you read those reports? How about your friends? Have they ever read such reports? Do you attempt to compare the performance of such athletes with the performance of able-bodied athletes? Imagine that you are an athlete experiencing disability. How would you feel if people who consume sport communication regarded your athletic performance as somewhat inferior to the performance of able-bodied athletes? Reflect on those issues and make sense of what you have read so far in Chapter 8.

WHAT WHEELCHAIR ATHLETES THINK ABOUT MEDIA COVERAGE

Earlier, the chapter noted that media coverage of persons experiencing disability tends to focus on those in wheelchairs and those who are amputees. But this focus on how media communicate about sport performed by those athletes is one end of the story. The other end is to recognize how those athletes, in turn, think about the way media report their sport performance.

Hardin and Hardin (2003) studied wheelchair athletes to find out how they feel about media coverage of their sport performance. They found four major themes that define these athletes and their relationships with sport media. The first is that wheelchair athletes avidly consume mainstream sport media. Despite poor coverage of their sporting performance in mainstream media, it did not discourage their consumption of such media. They want to consume sport communication, no matter the source. Moreover, some wheelchair athletes see some mainstream athletes as models to emulate. Hardin and Hardin (2003) conclude as follows: "The athletes use the mainstream publications to learn more about sports, to seek able-bodied sport role models, and to enhance their socialization with others" (p. 252).

But they did not solely consume mainstream sport media. Instead, several wheelchair athletes also consume sport media focused on the disabled community. The most mentioned sport publication is the *Sports n Spokes* magazine. They also consume sport through other sources considered specialized. Hardin and Hardin describe specialized publications as helping those experiencing disability to affirm "their role as 'athlete,' to connect to the disability sports community, and to find information specific to their needs" (p. 253). This type of sport communication is very important since mainstream media tend to diminish the "athlete" role of those experiencing disabilities.

Though wheelchair athletes are overrepresented in sport media coverage of athletes experiencing disabilities, wheelchair athletes express dismay with how mainstream media report their athletic performance. In fact, a major complaint is that sport media barely cover disability sport. The athletes consider *supercrip* coverage devaluing. They expect some criticism of their performance but not a focus on overcoming odds, which they consider patronizing.

Hardin and Hardin (2003) identified a fourth theme from their study of wheelchair athletes. This theme notes that most wheelchair athletes recognize that disability sport is poorly covered in the media, but they are split on whom to blame. Younger wheelchair athletes blame the media, citing ethical responsibilities requiring diverse coverage of various populations in the community. Older wheelchair athletes did not feel that it was the media's responsibility to cover disability sport. Instead, they believe that athletes experiencing disabilities must perform at an elite level in order to attract media coverage, because the media will focus on coverage that attracts revenue.

ABLEISM IN SPORT FACES CHALLENGE

She says its "nothing . . . I am playing the same lines as the others. And I have the same dreams and goals. It is not an issue. My coaches expect the same from me as from everyone else." Those are the words of Poland's Natalia Partyka, one of the world's best table tennis players. She was born without a right hand and forearm but participates in several competitions, such as the Olympic Games, that include able-bodied athletes. At the age of 11, she became the youngest participant at the Paralympic Games.

Watching Partyka play, you only notice her disability when she serves the ball. She cradles the tiny ball in the crook of her right elbow and drops it onto her swinging paddle, projecting it with speed over to the opponent's end of the table. Besides that, you hardly notice her disability, as she plays with the acute sight of one of the world's best players, following the ball as it rapidly moves from one end of the table to the other. Her game, clearly, is at the world level, and there is no surprise that she is one of the best players in the world, including those that are able-bodied.

At the 2000 Paralympics, when she was only 11, reports of her performance were based on a supercrip model. It was about how she overcame disability from a young age to compete in table tennis. It was about how she is able to effectively use only her left hand. There were hardly reports about how her play deserves being among the best athletes. Few focused attention on her accomplishments as a young athlete, and instead it was about her disability. Natalia shrugs off mention of her disability because she does not want people to focus on that. Instead, she wants people to focus on her athletic ability. As reported in the *Miami Herald*, Natalia stresses the fact that "I have the same dreams and goals (as able-bodied athletes). . . . My coaches expect the same from me as from everyone else." The *Miami Herald* goes further: "She (Natalia) admits it can get tiresome being asked about her missing hand, but she smiles and politely answers every time the topic comes up."

The *Miami Herald* reports that: "Because of Natalia's story, the television and media are paying attention to table tennis now." The newspaper reports that Natalia's accomplishments mean that the Polish media increasingly report on the team's competitions and results.

Natalia has not made a big deal of the way she and her team are covered in the media. For her, she just wants to be seen as a normal athlete. However, she recognizes that her abilities encourage others who may be experiencing disability to participate and do well in sport. She says, "I can show people that nothing is impossible. . . . Maybe being disabled makes things more difficult than for able-bodied people, and maybe we have to work a little harder. But we can do anything we want to do if we just try. Maybe someone will see me and realize their own disability is not the end of the world, that they can achieve bigger dreams than they imagined."

Natalia is one of few athletes experiencing disabilities who have competed successfully against able-bodied counterparts. She believes that all athletes are the same, they all work hard, and anyone can experience success by just working hard even at the elite level of sport. She hopes that media attention focuses on those aspects and not on an athlete's disabilities, but that is not always the case. It remains a challenge for the media when reporting on the athletic performance of those experiencing disability.

Discussion questions

1. Do you think that Natalia enjoys supercrip narratives of the media in describing performance of athletes experiencing disabilities? Why?
2. After reading the case, what do you think about athletic rules as far as creating a fair competition environment for both able-bodied and athletes experiencing disabilities?
3. What challenges do the media face when reporting the athletic performances of those experiencing disability?
4. What do young athletes learn from the story of Natalia Partyka?
5. Do you think separation of competition for able-bodied and those experiencing disabilities should continue as is presently with the Olympic Games and Paralympics, respectively? Please provide justification for the position that you take.

USING NEW MEDIA

Most discussions in this chapter on sport and communication focus on television and other mass media. However, as pointed out in previous chapters, new media are growing, whereas traditional media are declining. This also points to the emerging importance of new media in defining the relationship between sport participation/performance of those experiencing disabilities and communication of those sporting activities. This section explores the role of new media in the relationship between disability and sport.

Lindemann and Cherney (2014) explore the functions of new media in adapted sport and provide us insight into the role of new media in disability and sport. Obviously, a critical role of new media is **connecting athletes** experiencing disabilities with each other. This connection is a major barrier disrupter as it breaks geographic and physical barriers that ordinarily prohibit connection between and amongst athletes with disabilities. For instance, athletes, some of whom may have needed the assistance of a third person, can connect directly with friends using new media.

Connections among these athletes provide platforms to **discuss important issues** that affect them. One of those issues is help for sport injuries that typically affect athletes experiencing disabilities. For instance, injuries common to these athletes may be remarkably different from those that affect able-bodied athletes. Lindemann and Cherney (2014) note that: "simple bruises acquired from playing quad rugby could lead to severe skin infections, due to athletes' lessened sensation and healing capabilities. Stories of this kind of experience populate the USQRA (United States Quad Rugby Association) online discussion board" (p. 357). Athletes also use online connections to discuss insights pertaining to competition. Furthermore, they discuss the rules of their sport and debate the need for changes. Lindemann and Cherney found that a major issue of discussion is the rule guiding eligibility to participate in quadriplegic rugby. This is an important discussion for participants in quad rugby, because the sport is only one of two sports available to quadriplegics. The other sport is power soccer, which is played using motorized wheelchairs. Without new media, there may be limited and time-bound discussion on several important topics for this population.

A significant role of new media is that they provide an avenue for athletes experiencing disabilities to **frame their own sport stories**. This is a powerful instrument to have, and it is particularly important because traditional media have largely covered disability and sport. Most traditional media coverage focuses on the supercrip model and with poor quantity and poor quality coverage, among other vexing media coverage. However, new media provide enormous opportunities to change all of that. By having the ability to write their own stories about their sporting performances, these athletes resist the perspective of stories written or broadcast by traditional media. For instance, they may focus more on accomplished athletic feats and not on medical issues of the athlete. McNary and Hardin (2013) provide a example of this resistance model with an example of a mono skier, Josh Dueck, who did a backflip that went viral on YouTube. Josh was paralyzed from the waist down after a tragic ski incident in 2004. He began to practice a backflip on a foam pit, and then he did it in a dramatic documentary in 2011 out in the snow. The flip was such an athletic feat that accomplishing it for any athlete, able-bodied or disabled, is remarkable.

Importantly, new media also function to create visibility and legitimacy for disability and sport. By breaking through the storytelling bridge occupied by traditional media, athletes experiencing disability are able to tell their stories in such a way that it challenges stereotypes created by traditional media and begins to convince sport consumers that athletes experiencing disability can participate in elite sport and achieve high standards. Josh Dueck's YouTube backflip and skiing is an example because the YouTube video was seen by millions of consumers. Olympic sprinter Oscar Pistorius of South Africa (discussed in the case later in this chapter) has a Twitter handle with over 363,000 followers as of mid-2016. He can reach this massive number of followers with messages that challenge media stereotypes.

THE PARALYMPICS

There is much confusion between two big sporting meets for those experiencing disabilities. The two competitions – Special Olympics and Paralympics – were initially designed for different purposes. The Special Olympics was for athletes experiencing intellectual disabilities while the Paralympics was for athletes experiencing physical disabilities.

Special Olympics, which began in 1968, does not exclude anyone who wishes to compete, but it categorizes each athlete based on their qualifying scores in order to ensure fairness. On the other hand, the Paralympics increasingly includes athletes experiencing intellectual disabilities, but they must, like other Paralympic competitors, meet certain qualifying sporting criteria before they can participate. In essence, the Paralympics is designed for elite athletes.

This section describes the Paralympics and communication related to it. The Paralympics includes only elite athletes who have met qualifying criteria in the sport in which they plan to compete. The event, which mirrors the Olympic Games, divides qualifying athletes into six main disabilities: amputees, cerebral palsy, intellectual disabilities, visually impaired, spinal injuries, and others. Newlands (2012) identified 18 sports at the Paralympics that recognize categorization of those six disability groups. These sports include rowing, archery, skiing, cycling, equestrian, and swimming.

Newlands (2012) finds that sporting communication pertaining to the Paralympic involves a concentration on nationalism, supercrip, and framing of competition in unserious terms. The mainstream media exclusively focus on athletes from their own country, with little or nothing about other athletes. During the Olympic Games, there is also a focus on nationalism but far less compared to the Paralympics. During the Olympic Games, traditional media at least endeavor to report major accomplishments by athletes of other countries. Though the supercrip model is described elsewhere, its constant occurrence reflects its ubiquity in the way mainstream media cover sport participation by those experiencing disabilities. Moreover, the media largely ignore the Paralympics, using only sporadic reports from less media representatives at the games. This creates the perception that the Paralympics is not a serious international sporting event. Buysse and Borcherding (2010) note:

> During 15 days of Paralympic competition (Beijing, 2008), only 152 photographs appeared in 12 newspapers from five countries, an indication that Paralympic sport is not perceived by the media as legitimate sport. An examination of those photographs further revealed that Paralympians were not represented as competent athletes.
>
> (p. 316)

The IPC has made attempts to overcome communication problems such as those mentioned in this chapter. The organization has created an online media channel – Paralympicsport.tv. This channel covers a wide range of sports instead of the few selected for coverage by mainstream media. Newlands (2012) writes: "110 countries took advantage of the service, watching approximately four hours of sport" (p. 219).

Changes are already appearing. There was far more coverage of the Paralympics at the 2012 London Olympics, with a focus on athletic accomplishments. Ferrara, Burns, and Mills (2015) write that: "London 2012 Paralympics represented one of the biggest global exposures to the general public of people with disabilities displaying their abilities, as opposed to their disabilities" (p. 21). Lindemann and Cherney (2014) point out that use of online media helps publicize the Paralympics far more than previously. Furthermore, the IPC uses similar icons for Paralympic sports as those used by the IOC for the Olympic Games.

OSCAR PISTORIUS, MEDIA COMMUNICATION, AND SPORT

Oscar Pistorius is one of few athletes experiencing disabilities who participated in Olympic Games. Some of the others are Poland's Natalia Partyka, born without a right hand and forearm, who is a table tennis athlete, and swimmer Natalie du Toit of South Africa, who was amputated at the knee following a car accident. These athletes are widely known after they competed against able-bodied athletes at the Olympics.

To participate at the Olympics was not easy, particularly for Oscar Pistorius, because he is a double amputee who runs on spring blades attached to his two knees. Much of the sport communication involving Pistorius was whether his artificial limbs give him an "advantage" over able-bodied athletes and whether those blades present a danger to other athletes.

The issue of advantage is the reason for the IAAF banning Pistorius from the 2008 Olympics. However, the claim of advantage was from a single scientific study. The IAAF decision was later overturned with evidence from a team of lawyers and scientists who participated in an appeal filed before the Court of Arbitration for Sport (CAS). The CAS decision is framed as a triumph of human rights. Most of these issues are communicated through various types of media and bring Pistorius to the attention of the world. Buysse and Borcherding (2010) write about the Paralympics: "Forty of the photographs featured two athletes – Oscar Pistorius and Natalie du Toit – and the remaining 112 photographs were of other Paralympians" (p. 317). In essence, athletes who were already known by competing against able-bodied athletes tend to be a focus of communication at the Paralympics.

THE NORWEGIAN EXAMPLE

Some countries work hard to integrate sport performed by persons experiencing disabilities with sport performed by able-bodied persons. One of such countries is Norway. In this section, Sorensen and Kahrs (2006) report on integration work in Norway.

The Norwegian commitment to integration was begun in 1996, and it required merging three organizations focused on different types of disability in sport into a single organization – The Norwegian Sports Organization for the Disabled. Finances are provided to sporting federations to encourage integration, and increasingly the federations have begun to accomplish integration tasks. Apart from difficulties in classifying the sport and athletes, there are major communication issues. For instance, Sorensen and Kahrs (2006) stated that "there was only one sport federation that had a person who knew sign language among their employees, no federations had anybody with knowledge of Braille, and only 2 federations were familiar with the mobility services for people with blindness" (p. 195). These issues present monumental problems and require education and communication, not just within federations but also from the federation to the general public.

CHAPTER SUMMARY

A key issue of disability in sport requires understanding how ableism marginalizes every other body in sport. Thus, the chapter begins by not only defining disability in sport but also demonstrating the effect of ableism on how other sport participants are perceived. The chapter shows that there are specific sports created for disabled bodies apart from those that mirror sport that able bodies participate in.

The chapter delves into a major issue of discourse in the field, which is media coverage of sport and disability. It shows that there are troubling issues on how the media cover disability and sport. One problem is that the media describe disabled athlete participation in sport as a social event instead of a serious sporting contest. Other issues covered in that section include little or no media coverage of disabled sport participation, a focus on more visible wheelchair athletes while largely silencing the efforts of other participants experiencing disability, and the general attitude of *otherizing* sport for those experiencing disabilities by always viewing sport from a lens of ableism.

Partly because of troubling issues mentioned in the chapter, the chapter then discusses how athletes experiencing disability use new media. Their usage of media includes connecting with other athletes and discussing important issues including those that help them improve in their sport of interest. New media also help them frame their own stories instead of waiting for mass media to frame stories about them. In that sense, new media have been helpful to athletes experiencing disability.

Another section of the chapter focuses on describing the Paralympics and differentiating it from the Special Olympics. Quite often, the two sporting events are not understood, and some think that they are the same event while others confuse one with the other. The chapter points out that the Special Olympics is for all participants who are experiencing disability. Athletes are not restricted from entry to the Special Olympics. On the contrary, the Paralympics is a competition designed for elite athletes who are experiencing disability. Therefore, athletes must meet certain standards in order to participate at the Paralympics.

Finally, the chapter briefly describes a popular athlete experiencing disability who competed in the Olympic Games, Oscar Pistorius of South Africa. Additionally, the chapter identifies Norway as a country working towards full integration of sport for those experiencing disability. In this sense, the country seeks to create fair grounds in sport for everyone.

DISCUSSION QUESTIONS

1. How does ableism impact sport participation for athletes experiencing disability?
2. What does *supercrip* mean? Provide examples of *supercrip* and explain why it is decried?
3. Can an athlete participate in both the Paralympics and the Olympic Games? Why? Is it possible for an able-bodied athlete to participate in both Games?
4. Considering problems that occur when mass media cover sport involving athletes experiencing disabilities, how may such athletes avoid such problems of sport communication?
5. Why do mass media focus on wheelchair athletes, and how can such unequal focus become rectified?

ACTIVITIES

1. As a group, use a media database such as Lexis-Nexis to review and analyze media coverage of previous Olympic Games and previous Paralympic Games. You may cover only one year of each of those two games. Note differences in how the mass media cover each. Write a group report of what you found.
2. Attend a sporting event organized for persons experiencing disability in your city or nearby city. Considering what you have learned from reading this chapter, write a report of what you observed, being mindful of avoiding problems noted on how media cover such a sporting event.
3. Search for Twitter hashtags that identify the 2016 Rio Paralympics. Study the contents of tweets under two or three hashtags that identify with Paralympics. Report key themes under those hashtags.

VIDEO RESOURCES

Murderball (Documentary/1h 28 min.). This is a movie on quadriplegics who participate in full-contact rugby in wheelchairs at the Paralympic Games.
Resurface (Documentary/1h). This is about a quadriplegic who swims to surpass himself and trains hard with the hope of going to the 2004 Paralympics.

S9 – David Grachat (Documentary/45 min.). This is about a Portuguese athlete who is experiencing disability but participates in competitive swimming.

Blind Ambition (Drama/1h 48min.). This is a television drama on an athlete who aspires to make it to the Olympics, but a tragic accident leaves him blind.

RECOMMENDED WEB RESOURCES

Disability sports: Information on sport for the disabled. www.disabled-world.com/sports/
Official website of the Paralympic Movement. www.paralympic.org

REFERENCES

Buysse, J., & Borcherding, B. (2010). Framing gender and disability: A cross-cultural analysis of photographs from the 2008 Paralympic Games. *International Journal of Sport Communication*, 3: 308–321.

Disabled-world.com. (n.d.). Disabled world: Towards tomorrow. www.disabled-world.com/disability/statistics/

Duncan, M. (2001). The sociology of ability and disability in physical activity. *Sociology of Sport Journal*, 18: 1–4.

Ferrara, K., Burns, J., & Mills, H. (2015). Public attitudes toward people with intellectual disabilities after viewing Olympic or Paralympic performance. *Adapted Physical Activity Quarterly*, 32: 19–33.

Hardin, B., & Hardin, M. (2003). Conformity and conflict: Wheel chair athletes discuss sport media. *Adapted Physical Activity Quarterly*, 20: 246–259.

Leavitt, S. (2009). *Disability, identity, and media: Paralympians in advertising*. Thesis completed for a Master of Arts degree in Kinesiology from the University of Lethbridge in Alberta, Canada.

Lindemann, K., & Cherney, J. L. (2014). Communicating legitimacy, visibility, and connectivity: The Functions of new media in adapted sport. In Billings, A. C., & Hardin, M. (Eds.), *Handbook of sport and new media* (pp. 353–363). London: Routledge.

McNary, E., & Hardin, M. (2013). Subjectivity in 140 characters: The use of social media by marginalized groups. In Pederson, P. (Ed.), *Handbook of sport communication* (pp. 238–247). London: Routledge.

McQuail, D. (2010). (6th ed.). *McQuail's mass communication theory*. Thousand Oaks, CA: Sage Publications.

Murphy, N., & Carbone, P. (2008, May). Promoting the participation of children with disabilities in sports, recreation, and physical activities. *Pediatrics*, 121(5).

Newlands, M. (2012). Debunking disability: Media discourse and the Paralympic Games. In Schantz, O., & Gilbert, K. (Eds.), *Heroes or zeros: The media's perceptions of Paralympic sport* (pp. 209–224). Champaign, IL: Common Ground Publishing.

Smith, B., & Sparkes, A. (2012). Disability, sport, and physical activity: A critical review. In Watson, N., Roulstone, A., & Thomas, C. (Eds.), *Routledge handbook of disability studies* (pp. 336–347). London: Routledge.

Sorensen, M., & Kahrs, N. (2006). Integration of disability sport in the Norwegian sport organizations: Lessons learned. *Adapted Physical Activity Quarterly*, 23: 184–202.

CHAPTER 9

GENDER, RACE, AND ETHNICITY

> **LEARNING OBJECTIVES**
>
> After reading this chapter, you should be able to do the following:
>
> - Understand differences among concepts of gender, race, and ethnicity.
> - Appreciate how different types of communication create and re-create gender in sport.
> - Become familiar with challenges that result from media coverage of race in sport.
> - Understand how spectators communicate racism in sport.
> - Recognize the media's role in ethnocentrism in sport.
> - Become familiar with selected regulations and/or policies designed to control issues such as gender inequality and racism.
> - Critically analyze gender issues in sport.

The issues of gender, race, and ethnicity are associated with communication in sport. Each term needs to be defined in order to understand how it is used in this chapter. **Gender** refers to male and female roles that are often but not necessarily biological. These roles are constructed socially or culturally with power embedded in interaction between roles. For example, some sports are perceived as a male preserve, and there may be performance expectations of females who participate in certain types of sport. In essence, sport becomes gendered. **Race** assumes differences among people based on skin color, hair texture, as well as other physical characteristics. These characteristics socially divide people into groups and/or classes for socio-economic control. The divisions vary from one society to the other. For instance, someone considered "Black" in one community may be "mixed" or

"Colored" in another. In essence, race or racial classification is not based on biological reality and is, therefore, considered a social construct (i.e. it is constructed by particular societies or communities in order to achieve certain goals). **Ethnicity** refers to people who share a common or distinctive ancestry, heritage, or culture. Thus, while certain individuals may share similar biological traits, they may be considered members of separate ethnic groups because of a difference in heritage.

This chapter describes, subsequently, how each term is communicated in sport across the world. This leads to discussions of gendered, racialized, and ethnocentric coverage of sport in the media. Additionally, the chapter describes and reviews policy regulations in sport that are designed to create equality in sport.

GENDER AND SPORT COMMUNICATION

To understand gendering that takes place in sport communication requires understanding female participation in sport. Sport was historically considered a male preserve, where males exhibited masculinity and demonstrated "gender superiority." Messner (1988) argues that the rise of industrialization and businesses threatened the social basis of patriarchal property ownership and created a crisis of masculinity. He writes that males responded defensively by becoming preoccupied with "physicality and toughness," and organized sport became a space for denoting and validating masculinity and male toughness. Around the same period, feminism began to challenge assumptions of femininity through athletic participation. This challenge obviously confronts gender assumptions in an arena where masculinity reigned supreme. Notwithstanding, while male sport participation was widely perceived as a confirmation of male toughness and masculinity, female participation was frowned upon because it was in conflict with the social expectation of femininity.

In Britain and its colonies, for instance, women's participation in sport rose. By World War I, early in the twentieth century, women's participation in sport was high. Social changes, necessitated by the war, made this phenomenon possible. At the time, most young males became involved as fighters at the war fronts, while girls and women were hired to work in factories and in other areas previously occupied by males. Female participation in sport was particularly important during this era as part of the war effort. Games between females became a source of raising charity for the war. These games, tagged as charity or novelty games, attracted huge crowds, but the female participants were considered entertainers (not serious footballers) who provided humorous moments. In fact, while these novelty games were taking place, most females were still discouraged from playing the game. Williams (2003), citing a schoolgirl in the 1950s, reported the following: "Well, they wouldn't let us play football (soccer) at school; it wasn't ladylike" (p. 30). In a sense, masculinity remained strong despite an increase in women's participation in sport.

Importantly, sport media at the time helped build the image that sport was a male preserve. Williams (2003) cites an unnamed Scottish newspaper that supported the Football Association's ban of women playing football (soccer) in 1921. The newspaper claimed that women, in general, did not support girls' participation in the game, and it also claimed that in America, girls were not allowed to play the sport without passing a medical test. The logic was that women were unfit for the game, and to participate successfully it entailed women passing a medical test.

Hartmann-Tews and Pfister (2003) show variations on how women participate in sport. This can be found in a book that they edited on sport and women covering a wide range of countries. In many countries, women's participation was frowned upon, and space for participation was limited as was the case in Britain. Examples included places like Tanzania and Brazil. However, while female participation in sport was separated from male participation in the United Kingdom, mixed participation was possible in Norway.

As Lorber (1994) argues, gender is repeatedly created and re-created through interaction and social life and by everyone "doing gender." Therefore, differences in how women participate in sport, in various countries, became embedded in culture and are repeatedly re-created through various types of communication. In interpersonal and small group communication, the conversations reinforce cultural expectations about participation, and mass media reports also act as confirmation of those expectations. However, the relationship between gender and sport communication goes beyond participation. It includes naming practices in sport and how the media cover sport.

Naming practices

A remarkable phenomenon is the naming of male and female sport teams and how such practice projects masculinity and power. In the United States, it is the norm to have college women's athletic teams use a qualifier identifying them as women's teams, but this does not apply to men teams. For instance, the University of Tennessee had its male teams known as "Volunteers" and the female teams were "*Lady* Volunteers." The university recently changed the names in November 2014, when it decided to drop the qualifier "Lady" from the names of its women's teams. Curiously, the school decided that the exception was the women's basketball team, which continues to retain the qualifier "Lady" to its name. The university cites the decision as respect for the women's basketball team, which was national champion in the United States on several occasions.

In Nigeria, more than half of the teams in the top tier of the league for women's soccer are known as "Queens." For instance, the league has teams named Ibom Queens, Edo Queens, Inneh Queens, Delta Queens, Confluence Queens, Tokas Queens, COD Queens, and Sunshine Queens, among others. This naming practice for female athletic teams indicates that the female team's existence is only understood in its relationship to its male counterpart, which does not need a qualifier. In the Nigerian case, the urge is to provide a name identifying female teams as feminine, whereas such an identifier for male soccer teams is unnecessary.

The leagues and competitions face similar naming issues. For instance, leagues and competitions for men are usually not qualified as male. Instead, they are neutrally named, such as the World Cup, the National Basketball Association (NBA) in the United States, and the National Hockey League (NHL) in Canada/United States. Equivalent leagues and competitions for women have the qualifier "Women's" attached to them, such as the Women's World Cup, the Women's National Basketball Association (WNBA), and the Canadian Women's Hockey League (CWHL) in Canada.

The naming practice is not limited to teams and leagues. A study by Billings (2003) shows that sport broadcasters regularly identify female players by their first names but use last names for male players during commentaries. Billings argues that this variation in using player names gives the impression that male players are more professional, more skilled, and heroic. The use of last names creates a distancing effect, which the use of a first name does not. The distancing, in a sense, reifies the male athlete in the eyes of the consumer.

Gendering sport media coverage

Furthermore, media coverage of sport tends to re-create gender in various other ways. Some of the implicit media strategies for doing this are gender marking, sexual stigmatization, variations in performance labeling, silence in the face of unequal treatment, and underreporting of female athletic performance. Each strategy is discussed as follows.

Gender marking occurs when an athlete's performance is described by the media as residing within the scope and expectation of the ability of a particular gender group. In essence, performance is marked as belonging only within that gender group. It cannot transcend that group. For female athletes, gender marking is plentiful, whereas for male athletes this is rare. A good example of this media practice is demonstrated as follows with an excerpt from the website of ABC News Online (Australia) in November 2014:

> Western Sydney Wanderers goalkeeper Ante Covic missed the shortlist for the AFC Asian player-of-the-year award, while Australian star Katrina Gorry is one of three nominees for *women's* (sic) player of the year.

Notice that there is no indication that Covic, a male footballer, had missed nomination for an award restricted to only males, but Gorry's nomination is marked specifically as an award for *female* footballers. Gorry's achievement had to be marked or limited to a particular gender group but not Covic's achievement. In essence, Covic's award covers *all* footballers, but Gorry's is marked for *only* females. It is important to note, however, that this practice is not universal worldwide. For instance, a similar award in the Confederation of North, Central American and Caribbean Association Football (CONCACAF) clearly identifies one award as CONCACAF Female Player of the Year and the other as CONCACAF Male Player of the Year.

Sexual stigmatization refers to labeling of a biological sex group with extreme disapproval. A person who performs outside the expectation of his or her biological sex group is seen as being on the fringe and not part of the norm. This stigmatization promotes hegemonic masculinity in sport. Ashcraft and Flores (2000) broadly define **masculinity** as "images, values, interests, and activities held important to a successful achievement of male adulthood" (p. 3). Furthermore, Antonio Gramsci (1992) uses **hegemony** as the idea where a dominant class manipulates the value system of society so that the dominant class view becomes the worldview society. Therefore, hegemonic masculinity is a situation where males become perceived as dominant in sport performance and "masculine traits" are considered supreme. It explains situations where a poorly performing male athlete is described as girl-like and a high-performing female athlete is described as man-like and lesbian because her performance is not considered the norm. Awareness of these types of stigmatization led to dismissal of the then President of America's Professional Golf Association (PGA) board, Mr. Ted Bishop, who disparaged English golfer Ian Poulter, calling him "little girl" (Crouse, 2014). Media reports on Nigeria's dominant women's national soccer team focus much of its attention on suspected lesbianism among players and stigmatizes a number of women players by labeling them as anti-Christian and not deserving of being members of the team. These are women who are high performing and are no longer regarded as the norm.

There also exist variations on how **performances** of women and men athletes are described in the sport media. Graydon (1983) notes that media coverage of women athletes focuses on their physical desirability and photos in sport magazines like *Sports Illustrated*. Such magazines cover women athletes in seductive poses. Women's performances and successes in sport are described as "emotional," whereas men counterparts are described as "mentally tough, powerful." In essence, these media comments help maintain social conceptions of gender differences and affirm cultural and social beliefs.

Sport media coverage also involves **silence in the face of unequal treatment** and the **underreporting** of female athletic performance. An example of the first is the lack of media criticism of huge funding differences provided for women's compared to men's teams. These differences exist in several sports and across several countries, but the media are largely silent about such disparity. Instead, the lack of media criticism helps to legitimize the disparity as status quo. Additionally, there are numerous studies (Creedon, 1994; Boutilier and San-Giovanni, 1983; Kane, 1989; Lumpkin and Williams, 1991) of how sport media underreport performance of women athletes. For instance, sport media reports on women athletics is less

Photo 9.1 Women participating in sport perceived as a male preserve, like soccer, can lead to masculinity-type media reports.

Source: Dreamstime.com, reprinted with permission

than 10% in *Sports Illustrated*, television airtime, and newspaper coverage. Instead, most of the reports focused on men's sport. When women's sport are reported, they often appear in shorter reports or in less prominent space.

REFLECTION

Take out time to watch a live broadcast of a college basketball game for women (or any other college sport for women) where the commentators are mostly men. Listen carefully to the commentary of the game. Think about how those commentaries may be different from similar commentary on a men's college sport. What did you learn? What changes would you make?

RACE AND SPORT COMMUNICATION

The issue of race and sport is a significant focus for sport films that include popular features, such as *White Men Can't Jump*, *School Ties*, *The Jesse Owens Story*, *Game of Change*, *Invictus*, and *Race*. While race is amply communicated in films about sport, there is a significant number of examples of how race is communicated through media reports on sport. This chapter describes ways in which media cover race in sport under the following topics: underrepresentation of minorities in sport, portrayal of athletic abilities, language descriptors used for athletes of various races, and demonization of certain cultural artifacts. But beyond the media's racial representations of athletes are also public racial representation of athletes that are communicated in athletic venues. This is also discussed here.

One of the major issues with race and sport is **underrepresentation** of some racial groups in sport media coverage. Lumpkin and Williams (1991) as well as Claringbould, Knoppers, and Elling (2004) have found underrepresentation of racial minorities in sport media in places like the United States. In the case of Claringbould, Knoppers, and Elling (2004), they found underrepresentation of minorities in the field of sport journalism even in those sports with significant numbers of minorities. In recent times, media have improved in coverage of minorities, particularly in the coverage of Black athletes in the United States. However, the same cannot be said about coverage of other racial minorities in U.S. sport.

While improvement is evident in representation of some racial groups in sport, their **portrayal** when compared to Caucasians remains a topic of concern. For instance, scholars like McKay and Johnson (2008) point to portrayal of successful African American tennis players the Williams sisters as sexually erotic and bizarre. At the 2016 Olympics, the media criticized American gymnast Gabby Douglas in coded terms believed to have racial undertones. They focused on her hair and said she was not smiling enough (Rogers, 2016). In Australian Rules Football, the media culturally embed the belief that certain racial groups perform well in certain positions on the field. For instance, Hallinan, Bruce, and Coram (1999) and Hallinan (1991) note that Aboriginals do well in positions requiring speed and quickness. In essence, they become overrepresented in non-central positions. The central positions or those that require thinking and power are reserved for Caucasians.

Media portrayals, which are repeated through redundant projections, photographs, and other means can also be found in **language descriptors** that racialize athletes by placing them in different ability categories. In team sport, particularly soccer, the African athlete is described as naïve, lacking in organization, but endowed with natural ability, compared to the Caucasian athlete who is regarded as tactical and organized. Thus, sport performance and success for the African athlete is attributed to natural ability, whereas for the Caucasian it is attributed to superior tactics. These racialized conclusions are used not only for athletes but also for coaches. Stereotypical comments by the media affirm how the media juxtapose the athlete's race to a fixed anticipated behavior. The film *White Men Can't Jump* is a good example of such a media stereotype. The film is based on the widely held perception that Caucasian athletes are not as athletic as their Black counterparts, and this perception encourages stereotyping of all Caucasian athletes despite their athletic ability.

What also occurs frequently in the sport media is the **demonization of cultural performance** of athletes when such performance does not fit with the cultural norm of *Whiteness*. *Whiteness* refers to a tendency to legitimize, as normal, the culture of Caucasians and simultaneously otherize alternate cultures. Ultimately, Whiteness becomes privileged. In American football, for instance, celebration of a touchdown by a non-White athlete involves an elaborate jiving, styling, and dancing choreographed by teammates. While this celebration is not out of the ordinary in African American culture, it is condemned by much of sport media, White fans, and professional sport leagues. Obviously, it is a celebration that is not culturally expected by Caucasians and, thus, is not privileged. In soccer, African teams consult and use "Black Magic" (also variously known as *Juju* or *Muti*), which is considered an aspect of spiritual and religious power in traditional Africa. The sport media condemn this practice, demonizing it and labeling it "primitive." However, this practice is equivalent to prayers used in Western religion, which soccer teams use openly before games without negative comments by the media.

This chapter has focused discussions, thus far, on mass communication and sport regarding issues of race. However, there are also other types of communication that impact race and sport. These involve **communication from spectators about racism**. Warren and Tsaousis (1997) discuss an incident in Australian Rules football that demonstrates racial communication and football. They note that racist taunting of opposing aboriginal players is an accepted tactic. This is similar to reported incidents in soccer in disparate places like Italy and Russia. In Australian Rules football an incident in 1993 involving an aboriginal player, Nicky Winmar, became a watershed in change. Winmar was racially taunted during a game, but in defiance he faced the crowd and gestured about being proud and Black before blowing kisses to the crowd and jogging to embrace a fellow Aboriginal player. The images of that event became an iconic photograph in Australian media reports and generated nationwide debate. Some of the media then joined a vanguard calling for regulations to end racist taunts and called for regulation of racist speech. Eventually, the debate forced establishment of a Code of Conduct.

AN AMERICAN UNIVERSITY FACES BUDGET CUTS

"I am at a loss on why the institution decided to cut back on our budget for next season," Coach Angela Lamar complained to the Athletic Director, Mr. Wilson Welbon. Mr. Welbon has been Athletic Director for this Midwestern university in the United States for two decades and is credited with building sport programs to reputable positions in the athletic conference.

Mr. Welbon hired Coach Lamar eight years ago after learning about Lamar's ability to build winning programs from scratch. At the time, the institution's women's volleyball team was the worst in its conference. Mr. Welbon's reputation is such that he is more revered at the university than the President of the institution. After all, athletic programs bring in hundreds of thousands of dollars and, in the last ten years or so, it is one of the reasons given by prospective students for seeking admission to the institution. Mr. Welbon is a man who is confident about his leadership ability and his decision making. He listened coldly as Lamar made her complaint. He did not take kindly to Coach Lamar's statement.

"Look, I have to make the best decision for this university. Your program does not bring in a lot of revenue, and we need to cut back because our football team did not make as much money as we anticipated in the last two years," he said. Lamar was alarmed. Her volleyball team has been national champion for the last four years, and last year it broke even in terms of revenue associated with the team.

"Why didn't you take the money from the football team?" she asked.

"Well, that does not make sense. The football team, in spite of its recent problems, far outstrips any of our other programs in terms of bringing in money," Mr. Welbon responded.

Coach Lamar was even more surprised that the local newspaper, *The Daily Digest*, ran an editorial a day after Mr. Welbon explained budget cuts to the local media. *The Daily Digest* is influential in the community. The Newtons, a wealthy family that provides financial support to the university's athletics, owns the newspaper as well as a local radio station. The newspaper editorial provided full support for Mr. Welbon's actions and suggested that the university consider dropping athletic programs like volleyball, because they "drain the resources of the university." Additionally, it urged the university to find ways to increase resources given to men's football and basketball programs. *The Daily Digest* justified this analysis and recommendation by providing dollar figures demonstrating differences among the university's athletic programs in terms of revenue generation.

The radio station was not much different. It reported the budget-cut story with little or no concern for the girls and hardly mentioned the championships won or how scholarships in sport help girls stay in school to obtain college degrees. In many ways, the radio report is more annoying to Coach Lamar. Callers into the station made jokes about women and sport, and few callers appeared to support sport for women. Some callers felt that the school should focus on football and basketball to ensure that the university moves into the national rankings.

Lamar is frustrated. She feels alone. No one seemed to understand or care. Her team has won multiple national championships and is the only school team to do so for years. She now cannot provide the same value of scholarships that she offers to recruits. Importantly, she no longer can make recruitment trips as she did in the past. Yet, each trip is significant in getting top high school volleyball players to her institution. Moreover, she has to cut back on several annual activities that the girls enjoy.

She wonders, "What should I do next? How should I go about informing my staff and the girls?"

Discussion questions

1   What examples of power are embedded in sport at the Midwestern university described in the case? Are there traces of masculinity, and how are they communicated? If they exist, please specify them.
2   What do you advise Coach Lamar to do next? Why?
3   Is Mr. Welbon fair in his budget distribution to the athletic teams? Is there anything that you would do differently, and what might that be?
4   Earlier in the chapter we learned that media coverage of sport tends to re-create gender. Does this occur with *The Daily Digest* and the radio station? Support your position with examples from the case.

ETHNICITY AND SPORT COMMUNICATION

Ethnicity is discussed, along with race, when looking at how they both intersect with communication and sport. However, such discussion conflates ethnicity and race, creating perception that they are the same. In fact, scholars such as Davis (1992) acknowledge that researchers use terms like race, ethnicity, and minority interchangeably even though the concepts are distinctively different from each other. Armstrong (2011) cites Davis in providing distinctive conceptions of each term as follows:

> (a) Race should be used to describe biological characteristics such as skin color, hair texture, etc., (b) minority should be used to reference the condition of subordination, and (c) ethnicity should address cultural similarities such as language, religion, values, and others. (p. 96)

While one may argue about particulars of the definitions provided above, it is clear that race is distinctively different from ethnicity. Please refer to the definitions provided earlier in this chapter. Ethnicity is discussed separately because it is different from race, and its relationship with sport communication is significant on its own. Earlier, it was noted that ethnicity defines people sharing a common or distinctive ancestry, heritage, or culture. People may be from different ethnic groups even if they share the same race or racial identity.

Our discussion of relationship between ethnicity and sport focuses on media ethnocentrism that impacts sporting contests, media publicity of ethnocentric rivalry, and the ethnic stereotyping of sporting persons in media reports. While these ideas appear on the face of it to be quite similar, they actually differ from each other.

Media ethnocentrism refers to media reports and views of one's own ethnic group to be inherently superior to others. Ultimately, those media views impact sport communication. Reid (2008) and May (2011) describe how media ethnocentrism may be demonstrated. Reid claims that the Scottish media set out to demonize Catholics, a minority Christian group in Scotland. Reid, for example, cites media narratives pertaining to the coach of the Celtic Football team. In the example, the media focus on the coach's identity as Irish and his Catholic background, which effectively marked him as an "outsider" in Protestant-dominated Scotland. Media reports that do this are cited as responsible for mayhem and violence that follow in the football stands.

Media publicity of ethnocentric rivalry is different from media ethnocentrism that we discussed in the previous paragraph, at least in one key aspect. The publicity focuses directly on a sporting event or some sporting rivalry rather than being a generalized report. In Spain, for instance, there continues to be intense sporting rivalry between Athletic Bilbao in the Basque region and the Madrid clubs because Basque is an ethnic region in north central Spain and parts of southern France that has sought independence from Spain for a while. Athletic Bilbao represents the Basque identity, and for a long time the club signed only players of Basque origin. The political situation has created, over time, a rivalry with the Madrid clubs. Media promote and publicize the rivalry, sometimes in ethnic terms. This tends to create a fever pitch around the rivalry and generates unwholesome behaviors that include violence.

There also exists **media stereotyping of persons** involved in sporting activities. May's (2011) work on sectarianism in Scotland provides an example with the persistent Scottish media stereotype of Celtic coach Neil Lennon. The media refer to him as "controversial" when there was nothing in his record supporting such a portrayal. The media refer to his red hair and describe him as fiery, because these characteristics fit the stereotype of Irishmen. Of course, Lennon is Irish. Unfortunately, media stereotypes, particularly in a community where being Irish Catholic and coach of a team (Celtic) that is the fulcrum of Catholic identity, create a dangerous social boiling mix. The result was as May (2011) reports:

> He (Lennon) has twice been assaulted in Glasgow, and has received 'live ammunition through the post [and] bomb threats' since taking over as Celtic's manager in 2010.

(p. 5)

POLICY REGULATIONS

By now, you are probably wondering if there is anything to ensure positive changes in how the communication of gender, ethnicity, and race impact sport. Much has been done in terms of introducing positive change over the years. There are regulations that govern how sport relates to gender, ethnicity, and race. Much of those regulations positively affect how sport media and other types of human communication interface with gender, race, and ethnic issues in sport. This section briefly reviews two such regulations. These are by no means the only regulations, as there are similar regulations in several countries all over the world. The two discussed here are Title IX in the United States and the anti-racism policy of the International Cricket Council (ICC).

Title IX in the United States

Title IX is a section of Educational Amendments passed by the U.S. Congress in 1972 designed to prevent discrimination against women in federally funded education, which includes athletic programs. Title IX is cited as key to an increase in women's participation in sport. As you know, sport was historically perceived as a male preserve and a venue for masculinity. Title IX is a critical provision for breaking down this male preserve.

What are some of the key provisions of Title IX? (1) It prohibits discrimination on the basis of sex in all educational programs and activities, including athletic programs; (2) the law applies to all educational institutions that receive federal funding; (3) it requires funding for sport, in an institution, to be proportional to the ratio of female and male student body; (4) in lieu of number 3, the institution must show a trend of continuing expansion of athletic programs for the underrepresented sex; (5) sport scholarships must be awarded proportional to the number of female and male students participating in intercollegiate athletics in the institution; (6) it requires equivalence in provision of other sporting benefits in such areas as coaching, recruitment, practice times, equipment and competitive facilities, publicity, travel and daily allowance, academic tutoring, and other benefits; and (7) violation may lead to withdrawal of federal funding for the institution.

It is important to note that legal battles are necessary to maintain Title IX. In 1984, for instance, the Supreme Court in *Grove City v. Bell* ruled that Title IX does not cover all parts of an educational system and that it covers only those programs that directly receive federal funds. Athletic programs, which do not directly receive federal funds, are exempt from Title IX provisions, according to the court. This essentially made Title IX toothless because if federal funds are not earmarked for athletics, then the institution does not have to abide by Title IX. However, activist groups fought back through the Congress to pass the Civil Rights Restoration Act of 1988, which outlawed sex discrimination throughout all aspects of an educational institution if a part of that institution is a recipient of federal funding. Therefore, as long as that institution receives federal funds, it became irrelevant if such funds are or are not earmarked for athletics. Institutions could no longer practice sex discrimination in athletic programs. Ultimately, this move in 1988 restored the powers of Title IX.

Anti-racism policy of the ICC

In 2012, the International Cricket Council (ICC) approved an amended Anti-Racism Policy to govern international cricket. It is one of the toughest policies against racism in international sport. One of the incidents that demonstrates the importance of such policy was recurring racism among spectators at international cricket tests. In 2007, for instance, Indian fans racially abused a mixed-race Australian player, Andrew Symonds, making monkey chants and gestures during an international cricket series between India and Australia. One particularly ugly sign by the spectators read: "We treat our visitors like gods, but some of our gods are monkeys." This type of behavior was unnerving not only for players but also for other spectators. The ICC acknowledged that such racism was not uncommon in international cricket tests. The ICC determined to stop the behavior. It instituted an anti-racism policy to curb such excesses. The 2012 amended policy imposes two responsibilities on each member of the ICC. First, each member must develop a plan for dealing with racism exhibited on a match day, and second, it must also develop a plan for addressing the complaints of racism received outside of a game day.

What are some of the key provisions of the policy? (1) it prohibits racially offensive conduct by players, staff, spectators, or other stakeholders; (2) it requires that ICC members should educate all stakeholders within its jurisdiction on the ICC's Anti-Racism Policy; (3) all spectators must, prior to and/or during a match, be made aware of the ICC's policy on inappropriate racist conduct; (4) all venues must display prominently the ICC's policy against racism; (5) banners, signs, or any similar displays that include inappropriate racist messages must be removed from spectators and from match venues; (6) spectators involved in inappropriate racist behaviors must be immediately removed and subsequently prosecuted; (7) such spectators must be banned for a substantive period and required to attend attitude and behavior-change programs; (8) activities involving inappropriate and racist behavior must be recorded for evidence; (9) reports of all racist incidents must be filed to attention of the ICC; and (10) the ICC retains the right to act against a member in cases of failure or refusal to comply with provisions of the Anti-Racism Policy.

CHAPTER SUMMARY

This chapter focuses attention on the relationship between communication and gender, race, and ethnicity. It describes how naming practices and media coverage of sport creates and re-creates gender. It also discusses how sport communication reflects racial underrepresentations, creates certain portrayals of different racial groups, and demonizes cultural performances of some racial groups. Furthermore, the chapter shows how language descriptors help in how media portray racial groups. Beyond media communications, it also describes how spectators communicate racism at sporting events. It then describes ethnicity and sport, noting the difference between race and ethnicity. The chapter also discusses media ethnocentrism, publicity of ethnocentric rivalries, and stereotyping of persons from certain ethnic groups. The final section of the chapter is a brief review of key aspects of two policy regulations: Title IX in the United States, which focuses on gender issues, and the International Cricket Council's (ICC) Anti-Racism Policy.

DISCUSSION QUESTIONS

1 What are major differences among concepts of gender, race, and ethnicity?
2 What does masculinity refer to in sport communication? How does masculinity impact gender roles in sport communication?
3 What is gender marking? Please provide examples of your experiences with gender marking.
4 How do the media demonize cultural performances that they do not view as the norm? Give examples.
5 What is media ethnocentrism? How is it reflected in media coverage of sport?
6 What are key provisions of Title IX in the United States? How about anti-racism provisions of the International Cricket Council (ICC)?

ACTIVITIES

1 As a group, visit a youth sport league in your community. Report your findings to the class, focusing attention on racial representation in the league in comparison to racial composition of the community. How may your report help media coverage of youth sport in your community?
2 Review media coverage of local sport teams in your community. Choose a period for this coverage and compare how the local media use gender marking. Then write a one- to two-page description of what you observed.
3 Interview an ethnic or racial minority athlete in your community. This athlete should be one who has played competitive sport at the university level or professional level. Ask him or her about media coverage, ethnic/racial differentiation in media reports, and other issues of differences in media reports. Then write a one- to three-page report on the results of your interview, making sure that you apply the principles that you have learned from this chapter.

VIDEO RESOURCES

Racism and Sport: *White Men Can't Jump* (Movie). This is a movie about a White basketball hustler who exploits the stereotype that underestimates the skills of White men in basketball.

Ethnicity and Sport: *Hitler's Pawn* (Movie). This is a documentary of a Jewish athlete, Margaret Lambert, who trained to represent Germany at the 1936 Olympics but was withdrawn at the last minute by Germany in a discriminatory act.

Gender and Sport: *Bend It Like Beckham* (Movie). An 18-year-old Indian girl is forbidden from playing soccer by her parents, but she joins a women's team that makes it to the top of the league.

Gender and Sport: *She's the Man* (Movie). Viola disguises herself as her brother and gets into her brother's school team in the UK and is involved in entangled love affairs.

Gender and Sport: *A League of Their Own* (Movie). This is about a professional all-female baseball league that springs up in the United States, as the men have mostly gone off to fight in World War II.

RECOMMENDED WEB RESOURCES

International Cricket Council: www.icc-cricket.com/home

NCAA's Diversity and Inclusion: www.ncaa.org/about/resources/inclusion

Racism, ethnic discrimination and Exclusion of Migrants and Minorities in the European Union (2010) Report: http://fra.europa.eu/sites/default/files/fra_uploads/1207-Report-racism-sport_EN.pdf

REFERENCES

ABC News Online (Australia). (2014, Nov. 12). Australian Katrina Gorry nominated for Asian women's player of the year, Ante Covic not recognized. www.abc.net.au/news/2014-11-11/aussie-gorry-nominated-for-afc-women27s-player-of-the-year/5884004

Armstrong, K. (2011). 'Lifting the veils and illuminating the shadows:' Furthering the explorations of race and ethnicity in sport management. *Journal of Sport Management*, 25: 95–106.

Ashcraft, K., & Flores, L. (2000). Slaves with white collars: Persistent performances of masculinity in crisis. *Text and Performance Quarterly*, 23(1): 1–29.

Billings, A. (2003). Portraying Tiger Woods: Characterizations of a 'Black' athlete in a 'White' sport. *The Howard Journal of Communications*, 14(1): 29–38.

Boutilier, M., & San Giovanni, L. (1983). *The sporting women: Feminist and sociological dilemmas*. Champaign, IL: Human kinetics.

Claringbould, I., Knoppers, A., & Elling, A. (2004). Exclusionary practices in sport journalism. *Sex Roles*, 51(11): 709–718.

Creedon, P. (1994). Women in boyland: A look at women in American newspaper sports journalism. In Creedon, P. (Ed.), *Women, media and sport: Challenging gender values* (pp. 67–107). Thousand Oaks, CA: Sage.

Crouse, K. (2014, Oct. 26). Playing like a girl? It's about time: Ted Bishop's comments demonstrate golf's persistent sexism. *The New York Times*. www.nytimes.com/2014/10/27/sport/golf/

Davis, R. (1992). Black ethnicity: A case for conceptual and methodological clarity. *The Western Journal of Black Studies*, 16(3): 147–151.

Gramsci, A. (1992). (Buttigieg, J., Ed.). *Prison notebooks.* New York: Columbia University Press.

Graydon, J. (1983). 'But it's more than a game. It's an institution:' Feminist perspectives on sport. *Feminist Review*, 13: 5–16.

Hallinan, C. (1991). Aborigines and positional segregation in Australian Rugby League. *International Review for the Sociology of Sport*, 26(2): 69–79.

Hallinan, C., Bruce, T., & Coram, S. (1999). Up front and beyond the centre line: Australian Aborigines in elite Australian Rules Football. *International Review for the Sociology of Sport*, 34(4): 369–383.

Hartmann-Tews, I., & Pfister, G. (Eds.) (2003). *Sport and women: Social issues in international perspective.* New York: Routledge.

Kane, M. (1989). The post-Title IX female athlete in the media: Things are changing, but by how much? *Journal of Physical Education, Recreation, and Dance*, 60: 58–62.

Lorber, J. (1994). *Paradoxes of gender.* New Haven, CT: Yale University Press.

Lumpkin, A., & Williams, I. (1991). An analysis of *Sports Illustrated* feature articles, 1954–1987. *Sociology of Sport Journal*, 8: 16–32.

May, A. (2011). *The 2010–11 Scottish football season and its effect on political attitudes towards sectarianism in Scotland* (Working Paper Series No. 11). Kingston University. http://eprints.kingston.ac.uk/24219/1/May-A-24219.pdf

McKay, J., & Johnson, H. (2008). Pornographic eroticism and sexual grotesquerie in representations of African American sportswomen. *Social Identities: Journal for the Study of Race, Nation and Culture*, 14(4): 491–504.

Messner, M. (1988). Sports and male domination: The female athlete as contested ideological terrain. *Sociology of Sport Journal*, 5: 197–211.

Reid, I. (2008). 'An outsider in our midst:' Narratives of Neil Lennon, soccer and ethno-religious bigotry in the Scottish press. *Soccer and Society*, 9(1): 64–80.

Rogers, K. (2016, August 15). Gabby Douglas defends herself against the wrath of social media. *The New York Times.* www.nytimes.com/

Warren, I., & Tsaousis, S. (1997). The law in Australian Rules Football: A critical analysis' sporting traditions. *Journal of the Australian Society for Sports History*, 14(2): 27–53.

Williams, J. (2003). *A game for rough girls? A history of women's football in Britain.* London: Routledge.

CHAPTER 10

NATIONALISM, CULTURE, AND IDENTITY

> **LEARNING OBJECTIVES**
>
> After reading this chapter, you should be able to do the following:
>
> - Learn how nationalism is expressed at sporting contexts.
> - Become aware of the differences among various terms such as state, nation, and nation state.
> - Understand the subtle differences between an ethnic group and a nation.
> - Describe how sport communication may use nationalism for political means.
> - Understand how identity is communicated via sport.
> - Recognize difficulties in gender identification in sporting contexts.
> - Become acquainted with how culture affects sport in various parts of the world.
> - Be able to provide examples of sport communication that involves nationalism, culture, and identity.

The relationship among culture, identity, and nationalism in sport is widely studied in sport communication. Furthermore, mega sporting events require representation in colors of countries in many of those competitions, and playing of the national anthems is required prior to the start of the competition or after the award of medals. Moreover, spectators frequently identify with their country and their country's representatives at such events. Local culture may also reflect in the clothing of sporting teams as well as their behaviors and values.

Noting the above issues, this chapter is dedicated to describing and analyzing three critical concepts: nationalism, identity, and culture and how each impact sport communication. Additionally, the chapter describes how communication of those concepts can become politicized. The chapter also provides examples from different countries to demonstrate each concept.

NATIONALISM

Nationalism is a strong positive feeling that people have for their country. In sport, this is reflected in passionate support for representatives of one's country. The word *nationalism* is derived from nation, which differs from country. A **nation** strictly refers to a geographic territory inhabited by persons who share a long history, myth of common origin, traditions, culture, and often language. Nations are not necessarily countries (e.g. a nation of Igbos in the country Nigeria or Catalonia in Spain or Quebec in Canada). A modern **state** or country refers to a political entity that is geographically located with established governing instruments. A *state*, within a country, refers to a division of a federal state (e.g. Texas in the United States) that has an established governing instrument. Hargreaves (2000) argues that modern states, which are often not nations in a strict sense, attempt to overcome internal cleavages by finding ways to create a sense of unity and "national" identity that they lack. However, a **nation state** is essentially a state or country that shares a history, tradition, and culture (e.g. Germany, France, and Japan). It is also important to note the difference between an **ethnic group** and a nation. While nations and ethnic groups share common elements like history, myth of common origin, traditions, and culture, they differ on one important aspect. A nation is limited by territory. An ethnic group is not defined by territory (e.g. African American refers to an ethnic group that is spread all over the United States and shares territory with several other ethnic groups).

Expressing nationalism in sport

Though countries are different in their histories, with some like Germany and France representing nation states with a long shared history and language while others, many established through colonialism, representing modern states, each country still aspires to generate feelings of nationalism among its citizens. Sport, through various contexts, offers opportunities for expressing nationalism. These contexts include international competitions, sporting rituals, sport evaluations/judging, sporting venues, support for certain foreign clubs or teams, and media communication.

International sporting competitions, which take place regularly, involve athletes or teams that represent different countries. These competitions, beyond preparatory games, are based on elimination principles, which heighten interest in the results of such games. When competitions involve representatives of countries, support for athletes and teams is based on nationality in most cases. The IAAF World Indoor Championships, for example, involve athletes who represent countries, and results

Photo 10.1 Nationalism at play. A fan of the German national association football team expresses a tense moment during a game involving Germany.

Source: Dreamstime.com, reprinted with permission

are classified on a country basis. Spectators attending this type of event support athletes based on their relationship with the country. For instance, Chinese spectators support Chinese athletes at the event just as French spectators support athletes representing France. This type of support represents an expression of nationalism, and Tang (2013), writing about the Olympics, argues that "an Olympic victory implies the defeat of other nations, which instigates national pride and symbolizes national prowess" (para. 5.1).

International sporting competitions involve **sporting rituals**, which also communicate nationalism. For instance, spectators frequently dress in their country's colors when attending these events and take along flags and banners expressing support for their country and country's athletes. A common ritual involves playing of national anthems at international sporting events, and members of the team stand in rapt attention singing along. It is not unusual to see some of the athletes become emotional during this ritual.

Nationalism is also expressed or communicated by **judges at sporting events** who award generous points to athletes from their own country or to other athletes based on perceived effects that such points may have on competition involving athletes from their country. Duong (n.d.) confirms this practice after examining scorecards in five men's events at the 2008 Olympics and found incidents of nationalistic bias. He found that "one Korean judge scored Korean gymnasts 0.25 points higher than he would for the exact execution of a performance by a gymnast from a country that the judge felt indifferently towards" (para. 12). Furthermore, Duong writes: "Nationalism seems to be the strongest driver of bias. . . . The Korean judge's large negative bias towards Japan, Spain, Italy and Romania may be an attempt to lower the Korean competitors' scores to give Korean gymnasts a better chance of ranking higher" (para. 19).

Sporting venues also provide for unbridled expression or communication of nationalism. Stoeckel (2012) points out that "the stadium was one of the few public places where people could express themselves freely" (p. 6). In some modern states, people are forbidden from gathering to express nationalistic sentiments in support of ethnic nations within such states. However, sporting venues allow transgression of such rules. People gather for a sporting event without first expressing their intentions to use such events to express ethnic nationalism, which would have prevented such gathering in the first place. Moreover, the intention of gathering is to watch a sporting contest and not for political interest. However, because the venue is within the locality, it allows a large congregation of local sympathizers for ethnic nationhood to express support for their ethnic nationality. In such instances, politically minded rallies may take place within the stadium spontaneously during games, and nationalism may be expressed in passionate support for the local team perceived as the national representative against certain opponents that are seen as representatives of the oppressing state.

An emerging context for expressing nationality occurs during support for **nationals who play for foreign clubs**. This is increasingly noted and studied in team sports like basketball and association football. Watkins (2016) points out that the Houston Rockets are China's most popular NBA team, because of the presence of Chinese star Yao Ming as a member of the Rockets. This phenomenon occurs in other team sports as well. The same type of support can be found in Nigeria for Arsenal FC of London. Ross (2013) writes that "The love affair between Nigerians and Arsenal is an enduring one. . . . The attachment many Nigerian football fans formed with the club during Nwankwo Kanu's five year spell at Arsenal has withstood" (para. 1). Kanu was a star Nigerian footballer, and Nigerians began to support Arsenal when Kanu was playing at Arsenal. This type of support, prevalent in several team sports, expresses nationalism. While international sporting competitions provide nationals with an opportunity to exhibit nationalism by supporting athletes and teams in their national colors, nationals also exhibit nationalism in a different case by supporting an athlete who shares the same nationality but plays in the colors of a foreign team.

The **media** also exhibit nationalism in several ways. Tang's (2013) work on the 2012 London Olympics provides an example of nationalism in the sporting media. For instance, he notes: "the BBC was more likely to cover events that featured Team GB (Great Britain) athletes than any others. . . . It is not surprising then that out of the 20 most memorable moments of London 2012 chosen by the BBC, seven highlighted exclusively the performance of Team GB athletes" (para. 2.1). Tang points out further that Olympic broadcasters use the word "us" in reference to athletes or teams from their country and "them" for teams and athletes from other countries. He then shows that a significant number of comments about athletes are dedicated to athletes who share the same nationality as the broadcaster. This is true of American broadcasters (83.5%) and Chinese broadcasters (52.2%). In essence, the nationalistic fervor is not limited to spectators or fans but also extends to the media.

Examining nationalism and politics in sport

The previous section discussed various contexts in which nationalism is demonstrated in communicating sport. In this section are examples of sport nationalism from Catalonia in Spain, Igbos in Nigeria, and Korea.

Stoeckel (2012) provides insight on how the association football club – **FC Barcelona** – projects Catalan nationalism. Catalonia is an ethnic nation in the northeast of Spain made up of people who share a common history, culture, and language. It has agitated for independence from Spain for centuries following its last war with the Castilian Kingdom in 1714. It is a heavily industrialized and rich region. FC Barcelona, established in 1899, has become a symbol for Catalan nationalism. The club, according to Stoeckel's study, has on its crest the Catalan flag (La Senyera), and the same flag appears on the armband of its captain and shirts of the players. The club promotes this nationalism by celebrating the Catalan National Day on September 11 and makes sure all announcements in its home stadium are made using the Catalan language. FC Barcelona, which has a following of millions of supporters beyond the region, is able to promote Catalan nationalism through various communication channels that include a bi-monthly magazine (*Revista Barça*), radio (R@dio Barça), television (Barça TV), Facebook, website, Google +, and YouTube channel.

One of the most remarkable demonstrations of the club's Catalan nationalism occurred on October 6, 2012 (Stoeckel, 2012; Wilson, 2012) in the club's stadium. Barcelona was hosting arch-rival Real Madrid when at exactly 17 minutes and 14 seconds (commemoration of the last war of 1714), 95,000 spectators at the stadium waved their Catalan national flags and began calling for Catalan independence. The stadium itself had long been a venue of resistance to what Catalans consider Spanish oppression. Under the Spanish dictator Franco (1936–1975), use of the Catalan language was banned, but at the stadium the Catalans freely used Catalan language in defiance.

NATIONALISM REIGNS AS PAKISTAN MEETS INDIA IN CRICKET

Cricket brings out the depths of nationalism in two countries that share a border: India and Pakistan. Cricket is widely supported in both countries, and when they meet in the cricket World Cup, emotions run high. There is a saying in India that nothing unites people in the country like cricket. They do not have a single religion, the vast film industry in the country is divided based on the language of the film, and there is a caste system that divides people in terms of social class. Pakistan is similar except that a different religion is the most dominant one – Islam.

The Tribune of India describes how media from both countries fuel the cricket rivalry: "before their semifinal match at the 2011 World Cup, several Indian TV channels used war imagery in the days before the game. Images of missiles illustrated infographics. . . . Newspapers used words such as 'war' and 'battle' in the headlines." The games are usually tense with days of extreme stress for people of both countries before they meet on the sporting field.

Recently, there were threats of demonstrations and disruptions when both countries were scheduled to meet in India. The International Cricket Council (ICC) said: "Our concerns relate both to uncertainty as to the level of those threats as well as the level of commitment to implement any security plan developed to mitigate such threats." Pakistan refused to travel until the Indian government guaranteed the security of its team.

However, even the government cannot secure everywhere in such a highly charged atmosphere. It is an atmosphere where Indian Muslims are routinely threatened by their neighbors who believe that they (Muslims) do not show enough patriotism to India because they share the same religious roots as Pakistanis. In fact, in India there is a "cricket test," which refers to observing Indian Muslims to see how emotionally supportive they are of Indian cricket during matches against Pakistan. As ridiculous as it may seem, some believe that such unofficial tests are advisable. The reality is that despite the religious divide within the countries or other divides, people support the team from their country – and they do so with passion.

The matches between both countries are used for what is called cricket diplomacy, where governments of both countries attempt to take advantage of the matches to thaw relations, and top government officials meet to explore peace. However, nothing much has come from such attempts at using cricket for international diplomacy. But why would a sport hold so much impact in and for both countries? Why does it bring the deepest human emotions to bear on citizens of both countries? Why is there hope that it may help bring peace to a border strife that has gone on for scores of years?

Discussion questions

1. What role do the media play in building sport nationalism when India meets Pakistan in international cricket?
2. Considering that the countries have ethnic, class, and religious differences within each of their borders, how is it that cricket can generate nationalism?
3. Do you think that sport and its communication has the ability to help both countries find peace?
4. Why are people from both countries stressed because of India versus Pakistan cricket? Is it not about a sporting contest?

Just like the case of Barcelona, but with its own distinctive demonstration of nationalism, Enugu Rangers International FC also represents **Igbo nationalism** in Nigeria. The Igbos are small communities that reside in the southeast part of Nigeria and share a common language. However, Onwumechili (2014) argues that "while it could be argued that Igbos meet four of the six elements that describe an *ethnie*, they did not share a myth of common descent nor a sense of solidarity until the arrival of the British (in late 19th century)" (p. 118). After British colonialism and a feeling of shared oppression under the Nigerian state, Igbos developed strong ethnic connections, which culminated in a civil war against Nigeria from 1967 to 1970. Enugu Rangers was formed in 1970, a few weeks after the war, and derived its name from a surreptitious decision to name it after the Rangers military regiment, which fought against Nigeria in the war. Nigeria prohibited public political assembly in Igbo areas after the war, but Igbos used football stadiums, in games involving Rangers, to generate an identity with a perceived Igbo nation which they believed "cannot be destroyed by mere force of arms" ("Ojukwu's Call From Exile," 1970). Identity with the club was solidified by the club's decision to recruit only Igbos in its early years and the Igbos' belief that several Football Association decisions against the club were examples of continued Igbo oppression by the Nigerian state.

South Korea provides us with two different types of expression of nationalism through sport. In one case, Cho (2009a) points out that many South Koreans avidly follow American Major League Baseball. However, some fans support an American baseball team because of the presence of a South Korean player on the team. This Cho refers to as individuated nationalism, and this phenomenon was earlier identified under the concept of support for **nationals who play for foreign clubs**. Cho provides an example with Korean fans' support for the Los Angeles Dodgers because of the Dodgers' recruitment of South Korean pitcher Chan Ho Park. In another case, Yan and Watanabe (2014) describe expressions of nationalism in Korean media following the victory of the South Korean men's Olympic association football team over its Japanese counterpart in a bronze medal game at the 2012 London Olympics. They note emotional responses in Korean papers in support of a Korean player, Park Jung-Woo, who celebrated with a banner displaying *Dokdo* (Liancourt Rocks) *is our land*. Dokdo is disputed between South Korea and Japan. Yan and Watanabe (2014) note that "the perception of Japan being the special enemy and that this soccer game was situated in the sociopolitical animosity between the two countries remained evident after the game in the Korean newspaper narratives" (p. 503). Even after the Chairman of the Korean Football Association (KFA) wrote to his Japanese counterpart to douse tension, the Korean media eviscerated the Chairman, humiliating him by publicly and sarcastically correcting grammatical errors in his letter to Japan FA.

Politics is part of sport communication, and there are numerous examples of it beyond those already mentioned. From the relatively minor issue of Korean athletes being exempt from mandatory military service after winning a medal for the national team (Cho, 2009), to Nigeria's refusal to participate in the Africa Cup hosted by South Africa after a political clash between the two countries, to the refusal of Arab teams to compete against Israeli sport teams, to war between Honduras and El Salvador after an association football game.

The 1969 war between Honduras and El Salvador deserves further discussion as it demonstrates an insidious height of nationalism and politics that sometimes occurs. Honduras and El Salvador share a border in Central America, south of Mexico. Russell (2016) points out that even though football led directly to the 1969 war, there were other political and economic issues before the game that helped ignite the situation. More than 300,000 Salvadorans were expelled by Honduras in the late 1960s following land reform and resentment against migrant Salvadorans in Honduras, which has more economic opportunities although it has, by far, the smaller population. Additionally, the cross-border passage accord between both countries expired in February 1969 without renewal. In June, both countries met in a World Cup qualifier. Honduras won at home 1–0 with a goal in a controversial overtime. El Salvador then won 3–0 at home to force a tie-breaker. This was also controversial because of what happened the night before. El Salvador supporters besieged the hotel of the visitors "banging pots, honking horns, and shouting all night to prevent anyone from sleeping" (p. 1). The controversies and the political uneasiness created a volatile environment. Thus, it was not unexpected when Hondurans were attacked in El Salvador after the second game. The media communicated exaggerated stories of bloodbaths and Hondurans being held hostage. In Honduras, revenge began to take place with vandalization and burning of homes and businesses owned by Salvadorans, who were also raped and many were beaten, forcing thousands to flee across the border. These things all heightened tension between the countries. El Salvador complained of genocide and called for international help. El Salvador then won the tie-breaker in Mexico 3–2, but by then media reports on the game and other issues between the countries had become inflamed. El Salvador severed diplomatic ties with Honduras and soon bombed the Honduran airport and cities, with its soldiers advancing rapidly into Honduras and near the capital Tegucigalpa before Honduras retaliated by bombing El Salvador's airport and damaging its oil supply and petroleum ports, which cut off supplies to the Salvadoran army. It was then that the Organization of American States (OAS) stepped in to quell the four-day war. Russell (2016) reported that more than 300,000 persons lost their lives and hundreds of thousands were displaced.

ISSUES OF IDENTITY IN SPORT

Identity refers to a person's sense of belonging to a group membership. Often, the person expresses pride in this membership and feels a positive self-esteem. A person usually self-identifies with a group. Importantly, people do not only identify with one group but instead identify with multiple groups. For instance, a Uruguayan female athlete may identify with being female, with her type of sport, and with her country.

Identity is strongly tied with the concept of nationalism in sport, discussed earlier in this chapter. This means that a strong identity with the national team exemplifies nationalism, but identity is not always with nation but can be with race, gender, or sport, among others. Stuart Hall (1996) wrote that people's identities are constructed and reconstructed within and not outside of discourse or communication. What Hall means is that people come to identify with objects or subjects through interactions with others over time. In essence, Hall acknowledges that identities are not static. Instead, they are in flux. Based on this thinking about identity, this chapter discusses examples of identity in sport communication in the next section.

Exemplifying identity

In this section are two examples of identity and sport communication. The first focuses on team identity on Twitter and the second on identity issues pertaining to transgender athletes.

Smith and Smith's (2012) study on sport team identity on Twitter is based on tweets that they analyzed following the 2012 College World Series of Baseball in America. They found that sport fans use Twitter hashtags for team identification. The hashtags make categories of discussion searchable. In essence, fans of a team may use a particular hashtag that uniquely identifies their team, player, or event to categorize a particular sporting event. Those who use the hashtag self-identify as part of the group, and it may be used to identify not just members of the in-group but also members of the out-group (i.e. those who participate in the Twitter discussion but do not use the same or similar hashtag). Though, this is not always true because others may also use the hashtag even though they do not self-identify with the group. A hashtag group ensures that those who share similar sporting interest are able to communicate with each other, sharing the success and failure of their team. An interesting finding is that highly identified fans "attribute team successes to internal factors such as team skill, performance of specific athletes, and coaching, while they ascribe losses to external factors like inclement weather, referee bias, and even cheating by the opposing team" (p. 542). The researchers conclude that:

> hashtags can be seen as a way for fans to identify with teams – a virtual wearing of a team jersey. . . . By branding a tweet with a specific hashtag, a fan can use that not only as an identifier for themselves but also as a way to recognize and show favoritism toward other fans of the same team.
>
> (p. 551)

Transgender athletes face several identity issues when they participate in sport. Lucas-Carr and Krane (2011) elaborate on several of these issues in a rare academic report on transgender athletes. They make the issues clear in their description of transgender. They note that each sport creates a binary of male and female for sporting competition and often influence communication that results from sport. They also note that gender, which is socially constructed, refers to how one presents oneself regardless of biological sex. In this case, people are labeled masculine or feminine based on physical appearance, attire, or behavior. However, none of that fully accounts for those who are transgender. For those who are transgender, the issue becomes gender identity, which refers to

> one's self-expression of gender or the internal sense an individual has of "being either male, female, something other, or in between." Gender identity is not

always consistent with biological sex and cannot be deduced by the way a person dresses, moves, or looks.

(p. 534)

They also note that incongruence between that inner feeling or identity of self and the gender assigned at birth is called transgender. They note further that a transgender person who decides to undergo sex reassignment surgery (SRS) to change anatomy to match an inner gender identity becomes **transsexual**. They also point to the difference between transgender and **intersex**. An intersex person is born with both male and female anatomy and physiology but may not be transgender.

Unfortunately, current sport policies are mute about transgender and intersex athletes, yet these athletes compete in an environment that challenges their identity. Lucas-Carr and Krane (2011) report that affected athletes feel that the sporting environment is uncomfortable, and the clear delineation between male and female teams leaves no room for transgender and intersex athletes. The researchers note that even when a transsexual such as Michele Dumaresq won the 2006 Canadian downhill mountain-biking championship, the second-place athlete protested by stating that she was the 100% authentic woman champion of 2006. In essence, Dumaresq, despite her SRS, was not accepted as a female. SRS athletes are wrongly believed to have an advantage over other athletes despite scientific studies that dispute such claims. For instance, the perception is that female-to-male (FTM) transsexuals receive excessive testosterone treatment, but the scientific fact is that they only receive levels of testosterone equivalent to that of an adult male (Teetzel, 2006). For the postoperative MTF transsexuals, studies find that they had increased body fat similar to females and similar bodies to females. Yet in the athletic world, the communication about unfairness persists.

The strict delineation of male and female creates identity doubts in the minds of athletes who do not clearly fit into one of those two categories. Moreover, current science points to gender variations existing between those two extremes (Fausto-Sterling, 2000). Though sex testing, which was mandatory and embarrassing from 1966 to 1999, was stopped, it continues to be required for those whose sex are questioned. This further impacts the emotional health of concerned athletes. Following is an examination of the case of South African 800-meter athlete Caster Semenya.

Caster Semenya

Caster Semenya is a South African female middle-distance athlete who won the 800-meter Olympic gold in 2016 in Rio. The controversy surrounding Semenya began after she won the 800-meter race at the World Championship in 2009 with the fastest time of the year. The IAAF claims it was obligated to test her for doping and sex verification because of her rapid improvement in time that was as large as 8 seconds in the 800 meters and 25 seconds in the 1500 meters. However, results of the tests indicated that she is intersex, that she has no womb or ovaries, had internal testes, and that her testosterone levels are three times higher than most females leaked to the media (Lucas-Carr & Krane, 2011; Hart, 2009; Smith, 2009). Suddenly, whispers among athletes and a media barrage became overwhelming. Such scrutiny led to a difficult time for the athlete, and as Smith and Maclean (2009) point out: "Caster Semenya has gone into hiding and is receiving trauma counseling. . . . Every day she meets with psychologists who are trying to help her through what is happening around her. We are concerned for her wellbeing" (para. 1 & 7). Angry South African officials retained a lawyer for Semenya and charged IAAF for violating Semenya's privacy and human rights.

Though Semenya was cleared to participate in women's athletics in 2010, one can imagine how traumatic the 2009 events were for her. It is also conceivable that she never knew that she is intersex. Note that visually, her biological sex is female. Then suddenly, tests show otherwise, which creates a problem of identity for her. But it is not just the issue of identity and self-doubts; there are also issues of discomfort for others. Then there are issues of stigmatization and scorn for the athlete.

IMPACT OF CULTURE ON SPORT AND COMMUNICATION

While there is a significant amount of academic scholarship on sport communication and nationalism and on sport communication and identity, studies on culture and sport communication draw widespread global interest. It is likely that the interest is driven by the fact that culture permeates most of what we do in any community. This section discusses important points about the relationship between culture and sport communication.

The starting point has to be a definition of culture. **Culture** is the shared beliefs, values, and practices particular to a group of people. Those shared beliefs, values, and practices permeate the group's institutions and artifacts. Geert Hofstede (1980), in a seminal work on culture, notes that culture has four dimensions and reflects programming of a group's collective mind to differentiate it from other groups. Presently, Hofstede (n.d.) believes that there are six and not four dimensions of national culture. These include power distance, individualism versus collectivism, masculinity versus femininity, uncertainty avoidance, long- versus short-term orientation, and indulgence versus restraint dimensions. These dimensions make up core values of a national culture and guide practices in the culture's rituals, heroes, and symbols.

The **power distance** dimension ranges from cultures that have a high power distance to those that have a low power distance. In low-power-distance cultures, people strive for equality, whereas in high-power-distance cultures, people accept a strict hierarchy of power inequality. In cultures where a high power distance exists, sporting administrators are in authoritative positions that are rarely challenged by athletes, and communication is top-down with few policy contributions coming from the bottom. Countries like Guatemala, the Philippines, Sierra Leone, and Malaysia rank high in power distance, whereas low-ranking countries include Israel and Denmark. Pannenborg (2010) describes power distance in African sport and calls it the Big Man–Small Boy syndrome. He describes the relationship between sport administrators and athletes as a strict hierarchy where the Big Man (Administrator) gives orders and the Small Boy (Athlete) must obey without a speck of complaint.

The **individualism versus collectivism** dimension reflects differences in individual freedom and a person's relationship to his to her community or group. In individualist cultures, individuals are highly independent, whereas in collectivist cultures, people work significantly in a group and acknowledge the importance of the group. Hofstede (n.d.) notes that: "A society's position on this dimension is reflected in whether people's self-image is defined in terms of 'I' (Individualistic) or 'we' (Collectivist)." American culture is one of the most individualistic cultures, and sporting communication focuses on individuals. For instance, in team sports like gridiron football or basketball, the American media focus on specific star players and attribute team success to a star player while muting contributions by others.

A third dimension is the **masculinity versus femininity** index. Competitive cultures that value achievement and assertiveness are examples of masculine culture. Furthermore, masculine cultures make gender roles distinct. Feminine cultures value the overlap of gender roles and cooperation, caring for others, and modesty. Hofstede (1980) describes countries like Japan, Mexico, and Italy as representing masculine cultures. Hofstede (1980) finds that several Scandinavian countries, such as Norway and Sweden, rank high in femininity. It is important to note that there are also cultural differences within organizations in the same country. For instance, in the United Kingdom (ranked slightly high on the masculinity index), Shaw and Hoeber (2003) find high levels of masculinity within senior levels of sport management. They note resistance to women at management levels and persistent masculine culture and conclude that "in general, discourses of masculinity were associated with influential coaching and senior management roles" (p. 370).

Hofstede (n.d.) describes the **uncertainty avoidance** dimension as a measure of how comfortable members of a culture feel about ambiguity in their lives. High-uncertainty-avoidance cultures work hard to control the future and reduce ambiguity, and they hold onto rigid beliefs and practices. Low-uncertainty-avoidance cultures have rules and principles but are not beholden to them. According to Hofstede's findings, countries like Uruguay and Portugal reflect high-uncertainty-avoidance cultures, whereas Denmark and Sweden are at the low end. The process for captainship of Nigeria's national football team exemplifies the values of uncertainty avoidance. The captainship is frequently handed over to the most senior member of the team, where seniority is based on the athlete's first appearance for the team.

One of Nigeria's managers, Sunday Oliseh, upset this procedure in 2015, generating national controversy. Opara (2015) notes that

> A lot of commentators have queried the wisdom behind handing the captainship of the team to Ahmed Musa instead of Chelsea of England midfielder, Mikel Obi, who used to be Vincent Enyeama's assistant. That action inadvertently suggests that the likes of Mikel and other senior players are free to dump the team if they can't subject themselves to Musa's leadership.
>
> (para. 13)

Ultimately, Oliseh's action was reversed by a new manager.

Short- and long-term orientation is one of the newer dimensions found by Hofstede. Short-term orientation refers to cultures that prioritize tradition over change, whereas long-term-oriented cultures prioritize change when such change is a major improvement. Long-term orientation values persistence and adaptability. In short-term-oriented cultures, value is placed on immediate gratification. On Hofstede's ranking, countries like Indonesia, Nigeria, and Ghana are short-term oriented, whereas China, Japan, and South Korea are long-term oriented. In South Africa, which tends towards short-term orientation, there is reverence to tradition. This is exemplified in the use of *Muti* (traditional magic) in sport. Culturally, *Muti* is believed to protect the athlete from spiritual attacks by opponents, enhance performance, and also intimidate the other team. It is a traditional practice that has not changed for ages. Kariuki (2015) claims that:

> During group play in the 2010 World Cup, the South African national team sought the services of a traditional healer – a sangoma – for help in its final match, against France. The stakes were high: win, and the Bafana Bafana (South Africa) would have a chance of advancing. . . . South Africa subsequently defeated France 2–1, but saw Mexico advance to knockout play thanks to the overall goal differential. . . . Coincidence? Many in South Africa believe otherwise.
>
> (para. 1, 2, and 4)

REFLECTION

Think about some of the sporting events that you attended, perhaps in your neighborhood. You may have seen girls playing with a hijab around their head. What do you think about that? Perhaps you have also heard stories of persons who believe that there is spiritual control over the result of a sporting competition. What do you think about that belief? Your reflection on those issues should remind you that people do not always share similar beliefs and values.

Photo 10.2 Women in certain cultures may be required to cover parts of their body. Here, a Muslim woman covers her hair with a hijab.

Source: Dreamstime.com, reprinted with permission

Finally, the newest dimension is the **indulgence versus restraint** index. On this index, the indulgent culture supports the drive for basic human gratification in having fun, celebration, and enjoyment. These cultures have a leisure ethic, are more extroverted, have less moral discipline, have active participation in sport, and have looser sexual mores. Examples are America, Nigeria, Mexico, and Sweden. Restraint is the opposite where cultures value social practices that control excessive gratification. These cultures are more introverted and have stricter moral discipline, less sport participation, and stricter sexual mores. Examples are Egypt, Saudi Arabia, Russia, and China. Nakamura (2002) notes that in several Arab countries, there is cultural restraint on women's participation in sport depending on the suitability of the sport to Islamic beliefs. The belief is that the female body should not be unduly exposed. Thus, sport that is flexible in terms of dress code, allows sex segregation, and controls access to performance space is acceptable to female participation. This way, moral discipline is maintained.

CHAPTER SUMMARY

Culture, identity, and nationalism are three significant concepts that frequently appear in discussions on sport communication. They are three concepts that describe issues that are clearly defined in the minds of not just sporting organizations and officials but also in the minds of the sporting public, including consumers.

The chapter opens by discussing the relationship among the three concepts with each one defined. Nationalism is exhibited in sporting contests between countries, including at major global events such as the FIFA World Cup, Olympic Games, and the Rugby World Cup. However, the term *nation* is often misconstrued and, thus, this chapter differentiates *nation* from *state* and *nation* from *ethnic group*. It goes further to demonstrate how people express nationalism in sport through various means, including competition, sporting rituals, and media communication, among others. Importantly, the chapter provides examples of sport nationalism and its intersection with politics. Two examples come from the short-lived border war between Honduras and El Salvador, which followed an ill-tempered association football game, and the other example is FC Barcelona and its commitment to promotion of Catalan nationalism within the Spanish state.

On the issue of identity, the chapter delves into several topics. One of the topics is how a focus on gender binaries in sport creates identity problems for several athletes who do not neatly fit into those binaries. Examples are transgender, transsexual, and intersex individuals who are not easily categorized into the binaries of male/female predominantly used in defining sporting competition. A vivid example is provided with the case of South African star athlete Caster Semenya, whose biological sex has been publicly challenged.

The section on culture relies on Geert Hofstede's cultural dimensions in demonstrating the impact of culture on sport communication. It applies those dimensions to sporting norms in various parts of the world. For instance, it describes how high cultural power distance in Africa affects relationships between sporting administrators and athletes. It also uses the dimension of cultural restraint to demonstrate subdued and stricter moral discipline among athletes in countries such as Saudi Arabia and China.

DISCUSSION QUESTIONS

1 Can you differentiate among the concepts of culture, identity, and nationalism?
2 How do sporting media demonstrate nationalism in their communication during international sporting events?
3 If there is a difference between nation and state, why would support for a state constitute nationalism, or what should be an appropriate description of such support?
4 How may individuals resolve identity conflicts in a sporting context?
5 Considering the Caster Semenya case, how do you suggest resolving the conflict between an individual's privacy and fairness in a sporting context?
6 Though Geert Hofstede's work is used in analyzing and understanding cultural differences, do you think that high levels of cultural differences continue to exist globally? Or is the world moving towards globalization of culture in sporting contexts?

ACTIVITIES

1. As a group, identify predominant cultural values, beliefs, and norms in your country. Interview a few athletes who have represented your country in a sport. The interview should focus on how cultural values, beliefs, and norms impacted them during international competitions. Write a three- to four-page report of your findings.
2. Review news stories about sport participation of transgender, transsexual, and/or intersex athletes. These stories should include feature articles of their lives, feelings about other competitors, and their social identity. Present this report to your classmates.
3. Review broadcast tapes of your country's media coverage of the Olympic Games. Analyze comments made by the commentators and listen to how their use of words, symbols, and/or narratives identify nationalism. Present your findings in a report.

VIDEO RESOURCES

Miracle (Biography/Drama/2h 15min.). This is a documentary based on the coach who led a surprising American Olympic team to overcome the powerful Soviet Union Olympic ice hockey team.

Salute (Documentary/2h). This is an Australian movie on Peter Norman, who was on the medal dais with USA athletes Tommie Smith and John Carlos who did the famous Black power salute. It is a film recording Norman's own views about ethnicism in Australia.

The 16th Man (Documentary/52 min.). Based on the South African rugby team's victory at the 1995 Rugby World Cup that united a segregated nation.

RECOMMENDED WEB RESOURCES

Kim, M. (2014). The everyday psychology of nationalism. *The Atlantic*. www.theatlantic.com/health/archive/2014/03/the-everyday-psychology-of-nationalism/284188/

Houlihan, B. (1997). Sport, national identity and public policy. *Nations and Nationalism*, 3(1): 113–137. www.colorado.edu/geography/class_homepages/geog_4892_sum11/geog4892_sum11/materials_files/Houlihan%20-%20Sport.pdf

Geert Hofstede's website. www.geert-hofstede.com

REFERENCES

Cho, Y. (2009). The glocalization of U.S. sports in South Korea. *Sociology of Sport Journal*, 26: 320–334.

Duong, A. (n.d.). *Bias in the 2008 Beijing Olympics (Gymnastics)*. Unpublished work. www.stat.berkeley.edu/~aldous/157/Old_Projects/duong.pdf

Fausto-Sterling, A. (2000). *Sexing the body: Gender politics and the construction of sexuality*. New York: Basic Books.

Hall, S. (1996). Introduction: Who needs "identity"? In Hall, S., & du Gay, P. (Eds.), *Questions of cultural identity* (pp. 1–17). London: Sage.

Hargreaves, J. (2000). *Freedom for Catalonia? Catalan nationalism, Spanish identity and the Barcelona Olympic Games*. Cambridge: Cambridge University Press.
Hart, S. (2009, Aug 24). World Athletics: Caster Semenya tests 'show high testosterone levels.' *The Telegraph*. www.telegraph.co.uk/sport/
Hofstede, G. (1980). *Culture's consequences: Comparing values, behaviors, institutions and organizations across nations*. Thousand Oaks, CA: Sage Publications.
Hofstede, G. (n.d.). Geert Hofstede Web site. https://geert-hofstede.com
Kariuki, N. (2015, October 7). Black bags, blood, and pungent paste: South African soccer's muti rituals. *Vice Sports*. https://sports.vice.com/
Lucas-Carr, C., & Krane, V. (2011). What is the T in LGBT? Supporting transgender athletes through sport psychology. *The Sport Psychologist*, 25: 532–548.
Nakamura, Y. (2002). Beyond the hijab: Female Muslims and physical activity. *Women in Sport and Physical Activity Journal*, 11(2): 21.
Ojukwu's call from exile. (1970, January 16). http:www.dawodu.com/ojukwu2.htm
Onwumechili, C. (2014). Nigeria: Rangers, Igbo identity, and the imagination of war. In Onwumechili, C., & Akindes, G. (Eds.), *Identity and nation in African football: Fans, community and clubs* (pp. 116–132). London: Palgrave Macmillan.
Opara, J. (2015, Oct. 14). Enyeama: Another look at Oliseh's managerial skills. *The Nigerian Vanguard*. www.vanguardngr.com/
Pannenborg, A. (2010). *Football in Africa: Observations about political, financial, cultural and religious influences*. A pre-publication of a Ph.D. research project. Htttp:// www.sportdevelopment.org/
Ross, E. (2013, September 5). Nigeria's love affair with Arsenal. *The UK Guardian*. www.theguardian.com/
Russell, S. (2016, June 20). The real football war! When El Salvador invaded Honduras over a soccer game. *War History Online: The Place for Military History News and Views*. www.warhistoryonline.com/
Shaw, S., & Hoeber, L. (2003). 'A strong man is direct and a direct woman is a bitch': Gendered discourses and their influence on employment roles in sport organizations. *Journal of Sport Management*, 17: 347–375.
Smith, A. & Maclean, S. (2009, Sept. 12). Fears for Caster Semenya over trauma of test results. www.theguardian.com/sport/
Smith, D. (2009, Sept. 10). Report claims 800m world champion Caster Semenya is a hermaphrodite. *The Guardian*. www.theguardian.com/
Smith, L., & Smith, K. (2012). Identity in Twitter's hashtag culture: A sport-media-consumption case study. *International Journal of Sport Communication*, 5: 539–557.
Stoeckel, M. (2012, July 28). *How did the Football Club Barcelona promote Catalan nationalism in the period 2008–2012?* Master thesis for degree in International Relations at the Universiteit van Amsterdam.
Tang, L. (2013, May 31). The role of nationalism in the Olympics: Reflecting on the 2012 London Games. *Sociological Research Online*, 18(2).
Teetzel, S. (2006). On transgendered athletes, fairness and doping: An international challenge. *Sport in Society*, 9: 227–251.
Watkins, C. (2016, April 4). Yao Ming, the 'emperor' of Houston and Chinese basketball. www.espn.com/
Wilson, J. (2012, October 29). FC Barcelona, Catalan Independence Movement makes team more than a club. *The Huffington Post*. http://www.huffingtonpost.com/
Yan, G., & Watanabe, N. (2014). The Liancourt Rocks: Media dynamics and national identities at the 2012 Summer Olympic Games. *International Journal of Sport Communication*, 7: 495–515.

PART III

MARKETS AND SPORT AS COMMODITY

Source: Author

CHAPTER 11

SPORT PROMOTION AND ECONOMICS

> **LEARNING OBJECTIVES**
>
> After reading this chapter, you should be able to do the following:
>
> - Understand how sport is used to reach a mass audience.
> - Have an awareness of elements for effective sport advertising.
> - Understand sport sponsorship.
> - Recognize and appreciate branding in sport communication.
> - Recognize critical elements in selecting an athlete endorser.

The sport industry has changed tremendously in the last few decades. A primary area of change is the revenue source for the industry. Increasingly, the major revenue source has moved away from traditional gate receipts to media rights and sponsorships. In essence, it points to an increasing interdependence between sport and media and also between sport and corporations. The relationship between sport and media is of particular interest as it has created a sense that "across the world, we're seeing ever closer convergence between the sport and entertainment industries" (PwC, 2011, p. 4).

Similar to the entertainment industry, sport is increasingly becoming commodified. Commodification means making something into a commodity and putting a price on it. In essence, the product becomes commercialized and presented for sale and purchase with the intention to generate profit. Sport, up until the early 1970s, was largely recreational and amateurish. The few sports that were professional, at the time, depended largely on gate receipts. Tomlinson (2005) points out that it was not until the 1970s that major sports in the United States were "remade around the logic of commodification" (p. 35). He argues that this remaking is based on corporate and media interests that began to view sport as a site for their own expansionist ambitions. Tomlinson (2005) captures a moment in the 1970s when a top Coca-Cola official became enamored with the potential of sport in market expansion:

> The Coca-Cola company had a federal structure, and did not typically make central decisions concerning worldwide policy and investments. Nally (sales executive) took Killeen (Coca-Cola Executive) to a match at Brazil's Maracana Stadium, "which absolutely blew his mind. He couldn't believe these 110 thousand screaming Brazilians that were there for the warm up, before the real match." Thus converted to the marketing and branding potential of a sport that could mobilize commitment and passions on such a scale, and across the globe, Killeen battled inside the company at board level, with the support of the company's number one, JP Austin, and won the decision.
>
> (p. 42)

By 2015, global sport revenue was worth $145.3 billion (PwC, 2011). Sponsorship was $45.3 billion, media rights $35.3 billion, merchandising $20.1 billion, and gate receipts $44.8 billion of the global sport revenue. These expansionist moves into sport has made the sport industry a major player in world entertainment revenue earning. This chapter delves into the economics of sport promotion. By this, the chapter seeks out factors that determine how sport is promoted and distributed for revenue.

ECONOMICS OF SPORT PROMOTION

Though economics often encompass various factors that pertain to production, distribution, and consumption of goods and services, the focus here is strictly on promotion of a product or service (i.e. sport). The word *promotion* describes how sport is communicated to various publics with the goal of getting the publics to spend and consume sport or spend to obtain rights to reach consumers of sport. Thus, promotion involves sport-related publicity and/or advertising.

The economics of sport involves several issues in the last few decades. Several of those issues are discussed here, including media rights, use of subscription television, advertising revenue, vertical integration of media and sport, merchandising, and sponsorship.

Media rights have increased steadily all over the world, and in many places these rights have overtaken gate receipts as the primary revenue item in sport. These rights refer to the mass media (usually broadcasters) earning exclusive rights to cover a particular sporting activity over a specified period in exchange for cash or other compensation. The broadcast of a sporting event attracts thousands and millions of sport consumers, which (a) may be a sold audience by subscription and/or (b) enables the broadcaster to sell sport during the event to advertisers of various goods and services who wish to reach such a large audience simultaneously. The broadcasts that result from these rights are also valuable because the broadcaster has exclusive rights for 20 years to authorize re-use of their broadcast to the public. This means that re-use is a valuable commodity that can be re-sold. This latter exclusive right is derived from the 1961 Rome Convention under the International Convention for the Protection of Performers, Producers of Phonograms and Broadcasting Organizations. It helps to protect the broadcasters' costly investment in broadcasting sporting activities. For the sporting organization, the sale of media rights makes available huge sums of money to fund its sporting activities. For instance, in 2014, the National Basketball Association (NBA) in America signed a nine-year $24 billion media rights agreement with ESPN and Turner Sports (Draper, 2014). This breaks down to $2.6 billion annually starting from the 2016–17 NBA season, a 180% increase over the $930 million annual fee in the previous deal. The power of sport communication cannot be overstated, particularly from the perspective of media rights. In today's television consumption, the only live programming that has not faced a decline in audience is sport programming. This perhaps explains why the cost of purchasing sport media rights continues to increase. Weinmann (2014) writes that media rights was central to the jaw-dropping costs of purchasing the Los Angeles Dodgers and Los Angeles Clippers, American baseball and basketball teams, respectively. He also cites media rights as a condition that AT&T specified for a recently proposed $48.5 billion merger with DirecTV.

Related to media rights is the increasing importance of **subscription television** in the economics of sport promotion. Rowe and Gilmour (2010) argue that sport is the key programming that makes subscription programming acceptable to viewers. It is used in migrating viewers to subscription television because viewers consider live sport critical entertainment that is must-have. In fact, Rupert Murdoch, the Fox network mogul, describes sport as the battering ram, which his network uses to cream off viewers from rival networks. He demonstrated this back in 1992 when he established a fledgling BSkyB, which

> was integral to the creation, promotion and exclusive subscription television broadcasting of a new "breakaway" league involving the previous members of the Football League's First Division competition. Murdoch's retooled Premier League became an international broadcasting phenomenon, attracting viewers around the globe and cultivating new audiences and revenue streams in emerging markets across the Asian continent.
>
> (p. 11)

The success of this model encouraged several other sports including rugby, boxing, and cricket to sign up with BSkyB. Sports and leagues in other countries such as Italy, the United States, and New Zealand followed. Sport was no longer merely broadcast to consumers as a cultural product free over the air, but it was commodified and consumers were willing to pay for it. However, regulations in several countries prevent all sports programming to be on subscription channels. Major events like the FIFA World Cup and the Olympics are required to be available on free over-the-air broadcast because they meet government requirements of being in the public interest (Nicholson, 2007). Subscription television became the pay gate through which consumers could still obtain live coverage of their favorite sport. Draper (2014) points out that subscription fees are also on the rise because increases in costs of media rights are partly transferred to consumers.

Advertising on major sport programs brings in substantial sums to the broadcaster. Of course, this is not rocket science since sport programming frequently attracts the largest number of viewers and advertising costs depend on the number of persons that advertisement reaches. Media companies that shell out huge sums of money to secure sport media rights depend on selling advertising spots on sport programs in order to make a profit on the money paid for rights to cover the sporting activity. Crupi (2015) reports that 37% of advertising revenues earned by television networks in America is from advertisements on sport programs. The total revenue for 2014–15 was $8.47 billion for the four major networks. Among heavy advertisers on sport programs are automobiles, insurance, telecommunications, beer, and restaurants. Crupi writes that each of the top five advertisers spent at least $260 million for the year on advertisements on the four networks. In South and Central America, Neirotti and Bliss (2011) report increases in advertising expenditure on sport, with Brazil rising by as much as 40% from 2010 to 2013 and Mexico by 18% from 2010 to 2013. Essentially, these reports point to the increasing value of sport communication.

Already, several factors in the promotion and economics of sport have been identified, but there are many other factors. One of those is driven by the rising cost of media rights and the increasing popularity of sport among media consumers. Those two key elements fuel and continue to fuel **vertical integration of media and sport** wherever regulation allows. In this arrangement, the same entity owns the sporting and media organization. Vertical integration provides advantages that include cost control and competitive advantages that go beyond costs to include ability to differentiate product, access to a scarce resource or important market, organizational efficiency, and technical efficiency. Vertical integration in sport and media occurs through a media company purchasing sport teams or a sport team purchasing or establishing its own media outlet. Media ownership of sport teams is fairly common in Europe and America. In Europe, media companies own teams in England, Italy, France, and Greece, among other countries. In America, Comcast (media company) owns 63% of the Philadelphia Flyers, who play in the National Hockey League (NHL) in America, and News Corporation has full ownership of the Melbourne Storm in the National Rugby League in Australia. Recently, Liberty Media Group purchased Formula One auto racing for $4.4 billion (Reuters, 2016). It was a major buy considering that Formula One is watched by more than 425 million people, and Liberty Media, which includes satellite radio Sirius XM, has media interests across 30 countries in the Americas, Europe, and the Caribbean. Beyond backward vertical integration, which occurs when a media company buys a sport team, forward integration occurs when a sport team buys or establishes a media outlet. For instance, association football teams in England such as Arsenal, Manchester United, and Chelsea have a broadcasting outlet. In Portugal, Benfica owns broadcast media and Galatasaray in Turkey has its own television station.

Merchandising is another means of promoting sport. Pitts, Fielding, and Miller (1994) note that products included in such promotion "might be t-shirts, cups, key rings, caps, jackets, blankets, and an event program (a printed program). Other examples include lamps, bumper stickers, sweats, decals, and even shoes. Typically, the merchandise is printed with the logo or other identifying mark of the sport organization or product" (p. 22). Sporting organizations use these products to keep the name of the organization within the *evoked set* of the consumer, which means that they are visible and ubiquitous to the consumer after they are purchased. This is expected to solidify the consumer's relationship with the organization and build loyalty. Importantly, it also provides substantial revenue for the sporting organizations. Where merchandising is substantially developed, it may bring in a large percentage of the organization's revenue. In North America, for example, merchandising accounts for slightly over a quarter of revenue for sporting organizations. In some regions, for instance in Africa, merchandising is largely underdeveloped by local teams and revenue is insignificant. What is surprising about this is that merchandise of European and American sporting teams are found in several places in Africa and are purchased. Though some of the merchandise is counterfeit, it demonstrates existence of a market for sport merchandise in Africa even though it is largely unexplored by local sporting organizations.

Sponsorship is another element in sport promotion. Sponsorship involves "full or partial funding of sport-related expenses in return for certain promotional gains. This is an exchange relationship" (Pitts, Fielding, & Miller, 1994, p. 23). It was pointed out earlier in the chapter that sponsorship is the largest revenue segment in sport. In China, for example, sponsorship reportedly accounts for 48% of total sport revenue, according to PwC (2011). Many corporations jostle to participate in sport sponsorship, particularly in association football and in major sporting events that attract millions of consumers. Sponsors benefit by having their product visible during sporting events, either by association with the event, through signage, or by mention during the event. If the event is on television, the benefits multiply to reach a far greater number of sport consumers. Furthermore, PwC (2011) reports that "key motivation is no longer just about maximizing brand visibility and awareness, but is also about gaining deeper and more emotional engagement with fans and staff, and even managing the perception of the sponsoring company" (p. 20).

SPORT AND MARKETING

Marketing refers to the process of planning and implementing conception, pricing, promotion, and distribution of goods and services in ways to achieve exchanges that satisfy organizational and consumer goals. For sport marketing, this involves determining what to market and how that fits into the organization's mission. For instance, a sporting organization that seeks to host an international track meet would develop the concept of this track meet in terms of what athletic competitions may be involved, the athletes and teams to participate, and other component ideas. This concept stage involves a lot of activities and research. The pricing phase will involve a careful analysis of the target market to estimate the level of demand for the track meet and the price elasticity of such demand. The price elasticity always refers to how much of that demand is sensitive to price adjustments. The idea is to find the right balance where profit exists without dampening demand for the meet. The promotion phase involves personal selling, advertising, sales, and public relations related to the track meet. This is the phase that we focus our attention on in this chapter. The final phase, distribution, refers to getting the product to the consumer.

The **sport marketing strategy** is an important step in sport marketing. This usually involves specifying a target market for the product or service. This choice must be made carefully because it determines the success or failure of the marketing process. Many considerations take place during the process of strategizing. The organization cannot market to everyone. Therefore, the target market must be clear and why it has been selected explained. Does the organization have the ability to meet the demands of this target market? What is the cost of serving them? Answering questions like those help the organization make important decisions about a target market and how best to serve that market.

There are numerous studies on **consumer buying behavior,** so there is a lot of information available to marketers on how to market to consumers. There are two major buying decisions that consumers often make – complex and programmed. **Complex decisions** require deliberation by the consumer and result from extensive personal research by the consumer. For instance, purchasing a season ticket is a complex decision because the ticket is expensive and season attendance at games takes away from other things. Therefore, such a purchase is regarded as a high-involvement purchase because it demands gathering as much information as possible, talking to friends, and asking a lot of questions, among others. A complex decision such as purchasing a season ticket involves becoming aware of the need for the ticket. Thus, the individual has to be someone who is a highly involved fan of the sport and the team and now wants to be at all the games involving the team. As soon as the individual becomes aware of this need, he or she may proceed with gathering as much information about the ticket purchase as possible and evaluating the gathered information. At a certain point, the individual decides to proceed in purchasing the ticket or simply discontinue the idea of purchasing a season ticket. If the decision is to purchase, then he or she will act on this decision by making the actual purchase. The process does not end there, because the individual will evaluate the utility of the purchase in order to determine whether such a decision would be made in the next season or not.

A **programmed decision** is different from the complex decision that was just described. It is routine and involves little thought and revolves around a low-involvement purchase like a low-cost sport memorabilia item. There is no active searching for information about memorabilia or an evaluation of it. Decisions that are programmed can be taken by noting availability of the product. For instance, the fan may come across memorabilia while stopping in a shop to purchase something else.

Segmenting the market is also a vital process that allows the organization to focus on an appropriate market or markets rather than simply marketing to all and sundry and hoping for luck in reaching some persons. To segment a market requires identifying groups of people or organizations that a product will be directed to. The subjects in each segmented market share characteristics common to that segment. These shared characteristics may stem from geography, demographics, psychographics, or product/service-related variables. Organizations often make segmenting decisions based on research of the market.

SPORT PROMOTION

As mentioned earlier, sport promotion is the focus of this chapter. The relationship between sport promotion and economics was already discussed in the earlier section of the chapter. This section discusses the fundamentals of sport promotion with a focus on the sport promotion mix and the objectives of promotion activities.

The sport promotion mix involves integration of advertising, personal selling, sales, and public relations. **Advertising**, which is discussed in detail in the next section, involves a paid type of promotion. The sporting organization pays a mass medium to provide space for the organization to promote its good or service to a mass audience. **Personal selling** involves a direct sale to a person or an organization. In such a case, it is important to obtain information on what the prospective buyer wants or wishes to satisfy, and then a sale can be made to that buyer. In sport, this is what sponsorship represents. **Sales** involve the offer of incentives for a defined period to the consumer in order to generate a response-enhancing promotion of the good or service. Sales may involve consumer contests, for instance. **Public relations** ensure that the organization maintains goodwill among its various publics. This goodwill is essential in order to ensure the organization's marketing success. Public relations involve various strategies and tactics. One aspect of public relations is publicity, which may come from press releases such as those discussed in an earlier chapter of this text. All of these aspects of the promotion mix work in tandem with each other to optimize success.

There are usually several reasons that sport organizations undertake promotional activities. These include creating awareness, providing information such as a change of name or participating in a major competition, retaining loyal consumers, explaining actions that the organization has taken, generating trials of a new service or goods, and increasing the amount and frequency of use.

PROMOTION THROUGH ADVERTISING

Pederson, Miloch, and Laucella (2007) wrote extensively on sport advertising. As mentioned earlier, sport advertising is part of the sport promotion mix and is one type of messaging that is critical to the economics of sport. It is central to the purchase of media rights, which is a large part of revenue earned by many professional sporting teams today. In essence, the media purchase rights to cover sport because they intend to sell advertising spots to corporations seeking a mass audience consuming the sport that the media intend to cover. Sporting teams also find the need to purchase advertising spots themselves in order to promote their activities. Pederson, Miloch, and Laucella (2007) describe those two types of advertising activities as (1) advertising through sport and (2) advertising for sport. Those categorizations are essential in describing sport-related advertising.

Advertising through sport

As mentioned earlier, the cost to secure media rights has continued to rise because sport is a singular event that provides access to the largest number of persons for advertisers. Moreover, as Nicholson (2007) notes: "Sport events and games are ephemeral products or perishable goods, which means that they endure or last for a very brief of time" (pp. 58–59). Nicholson also points to the fact that a sport is limited and unique, and often there is no substitute for live sport in the mind of consumers. These characteristics of live sport have led to incredible surges in the cost to secure rights to sport. Nicholson writes that the rights to the FIFA World Cup and the Olympics rose by 900% and 380%, respectively, in a decade!

Earning media rights is just the first step for media organizations. These rights can be exclusive, which means the organization pays a premium for it, or it may be nonexclusive, which brings down the price but increases competition between several media organizations. The next step is to generate profits from owning the rights. This is where **advertising** and **subscription fees** come in.

Media organizations recoup expenditure through charging subscription fees to access sporting events. However, that is not the primary mode for recouping expenditure and making profit. Instead, the primary mode is by selling **advertisement spots** in the programming of the sport for which they purchased media rights. These advertisement spots are valuable because corporations compete for them in order to reach a large number of consumers who have large disposable income. Nicholson

(2007) writes that: "sport usually attracts male viewers aged between 16 and 35 years of age, who are both difficult to reach and typically have high disposable incomes" (p. 60). He notes that companies "spent approximately $155 million during the broadcast of the (American gridiron football) Super Bowl to promote their products to an audience of 130 million people throughout the broadcast. Anheuser Busch, the company that owns Budweiser beer, spent US $20 million on eight commercials advertising beer" (p. 72). Usually companies that market alcoholic beverages, automobiles, restaurants, and sporting products, among others, are interested in purchasing advertisement spots during sport programs.

Advertising sport

Beyond advertisement through sport that arises from the sale of media rights for coverage of sport, sporting organizations advertise their organization in the media. This is what Pederson, Miloch, and Laucella (2007) labeled advertising sport. Though sporting organizations can create awareness of their activities through **publicity** instead of advertisement, there are still occasions when they must advertise. These occasions vary but they include informing the public, through the media, about major organizational events such as a change of name, and another occasion is marketing the organization's merchandise. It is important, however, to note that a sporting organization may advertise using other media besides the mass media. They may, for instance, put up signage about upcoming events in their own sporting venue or may also include advertisement in publications available to consumers.

Sporting organizations seek effectiveness in advertisement by focusing on two major principles. The first is to focus on the consumer experience at a sporting event and the other is creating the impression in the consumer's mind that the sporting event is of high quality. Focusing on consumer experience at a sporting event is important in advertisement, because a sporting event is perishable. It is not a tangible product that a consumer can purchase and keep over a long period. Thus, it is critical to present it as a great experience that resides in the consumer's mind over a long period. The experience is integrated with the sense of being a high-quality one. This sense of high quality is sold by presenting the star quality of performers and their previous accomplishments.

Athletes or teams as endorsers

Teams and/or athletes are used to endorse advertised products. Athletes are considered credible, attractive, and likeable endorsers. **Endorsement** of a product involves the endorser speaking positively about a product or using the product in exchange for payment. Endorsement of a product, idea, or service by a team or an athlete is effective when the product and the endorser fit each other. A good example of this is an athlete endorsing sporting equipment. Feloni (2015) and McCormick (2013) provide examples of effectiveness of athlete endorsement of products. Feloni (2015) points out that Under Armour has risen quickly to number two in the United States sport apparel industry based on its use of sport celebrities to endorse athletic wear. McCormick claims that "When Michael Jordan announced his return to basketball in 1995, the five firms he was endorsing (reported) a 2% increase of stock returns, which resulted in more than $1 billion in market value" (p. 10). The companies were Nike, Gatorade, McDonald's, Hanes, and Wheaties.

However, athlete endorsers, like celebrity endorsers, can be risky. All it takes is one incident of poor public behavior by the athlete, and such behavior becomes associated with the endorsed product and company. Therefore, companies include a behavior clause in contracts with an athlete endorser. This allows the company to quickly drop an athlete if a scandal occurs. Coca-Cola and the Asian beer Tiger did not renew a contract with Manchester United's Wayne Rooney after it was alleged that Rooney was visiting prostitutes and cheating on his pregnant wife. Champion cyclist Lance Armstrong lost lucrative contracts with Nike, Trek Bicycle Corp., Honey Stinger, Anheuser-Busch, and other companies in 2012 following news that he was using performance-enhancing drugs. Therefore, companies are careful in selecting an athlete to endorse their product. The company must consider the athlete's reputation.

Companies consider several key things about an athlete before making the decision to sign him or her as an endorser. Beyond evaluating the athlete's reputation, the company considers the athlete's accomplishments, popularity, and personality. Above all, the company also considers affordability because athlete endorsers are expensive. McCormick (2013) provides a list of top endorsement earners who are athletes, and the figures are in the hundreds of millions. For instance, McCormick provides 2012 figures showing that David Beckham, a soccer player, was paid $160 million by Adidas, golfer Tiger Woods was receiving $100 million from Nike, and retired boxer George Foreman was earning $137.25 million from Salton Incorporated.

Challenges of advertising sport

Though the advertising industry has been critical in the commodification of sport, it has challenges using sport for advertisement. Pederson, Miloch, and Laucella (2007) point to the following challenges that sport presents to advertisers: intangibility, heterogeneity, and perishability.

Sport is **intangible** as mentioned previously (i.e. it is a product that cannot be touched, grasped, and stored for later use). This inability to re-use a product creates a challenge as the product's impact is in the memory. In order to persuade the consumer to attempt a re-purchase of the product, he or she must be reminded how memorable the product is. This is what makes sport similar to other entertainment that is experienced or felt. In fact, sport is more intangible than a music show. In a music show, you may see the same talent perform similarly again, whereas every sporting competition is different because of different opponents, non-choreographed actions, and myriad other variables. Thus, advertisers can only market sport by persuading prospective consumers that the product will provide a high level of experience, which will be memorable (i.e. an experience that they would remember for some time).

The high level of changeability in sport referred to in the previous paragraph demonstrates a related challenge that Pederson, Miloch, and Laucella (2007) label sport **heterogeneity**. For instance, watching Annekatrin Thiele of Germany row is an enthralling experience, but watching her multiple times can produce multiple experiences because one performance varies from the next. Pederson, Miloch, and Laucella (2007) note that: "Numerous factors make the sport product heterogeneous, including but not limited to player injuries, weather, facility amenities, and team performance. As the sport product changes, so too do consumers' perceptions of the product" (p. 242).

Furthermore, Pederson, Miloch, and Laucella (2007) write: "The sport product cannot be stored and has no shelf life. Again, it is consumed at the same time it is produced, and therefore it is **perishable**" (p. 242, emphasis added). The moment a sporting contest is over, it is completed and cannot be re-played live again. This explains why sport consumers prefer to watch a sporting contest live. When watching a re-play of a recorded sporting contest, there is a feeling of something missing. There are, in fact, missing elements that differentiate a live from a recorded sporting contest. A key one is the feeling of unpredictability and associated tension and excitement, which are critical to live sport, but they are lost and not recoverable (they perish with the live event).

SPORT SPONSORSHIPS AND CHALLENGES

Sponsorship in sport has been increasing for awhile. PwC (2011) notes that sport sponsorship is the largest percentage of sport revenue in Asia Pacific, accounting for 43.2% of all revenue. In Europe and North America, it is the fastest growing sector, with 5.3% and 6.1% rates, respectively. Though there is little data provided on Africa, reports indicate that sponsorship, at the very least, is a significant portion of sporting revenue in that region, where most sporting finance comes from state-supported funds.

Sponsorship is visible in a few ways. Three of those ways is through sponsorship via naming rights, placement rights on signages at the sporting venue or on team apparel, and showcasing a company's products in exchange for fees. **Naming rights** refer to the purchase of rights to name a sporting facility or event. For sporting facilities, such rights frequently cover periods from three to 20 years, and there are examples of its use all over the world. Examples exist in the United States, Germany, Britain, Finland, Japan, China, Israel, Canada, and Australia. The home of the Surrey County Cricket club in England is presently named Kia Oval after its sponsor, Kia Motors. Kia paid an estimated $5.44 million to purchase the rights to name the oval for five years beginning the first day of the year 2011. The top division of the soccer league in Ghana is named the First Capital Plus Bank Premier League after First Capital Plus Bank, which paid $10 million in February 2014 to sponsor the league for a five-year term. Naming rights provide advertising repeatedly for the sponsor because the sponsor's name is attached to the facility or the event and, thus, is frequently mentioned during a sport event and report. In exchange for rights, the sporting league or organization receives cash for its operations.

Alternatively, a sponsor may receive **placement rights** (in exchange for cash) to have its name placed on signages around the sporting venue. This has the publicity effect of appearing in photographs taken by sport reporters during a sporting event. Consumers also view signages while attending events at a sporting venue. Additionally, sponsors may have their names on sporting apparel of a team in exchange for cash. Coca-Cola appears on the shirts of Club America and Banamex, a financial service provider, is placed on the shirts of Cruz Azul in Mexico. However, it is not just commercial interests that provide this type of sponsorship. In a surprising but widely distributed report, the government of Chad announced a $4.5 million sponsorship of a premier league soccer club in France – FC Metz (Monks, 2016; Nathan, 2016). FC Metz will have on its shirt *Chad: Oasis of the Sahel*. The deal was widely criticized because Chad is the fourth poorest country in the world and had withdrawn from sporting competitions because of lack of funds. However, Chad

Photo 11.1 Corporate signages in the stadium. Signages include those from global automaker Toyota.

Source: Author

government representatives claim that "the deal will improve their public image and encourage tourism to the Central African state" (Monks, 2016, para.2).

> **REFLECTION**
>
> Think about a recent sporting event that you attended. Who sponsored the event? At the event, you may have noticed signages all around the event grounds. While those signages convey messages to us, they also pay for the sport we love. Perhaps they also made you think of purchasing the sponsor's products and/or services. Think back, reflect on the event, and challenge yourself to recall signages that were at the event.

Showcasing a company's products occurs when companies, usually manufacturers of sporting apparel, provide sporting apparel and equipment for use to a sport team or leagues. In many cases, the company attaches a financial package to the deal encouraging use of the product(s). In return, the team or event agrees to use the products exclusively. This way the product is showcased to sport consumers during competition. The apparel, with the team colors, is offered for sale to the team's supporters at premium prices as authentic team uniforms. Nike, a sporting apparel maker, has team uniform sponsorship deals with sporting teams and athletes across multiple sports. For instance, its team deals include Argentina's national rugby team since 2012 and with Dinamo Bucuresti soccer club in Romania. It has official tournament ball deals with football associations in Malaysia, Brazil, and Saudi Arabia. Its deals with athletes include distance runner Mo Farah of Britain, basketball player LeBron James of the United States, boxer Gennady Golovkin of Kazakhstan, soccer player Neymar of Brazil, golfer Thorbjorn Olesen of Denmark, handball player Filippos Veria of Greece, mixed martial artist Junior dos Santos of Brazil, and tennis player Victoria Azarenka of Belarus.

Why companies sponsor

Companies have various reasons why they participate in sport sponsorship. Some reasons are obvious, which include increasing the company's visibility and driving company sales. However, there are many other reasons why companies participate in sponsorship, and Pederson, Miloch, and Laucella (2007) mentions some as follows:

- Shaping new and/or reinforcing existing attitudes about company's products or services
- A way to differentiate company's products from those of close competitors

- A way to showcase product attributes of the company
- A strategy to counter budget advantages of competitors, particularly in the area of advertising
- A way to participate in business-to-business marketing

Relationship marketing in sponsorship

With increasing reliance on sponsors for a substantial part of a sporting organization's revenue, maintaining a positive relationship with sponsors has become a premium. Nufer and Buhler (2009) describe relationship marketing as "the establishment and maintenance of positive, enduring and mutually beneficial relations between professional sporting organizations and their stakeholders" (p. 158). They claim five major factors in building successful relationships with stakeholders and ensuring sponsorship success. These factors are building trust, mutual understanding, having a long-term perspective, communication, and cooperation.

Trust is critical to a positive relationship and goodwill. However, to build trust requires a relatively long period where parties establish reliable and transparent behavior that brings them together as partners. This furthers **mutual understanding** among parties. Mutual understanding requires that each party respect the goal of the other. A **long-term perspective** among parties that are linked in a sponsorship relationship requires that each party contemplate a relationship for the long haul and not just for the contracted period. Sponsorship contracts specify a contractual period, but they are often renewable. When parties build a strong and positive relationship, they are more likely to renew their sponsorship contract. Nufer and Buhler (2009) provide an example of a long-term relationship by citing the sponsorship relationship between Liverpool FC in England and Carlsberg, which began in 1992. A fourth factor is **communication**, where effective communication requires a frequent exchange of information among parties. This information should go beyond business to include social-type communication, which brings key persons closer to each other and strengthens the bond among parties. Additionally, key partners receive preferred information, indicating a partnership that is highly valued. Nufer and Buhler (2009) note that a strong communication relationship exists when "the main sponsors of the German professional basketball club Deutsche Bank Skyliners Frankfurt receive information regarding new players or other important issues before the information is made public" (p. 167). The final factor is **cooperation**, where each party works together on each other's marketing efforts. In such a case, each partner brings to the table its expertise to complement the other's efforts.

Challenges with sponsorships

Pederson, Miloch, and Laucella (2007) cite three challenges with soliciting sport sponsorships. The challenges are differentiation, research, and meeting the needs and desires of sponsoring companies. Understanding each challenge is important because of a rapid increase in the amount of sponsorship revenue. Even in regions where sport has largely relied on state funds for annual operations, the first type of commodification in such areas is corporate sponsorships.

Differentiation in sponsorship categories is important because sponsors seek exclusivity in most cases. However, sponsorship categories are finite, whereas sporting organizations seek as many sponsors as possible. This situation creates a dilemma for the sporting organization. The most effective way of creating categories and attracting multiple sponsors is often to ensure that each category does not have sponsors who compete directly against each other in the same market. For instance, you should not have two financial institutions as sponsors within the same category of sponsorship.

The **research** challenge pertains to how much information the sporting organization has about its own market and consumers in order to persuade sponsors to sign on. While many companies participate in sport sponsorship, their interest is based on reaching consumers who are interested in the company's products. Thus, companies want to find detailed research on the sporting organization's consumers in order to determine whether those are segments that the company wants to reach or not.

Finally, while the above discussion points to reasons why a company is interested in a sporting organization's consumer researcher, it is important to realize that companies participate in sponsorship for several other reasons. Earlier the chapter noted several of those reasons. What is important, therefore, is for the sporting organization to understand which reason applies for a prospective sponsor and how the sporting organization may help the prospect **meet desires and/or needs**.

BRANDING ISSUES

Branding refers to the process of trying to create a unique name, an identity, and an image for a product in the consumer's mind. It is a marketing process that applies a consistent theme intending to differentiate the product from others in the market in order to attract and maintain loyal consumers.

The process of branding a product requires careful planning and a campaign that maintains a consistent theme. This involves how the brand is communicated to a specific segment of consumers and the choice of communication channel. During the process of branding, the company or team logo is displayed prominently and consistently to help consumers associate the product with a consistent message. A tagline also accompanies the logo.

An example of a sport brand that is communicated worldwide is Under Armour, maker of sport apparel and sporting equipment. Hobbs (2016), in an interview with the company's executives, points to how Under Armour is branded. The company's goal is to differentiate itself from the industry leader by appealing to younger consumers and creating a message that Under Armour is the new sporting fashion that is the choice of top-flight athletes. The company supports this brand by using young and high-quality athletes as endorsers, producing novel sport wear, and using vibrant advertisements. Its logo is consistently shown with the tagline "Protect This House" and the slogan "I Will." Those have become a catchphrase among the youth, and the company's sales have grown for 23 consecutive quarters with at least 20% net revenue (Grill-Goodman, 2016). International growth is 70%, according to Grill-Goodman (2016).

SPONSORING A SPORTING EVENT IN THE COMMUNITY

Ingrid Mjelde has always organized a local sporting event for youth teams from all over the country. The annual event is one of few elite youth events in the country, and it attracts a reasonable attendance from the local community.

This year, the event attracted a few sponsors. The major one is a chemist or drugstore in the community established barely two years ago. The store became interested because the owner, Anders Herlovsen, believes the tournament will bring in many customers and grow the store's revenue faster than its current growth. Herlovsen needs to make his store known in the community because it is not one of the big four drugstores in the country – Apotek 1, Boots Apotek, Ditt Apotek, and Vitusapotek. Those four are the dominant drugstore chains in the country where truly independent stores are few and far between.

Herlovsen's sponsorship involves naming Ingrid's tournament for the next three years. This was a first for Ingrid. In fact, she did not seek to have her event named after a store or some other commercial entity. However, Herlovsen offered a lot of money upfront to cover tournament expenses for the next three years. Ingrid is elated, and she accepted the offer because it makes it much easier to organize events and provide opportunities for the event to grow.

Herlovsen obtained permission to have his store's signages at critical points at two locations where the event is held. For example, signages are placed at the entrance to the locations, the event center, and the playing areas. These signages have the logo of the store, the contact number, email, and a short statement indicating that the store's goal is to provide caring services. Families and athletes leaving the event centers receive a giveaway package containing a t-shirt with the company's logo and a message similar to the message on the signages. However, the store's addresses are on the back of the T-shirt. In the giveaway pack is also a coupon offering a six-month discount for purchasing store products. For Herlovsen, he hopes that it is money well spent.

This year's event is well attended, particularly by people from the community and teams located nearby. Attendees mention how much they enjoyed the competition. At the end, they took home the giveaway packages, and some of them immediately wore the t-shirts. For others, they would wear the shirts at home and on other occasions.

Herlovsen is happy. He believes that sponsoring the event makes a difference. Shortly after the tournament, his store experiences an increased number of people coming in, and some of them end up purchasing the store's products. Moreover, he also notices that people are wearing the t-shirts in the community. He makes sure that consumers experience the in-store caring promised in the promotional messages. It is the primary image he wishes to create of his store.

Discussion questions

1 What do you think are the effects on the community of Herlovsen's sponsorship?
2 In which ways did Herlovsen go about branding his store?
3 Do you think people who attended the sporting event sponsored by Herlovsen will recollect or become aware of the sponsor? Why?
4 Apart from event attendees, what opportunities or chances do other community members have to become aware of Herlovsen's store?
5 What kinds of benefits do you think Ingrid Mjelde's organization will get with the event sponsorship?

CHAPTER SUMMARY

There is no doubt that sport has increasingly commodified to become a business of hundreds of billions of dollars annually. Most of the revenue comes from four key sources, which are sponsorships, media rights, merchandising, and gate receipts. However, it is clear that dependence on gate receipts, which used to predominate sport, is waning while revenue from the other three areas are rising.

The chapter discusses, at length, the economics of sport promotion. It points out that sport promotion has the ultimate goal of encouraging consumption, whether it is consumption of sport or consumption of products associated with sport. The chapter's discussion includes media rights, subscription television, advertising revenue, vertical integration of media and sport, merchandising, and sponsorship.

It also reviews the relationship between sport and marketing. In doing so, it discusses strategy, consumer buying behavior, complex decision making by consumers as opposed to programmed decision making, and then how to segment the market. It is under the general understanding of sport and marketing that the chapter discusses sport promotion. This is introduced by defining marketing mix, which constitutes promotion. That mix involves advertising, personal selling, sales, and public relations. Each component is discussed, with special attention paid to advertising by discussing two key types of advertising pertinent to its relationship with sport: teams and athletes as product endorsers and special challenges of advertising sport.

The chapter also discusses sport sponsorship and related challenges in signages, naming rights, and showcasing company products. Importantly, it provides information on why companies are involved in sport sponsorship. Additionally, there is a section on branding. That section describes what branding means and provides an example of the Under Armour sport apparel and equipment brand, which spread globally by taking advantage of unique messaging targeted at a younger segment of the sport market.

DISCUSSION QUESTIONS

1. Has commodification helped development of sport globally? How has it affected consumers? How has it impacted other stakeholders such as sporting organizations and corporations?
2. What do you think of vertical integration of sport and media? Provide examples and discuss how integration impacts consumers.
3. How would a consumer's buying behavior in sport become affected when a product requires complex decision making as opposed to programmed decision making?
4. How does sport heterogeneity and perishability impact advertising?
5. Which ways can a sporting organization provide the consistency required to effectively brand a product?
6. What is the difference between advertising sport and advertising through sport? Provide examples to support your key points.
7. How effective is athlete endorsement of a product, and what kinds of downsides may come with such endorsement?

ACTIVITIES

1. Find an example of naming rights involving an elite sport league, team, facility, or other sporting object. Review the negotiated deal for such rights and then share your report with the class.
2. Attend a sporting event in your neighborhood. Observe sponsorship of the event, signages, product giveaways, and related sponsorship activities at the event. Also interview other event attendees with the goal of finding out their awareness level of sponsorship related to the event. Then write a three- to four-page report.
3. Consume an elite sporting contest on a communication media platform (television, radio, YouTube, etc.). Write down the number of advertising messages that appear during presentation of the contest through the platform. How many

such messages occur? What were they selling? Do you think the advertising of products/services during that particular sporting contest appeals to consumers of the contest? Write a report of your finding.

VIDEO RESOURCES

Value of Corporate Sponsorship of Sports (CNBC Africa/YouTube/12.42 mins.). Video on sponsorship in South Africa.
Sport Marketing, Sport Sponsorship, and Sport Event Bidding (Trinidad & Tobago/YouTube/32.14 mins.). This video focuses on bringing auto racing to Trinidad and Tobago.
SSAC 14: Business of Sports (USA/YouTube/1:02:40). Discusses business of sport industry in America.

RECOMMENDED WEB RESOURCES

Belzer, J. (2014, February 5). Sports industry 101: Breaking into the business of sports. *Forbes*. www.forbes.com/sites/jasonbelzer/2014/02/05/sports-industry-101-breaking-into-the-business-of-sports/#5a3319de5491
Radd, D. (2007, February 22). Sports and in-game advertising. *Bloomberg*. www.bloomberg.com/news/articles/2007-02-22/sports-and-in-game-advertisingbusinessweek-business-news-stock-market-and-financial-advice
The Forbes fab 40: The world's most valuable sports brands. *Forbes*. www.forbes.com/pictures/mlm45jemm/2-espn/#260af8092f41

REFERENCES

Crupi, A. (2015, Sept. 10). Sports now accounts for 37% of broadcast TV Ad spending: Big Four nets $8.47 billion in Ad sales. *Advertising Age*. http://adage.com/
Draper, K. (2014, Oct. 6). What the NBA's insane new TV deal means for the league and for you. *Deadspin*. http://deadspin.com/
Feloni, R. (2015, Jun. 16). The athlete endorsements that are turning Under Armour into Nike's strongest competitor. *Business Insider*. www.businessinsider.com/ the-athlete-endorsements-helping-under-armour-compete-with-nike-2015–6
Grill-Goodman, J. (2016, Feb. 5). Under Armour sees explosive growth for 23rd time. http://risnews.edgl.com/retail-news/
Hobbs, T. (2016, May 4). How Under Armour plans to become the world's biggest sports brand. *Marketing Week*. www.marketingweek.com/
McCormick, K. (2013). Athletic endorsements and their effect on consumers' attitudes and consumption. www.nsga.org/globalassets/management-conference-archives/2013/karla-mccormick.pdf
Monks, K. (2016, Sep. 7). Chad seeks salvation through soccer. *CNN*. http://edition.cnn.com/
Nathan, F. (2016, Sep. 5). Fourth poorest country in the world Chad are sponsoring French team Metz to improve its image. *The Sun*. www.thesun.co.uk/
Neirotti, L., & Bliss, J. (2011). Covering sports in Latin America. *Americas Quarterly*.
Nicholson, M. (2007). *Sport and the media: Managing the nexus*. Oxford: Linacre House.
Nufer, G., & Buhler, A. (2009). Establishing and maintaining win-win relationships in the sports sponsorship business. *Journal of Sponsorship*, 3(2): 157–168.

Pederson, P., Miloch, K., & Laucella, P. (2007). *Strategic sport communication*. Champaign, IL: Human Kinetics.

Pitts, B., Fielding, L., & Miller, L. (1994). Industry segmentation theory and the sport industry: Developing a sport industry segment model. *Sport Marketing Quarterly*, III(1): 15–24.

PwC (2011, December). Changing the game: Outlook for the global sports market to 2015. www.pwc.com/gx/en/hospitality-leisure/pdf/changing-the-game-outlook-for-the-global-sports-market-to-2015.pdf

Reuters. (2016, Sept. 7). Liberty media to buy Formula One racing for $4.4 billion. *Fortune*. http://fortune.com/2016/09/07/liberty-media-formula-one/

Rowe, D., & Gilmour, C. (2010). Getting a ticket to the world party: Televising soccer in Australia. In Hallinan, C., & Hughson, J. (Eds.), *The containment of soccer in Australia: Fencing off the world game* (pp. 9–26). London: Routledge.

Tomlinson, A. (2005). The making of the global sports economy: ISL, Adidas and the rise of the corporate player in world sport. In Silk, M., Andrews, D., & Cole, C. (Eds.), *Sport and corporate nationalisms* (pp. 35–66). Oxford: Berg.

Weinmann, K. (2014, May 21). Cash-Cow sports media rights help shape bigger M & A picture. *Law360*. www.law360.com/

CHAPTER 12

THE SPORTING MEGA EVENT

LEARNING OBJECTIVES

After reading this chapter, you should be able to do the following:

- Understand what a mega sporting event is.
- Be aware of why mega sporting events have grown in recent years.
- Recognize how boosters for mega sport events communicate persuasive messages to the public.
- Become acquainted with resistance strategies of those who oppose mega sporting events.
- Show an ability to describe and explain intricate relationships between mass media and mega sporting events.
- Describe how sport communication is applied to a mega sporting event.

Delineating the scope and boundaries of what is known as a mega sporting event is not simple. The difficulty stems from various issues that make fuzzy what is and what is not a mega sporting event. Despite these difficulties, a mega event is defined as: "large scale cultural events, which have a dramatic character, mass popular appeal and international significance" (Roche, 2000, p. 1). A mega sporting event, therefore, refers appropriately to periodic large-scale sporting tournaments that attract huge media attention across international boundaries.

The definition provided above discriminates between what is and what is not a mega sporting event. First, note that it must be a tournament (i.e. a short-term sporting competition that involves a relatively large number of competitors in few venues). Second, a mega sporting event is held periodically, which means that it takes place after regular intervals. Third, it is large scale, which means that it involves a large number of persons and a large number of competitions among persons and teams that are in few venues. Fourth, media attention is critical to a mega sporting event because attention demonstrates large interest beyond the host city and country. Fifth, media interest is not limited to a single country. Instead, media attention occurs across several countries.

The Olympic Games, the FIFA World Cup, the Rugby World Cup, the Copa America, the IAAF World Championships, and similar sporting events meet the definition of mega sporting events. However, the English Premier League, which is watched by millions of people all over the world, does not qualify. Why? The English Premier League is not a tournament, and it is made up of a large number of matches played in 20 different locations year round.

WHY HAVE MEGA EVENTS GROWN?

Clearly, hosting a mega sporting event is an expensive endeavor, and countries spend years to prepare for bidding and hosting a mega sporting event. Despite this cost, interest in hosting a mega event has risen. Horne and Manzenreiter (2006) note that "the enthusiasm to host and participate in sports mega-events like the Olympic Games and the FIFA World Cup has grown in the past twenty years" (p. 3). In many cases, cities and countries become involved in a bidding contest to host a mega event. For instance, the bidding to host the 2018 and 2022 FIFA World Cups were so tense and acrimonious that countries pointed accusing fingers against others, and there were claims of bribery and corruption in the bidding process.

Zimbalist (2010) reports that the costs of hosting these events are astronomical and often underestimated. For instance, the 2004 Athens Olympics, the 2008 Beijing Olympics, and the 2012 London Olympics were projected to cost $1.6 billion, $1.6 billion, and $4 billion respectively but eventually cost $16 billion, $40 billion, and over $20 billion respectively. The question is why such huge interest in hosting a mega event that is clearly very expensive? Three key factors increase interest in hosting and participating in these large events, according to several academic scholars. They are new media technology, promotional opportunities for the host, and internal development opportunities.

Horne and Manzenreiter (2006) and Nauright (2013) point to **development of satellite television** as key to interest in hosting these events. According to Horne and Manzenreiter (2006), satellite television allows simultaneous access to millions of consumers all over the world. Close to 4 billion people watched parts of the 2004 Athens Olympics, and that cumulative audience was estimated at 40 billion people. Therefore, access is not only of interest to the mass media and corporations but also to governments that wish to host the event. Hosts seek the opportunity to take advantage of such an audience that is scarce and, thus, place a high premium on competing against others for rights to host. It is difficult to find a non-sporting event that matches the attraction of sport for millions of people.

Photo 12.1 A packed athletic stadium at a mega sporting event. Note flags of several countries hanging on the stadium roof. Note also the number of media members working behind their electronic media communication equipment.

Source: Roxane Coche, reprinted with permission

Access to millions of consumers presents **promotional opportunities** that are rare. These opportunities exist in terms of media rights that grant direct access to a huge audience. The host city or country will be mentioned repeatedly throughout the mega event and, thus, attract unprecedented publicity. Places like Nagano in Japan and Sochi in Russia were largely unknown to most parts of the world until they became host cities for the 1998 Winter Olympics and the 2014 Winter Olympics respectively. A city or country, through publicity, creates a good image for itself. Nauright (2013) and Hebein (2012) point to cities and countries bidding for host status for a mega sporting event assuming that the publicity from hosting will improve tourism post-event. Nauright (2013) also cites governments that use their hosting status for international diplomacy.

Third, hosting a mega event allows cities or countries to implement massive **physical development** that includes a major facelift of existing facilities and new construction of sporting venues, transportation systems, and hotels, among other constructions. Cities, particularly, use their host status to persuade the national government to provide money for major infrastructural development that would not have been possible without the status of hosting a mega event. Shahwe, Davies, and Carson (2013) argue: "Cities which may have found it difficult to justify spending money on 'aspirational' projects as part of their normal operations may use the guise of a mega event to support large capital expenditure" (p. 2).

Ultimately, these factors motivate cities and states to bid for hosting rights. Thus, economic benefits are not always the major consideration in many bids, even though they are often highlighted. The fact that they are highlighted indicates the belief that effective communication in winning support for a bid lies on adding economic justification.

COMMUNICATION: RATIONALIZING PUBLIC SUPPORT FOR MEGA EVENTS

Communicating in persuasive ways remains essential to earning support for bidding to host a mega event. The previous section mentioned key factors that motivate cities and states to seek hosting rights for mega events. In this section, the focus is the support that prospective hosts (i.e. the cities and states) frequently use in communicating persuasively to publics about the need to serve as host.

Mega events are such large-scale sporting meets that they are rarely financed through private funds. It requires public money in many cases to host the events and, therefore, the public or representatives of the public must be persuaded to support hosting. This is not an easy process, as there are those who oppose hosting of mega events and, thus, boosters for the event must be well prepared with figures, usually estimated, to win the communication contest and earn public support. Boosters often cite local job creation, tourism, and increased local tax revenue as critical aspects of their persuasive communication to the public. Those elements are in addition to the three already mentioned in the previous section.

The citation of increased employment, as a benefit of hosting, appeals directly to public interest. In essence, the argument is that hosting provides you or perhaps a friend or family member with the opportunity to secure a job that would not ordinarily be available. It is an emotional appeal but often couched as a logical appeal. Most employment is in construction of facilities to host the event. These include stadiums, hotels, roads, and similar types of construction. However, there are also employment opportunities in hospitality, security, and transportation sectors. Konrad Adenauer Stiftung (2011) issued an employment report covering three mega events: the 2010 World Cup in South Africa, the 2010 Commonwealth Games in India, and the 2016 Olympics in Brazil. In South Africa, the forecast was almost 700,000 new jobs and in India about 2.5 million new jobs.

Opportunity to boost tourism is another claim put forward by boosters seeking to host mega events. The tourism argument is directed to small businesses in the host city or country. Why is tourism important to small businesses? First, note that mom-and-pop businesses depend on visitors to make increased profit in their daily business. Visitors buy drinks from local bars, food from neighborhood restaurants, and toiletries from next-door stores, among other small business purchases. Thus, appealing to owners of such business is important in winning community support for mega events. While many scholars point to tourism as important to hosting mega events, Fourie and Santana-Gallego (2011) argue that actual gain of tourists during mega events depend on the type of event and country. Furthermore, sport tourists displace the usual annual tourists if the sporting event is in a big urban center. Moreover, the estimated number of tourists is not sustainable over time.

Increased local tax revenue is an additional claim used in persuading the local population. These taxes are expected to come from various sources, including income from new jobs, hotel taxes, and tourist taxes, among others. Additionally, taxes accrue from use of facilities after the mega event. Such persuasive messages by boosters create expectations that surplus taxes would improve the quality of life in the community.

Unfortunately, several economic studies show that revenue expected from hosting these mega events fails to materialize. Zimbalist (2015) argues that economic analysis of hosting sporting mega events shows that it is not cost effective to use public money to subsidize the events. These analyses force boosters to gradually move away from making a hosting case based on economics. Instead, they have shifted towards soft and more qualitative benefits that include image building for the host city and/or country. What we should learn is that sport communication has powerful persuasive effects on the public whether it involves making a hard case via economic numbers or making a soft case via qualitative arguments.

> **REFLECTION**
>
> Think about a recent mega sporting event that you either attended or watched via a mediated platform. Think about arguments used in winning the bid to host the event. What host image is demonstrated by hosting the event? Think of mega events that made you aware of places that you had no idea existed. Do you feel like visiting those locations?

INCREASING RESISTANCE

Sport mega events involve communication from various stakeholders. Boosters for mega events make a case for hosting through strong and persuasive proposals, which a significant number of economists believe are overstated. Beyond economists, the general public (especially those directly affected by mega events) also resist in the best way that they can. Some of the resisters are groups that work in construction but feel that labor conditions are not favorable. Another is a large number of people who are displaced during building of new facilities to host the mega event.

The Centre on Housing Rights and Evictions (COHRE) issued a study report in 2007 noting displacement of marginalized populations during preparation for hosting mega events. The report notes: "The inner city areas which are targeted for redevelopment, gentrification and beautification are areas which usually house the highest concentration of low income earners, often renters and/or those with limited or no security of tenure" (p. 77). These groups, according to the report, include ethnic minorities such as the Roma at the Athens Olympics 2004, the elderly and sex workers at the Olympics of Barcelona 1992, the elderly at Sydney 2000, people with disabilities and street vendors at Seoul Olympics 1988, migrant workers at Beijing Olympics 2008, and low-income people at Rio de Janeiro Olympics 2016.

Before the start to the Rio Olympics 2016, there were several protests against the games. One protestor extinguished one of the Olympic torches as a runner was holding it. The protestors, angry over the recession in Brazil, stoned cars and fought with police. They were unhappy over the city's decision to host the Games while many in Brazil were under economic hardship. Phillips (2016) cites a protestor who claimed: "the Olympic Games in themselves were a worthwhile event, but the declaration by Rio's cash-strapped state government in June (2016) of a 'public calamity' in its finances proved that the city couldn't afford to stage them" (para. 6).

COHRE reports that about 1.5 million people were evicted in Beijing to make way for new facilities built for the 2008 Beijing Olympics. The same was the case in the *favelas* of Rio where thousands were forcibly removed, leading to unrest and protests by those affected and their supporters. Romero (2012) reports resistance in Brazil at sites designated for construction of the 2016 Olympics. He wrote:

> There was just one problem: the 4,000 people who already live in that part of Rio de Janeiro, in a decades-old squatter settlement that the city wants to tear down. Refusing to go quietly and taking their fight to the courts and the streets, they have been a thorn in the side of the government for months.
>
> (para. 3)

Apart from resistance by the general public affected by construction displacements, protests also come from labor. The communication goal of labor protests are similar to those previously mentioned (i.e. the economic status of protestors juxtaposed with the gigantic expenditure for hosting a mega event). The hosting of the 2010 World Cup in South Africa provides examples of labor protests. In South Africa, there were protests from several workers in varied types of work but mostly related to World Cup service. Hytner (2010) reports protest by stadium workers and stewards in Cape Town over wages. Protestors know that protests concerning a mega event will be communicated to a worldwide audience by global media, and they take full advantage of this reality. Hytner's report focused on a major stewards' protest over pay where stewards believe that they were being underpaid after promises of larger pay.

MEGA EVENTS AS MEDIA SPECTACLE AND GLOBALIZATION

A major study on mega events comes from Professor of Sociology Maurice Roche (2000, n.d.). Roche published a 2000 book on mega events and modernity that is widely cited by other scholars, and his philosophical work in the area of popular culture has attracted notice. Roche claims that mega events demonstrate the idea of globalization. The importance of this work for sport communication is enormous. It makes us re-think sport communication but also begin to understand the reality of everyday globalization. That work forms the basis of discussion in this section.

Photo 12.2 At a mega sporting event, booths are allocated to several media representatives from which to watch and report on the event. The photo shows media representatives at their booths ready to cover a rowing event.

Source: Roxane Coche, reprinted with permission

Roche's work challenges current work on the study of globalization. **Globalization** is a relatively new term that describes the process of increasing interaction, migration, and integration of peoples, cultures, corporations, and communication systems all over the world. This development is driven by many changes in international trade, sporting engagements, and technologies, and leads to observable effects on culture, political systems, and economies worldwide. While the term *globalization* is new, the actual process has been ongoing for centuries, particularly in international trade and human interaction.

Roche notes that globalization discourse in various academic fields largely ignores sport. He, however, believes that sport and its interaction with the media and particularly the existence and performances of sporting mega events provide great examples of the process of globalization. But how does this relationship occur?

He argues that we should see mega events, such as the FIFA World Cup or the Olympic Games, as "media events" within the global village. He writes that this phenomenon is visualized through each person's experiences of social time and space. Using examples of the Olympic Games and the FIFA World Cup are particularly excellent because those two mega events attract the largest viewership in the world.

Millions of people are transfixed on the same mega event simultaneously all around the world, shrinking the limitation of distance. In Roche's own words:

> the periodic sociological realities of simultaneous world-wide mass spectatorship in mediated sport mega events like the Olympics create a unique cultural space and provide unrivalled opportunities to dissolve spatial and temporal distance, to participate in a notional global community, and to promote, albeit transitorally but recurrently, a "one world" awareness.
>
> (p. 2)

Notably, he reminds us that there are no comparable ceremonial events that capture the same sense of "globality" in any other sphere of global life and activities. If you think about it for a moment, you realize that what Roche identifies is a special intersection between sport at the global level and the communication of sport to a global audience. In a sense, it is a strong demonstration of the "global village" where villagers may participate in an event simultaneously. That is the zenith of globalization.

Roche goes further to analyze this sense of globalization. He notes that four main factors help in defining globalization when viewed from the perspective of a sporting mega event (see Table 12.1). These factors are technological/economic dynamism,

Table 12.1 Adapted from Maurice Roche's perspective of globalization that is viewed through the lens of a mega sporting event.

Factors Defining Globalization	Globalization Perspectives	
	Basic View	*Complex View*
Technological Development and Economic Efficiency (*Dynamic Processes*)	Developments in media technology and search for efficiency enable simultaneous communication of sporting mega events to the global "village."	While technology development exists, states, cultures, organizations, and persons have agency to make choices on what and when to view sporting mega events.
Global Standardization	Sport rules and media transnationalism create standardization of sport presentation for global consumption.	While standardized sport rules and media transnationalism exist, differences in local and cultural styles modify how sport is presented for local consumption.
Time & Space Compression	Simultaneous viewing of sport mega events mute time differences and shrink distances.	Unique local choices mean differences remain on what event is accessed and when.
Epicenter of Globalization	Characteristics of different nations disappear, and the globe assumes a single epicenter.	Multiple epicenters exist reflecting localized and regionalized differences.

Source: Adapted from Roche (2000)

standardization, compression of time and space, and the epicenter of globalization. Each of these factors can be seen either from a basic or from a complex perspective.

The first factor, when seen from a basic perspective, assumes rapid **technological developments** and subsequent pressures toward **economic efficiency** impact all parts of the world similarly and pulls everyone towards globalization. This implies that nation states and people barely resist these developments and pull towards globalization. They merely comply. From a complex perspective, the interpretation is vastly different. From this view, nation states, political and cultural organizations, and people have agency. That is, despite technological developments and opportunities for economic efficiency, institutions and people remain active and make choices that are technologically rational.

On the issue of standardization, he argues that the basic perspective assumes that true globalization requires promotion of **standardization** and uniformity in global life. International sport, somewhat, already does this with uniform rules and cultural styles being melted together through migration of coaches and athletes. From the complex perspective, the idea is that globalization involves "differentiation and particularization," which is widely referred to as glocalization. Here, unique characteristics of places are retained even as they participate in a more globalized world. In sport, the argument would be to insist on retention of certain local characteristics despite migration of coaches and athletes mentioned previously. Importantly, and despite the standardized rules of several sports, media communication is still largely nationalistic, which stresses differences and unique aspects within a globalized world.

The third factor, involving issues of **time and space**, is generated through impact of communication technologies. The basic perspective claims that "one world" is ultimately created through compression of time and space, where time differences and distances are overcome universally in this "one world." Roche provides an example by arguing

> the global broadcasting of the "live" Olympic media-event can be said to exemplify space-time compression, namely that, with due allowance for over-emphatic simplification, "the whole world" can be said to watch "the same thing at the same time," and thus in some sense to be in communication or at least to co-exist and be co-present in "the same (mediated) place" at "the same (mediated) time," a global "here and now."
>
> (p. 3)

A more complex assumption of a "one world" is one in which diversity exists on the issues of time and space. Productions differ and support for certain sports by certain places, unequal distribution of broadcast, among other differences indicate a diverse view of this globalized world. Watching sport in the stadium "live" differs from watching sport "live" on television. Furthermore, some parts of the world may choose how much distance to keep and how much participation will occur for them in the "one world." In essence, it involves "the reconstruction of temporal and spatial distance and differences" (p. 3).

The final factor is the **epicenter of globalization impact**. The basic perspective focuses attention at the national level and assumes that characteristics of nations (particularly those things that differentiate one nation from the other) will disintegrate and the existence of "nations" will pass into history as globalization becomes fully instituted. In essence, national sport teams as we know them today will disappear, and competition might be those that exist at club levels. But the complex perspective indicates that the epicenter is more broadly spread and involves not just national levels but also sub-national, organizational, and transnational levels. New social networking platforms impact national structures and characteristics. They also impact organizations at sub-national levels and transnational relationships.

Roche's work shows us how mediated sport mega events demonstrate a globalized world. In essence, we are able to imagine this world through the lens of mass media communication using sport as attraction. Additionally, Roche shows competing views of a globalized world. At one end is the basic perspective that assumes a standardized and technologically determined world where human agency is unimportant. At the other is a complex view where globalization acknowledges a largely integrated world but allows for human agency in negotiating differences and unique characteristics that exist in such a world. No matter which of those views becomes dominant in the future, it is clear that sport communication will be a central feature.

CONFLICT ESCALATES FOR AND AGAINST HOSTING

Though the Rugby World Cup is a relatively new sporting mega event, with New Zealand and Australia hosting the inaugural in 1987, countries increasingly are interested in serving as host. However, the requirements of a host country are not easily satisfied because the host must have stadia with at least 15,000-person capacity, and the final game requires no less than a 60,000-person capacity stadium. It may not sound like much for a FIFA World Cup, but Rugby World Cup is relatively new and not many countries participate in the sport. However, rugby is experiencing a surge in its growth and popularity, with the Rugby World Cup and its global broadcast coverage playing a central role.

Oceania consists of islands in the southeast seas of the Indian Ocean with great rugby traditions. Mr. Ratu Rubuti and his partners Maraia Rokouono and Rupeni Vuni have dreamed for years about bringing the Rugby World Cup to their country. After all, their country has a great tradition in rugby and is a strong challenger for the Cup, even though it has yet to win one. Importantly, they feel that hosting the sporting event will do a lot of good for their country. They recently hired a consultant, Ms. Nanise Moto, to study the likely benefits of hosting a Rugby World Cup.

Ms. Moto carries out a 14-month study and her report is positive. It claims that a Rugby World Cup would bring increased tourism, tax opportunities, and job opportunities, among other benefits. Tourism is a great reason to host the event because little of the country is known, and most tourism to the islands in this part of the Indian Ocean often goes to much bigger Australia or New Zealand. The Rugby World Cup could at least make the country competitive against those two. Employment is particularly important, and as Mr. Rubuti acknowledges: "those jobs could help the country get out of the current economic rut that has been very hard on people."

However, there are those in the country who are unhappy that it is planning to host a Rugby World Cup in the midst of economic difficulties. For them, "It is simply heartless. Instead of seeking solutions, Mr. Rubuti and his colleagues are planning to set up festivities on the back of long suffering citizens." Ms. Miriama Wai and Mr. Mara Rowati have taken up the fight against a Rugby World Cup, pointing out that Mr. Rubuti and his colleagues plan to build the World Cup facilities on pristine lands, some that have been under environmental protection for years. Moreover, the Rugby World Cup is likely to displace several poor people who live near the big cities where the games are planned.

Mr. Rubuti labels the anti-Rugby group as mischief makers who "stand by and do nothing. They have no solutions to our economic situation and are simply out to criticize every possible solution." He says, for instance, that most accommodation for the World Cup will be built without state funds. The housing will be built through a Build-Operate-Transfer (BOT) agreement with private companies, but the state will forgo taxes on those. The state will, however, agree to host international competitions at least once every two years for the next decade in the cities where new housing will be constructed. The BOT companies will engage local organizations to plan international conferences more frequently with attraction of lower rates on housing. Furthermore, Mr. Rubuti argues that airlines from neighboring countries and elsewhere will get tax breaks to provide transportation during the competition. Above all, global media coverage will put the country's name in front of global citizens and is likely to generate sustainable tourism in the long run, Mr. Rubuti argues. The statistics show more than 120 million potential global viewers and almost 500,000 estimated travelers.

While Mr. Rubuti and his group are undeterred and plan to go ahead, Ms. Wai and Mr. Rowati plan major protests in big cities and are likely to work with labor to point out that the job opportunities are a "fluke" and will not materialize. If the country wins hosting rights, then Wai and Rowati will move to the next stage of engineering labor protests for pay increases. It seems that conflict between those for hosting and those against will solidify in the coming months. What is left is to examine arguments on both sides and ascertain their values.

**This is a fictitious case.

Discussion questions

1 Considering economic difficulties, should the country bid to host the Rugby World Cup?
2 Is hosting the Rugby World Cup an opportunity to put people back to work? Provide support for your answer.
3 Should hosting the Rugby World Cup lead to a reasonable expectation of increase in sustainable tourism figures?
4 Considering the expenditure for accommodation and stadium facilities, who will use those capacities after the mega event? Do you think that there is reasonable planning for this? What would you recommend if you are to disagree with existing plans, and if you agree with existing plans then indicate why you agree.
5 A mega sporting event should bring free global media mentions that bolster the country's image. Is that enough value and reason to host?
6 Do you think negotiating the BOT is beneficial to the state? Beneficial to the private companies? Provide support for your answers.

THE IAAF WORLD CHAMPIONSHIP

Nylund's (2009) study of press coverage of the 2005 IAAF World Championship in Helsinki provides insight into how a mega event is communicated to consumers. Nylund studied coverage in the Finnish media and compared that to a study of international media covering the same championship. Importantly, the study of the championship is especially important because it is the third-most-covered mega sport besides the FIFA World Cup and the Olympic Games. The study, once again, reminds us that the great majority of elite sport consumers do so via mass media. In the IAAF Championships, 91% of the Finnish people consumed the sport through the media while only 3% went to the stadium (Nylund, 2009).

The Finnish media largely depend on press releases from local organizers. This overwhelmingly tilts the tone of their reports, particularly before the Championships, to positive. They focus attention on reporting on how big the Championship is and that the global interest is going to be huge. This, perhaps, justifies their concentration on how the Championship provides an opportunity for Finland to create a positive image. They also report that the championship is a matter of national pride and that it will create tourism for the city, noting how the marathon route is designed to take athletes through the city's waterfront. They also communicate about the championship bringing huge economic returns to the city. There is very little reporting of sport. In fact, Nylund writes: "Of the entire (local) press material studied, 21 percent concerned sports" (p. 129). In essence, sport is not the main focus. From this example of the focus of the Finnish media, it is clear how powerful boosters of mega events are influencing the sport media.

The foreign media report the Championship from a different perspective. They are more interested in preparation of their national athletes and not on Finland. Their focus is not on things like tourism and the economic benefits of hosting for Helsinki or Finland. Instead, they focus on how prepared their national athletes are and the conditions for competition at the Championship. For instance, they complain about rains that led to delay, postponement, and/or cancellations of some events. On the marathon route, the Finns expected newspapers to report on the surrounding scenery, but the foreign media focus attention on how winding, narrow, and hard the surface is and that it made the marathon more difficult. Not a single article discusses tourism. The few stories about the host are stereotypical.

CHAPTER SUMMARY

Chapter 12 takes a deep look at mega sporting events, particularly as they relate to sport communication. The first challenge is effectively defining what is a mega event in order to differentiate it from other sporting events. The definition points to several key factors that serve as indices for identifying a mega event. Those factors are that it must be a short-term tournament, be periodic, be on a large scale, and attract international media interest.

The chapter explains why mega sporting events have grown in recent times. A major explanation is development of new media technologies that help in communicating the event to a worldwide audience. Other explanations are promotional opportunities for countries that host the event and then opportunities to develop host locations. This explanation is related to rationalization, communicated to the community, about hosting mega events. The chapter also recognizes that while countries increasingly seek to host mega events, there is also some resistance to hosting communicated in protests against displacement of marginalized communities. The chapter provides examples to support those claims.

Roche (2000) is cited for the idea that sporting mega events demonstrates and explains globalization. Roche's argument focuses on how media cover mega events and create pictures in our heads. For instance, the coverage shrinks time and space in ways that the sporting event is seen as occurring in a global village with villagers able to watch simultaneously. Furthermore, such events and rules introduce the idea of standardization and captures for us how technological development brings us together.

DISCUSSION QUESTIONS

1. Which factors differentiate mega sporting events from other major sporting events?
2. What are key reasons why mega sporting events have grown in recent times?
3. What do cities or countries stand to gain by hosting mega sporting events, and do they achieve those goals? Provide support for your answers.
4. How do groups within cities and countries resist attempts to host mega sporting events? How do they communicate such resistance?
5. Demonstrate the relationship between media coverage of mega sporting events and the idea of globalization.

ACTIVITIES

1. Conduct research on various communication of hosting resistance to hosting the 2010 World Cup in Africa or the 2014 World Cup in Brazil. Write a three- to four-page report on your research findings.
2. Use your Internet browser to search for information related to Brazil winning the bid to host the 2016 Olympic Games. Focus especially on how the local Olympic Committee communicated reasons for hosting the Games. Write a report of your finding.
3. As a group, determine a mega sporting event that you want your city or country to host in the coming years. Do some research to determine how such event benefits your city and country. Design a written package on how to communicate to your community the plan to host and its benefits, among others.

VIDEO RESOURCES

2016 Olympics Bid Announcement (YouTube/29.23 mins.). This video discusses nations waiting for announcement of the host city for the 2016 Olympic Games eventually won by Rio de Janeiro, Brazil.
Contra A Copa: The Other Side of Brazil's World Cup/Full Length (YouTube/36.13 mins.). This video shows protests against hosting of the 2014 World Cup in Brazil.
NBC Olympics Preview: 2016 Rio Olympic Games (YouTube/47.39 mins.) Speaks on media coverage of mega events.

RECOMMENDED WEB RESOURCES

Homepage for the Olympic Games. www.olympic.org FIFA Official site. www.fifa.com
Rugby World Cup – Official Site. www.rugbyworldcup.com
IAAF World Championships. www.iaaf.org/competitions/iaaf-world-championships

REFERENCES

Centre on Housing Rights and Evictions (COHRE). (2007). *Fair play for housing rights: Mega-events, Olympic Games and housing rights.* Geneva, Switzerland: Author.

Fourie, J., & Santana-Gallego, M. (2011). The impact of mega-sport events on tourist arrivals. *Tourism Management*, 32(6): 1364–1370.

Hebein, J. (2012). *The impact of mega-events on inbound tourism demand.* Paper presented to the Pomona College Department of Economics. http://economics-files.pomona.edu/

Horne, J., & Manzenreiter, W. (2006). An introduction to the sociology of sports mega-events. *The Sociological Review*, 54(2): 1–24.

Hytner, D. (2010, June 14). World Cup 2010: Riot police break up stewards' protest. *The Guardian.* www.theguardian.com/

Konrad Adenauer Stiftung. (2011). *Sustainable mega-events in developing countries: Experiences and insights from host cities in South Africa, India, and Brazil.* Johannesburg, South Africa: Author.

Nauright, J. (2013, Winter). Selling nations to the world through sports: Mega events and nation branding as global diplomacy. *PD Magazine*, pp. 22–27.

Nylund, M. (2009). Mega-sporting events and the media in attention economies: National and international press coverage of the IAAF World Championships in Helsinki 2005. *Nordicom Review*, 30(2): 125–140.

Phillips, D. (2016, August 5). Thousands join anti-Olympic protest in Rio before Games begin. *The Washington Post.* www.washingtonpost.com/news/worldviews/

Roche, M. (2000). *Mega-events and modernity: Olympics and expos in the growth of global culture.* London: Routledge.

Roche, M. (n.d.). Olympic and sport mega-events as media-events: Reflections on the globalization paradigm. http://library.la84.org/SportsLibrary/ISOR/ISOR2002c.pdf

Romero, S. (2012, March 4). Slum dwellers are defying Brazil's grand design for Olympics. *The New York Times.* www.nytimes.com/2012/

Shahwe, T., Davies, K., & Carson, C. (2013). *The impact of mega events on construction planning, processes and performance – Auckland's experience of the Rugby World Cup 2011.* Paper presented to the International Council for Research and Innovation in Building and Construction (CIB). http://research.digitalnz.org/

Zimbalist, A. (2010, March 10). Is it worth it? The International Monetary Fund (Finance & Development). www.imf.org/external/pubs/ft/fandd/2010/03/zimbalist.htm

Zimbalist, A. (2015). *Circus maximus: The economic gamble behind hosting the Olympics and the World Cup.* Washington, DC: Brookings Institution Press.

CHAPTER 13

IMAGE AND CRISIS COMMUNICATION

LEARNING OBJECTIVES

After reading this chapter, you should be able to do the following:

- Be aware of crisis situations in sport.
- Be aware of the effects of crisis situations in sport.
- Understand how to respond to crisis situations in sport through effective communication.
- Know communication strategies that are used proactively to prevent crisis situations.
- Be able to identify, describe, and explain elements necessary for image repair following the onset of a crisis.

SPORT CRISIS COMMUNICATION

Crisis is usually a situation that is critical and believed to lead to an undesired end. Crisis is caused by an event that occurs and portends dire consequences. Usually, crisis has the potential to damage an athlete or sporting organization's image and/or reputation or other negative outcomes. Numerous crises can occur for a sporting organization or an athlete. **Image** refers to how an organization or an athlete wishes to be perceived by others. Image is what an organization and/or athlete wishes to create, through messaging, in the mind of its consumers. It is often short-term and formed via messages of the organization. Thus, it can be inconsistently held among consumers because they perceive the organization's messages differently. **Reputation**, on the other hand, is a longer-lasting belief that consumers have about an organization based on consistent actions that the organization/athlete has taken in the past.

It is considered a social capital that the organization has built over a long period based on its activities in the community. Some scholars view reputation as an accumulation of various images held by consumers. Thus, organizations may cite past examples of actions to support their reputation.

Sport crisis communication is an aspect of public relations that helps to protect the athlete and/or organization's image and reputation from adverse outcomes. It involves "collection, processing, and dissemination of information required to address a crisis situation" (Coombs, 2010, p. 20). Coombs went ahead to identify three **types of crises**, which he labeled victim, accidental, and intentional, with each type divided into subtypes.

The first type, **victim** crisis, occurs in an organization or to an individual but is not perceived as emanating from the organization or individual. Instead, the organization or the individual is considered the victim of such crisis. These types of crises have a low likelihood of affecting reputation. Examples of such crises are natural disasters, workplace violence, or rumors. For instance, there may be a rumor circulating that a neighborhood sporting organization has a policy of not hiring immigrants. Although this is damaging information about the organization, if there is no truth to it, then the organization can move quickly to address the falsehood and keep its reputation intact. However, if left unaddressed, it may spiral into adverse consequences for the organization.

The **accidental** crisis type points to crisis for which the organization or the athlete has responsibility but the responsibility is considered minimal because it is caused by a genuine technical accident or by an act that is not a violation of law or statute. These types of crises have moderate reputational consequences. Examples of an accidental crisis include technical failure of cash cards distributed as part of ticket discounts to season ticket holders. In this case, the failure is attributed to card technology and not human error from the sporting organization. Again, although the consequence to the organization may be mild, it still has to be addressed in a timely manner.

The third and most damaging crisis type is **intentional** crisis. This has severe consequences for a sporting organization or an athlete in the area of image and reputation. Intentional crisis involves misdeeds that result from knowingly violating laws and regulations. It may also involve negligence or other types of human errors such as poor judgments. Kulkarni (2014) provides an example of an intentional crisis involving Indian badminton players over violations of age regulations. These athletes were using false birth certificates to enable them to compete in younger age brackets. They were discovered when they failed X-ray verification tests evaluating skeleton age and bone maturity. The acts of those players were criminal and have a substantive likelihood of severely damaging the reputation of each of them.

Recent athlete crisis situations

New social contexts, which are difficult to control, currently expose athletes to adverse effects on their public image. Athletes are increasingly in the public eye via social media. In the past, athletes were largely away from the public eye and mostly seen when playing sport. This reduced the possibility of athlete misbehavior that endangers public image. However, social media have meant that public relations professionals, who help to protect athletes from behavior that is likely to tarnish their image, are finding it increasingly difficult to protect athletes. In this section are two examples of situations that create image problems for athletes.

The first situation involves swimmer Ryan Lochte of the United States. Lochte is perhaps America's second-most decorated male swimmer. However, it was not his swimming ability that brought him to the attention of the world. Instead, it was his behavior during the 2016 Summer Olympics in Brazil and the presence of a security camera that brought his misdeed before the eyes of a global audience. Lochte and one of his teammates claimed that they were robbed, at gunpoint, by men in security uniforms who sideswiped and stopped their taxi. The news spread quickly, as it appeared to confirm earlier media framing of Brazil as a dangerous place despite efforts by local Brazilian authorities to paint an image of a safe Olympics. However, a Brazilian police investigation soon began to unravel Lochte's claims. Importantly, the security camera at the gas station captured significant aspects of the incidence. It turned out that Lochte and his friends had been drunk and vandalized the restroom of the station where their taxicab stopped, and as they got back into the car to flee the scene they were stopped by a security personnel who brandished a handgun to prevent their escape. "The swimmers gave money to the manager before leaving, witnesses said" (Romero, Buchanan, and Keller, 2016, para. 5). Lochte had to admit that his story was fabricated, but it had created a major international storm enraging Brazilians who thought that their city had been unfairly smeared. Faced by the situation, four major sponsors of Ryan Lochte walked away from his sponsorship. Isidore and Wattles (2016) report that: "Speedo, Polo Ralph Lauren, and Gentle Hair Removal and mattress maker, Airweave all said that they would be cutting ties with Lochte after the swimmer admitted to lying about being robbed at gunpoint while in Rio" (para. 2). Though two new sponsors signed up with Lochte, there was no doubt that his image had taken a major hit. Interestingly, one of the sponsors was to use Lochte on a media campaign focused on forgiveness. But Lochte's problems did not end with sponsors walking away. In addition, the United States Olympic Committee (USOC) and USA Swimming suspended Lochte for 10 months for the embarrassment he had caused authorities and the country, according to Vasser (2016). The USOC cited unacceptable behavior, unfair maligning of the host country, and diverting attention from the achievements of Team USA.

The second situation involves a Nigerian athlete who took to Twitter to express his disappointment for not being invited to be part of the country's team to the 2013 Cup for African Nations. Peter Odemwingie, a soccer player who plays professionally in England, was disappointed by his non-inclusion in the team and decided to vent his frustrations on Twitter. This was an unusual move in the country. Though

Peter was a regular member of the team for years, a player's non-inclusion is something Nigerian players may discuss with their coach or authorities in private settings, but it is rare to have an athlete go public to discuss this issue. Peter chose differently. He lashed out at several coaches and authorities and cited his long record with the national team. He did not stop there. He attacked the captain of the team and journalists. It was a wide-ranging attack that triggered adverse public reaction. Days after he had grasped the enormity of his unexpected reaction, Peter recanted by meeting selected journalists to issue an apology, attributing his tweets to a fit of anger. Ogunleye (2012) reports that Peter concluded as follows:

> I am human and open to error by the way I may have taken the issue, and regret the whole controversy, and want to put all this behind me now and focus on my club career, while wishing the team the best of luck as a Nigerian.
>
> (para. 17)

These two athlete examples identify two different crisis situations. In one case, the athlete's fabrication of a story negatively impacts an image that a country worked hard to create and ends up embarrassing the sporting authority of the athlete's country. The fabrication ended up affecting the athlete's image and endorsements that he signed with several sponsors. In the other situation, an athlete goes off on an emotional rant on Twitter, attacking a list of sporting stakeholders. Public response to the athlete forces him to retreat from his public ranting. Both acts create crisis situations for the athletes and require them to take action to reverse damage to their image or reputation.

Importantly, actions like those described by elite athletes attract media interest and coverage. The coverage is often adverse to the athlete, who is likely to lose public goodwill, and there is damage to image and reputation if there is no attempt by the athlete to respond. Thus, in many cases the athlete would respond by holding a media conference or issuing a media release. What should be in the content of that media release is discussed in detail in a subsequent section.

PREPARING FOR CRISIS WITH COMMUNICATION

One of the major scholars in the area of crisis communication is William Benoit (1997), and he outlines how organizations should prepare for crisis communication. This plan is predicated upon the assumption that crisis situations come with major damage to the organization that is far-reaching and lasting, if not addressed. For a sporting organization, the consequence is damaging because of intense media interest and coverage of sport. Benoit states that his recommendation comes from years of research in the field, which identifies four stages that cover preparation all the way to taking action to repair an organization's image. The stages are discussed as follows.

Making contingency plans

This is the first stage, and the assumption is that crisis can be anticipated. Of course, other crises are difficult to anticipate. For those that can be anticipated, organizations set up detailed contingency plans on how to respond to the crisis. For instance, a sporting organization should anticipate social, regulatory, and legal violations by its athletes as well as its staff. While the specific violation may not be known, anticipating occurrence of some sort of infraction provides an edge to the organization.

The contingency plan includes identifying a staff member responsible for providing leadership during a crisis response. Of course, this individual will have a team to provide support for this task. The organization should have a written document that guides response to crisis. This contingency plan helps the organization avoid delays in responding to a crisis situation. Bear in mind that delays can be harmful to the organization. The contingency plan should be reviewed and updated periodically in order to have a guideline that is effective. Benoit points to the importance of periodic review by reminding us that "elements of the actual (crisis) problem may differ from the anticipated problem, so plans should be modified as needed" (p. 182).

Full analysis of crisis situation

This stage occurs when an actual crisis occurs. The contingency plan established by the organization becomes applicable at this stage. However, it is important that the crisis situation is fully analyzed by identifying the crisis, its scope, its source(s), and other related issues. The organization should also become aware of what type of crisis it is facing. Is the organization a victim, is the crisis accidental, or is it intentional? Furthermore, the organization should quickly obtain data relevant to the crisis. If the analysis and obtained data indicate that the current contingency plan is not adequate in addressing the crisis, then the organization should modify its plans for responding to the crisis.

Let us assume that a sporting organization faces a financial problem that leads to significant delays of paying promised winning bonuses to its athletes and coaches during an international competition. The local media break the story, citing unnamed sources from the organization. Several other media organizations call for interviews related to the story, and calls have come from sponsors and some season ticket holders who are concerned about the team's long-term survival and the psychological state of the athletes. This is a crisis situation where the organization may be a victim or the crisis may be intentional. The organization must be diligent and thorough in investigating the issue to determine the nature of the crisis. If the situation is due to the act of an external party (e.g. a sponsor not fulfilling a financial obligation), then the response would be different compared to a situation that is intentional (e.g. an organizational officer mismanaging funds).

Identification of relevant publics

After a full understanding of the crisis and obtaining relevant information surrounding it, the next stage is identifying publics to whom the response should address. This is a careful process in order not to leave out any important public. The identification of publics is critical because each public may require a different kind of message response, and it is also important to avoid a situation where messages can become contradictory.

Using the example provided in the previous stage, the sporting organization should identify at least three key publics: players/coaches who are directly affected by the financial situation, sponsors of the club, and the fans/community. If the organization is publicly owned, then a fourth public would be stockholders. Each of the publics identified above has its own unique interest in the crisis. For instance, stockholders and sponsors are more concerned about financial stability and viability of the organization in both the short and long term. Fans and the immediate community are more concerned about competitiveness of the team, while the players/coaches are concerned about when their bonuses will be fulfilled. With differing interests, the organization must be prepared to address each interest in such a way to stem the crisis.

The organization must prioritize the publics. In this case, it is important to quickly address the players/coaches first and then the sponsors in private communication sessions. Right after such address, the organization must then use the media to address fans. The interval must be minimal between addressing separate publics in order to avoid leaking information and to control rumors.

Repairing a tarnished image

This is the stage where response to crisis occurs. A message is carefully crafted for the publics and then delivered with the goal of protecting the organization's image. It is important to note that protecting the organization's image does not mean lying to the public. The organization should be truthful about its role in the crisis and apologize if necessary and then provide information on how it plans to proceed in the future in order to prevent a re-occurrence of the crisis. This must be communicated persuasively in order to win back the public's trust.

Though Benoit (1997) provides these steps towards preparing for and addressing crisis situations, it is important to note that an organization does not have to go through all the four steps as stated by Benoit. In fact, Benoit (1997) acknowledges that an organization does not have to respond to all crisis situations. First, recall the different types of crisis, including a crisis where the organization may actually be a victim. Instead, Benoit refers to other possible responses to a crisis situation. He offers the following:

> First, it is possible to redefine the attack. Second, instead of altering the nature of the accusations, the business may attempt to refocus attention on other issues.

Third, it is possible that each accusation is not important to the audience. Of course, if a charge is important to the audience, or if it is repeated enough by the attackers, a business may well be forced to deal with that accusation.

(p. 183)

> **REFLECTION**
>
> Recall a recent sporting crisis that occurred in your country. It may have involved an athlete or a sporting organization. Now that you have read about crisis types, what type of crisis was it that you recall? What key things come to mind as you recall the crisis?

CONFRONTING CRISIS

Beyond the knowledge of steps that organizations take to prepare for crisis and deliver a communication response, there is a need to become aware of how sporting organizations and athletes have responded to crisis. Therefore, this section focuses on how sporting organizations and athletes respond to crisis. Additionally, a third subsection provides an example of an international sporting organization and its attempt to create a positive image after a major crisis.

The organization

Sporting organizations are unique when it comes to confronting crisis. They are unlike other corporations or organizations. For instance, there is a separation between employees at a sporting organization and elite athletes. One set of employees is the athlete who is employed on a contract basis. This employee is different from the regular employee hired for administrative duty. For most other organizations or corporations, employees work on administrative-type tasks.

The separation of types of employees in a sporting organization provides leeway for organizations to respond to crisis. Since most athletes are employed based on contracts, the sporting organization can easily distance the action of athletes from that of the organization, especially when such action is not pre-approved by the organization. This possible separation is difficult in the case of an administrative staff whose action is more directly linked to the organization.

There are several examples of sporting organizations that have faced severe crisis, and each one has attempted to deal with possible damage to its image and reputation. Benoit (2015) provides two examples. One is the Canterbury Bulldogs, who were accused of violating the Australasian men's rugby league salary cap restrictions. The other is the New Orleans Saints in the National Football League (NFL) in America that ran a "bounty" program, encouraging players to injure opponents.

A third example comes from the work of Compton and Compton (2015) on the NFL facing accusations that it was not doing enough to address unhealthy conditions in its league due to concussions sustained by athletes. Each case involves direct accusation of administrator involvement in the crisis and, thus, it means a direct attack against behavior of the organization. In none of those cases could the organization be separated from the act. The organization had to respond in order to protect its image. For instance, the Bulldogs tried to deny cheating, but such a position became untenable as more facts came out leading to the resignation of CEO Raelene Castle, which forced the organization to admit guilt, apologize, and scapegoat Ms. Castle. Denial is always a dangerous strategy to use, particularly when an organization committed the act.

However, Len-Rios (2010) reports on a sporting crisis faced by an educational institution where the institution did separate athlete behavior from values of the organization. In Len-Rios's case, she studied Duke University's lacrosse team members' involvement in an alleged sexual assault of a female dancer. Len-Rios is able to show how the university separated its image and reputation from acts of the athletes. Len-Rios writes as follows:

> separation is about placing responsibility on a group member and dissociating the organization from the member. . . . The university used expression of disappointment several times in its public statements. These types of statements are used to show that the university administration did not condone the behavior or alleged behavior of its students. Thus, the university suggests that the players' poor behavior should only be a reflection on them and not the school.
>
> (p. 279)

Sporting organizations like those involved in the type of crisis identified above face difficult situations. The media are hungry for sport news because of huge public interest in sport and, thus, crisis news attracts hordes of media. This means that crisis for a sporting organization can quickly become national news, with thousands of people showing interest in following each development. Organizations must be ready and prepared to face the media in order to explain their side of the story and issue an apology or corrective action when necessary. Importantly, there is always an organizational concern for maintaining a good image and reputation as a way of retaining the goodwill of its key stakeholders.

The athletes

There are several studies on how athletes respond to crisis. Most of them are on athletes in the United States and, just like organizations, athletes stand to lose sponsorship if they encounter crisis. For instance, the story on Ryan Lochte discussed in a previous section pointed to four companies withdrawing support for Lochte immediately after it became public that Lochte lied about a robbery during the 2016 Olympic Games in Rio. Top elite athletes make a substantial percentage of their income from endorsements and, thus, losing an endorsement is a huge financial loss. Phillips (2016), for example, reports that tennis star Roger Federer's $60 million in endorsements was 89% of his total earnings. Though that figure is an aberration, it points to the importance of endorsement to the athlete. The more reasonable figures for the top athletes are those related to basketball star LeBron James and soccer star Cristiano Ronaldo, who saw their endorsements form 70% and 57% of their total earnings, respectively. In any case, no sponsor likes to associate with an athlete who violates the law or participates in an indiscretion. A sponsor may lose consumers if it stands by an athlete who has very little public support. Those situations encourage athletes, who find themselves involved in a crisis, to seek appropriate ways to respond to such crisis and restore a good image and reputation.

In this section are two examples of image repair attempts by two athletes. In one case the attempt to repair image fails and in the other it is a success. The section demonstrates why one attempt may have worked and the other failed.

The first is American cyclist Floyd Landis, who failed a drug test for using performance-enhancing drugs. He failed multiple tests, including one that found synthetic testosterone in his system. According to Glantz (2010), Landis failed to admit his use of performance-enhancing drugs and did not offer an apology. Instead, he makes several media appearances where he steadfastly denies his use of performance-enhancing drugs. Sponsors withdrew from the Ouch Pro cycling team after the team signed Landis. Landis first calls a press conference when rumors spread that he failed a drug test. He was intent on protecting his image as a successful cyclist who won the challenging Tour de France. He initially characterized the first test result as an abnormality, but not one that rises to the level where he could be accused of being a drug cheat. However, a second test later shows that there is a significant and elevated presence of synthetic testosterone in his body, which means that his attempt to frame the initial test result as a simple abnormality was no longer tenable. This time, he changes his defense by denying ever using a performance-enhancing drug. By denying, he still has to explain the results, but he attempts to do so by claiming that he had no control of the tests and attacks the competence of the Anti-Doping Agency. He tries to also bolster his image by mentioning how hard he worked and trained. Then he sought sympathy from the public by mentioning how the media have hounded him since the test results came out. However, Landis's attempt at persuasive communication about his failed drug test lacks credibility. First, there is no reason for the Agency to have willfully failed Landis. Moreover, the Agency runs a reputable laboratory and tests with well-qualified persons. Furthermore, the cycling sport is already known to involve athletes using performance-enhancing drugs. Those situations combine to make Landis far less credible than the agency carrying out the tests. Ultimately, the media, sponsors, and the public do not believe Landis.

For another American athlete, Michael Vick, the result of his image repair attempt is considered successful. Vick was a popular quarterback for the American gridiron football team the Atlanta Falcons. Vick was charged by federal officials with a crime involving illegal dog-fighting and related offenses. There was a barrage of negative media reports on Vick and attacks from organizations advocating for animal rights. Holdener and Kauffman (2014) examine Vick's attempts to rebuild his image following his guilty plea. Vick adopted a humble tone in his media conference by asking the media for patience "due to his inexperience in public speaking" (Holdener & Kauffmann, 2014, p. 95). He admits guilt and apologizes for not being truthful to the league, his team, and his teammates at the onset of the crisis. He then apologizes to his fans. He asks forgiveness and said that he has turned his life to Jesus. Vick's strategy, particularly his appeal to a higher power, is unusual in a sporting organization's or athlete's image repair attempt, but it is a critical move. By appealing to a higher power and claiming that he has changed , Vick spoke powerfully about taking corrective action in a way that his message is difficult to attack. Ultimately, Vick's image-rebuilding attempt works because he subsequently receives "mostly positive reviews for his apology from the general media," according to Holdener and Kauffmann (p. 96). Then he is swiftly accepted to rejoin the league after he served his sentence.

Athletes, like organizations, must carefully evaluate a crisis and respond appropriately. The cases of Lochte, Odemwingie, Landis, and Vick represent crisis that athletes may face, and success at rebuilding an image depends on a careful analysis of the crisis and creating an appropriate response. Michael Vick's choice of not denying guilt when he knew he was responsible for the act is an important move. His decision to ask for forgiveness and indicate that he was in the process of change helps his publics to accept his position and offer him another chance.

The international organization

An international sporting organization, in some ways, differs from the usual sporting organization. The international sporting organization is usually not answerable to any other organization. Not only does it regulate others, but it also regulates itself. However, like other sporting organizations, the international sporting organization relies on sponsors for its revenue, among other sources of revenue. In this subsection, the focus is on the International Federation of Association Football (FIFA), which faced its severest crisis in May 2015. How did the organization counter the threat to an image that it was working hard to create? That's what this section reviews.

In the early morning hours in May 2015, Swiss police arrested several top executives of FIFA who were in Switzerland for FIFA's presidential elections. The officials are charged with several crimes including ticket racketeering and corruption by the U.S. Department of Justice. Onwumechili and Bedeau (2016) report that

FIFA, through its President Sepp Blatter, began immediately to respond to the crisis by speaking to the media in order to reach out to several of its publics. FIFA's case is a special one. Sponsors, for instance, could not easily withdraw from FIFA as they did with examples of the athletes who were discussed in the earlier section or as they could do with other sporting organizations. FIFA has a global reach and regulates the world's most popular sport, and there is no real substitute for FIFA. A sponsor could leave one athlete and immediately sign up another one. A sponsor can also do the same with another sporting agency, but with FIFA, there is no close substitute. The closest substitute is the Olympic Games, but soccer for the Olympics is a four-year periodic event, and it is just one of several Olympic sports, whereas FIFA's association with soccer is 100% and on a daily basis. But FIFA is not immune from damage to its image, which could lead to decline in revenue from consumers as well as other financial losses. As Onwumechili and Bedeau (2016) point out, FIFA faced adversaries from the media, public, and interest group organizations.

FIFA's attempts to create a good image were quite unsuccessful right after the arrests. Onwumechili and Bedeau (2016) find that FIFA attempted to separate itself from the actions of those officials who were arrested, and FIFA chose, instead, to attack the accuser (i.e. the United States). Additionally, it offered to take corrective action by reforming. Ultimately, FIFA took several desperate actions, including the resignation of President Sepp Blatter, but with little effect as its public image plummeted.

FIFA's travails led to deep reforms in the organization. It reformed with remarkable changes, including diluting the power of a FIFA President and introducing a new position of Secretary General to run the daily administrative work of the organization. Importantly, FIFA diversified its executive makeup that was solely male and appointed a woman as the first Secretary General, and reserved positions for women representatives on a new FIFA Council. Furthermore, it introduced term limits for the position of President. These are remarkable changes that resulted from crisis and forced FIFA to rebuild a damaged image.

COMMUNICATION: APOLOGIA AND PRIOR REPUTATION

At this point, it is important to address two issues that are important during an attempt to repair a public image or restore reputation. The two – apologia and reputation – are not the only important issues, but they are selected for review because the two are regularly mentioned during a process of image repair and reputation restoration.

Apologia refers to speech or statements made in self-defense after an accusation takes place. It is different from making an apology. An **apology** refers to stating that a person is sorry or expresses regret for doing something wrong. On the other hand, an apologia involves not just an apology but includes a host of different things that a person may include while defending him or herself against an accusation of having done something wrong. Thus, while an apology may be included in an apologia, an apologia is not the same as an apology. Apologia, therefore, is what athletes or sporting organizations produce when they appear before the media following a crisis.

Prior reputation, as you can imagine, has its own impact on an organization or an athlete's attempt to repair an image. A positive reputation is, perhaps, the single most important factor when attempting to respond to a crisis situation. In fact, it is so important that some studies find that an organization with a good reputation may use a defensive response strategy successfully, especially if the CEO is visible (Turk, Jin, Stewart, Kim, & Hipple, 2012). In such a case, a defensive strategy is as good as an apologetic one. Without prior good reputation, using a defensive strategy is a weakness and one in which the audience is likely to reject attempts to build a positive image.

CYCLIST LANDIS STRUGGLES TO REPAIR IMAGE

American cyclist Floyd Landis was considered a rising cyclist worthy of note after he won the Tour de France in 2006. By July of the same year, there are media reports of Landis failing a urine test, but it is unclear whether the failure is due to use of a banned substance. Instead, the reports state that the test showed some peculiarities. However, a second test by the Anti-Doping Agency confirms that Landis indeed used a prohibitive amount of a banned substance that elevated his testosterone. The testosterone found in his body is not naturally occurring but a synthetic type.

Landis is faced with a serious crisis that threatens not only his victory at the prestigious Tour de France but also his image as one of the world's best cyclists who is clean. He also faces a loss of sponsors. For Landis, it is a difficult time. His public relations team immediately arranges for Landis to begin a media blitz with the goal of restoring his image in the minds of the public. He holds a press conference on July 28, 2006, a day after the report of the first test, and he has several television appearances for almost a full year afterwards as he struggles to repair a shattered image.

During his first press conference after accusations surfaced, Landis denies taking banned substances and claims that his positive test result could have been due to alcohol consumption and prescribed thyroid medication. He claims: "I declare convincingly and categorically that my winning the Tour de France has been exclusively due to many years of training and my complete devotion to cycling."

But after the second test also turns out positive, Landis begins his various media appearances by flatly denying taking any banned substance. He no longer claims that it could have been a result of alcohol. In this case, he begins to claim that his samples may have been altered at the lab and that the files pertaining to the test were altered or destroyed. His physician, Dr. Brent Kay, also states that the positive results could be "due to a variety of other factors with handling and specimen contamination and various other things." The French lab, in response, announces that it welcomed an independent audit of its activities.

Landis asks the United States Anti-Doping Agency (USADA) to dismiss doping charges on two claims: (1) that the urine samples taken from him at Tour de France did not meet the established criteria for positive doping offense and that it was full of errors, and (2) that the second test came from a sample number not assigned to Landis. The USADA set up an independent arbitration panel to hear the Landis case. After a nine-day hearing, the arbitration panel finds Landis guilty and strips him of the Tour de France title and suspends him for two years. But Landis refuses to give up. Instead, he appeals the USADA ruling to the Court of Arbitration for Sport (CAS). He loses the appeal in June 2008 but then moves to the U.S. Federal Court claiming partiality and conflict of interest by the CAS. By the end of the year, the USADA and Landis finally settle and Landis agrees to withdraw the case.

In May 2010, Landis admits to doping but continues to deny taking testosterone at the 2006 Tour de France. In 2011, he is convicted *in absentia* for hacking into the computer of the French Anti-Doping Agency in an attempt to steal documents to help his case.

Discussion questions

1 Why did Landis go on a media blitz when there are institutional processes with expertise to evaluate his case?
2 What type of crisis did Floyd Landis experience in this case and why?
3 Would you say that Floyd Landis and his team went through a full and thorough analysis of the case before embarking on a media blitz? Please support your position with facts drawn from the case.
4 Did prior reputation play a part in this case, or not, based on your knowledge?
5 Do you think that Landis is believable in the specific case of Tour de France urine tests? Please provide support for your answer.
6 What did we learn about image repair by how Floyd Landis went about his case? Is there anything that he should have addressed differently?
7 Why do you think that USADA and Landis agreed to settle out of court? Support your opinion with reasoned answers based on information from the case.

CHAPTER SUMMARY

Communicating image during a crisis situation is quite common as an aspect of sport communication. This type of communication is undertaken at various levels, including at the athlete and organizational levels. This chapter dedicates its discussion of communication during crisis to messages disseminated after a crisis takes place with the goal of repairing an image.

The chapter opens by defining three key concepts, which are crisis, image, and reputation. Based on those concepts, the chapter defines sport crisis communication as a way to protect the image and reputation of the athlete and/or organization from adverse outcomes following a crisis. It also goes ahead to identify three types of crises as victim, accidental, and intentional. Of the three, the intentional crisis is the most challenging for an organization because it has great potential for damaging the image and/or reputation of the organization. Two examples of athlete crises are also presented to demonstrate the types of crises that occur in a sporting context.

A section of the chapter delves into how sporting organizations may prepare to communicate in a crisis situation. Four phases are identified, with the first phase dedicated to contingency plans for countering adverse communication during crisis. Essentially, it requires that a plan already be in place. The second phase requires analysis of a particular crisis situation, and the third requires identification of relevant publics that an organization plans to reach with its communication. The final phase involves taking action, including communication, to repair the tarnished image of the organization.

Other sections of the chapter focus on levels at which a crisis is confronted. These contexts are at the athlete level, organizational level, and international organization level. Each level requires a unique way of confronting crisis. The chapter also defines apologia and discusses the importance and impact of prior reputation. In essence, whether a reputation is positive or negative impacts the chances of repairing a damaged image.

DISCUSSION QUESTIONS

1 What are critical differences between image and reputation?
2 Of three types of crises, which of them could be problematic for a sporting organization seeking to protect its image and reputation? Why?
3 Why is it important to have contingency plans for crisis communication? How effective is such a plan when it is unknown which type of crisis may occur in the future? Please provide support for your answers.
4 Reviewing the Ryan Lochte case, which occurred during the 2016 Olympic Games, how would you advise Lochte and his handlers to address the crisis in which Lochte found himself?

5 What are the differences among crises that occur at the athlete, organizational, and international organizational levels?
6 What is the difference between an apology and an apologia? Demonstrate the differences by providing examples.
7 How does prior reputation impact a sporting organization's ability to repair its image after a crisis?

ACTIVITIES

1 Identify a recent crisis involving an international sporting organization. Review the crisis situation and how the organization confronted it. What type of crisis was it and was the organization successful in repairing its image?
2 As a group, identify two sporting crises that may be both at the athlete level or both at the sporting organization level. One situation must involve an organization with negative reputation and the other an organization with positive reputation. Study how the media react to both situations and write a brief report.
3 Research a recent athlete crisis generating media interest. In your review, identify the type of crisis, and address how the athlete should communicate about it.

VIDEO RESOURCES

Situational Crisis Communication Theory (YouTube/7.03 mins.). Theorist Timothy Coombs explains how to approach crisis situations.
South Africa: Cronje Cricket Inquiry (YouTube/5.48 mins.). Disgraced South African cricket captain Hansie Cronje's press conference apologia.
FIFA Press Conference of May 27, 2015 (YouTube/29.28 mins.). FIFA press conference following arrests of its officials on corruption charges.

RECOMMENDED WEB RESOURCES

Frandsen, F. *The apology of a sports icon: Crisis communication and apologetic ethics.* www.academia.edu/2085251/The_Apology_of_a_Sports_Icon_Crisis_Communication_and_Apologetic_Ethics
Crisis communication plan. www.ready.gov/business/implementation/crisis
Winters, R. (2015). Image repair and crisis response of professional athlete Adrian Peterson. *Elon Journal of Undergraduate Research in Communications,* 6(2): 16–23. www.elon.edu/docs/eweb/academics/communications/research/vol6no2/02_ryanwinters.pdf

REFERENCES

Benoit, W. (1997). Image repair discourse and crisis communication. *Public Relations Review,* 23(2): 177–186.
Benoit, W. (2015). (2nd ed.). *Accounts, excuses, and apologies: Image repair theory and research.* New York: State University of New York Press.

Compton, J., & Compton, J. (2015). Open letters from the National Football League, concussion prevention, and image-repair rhetoric. *International Journal of Sport Communication*, 8: 266–275.

Coombs, T. (2010). Parameters for crisis communication. In Coombs, T., & Holladay, S. (Eds.). *The handbook of crisis communication* (pp. 17–53). Malden, MA: Wiley-Blackwell.

Glantz, M. (2010). The Floyd Landis doping scandal: Implications for image repair discourse. *Public Relations Review*, 36: 157–163.

Holdener, M., & Kauffmann, J. (2014). Getting out of the doghouse: The image repair strategies of Michael Vick. *Public Relations Review*, 40: 92–99.

Isidore, C., & Wattles, J. (2016, August 22). Ryan Lochte ditched by four major sponsors. http://money.cnn.com/

Kulkarni, M. (2014, Aug. 13). Badminton Association uncover multiple age violations and boxing India delay elections. www.lawinsport.com/

Len-Rios, M. (2010). Image repair strategies, local news portrayals and crisis stage: A case study of Duke University's lacrosse team crisis. *International Journal of Strategic Communication*, 4: 267–287.

Ogunleye, A. (2012, December 30). Why I blasted Keshi, NFF, Osaze reveals; apologises for outburst. *Premium Times*. www.premiumtimesng.com/

Onwumechili, C., & Bedeau, K. (2016). Analysis of FIFA's attempt at image repair. *Communication & Sport*. DOI: 10.1177/2167479516633843

Phillips, R. (2016, June 8). Cristiano Ronaldo tops Forbes List of highest-paid athletes in 2016. http://thebiglead.com/

Romero, S., Buchanan, L., & Keller, J. (2016, Aug. 18). The evidence that Ryan Lochte lied about an armed robbery in Rio. *International New York Times*. www.nytimes.com/

Turk, J., Jin, Y., Stewart, S., Kim, J., & Hipple, J. (2012). Examining the interplay of an organization's prior reputation, CEO's visibility, and immediate response to a crisis. *Public Relations Review*, 38: 574–583.

Vasser, S. (2016, September 8). Ryan Lochte will be suspended 10 months, source says. www.cnn.com/

PART IV

SPECIAL ISSUES IN SPORT COMMUNICATION

Source: Dreamstime.com, reprinted with permission

CHAPTER 14

SPORT HEROES AND CELEBRITIES

> **LEARNING OBJECTIVES**
>
> After reading this chapter, you should be able to do the following:
>
> - Identify and define who a sport celebrity is.
> - Be able to differentiate a sport hero from a celebrity.
> - Describe and explain how sport heroes emerge and the role of media in such emergence.
> - Become aware of the impact of sport celebrity on society at large.
> - Understand how a sport celebrity impacts endorsed products.
> - Be able to identify and describe major sporting celebrities.

There is a tendency to equate every sporting hero to a celebrity. However, as you will discover, the terms *hero* and *celebrity* are different, and a hero does not automatically become a celebrity, and neither does a celebrity automatically become a hero. However, heroic athletes can achieve celebrity status. Let us first define what each of those terms means in order to clarify their differences.

A **hero**, in the classic sense, is a person who sacrifices his or her own safety or personal concerns for the greater good. It is someone who faces danger but combats and overcomes it to help others. This definition makes it difficult to describe an athlete as a hero in the purest sense. However, the term still applies to athletes. So, who are **athletic heroes**? On the athletic field, a hero is an athlete who performs an extraordinary feat that is the reason for a victory or major accomplishment. The word may be used in a dynamic sense for an athlete who is a hero for a particular sporting encounter. For instance, an athlete who goes on to win the first-ever medal for her country at the Olympics is a hero because it is an extraordinary accomplishment for that country. An athlete who performs a similar feat repeatedly is a hero in the eyes of people for a lengthier time period. Thus, a hero may define a singular achievement or repeated achievement.

On the other hand, a **celebrity** is someone who becomes famous for a certain act or achieves fame based on an attribute. The person becomes widely known, prominent, and celebrated by a significant number of people. Thus, a sport celebrity has to be an athlete who is widely known and celebrated, but this does not require the athlete to be a hero. A good example of this is Anna Kournikova, a former Russian professional tennis star. In her 14-year professional career, Anna never won a World Tennis Association (WTA) singles title, but she became a famous tennis player. She is not a sporting hero, at least not at the global level. However, she attained fame because of her beauty and attractiveness, which led to several product endorsements, including the renowned absorber sport bras. She, ultimately, became a famous face in the media. For years, *PR Newswire* (2005) named her one of the most-searched athletes on the Internet, and she subsequently earned several roles in movies and occupied the cover pages of popular magazines. Beyond that, her name is used in *poker* (a computer virus), which appeared in 2001 (Kizza, 2005).

THE SPORTING HERO

Shuart (2003) points to Orrin Klapp's work of more than a half century ago as the basis for the general understanding of a hero. As we shall see, communication is critical in the emergence of a sporting hero. Klapp (1962) argues that a sporting hero requires certain characteristics, which includes a high level of physical ability and the ability to establish a certain notoriety, among other qualities. As mentioned in the definition of a hero, the sustained athletic hero possesses elite talent that allows him or her to remain a hero for a lengthy time rather than the ephemeral hero who results from one heroic performance. Sustained elite performance leads to a level of notoriety necessary to earn the label. The notoriety is advanced through interpersonal and mass communication that disseminates positive analysis of the athlete's performances. An athletic hero also performs at an elite level despite obstacles that may include injury, emotional loss, and other types of impediments. There is also an athletic hero who has the physical talent and performs his or her craft with charisma and/or flair, which observers admire. In essence, there are several paths to heroism under the sport hero definition.

Klapp also identifies stages that define how a sport hero is developed. This is called a five-stage process in hero development. The stages are outlined as follows:

1 The athlete is recognized at the initial stage as having the necessary physical qualities to play at an elite level compared to teammates and competitors.
2 The athlete then performs heroic acts that fulfill initial expectations. The athlete is formally labeled a hero at this stage.

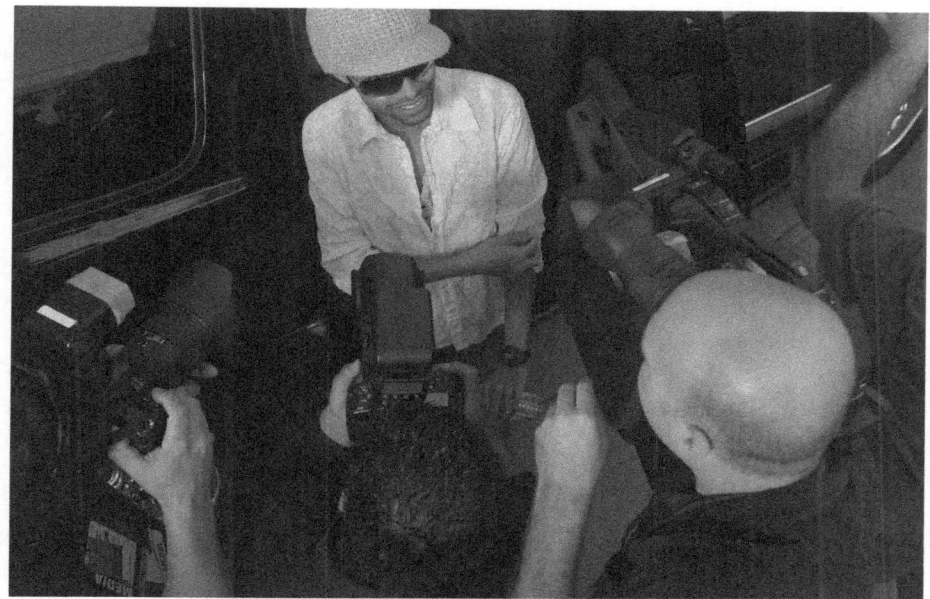

Photo 14.1 A sport hero or celebrity attracts media attention, as seen in this photo.
Source: Dreamstime.com, reprinted with permission

3   The mass media become important at the third stage, which is where hero status begins to solidify. This stage involves image-building by the media involving storying the athlete and his or her performances, hyping the athlete's subsequent performances, and comparing it with the accomplishments of legendary athletes.
4   The fourth and fifth stages occur after the athlete has retired from peak competition. However, both stages are important in the development of a hero. The fourth stage involves commemoration/celebration of the athlete and his or her performances and contributions to the sport. This is noted through special ceremonies (e.g. induction into the Hall of Fame) to honor the athlete.
5   Finally, the athlete reaches cult status. Again, the mass media are important at this stage. An athlete reaching cult status develops a fanatical following from the general public. Media narratives describe the athlete as perfect, faultlessly playing the sport, and continually achieving. This media description rarely occurs while the athlete is still competitively active. Instead, it is reserved for athletes who have retired from active sport participation.

THE SPORTING CELEBRITY: FACTORS AND CELEBRITY TYPES

As pointed out previously, a sport celebrity differs from a sport hero, even though there are athletes who achieve both the status of hero and celebrity. This section takes a closer look at sport celebrity. It describes major factors that help our understanding of a sport celebrity and three categories of sport celebrity.

Major factors in sport celebrity

Digance and Toohey (2011) studied sport celebrity and identify four themes that help us understand sport celebrity. Both scholars list the four as follows:

1. The capitalist market commodifies the athlete in the media, where the athlete appears regularly in advertisements as an endorser. These advertisements are disseminated to wide audiences across national borders.
2. Media analysts and other media types hype the athlete and frame him or her in ways that are notable and attractive to the audience. However, it is not always that the media creation is positive. In certain cases, the creation is anti-heroic, but the hype creates such a notoriety that a following for the athlete develops.
3. Digance and Toohey (2011) add: "the appropriation of the celebrity persona by fans (which) in the extreme can lead to stalking and violence" (p. 350). Appropriation does not mean that the fan adopts the athlete's celebrity persona. Instead, the fan worships the persona and expects the athlete to maintain it.
4. Abundance of new technologies, particularly ubiquity of social media networks, helps disseminate stories, narratives, and hype that surround the athlete and quickly spread notoriety and fame of the athlete persona. It is not just traditional media that control messaging and framing of the athlete. Instead, social media networks allow participation of the general public in developing mythologies that help cement the celebrity's persona.

Celebrity categories

Rojek (2001) writes extensively on celebrity and categorizes three types of celebrities. This typology is based on how the individual achieves fame and becomes a celebrity. The three categories are ascribed, attributed, and achieved.

The **ascribed celebrity** achieves celebrity status based on family. In essence, the individual's parent was a celebrity, and the individual grows up to become a celebrity as well. However, examples of this are rare in sport. While sporting celebrities such as Michael Jordan have sons who play sport, their sons rarely achieve hero status or become celebrities themselves. On the other hand, there are sport celebrities with an athletic parent, but that parent may not have been a celebrity.

Attributed sport celebrities attract a high level of media attention not necessarily for their talent but for other reasons. Anna Kournikova, mentioned previously, is an example of attributed celebrity. Many anti-heroes or infamous celebrities fall under this category of attributed celebrity. In essence, they are created solely by the mass media or new media and have not developed their status based on elite performance in a sporting arena.

Most sport celebrities fall under the category of **achieved celebrity**. This category of sporting celebrities achieve hero status in their sport and transcend that status through media coverage that has exploded beyond sporting performances to coverage of other activities leading to the athlete participating in product endorsements.

It is most important to realize that a sporting celebrity is largely the creation of mass communication in the form of advertising, publicity, and/or public relations. This type of sport communication creates fans or consumers dedicated to the athlete celebrity. The casual consumer of such celebrity may not be emotionally invested in the celebrity but will consume information about the celebrity when it is immediately available. Dedicated consumers of the celebrity become addicted to the celebrity and constantly seek information on the celebrity through various types of media. A dedicated consumer may range from exhibiting mild to severe attachment to the celebrity. Those who exhibit severe attachment may impinge on the celebrity's right to privacy, which becomes a major problem.

SPORT CELEBRITY AS PRODUCT ENDORSER

The wide popularity of a sport celebrity means that marketers and advertisers seek to have a sport celebrity endorse products in order to attract a large number of consumers to adopt the endorsed product. Andrews and Shimp (2012) note that 20–25% of all advertisements feature a celebrity. This, without doubt, affirms the importance of celebrity endorsers. The question is how do sport celebrity endorsers impact a product? Are there risks associated with such product endorsers? How best to select a sport celebrity endorser to ensure that positives are accentuated over any possible risks?

Impact of sport celebrity endorsers

The impact of sport celebrity endorsers is well known because it has been studied for a long period. The impact includes increasing attention to the product, leading to favorable evaluation of the product, helping to polish the product's image, establishing a brand name, making huge financial returns to companies, and helping overcome cultural barriers. Though this list is not exhaustive, each is reviewed in some detail as follows.

The fact that a sport celebrity is in an advertisement **attracts the attention** of consumers immediately. Belch and Belch (2001) describe this as having stopping power. By this, they mean that sport celebrities draw attention to communication messages in the advertisement and increase message recall by consumers. It is a pull that gets consumers to view the advertisement and listen to the celebrity. In an environment where there is a clutter of advertisements, the use of a sport celebrity makes the difference for a particular advertisement to get consumers' attention.

Popularity of a celebrity is transferred to the product that he or she is endorsing. This means that if the viewer likes the athlete, there is a high probability that the viewer will also like the product. Therefore, the viewer or consumer would **positively evaluate the product**. This transfer of liking is a key reason for corporations signing popular athletes to endorse their product, which communicates to the athlete's fans to follow suit in liking and possibly purchasing the product.

Association of a celebrity athlete with a product **polishes the product's image** in the consumer's mind. This is particularly true where the athlete is viewed as having a good image and is also popular. A good example of this is the image of products endorsed by golfer Tiger Woods before Woods' personal relationships were exposed in the media. At the time, Tiger Woods was popular and perceived as a good role model with a clean image. This image rubbed off on the products that Tiger endorsed, including Gillette and Gatorade.

Celebrity athletes also help **establish a product's brand**. An example is Michael Jordan's endorsement of Nike shoes. At the time, Jordan wore Converse shoes which, along with Adidas, were the most popular sneakers. Nike offered almost its entire budget to sign Jordan with the belief that he would be an outstanding professional basketball player, and the company began a massive advertisement of Jordan endorsing the shoes. Nike's shoes (especially the Air Jordan shoe) quickly became popular among consumers, and Nike became the number-one sneaker. Nike's brand image as the shoe for an elite athlete or for someone who wants the best shoes became established.

In addition, it is important to note that creating awareness of the product, attracting consumers, and creating an image, among others, lead to the difference in a company's bottom line (i.e. the difference in the **financial** statement). McCormick (n.d.) provides financial figures to demonstrate the financial impact of using sport celebrities. For instance, the return on investment for companies endorsed by Tiger Woods increased 1%, and for Jordan's products it was over $1 billion upon his return to basketball in 1995. Jordan's brand continues to grow, and in 2012 it grew an astonishing 25–30% even though he is retired.

Finally, using a sport celebrity as a product endorser allows companies to **overcome cultural barriers**. Usually, products sold across national borders require the creation of different advertisements and talents in order to be effective in various geographic locations. However, this situation is ameliorated through use of a sport celebrity because sport celebrities are recognizable and likeable across national borders. Their impact on consumers across borders is also positive.

> **REFLECTION**
>
> Recall a recent advertisement that uses an athlete endorser that you have seen on television or another mass medium. As you reflect on that advertisement, think of why the athlete was selected to endorse that particular product. Then ask yourself whether you find the athlete effective in advertising the product and why. Were you impacted by the advertisement to the extent that you could immediately recall it? Would you purchase the product based on the advertisement? As you reflect on these issues, recall what you have read so far in this chapter.

Risk of celebrity endorsement

As pointed out in a previous chapter, using an athlete for product endorsement is risky, and that also applies to use of a sport celebrity. The risk has three possible sources, which are celebrity-related, product-related, and financial.

Chapter 11 provides examples of athlete behavior that could ruin a product endorsement. Most of those behaviors are similar to **celebrity-related risks**. These risks involve poor or socially unacceptable behavior by a sport celebrity. Because a sport celebrity is intricately linked to the product that he or she endorses, such behavior has a high probability of harming the product. It attracts negative publicity to the product and product sales may plummet. But celebrity-related risks are not limited to poor behavior by a sport celebrity. It may also involve what is labeled celebrity extinction. This refers to the athlete suddenly losing celebrity status. A classic example occurred recently in professional basketball in America involving Jeremy Lin. Lin, an Asian American point guard, exploded into prominence in 2012 when he scored over 20 points for the New York Knicks in successive games as a surprise starter because of injuries to other players. Suddenly, the media began to promote Lin and he became famous, and even non-basketball fans became aware of who he is. However, this did not last; Lin signed a big contract the next season to play for the Houston Rockets, but his performance was not at the level the media had built, and he faded as a celebrity. Such a drop in celebrity status may harm a product that becomes associated with the player.

There are also **product-related risks**. There are three sources for product-related risks, according to Belch and Belch (2001). These include the celebrity overshadowing the product, which occurs when consumers focus attention on the athlete and are unable to recall the product that the athlete is endorsing. Thus, it is important that copywriters and others who work on the advertising message ensure that product prominence is established in the advertisement copy. Another source of a product-related risk is overexposure of the celebrity endorser. If the celebrity endorses several products, consumers may become confused and forget particular products endorsed by the athlete. Finally, a third source is confusion, which is somewhat related to overexposure. However, in the case of confusion, multiple celebrities endorsing a particular product can confuse the consumer in terms of both recall and imaging the product.

Financial risk occurs because sport celebrities are expensive to contract, and yet celebrity-related risks come with sport celebrities. That combination increases the financial risk for the advertiser, which requires some risk balancing and protection through contract clauses. Furthermore, a risk occurs when the celebrity endorses a product but uses a competing product. This occurred with the Nigerian national football team – the Super Eagles – leading Adidas to withdraw its sponsorship of the team. Jideaka (2014) reports that: "Adidas blamed their withdrawal on the players and officials of Super Eagles, especially one of the team's coaches who breached the contractual agreement during the World Cup in Brazil by wearing kits of rival kit supplier, Nike" (para. 4).

Selecting a celebrity endorser

There are many considerations in selecting a sport celebrity endorser to communicate with prospective consumers of a product. Some considerations for selecting an athlete endorser are mentioned in an earlier chapter. The same considerations apply to selection of a sport celebrity endorser. These include credibility of the celebrity, attractiveness, Q-rating, and the No Tears model. Those considerations are not exhaustive, but they represent what many advertisers use in selecting a celebrity endorser.

Credibility revolves around whether the celebrity is appropriate in speaking on a particular product. For instance, a sport celebrity who is an elite ice hockey player is credible endorsing a sport equipment product compared to endorsing educational equipment. Another aspect of credibility is the issue of trust. Is this celebrity trustworthy? If the celebrity was unreliable and untrustworthy in the past, then it will rub off on the product.

The **attractiveness** of the celebrity endorser relies on three dimensions of measure. These dimensions are (1) how likeable is the endorser? (2) is the consumer segment for the product familiar with the sport celebrity endorser? and (3) does the sport celebrity's attributes indicate similarity with consumers? All three dimensions are important for the endorser to be effective when communicating with a prospective product consumer.

A third selection model uses what is called **Q-rating**. The Q-rating is a mathematical formula that determines the effectiveness of a sport celebrity in reaching a particular audience. It involves a simple calculation that divides the popularity percentage of the celebrity among consumers by the familiarity percentage. These percentages are obtained via survey of prospective product consumers and then used in the formula. Ultimately, the formula is a measure of the sport celebrity's appeal to consumers of the product.

Finally, the **No Tears** model is exactly what the name says. You use this model to avoid tears. The model, mentioned by Miciak and Shanklin (1994), attracts attention from several advertisers. It is a model that includes factors such as credibility and attractiveness of the sport celebrity to prospective product consumers. It also includes: What are the costs of working with the celebrity? What is the ease of working with the athlete? How expensive is the athlete? Does he or she have multiple endorsements? What is the likelihood that the celebrity is controversy-free in the future?

THE CELEBRITY ATHLETE AND CHOICES IN THE FUTURE

Landon Schultz's shirt is the number-one selling merchandise in the league for the last two years. He seems constant in the mass media. If he is not appearing in a family television show as a guest, then he is being interviewed or he is endorsing a product. One sport analyst claims: "He is the most important athlete of this era. It is hard for me to identify another athlete that is so loved and an athlete that many parents consider a role model for their children." However, while he is lauded for his personality and his popularity, he is clearly not among the top-performing athletes on the sporting field.

But how did Landon get to this point? At the professional level, Landon is not the star of his team. He does not lead in several statistical areas, but he is well known for his aggression, tenacity, and grit. The spectators love him for that. However, he is not the only athlete who has done well in those areas. At least two other teammates receive accolades for their overall efforts. However, neither of those two are recognizable beyond the gaze of committed fans of the sport. Thus, it is difficult to claim that Landon's fame has come from the way he plays the sport.

So what put Landon in the public limelight? Landon's personality is cited as a major reason. Landon is an extrovert with an infectious personality that makes people around him happy. He is not only popular among teammates, but he is also loved in his community and the media. Landon always stays back after a game and participates in media interviews, and he always provides the media with memorable quotes. While some of his teammates present themselves as aloof, he is approachable. In the community, he finds time to participate in activities in various places such as the elementary schools, churches, and local fairs. He is a face that people are used to, and he is always available to sign autographs with a smile.

His personality and media activity make him a natural choice to represent the team and organization at various events. The media increasingly write positive stories about him, and he is frequently cited in stories about the team. His photographs are sometimes included in those stories. Importantly, his team shirt number is popular on several pieces of team merchandise, and the team's rise in revenue is associated with the large sale of merchandise associated with his number. Corporations seek Landon for product endorsements because his endorsement is associated with selling of products and services.

But Landon is approaching his 34th birthday, and there are talks of his decline on the sporting field. The team coach knows that he is popular, but the coach has younger players pushing for starting spots ahead of Landon. The coach has a tough decision to make on whether to continue starting Landon when there may be better players on the team or to use Landon as a substitute. But it is not just the coach who is worried. Top administrators in the organization are worried about a negative impact on the organization's revenues if Landon is moved into the team's reserve. Advertisers are concerned and are beginning to discuss how best to find a substitute and an appropriate athlete endorser if the need arises. Several decisions are likely to be made in the coming months.

Discussion questions

1. What type of celebrity is Landon Schultz? Why?
2. Why would someone, who is not regarded as the top athlete on his own team, become as famous as Landon? Are there real-world examples that you can provide similar to Landon?
3. What should the team's administrators do considering the future of Landon and the club's marketing success?
4. What type of endorsement risks does this case demonstrate and why?
5. Using Digance and Toohey's sport celebrity development model, show how Landon Schultz developed into a sport celebrity.
6. Advise advertisers on how to proceed in selecting the next sport celebrity endorser.

EXAMPLES OF SPORT CELEBRITIES

There are many sport celebrities, including Cristiano Ronaldo, LeBron James, Anna Kournikova, Serena Williams, Lionel Messi, Tiger Woods, and David Beckham, among others. This section discusses five sport celebrities. Each is carefully chosen for various reasons. The five are Brian Lara, Li Na, Diego Maradona, Hines Ward, and Dennis Rodman.

Brian Lara

Brian Lara is believed to be the best batsman ever in cricket. He represented Trinidad and Tobago and amassed several international cricket test records. These records include the highest individual score in cricket without being out. He also became the only batsman to score a hundred, a double century, a triple century, a quadruple century, and a quintuple century in elite games over his career.

Lara's sustained sport performance makes him an achieved celebrity to the point that his current net worth is estimated at $60 million. For someone who played cricket, that is a substantive net worth. He received an honorary member of the Order of Australia in 2009, and then he was inducted into the International Cricket Hall of Fame in 2012. He received an honorary degree from the University of Sheffield in the United Kingdom in 2007. His country named him Ambassador of Sport, issuing him a diplomatic passport. U.S. President Barack Obama met Lara in 2009, describing Lara as the Michael Jordan of cricket.

Brian Lara's fame led to his endorsement of a video game on cricket titled after his name; it was first developed in 1994, and newer versions continue to enjoy success among consumers, particularly in the United Kingdom. He also endorses Oakley sunglasses, bmobile telecommunications, and Angostura's LLB in his country. Baksh (2009) writes: "his shrewdness in money matters created an awareness of financial values that was never quite as pronounced in the regional game. . . . No other player in West Indies cricket history has benefitted as handsomely from sponsorships and endorsements as Lara" (para. 23).

Li Na

Li Na, now retired, is the only Asian female tennis player to win a Grand Slam event. She won both the Australian and French Opens in different years and rose to the rank of number two in the world in 2014. Li Na is a sport celebrity in China, where her accomplishments on the court led to a large increase in the number of tennis players in China. Former tennis star Chris Evert (2013) describes Li's influence as follows: "Tennis has exploded in China. The country now has some 15 million tennis players; 116 million watched Li win the French Open . . . and it never would have happened without Li." She began as a badminton player but later changed to tennis. Her historic break came in 2011, when she won the French Open in a match over Francesca Schiavone that was watched by 330 million people worldwide, according to Chambers (2011).

Her accomplishments on the court make her one of the most celebrated Asian athletes. Apart from being named one of only four athletes in *Time*'s 100 most influential people in the world in 2013, she is only one of three female athletes to crack the *Forbes Celebrity* 100 list. She endorsed seven major products after her French Open victory to add to her endorsements. The seven include Nike and Babolet Pure Drive GT rackets. In fact, one of the remarkable endorsement deals allows her to include patches of other donors on her Nike tennis shirt. The ability to negotiate such an unusual deal with Nike communicated her strong leverage as a celebrity. Additionally, there is a movie on her life.

Li Na's celebrity status is one of an elite celebrity. She has more than 23 million followers on her Sina Weibo micro-blogging site as of late 2014. Sina Weibo is a Chinese micro-blogging site that is a hybrid of Facebook and Twitter. She has a rose tattoo on her chest in a culture where tattooing is not widely accepted. Furthermore, she has clashed with authorities and at one time quit the Chinese national tennis team. Followers adore her and many believe that her rebellious image attracts several followers. In 2016, it was rumored that she died and Twitter exploded over the hoax, with hundreds sending condolences before a quick response pointing out that no story of her death appeared in the Chinese media (Simpson, 2016).

Diego Maradona

Maradona is probably one of the greatest athletes to play association football. He was an incredible talent who rose to legendary celebrity status only to crash because of drug abuse and poor financial choices. His celebrity status was across the world and beyond his home country of Argentina. Diego is an exceptional talent who played for his country's national team just before his 16th birthday and went on to amass scoring feats from a position on the field that is not known for producing scorers. He was named footballer of the century, and his goal at the 1986 World Cup against England is recognized as the best goal in a World Cup final. He took the ball in his own half and dribbled through half the English team before scoring. He also led Napoli of Italy to its first-ever league championship and, upon his retirement, Napoli retired his Number 10 shirt, never to be worn again by a Napoli player. His country Argentina applied to FIFA to have the No. 10 retired, but FIFA denied the request.

Maradona's fame is global. He held the world record transfer fee twice, being the only player to do so. Many parents in both Argentina and Brazil name their male child after Diego. In Nigeria, a President became known as "Maradona," referring to the President's style of dribbling around in decision making. His biography *Yo Soy El Diego* became a bestseller in his homeland. Argentinos Juniors named its stadium after Maradona. His talk-variety television show in Argentina *La Noche del 10* achieved exceptionally high ratings. His look-alike appeared in cartoon books. He has a film made about him by a Serbian filmmaker. A parody religion on the Internet, "The Church of Maradona," with 200 founding members, attracts thousands of memberships via an official website.

Maradona's talent is unquestioned, and it led to endorsements with Puma, Coca-Cola, and Louis Vuitton, among several others. But all of that was largely frittered away by persistent drug and alcohol abuse and other health problems.

Hines Ward

Jun and Lee (2012) describe how Hines Ward, an American gridiron football player, emerges as a sport celebrity in South Korea. Hines has mixed heritage, with an American father and a Korean mother. In such a circumstance, Hines was not considered a citizen of Korea because Korean citizenship is based on pure Korean bloodlines. However, Korean journalists changed the narrative for Hines Ward and built not only a case for his Korean nationality but also turned him into a sport celebrity in Korea.

Ward's Korean classmates in America discriminated against him because of his mixed heritage. He overcame that to become an accomplished American gridiron football player. In 2006, he was named Most Valuable Player (MVP) of the Super Bowl, the football championship game, against the Seattle Seahawks. From that moment, the Korean media began to focus on Hines using the frame of his Korean nationality. This allowed Korean consumers of sport media to "associate and identify themselves with symbolic meanings embedded in such mass-mediated identities," according to Jun and Lee (2012, p. 105). Media coverage of Hines was not only in the sport section but also in editorials, talk shows, and feature sections. Remarkably, as Jun and Lee note, "Many news stories focused on his Korean identity, rather than his athletic performance. His Korean identity was often emphasized in association with his Korean mother" (p. 106).

A few months later, Ward arrived in Korea as a celebrated figure well known to Koreans, many of whom had little interest in American gridiron football. He and his mother were invited to lunch with Korean President Roh Moo-Hyun. Then he became only the second person to receive honorary Korean citizenship. The first was Dutch football coach Guus Hiddink, who led Korea to the semi-final of the FIFA World Cup and influenced cultural changes to business and education in Korea (Lee, Jackson, & Lee, 2007). Jun and Lee (2012) also report that a film was made of Hines, and many South Korean corporations sought Hines to endorse a variety of products because of his popularity in Korea. Some of these corporations include Korean Air, Korea Exchange Bank, and Kia Motors.

Dennis Rodman

Dennis Rodman is an anti-establishment hero who climbed quickly to celebrity status based on his antics. Rodman was not a superstar American basketball player, but he regularly made sport news for eccentric behavior and became widely known in America and outside of American borders. Though his defensive abilities led to his Hall of Fame induction, his behavior is what many readily recall and what made him a celebrity.

Rodman built up an image of a bad boy, dying his hair, piercing his body, and tattooing it. Among his antics are wearing a bride's wedding dress to promote his autobiography and developing high-profile affairs with actress Carmen Electra and the infamous singer Madonna. Rodman is the classic anti-hero who does all the wrong things but yet is a celebrity. Many people believe that Rodman, who was a typical college athlete prior to his draft into the American professional basketball league, intentionally created the image of anti-hero in order to generate publicity. Whether this is true or not, it is clear that he succeeded.

Rodman became better known than many more talented basketball players. After his retirement, he went on to garner publicity by acting in a few films, earning appearance fees, appearing on several television shows, and having his own reality television show. He also partnered with Premier Brands to develop Bad Boy vodka.

CHAPTER SUMMARY

This chapter is on both sport heroes and celebrities, but a large part of the chapter is devoted to discussion on sport celebrities. Importantly, it clarifies the difference between a sport hero and a sport celebrity. A hero is an athlete who performs an extraordinary feat in a competitive environment, and the hero tag may either be temporary for a particular feat or long-term when the feat or similar ones are performed for a longer period of time. A sport celebrity does not need to accomplish an extraordinary feat. Instead, a celebrity is one who becomes famous for an act or is perceived to be famous for an attribute. An example of a famous athlete, who is not a hero or an extraordinary athlete, is also provided.

The chapter provides a five-step process for developing a sport hero. The process is based on Klapp's 1962 work, which identifies an athlete's life cycle from a young age of physical and athletic development through performing a heroic act, which the media widely publicizes, to the retirement period when the athlete is commemorated and a cult following is built and sustained around the athlete. There is also identification of key factors in sport celebrity, including marketing of the athlete and subsequent media hyping of the athlete, which builds a large public following for the athlete. The large following creates, with an abundance of media technologies, additional narratives that sustain the athlete's notoriety. The discussion recognizes the existence of at least three types of sport celebrities, which are ascribed, attributed, and achieved sport celebrity.

Other sections of the chapter identify benefits that accrue from an athlete who endorses a product. These benefits include attracting attention to the product, creating a positive evaluation of the product, polishing the product's image, assisting in establishing a product brand, helping overcome cultural barriers among consumers, and making a difference in the financial standing of a product's marketer. The chapter also recognizes that celebrity endorsement includes risks related to choice of celebrity, the product being endorsed by a particular celebrity, and financial-type risks like overvaluing the celebrity. Based on such risks, selection of a celebrity endorser becomes a major decision for marketers where factors like credibility, attractiveness, and the celebrity's Q-rating are considered.

The final part of the chapter provides examples of sport celebrities and products that they endorse. This gives the reader examples of product fit, issues of credibility, and other important factors that marketers consider before selecting sport celebrity endorsers. Athletes described in this section are Brian Lara, Li Na, Diego Maradona, Hines Ward, and Dennis Rodman. In Rodman's case, he provides an example of an anti-establishment celebrity.

DISCUSSION QUESTIONS

1. What key factors differentiate a sport hero from a sport celebrity? Provide examples of athletes that define each category.
2. Differentiate the process for developing a sport hero from the process for developing a sport celebrity.
3. What is an ascribed sport celebrity? How does an ascribed sport celebrity differ from an achieved sport celebrity?
4. How does a sport celebrity endorser help polish a product's image and establish a product's brand?
5. In which ways do sport celebrity endorsers help overcome cultural barriers in a product's marketing?
6. Identify various risks associated with using a sport celebrity product endorser.
7. What is Q-rating used in selecting a sport celebrity endorser?
8. What factors should a marketer consider before selecting a sport celebrity endorser for a product?

ACTIVITIES

1. Identify three athletes who are either heroes or celebrities or both. You must select at least one female and one male athlete. Then identify the risks associated with each selected athlete in terms of product endorsement. Write a report of your finding and present it to the class.
2. Identify at least five products that a selected sport celebrity endorses. Analyze each product in terms of its fit for the endorser. Write a report on your findings that includes whether each product is a fit or not.
3. Identify two famous athletes that are anti-establishment or socially non-conforming. Find out which types of products they endorse and analyze why they endorse those products. Submit a report of your analysis and findings to the class.

VIDEO RESOURCES

Linsanity (Documentary/1h 29min.). This is a story about Jeremy Lin, who was not expected to start for his professional basketball team, but starts because of injuries to key players and then takes the league by storm with spectacular displays that earn him celebrity status.

Anna Kournikova – Beyond the Glory (Documentary/40.43 min.). This a story of Anna Kournikova from her young age and the media focus on her physical attractiveness and then the celebrity status.

Ronaldo (Documentary/1h 32min.). Story about one of association football's greatest athletes.

Bad As I Wanna Be: The Dennis Rodman Story (Drama/2h). Biography of American basketball player Dennis Rodman.

Serena (Documentary/1h 30min.). This is an intimate story about the life of one of tennis's greatest players, Serena Williams.

RECOMMENDED WEB RESOURCES

Srivastava, R. (2011). Will multiple endorsements communication strategy by a celebrity work in educated consumer segment? *Innovative Marketing*, 7(2): 99–105. http://business perspectives.org/journals_free/im/2011/im_en_2011_02_Srivastava.pdf

Roll, M. (2010, October 2). Celebrity endorsement guide. www.brandingstrategyinsider.com/2010/10/celebrity-endorsement-guide.html#. WCIO0TLMxo4

Simmers, C., Damron-Martinez, D., & Haytko, D. (2009). Examining the effectiveness of athlete celebrity endorser characteristics and product brand type: The endorser sexpertise continuum. *Journal of Sport Administration & Supervision*, 1(1). http://quod.lib.umich.edu/j/jsas/6776111.0001.110/ – examining-the-effectiveness-of-athlete-celebrity-endorser?rgn=main;view=fulltext

UNICEF. (2007). Sport for development in Latin America and the Caribbean. www.unicef.org/lac/deporte_para_el_desarrollo_ing(1).pdf

REFERENCES

Andrews, J., & Shimp, T. (2012). (9th ed.). *Advertising promotion and other aspects of integrated marketing communications.* Independence, KY: Cengage Learning Custom Publishing.

Baksh, V. (2009, November/December). Brian Lara: Legend in his own lifetime. *Caribbean Beat.* http://caribbean-beat.com/

Belch, G., & Belch, M. (2001). (5th ed.). *Advertising and promotion: An integrated marketing communications perspective.* New York: McGraw-Hill.

Chambers, S. (2011, June 6). Li Na of China keeps feet on ground after historic French Open victory. *The Guardian.* www.theguardian.com/

Digance, J., & Toohey, K. (2011). Pilgrimage to fallen Gods from Olympia: The cult of sport celebrities. *Australian Religion Studies Review*, 24(3): 342–360.

Evert, C. (2013, April 18). The 2013 TIME 100 List – Li Na. *Time.* www.time100.time.com/

Jideaka, R. (2014, December 2). 2015 AFCON crash: Nike, Umbro, Puma reject Super Eagles. *Complete Sports.* www.completesportsnigeria.com/

Jun, J., & Lee, H. (2012). The globalization of sport and the mass-mediated identity of Hines Ward in South Korea. *Journal of Sport Management*, 28: 103–112.

Kizza, J. (2005). *Computer network security.* New York: Springer.

Klapp, O. (1962). *Heroes, villains and fools.* Englewood Cliffs, CA: Prentice-Hall.

Lee, N., Jackson, S., & Lee, K. (2007). South Korea's global hero: The Hiddink Syndrome and the rearticulation of national citizenship and identity. *Sociology of Sport Journal*, 24: 283–301.

McCormick, K. (n.d.). Athletes endorsements and their effects on consumers' attitudes and consumption. www.nsga.org/globalassets/management-conference-archives/2013/karla-mccormick.pdf

Miciak, A., & Shanklin, W. (1994). Choosing celebrity endorsers. *Marketing Management*, 3(3): 51–59.
PR Newswire. (2005, December 12). "Web users have spoken:. . ." http://www.prnewswire.com/
Rojek, C. (2001). Sports celebrity and the civilizing process. *Sport in Society*, 9(4): 674–690.
Shuart, J. (2003). *The media dichotomy of sport heroes and sport celebrities: Marketing of professional women's tennis players*. Paper presented at the Northeastern Recreation Research Symposium.
Simpson, J. (2016, September 26). 'Li Na dead 2016': Tennis player killed by Internet death hoax. *Mediamass*. http://en.mediamass.net/

CHAPTER 15

HEALTH, SPORT, AND COMMUNICATION

LEARNING OBJECTIVES

After reading this chapter, you should be able to do the following:

- Identify emerging health issues in various sports.
- Understand how sporting organizations communicate about athlete injuries to sport consumers.
- Understand how athletes report health issues and injuries.
- Become aware of injury issues, including musculoskeletal injuries, concussions, and mental illnesses, and how they are communicated in the media.
- Discuss issues surrounding media discourses of performance enhancement drugs.
- Understand how health epidemics like Ebola impact sport and how they are communicated to the larger public.

Sport communication about health issues is increasing, particularly in popular communication media. Ostensibly, the reason for this is sport consumers' need to know everything about sport, including the health of athletes. Obviously, with the rise of fantasy sport, which is discussed in Chapter 16, it makes logical sense to report an athlete's health status, which affects the outcome of sport competition. This interest in sport communication about health is reflected in this chapter's focus.

HEALTH ISSUES IN SPORT

Of course, there are numerous types of health issues that pertain to sport. For instance, competitive sport is frequently associated with injury issues such as brain injuries, ligament strains and damage, and musculoskeletal injuries, which are notable. There are health issues that do not result from the competitive field but are increasingly associated with sport participation. These include drug and substance abuse, mental illnesses, and the wider social health epidemics that affect sport and the larger population. Most of these health issues require interpersonal and group communication among athletes and their supervisors, and they are increasingly communicated to the wider publics and consumers.

This chapter discusses several health issues related to sport, particularly at the elite level. Especially important is examining how the athlete's health is communicated and discussing key health issues such as concussions, drug abuse, and the impact of epidemics.

SPORT ORGANIZATIONS AND COMMUNICATING ATHLETE HEALTH

Communicating about an athlete's health is not as simple as one may think. To disclose or not to disclose depends on what the health issue is and what interest the organization or the athlete may have on the matter. There are privacy concerns even though an athlete, at the elite level, is a public figure. For instance, some countries require a person's (including athletes) HIV status to remain confidential. Confidentiality is critical because revelation may create a climate where the athlete faces stigma or discrimination from others. Take the example of American basketball great Magic Johnson, who announced in a 1991 press conference that he had contracted HIV. Some of his fellow athletes made uncomplimentary remarks to the media regarding Magic's decision to continue playing. They were afraid of contracting AIDS. Those protests forced Magic to retire for four years. The following subsections examine the motivations of sporting organizations and athletes in communicating about health issues.

Sporting organizations

Sport organizations take into consideration various reasons before communicating about an athlete's health. These reasons include tactical issues, obsession with winning, promoting heroism culture, responding to consumer concerns, and covering up other decisions.

Coach Bill Belichick of the New England Patriots, an American gridiron football team, is regarded as a coach who uses injury communication to **achieve tactical goals**. Belichick is, perhaps, one of the game's best managers, but he is perceived as someone who will do anything to gain an advantage over his opponents. In American football, the league requires teams to announce the injury status of players prior to each game. Not doing so attracts a fine from the league. These injuries are graded in terms of the player's percentage likelihood of participating in an upcoming game. In Belichick's case, he takes advantage of this to send tactical messages to opponents. For instance, Florio (2016) writes: "there's a chance that the Patriots are deliberately overstating Gronkowski's health condition in an effort to confuse the Chiefs as they finalize a game plan for Saturday. . . . It causes the Chiefs to assume that they'll see an impaired Gronkowski when in fact he'll be fine" (para. 5 & 7).

Teams also use persuasive communication to get a player to play while injured. This occurs when the player is critical to the team's competitive status. Such persuasive communication takes place at the interpersonal communication level, where the coach persuades the player or the team's trainer makes an optimistic medical report about the player's readiness to participate. This issue has attracted negative responses from the media and sport consumers. Jacobs (2015) points out that pressure to play comes from more than just the coach or trainer. Instead, Jacobs cites pressure from fans, parents, and teammates. He argues: "the pressure that really impacts their (athletes') decision-making comes from 'others in the sport environment,' including family members who are cheering them on from afar" (para. 11).

The team's interest in communicating a player's health status is sometimes intended to communicate a **heroism culture** to the larger public. The American professional basketball league (the NBA) creates an injury narrative about Willis Reed of New York Knicks, who took a painkiller for a torn thigh muscle in order to play against the Los Angeles Lakers in a 1970 NBA final game. That narrative demonstrates the culture of heroism associated with athletes playing through poor health. However, Mullen (2014), citing a research study by Sanderson and Weathers, notes that such heroism culture, built up by the mass media, is gradually eroding. The media now support actions of athletes to sit out because of major injuries. However, this shift in media attitude and coverage is only at an early stage because some media still associate playing through poor health as a mark of toughness.

Teams also communicate the health status of athletes to **consumers** in order to assuage health concerns. This is particularly important when an athlete is injured in a competitive environment. This situation creates emotional concern for consumers that is only assuaged by timely information on the player's health status. Sometimes such information may not be good news, but it remains important that it is shared with consumers in a timely manner. For instance, the German Olympic Sports Confederation timely announced the death of its canoe slalom coach Stefan Henze, who died in a fatal car crash during the 2016 Rio Olympics. Henze was taken immediately to a hospital for emergency brain surgery after the crash but did not survive (Goldman, 2016). Though the incident occurred outside the competitive arena, fans learning about the crash and hearing about the surgery waited for the result. It is important news for them because many hoped that he would make it out alive.

Finally, a sporting organization may provide false information concerning a player's health in order to **detract attention** from a decision. This was the case when Nigeria's national football team coach, Sunday Oliseh, informed the media that he had substituted a player, Rabiu Ibrahim, because of an injury. Opara (2015) writes that: "Oliseh was not particularly pleased with midfielder, Rabiu Ibrahim, who came in as a substitute and was removed shortly after" (para. 5). However, other sources confirm that the player was fit, but the coach's communication to the media was intended to detract attention from his decision to bring in Rabiu as a substitute and shortly replace him afterwards, which would have led to media flak.

Athlete's motivation on health issues

Athletes have motivations for communicating a particular health status. Just like sporting organizations, much of the motivation is based on self-interest, such as a drive to participate in action during an important game, wishing to be heroic or tough, and a way to resist regulation by authority.

Ordinarily, most athletes **want to participate in sport** even during times of poor health. Thus, athletes generally have to be saved from themselves in such situations. Interpersonal sport communication between an athlete and his or her coach requires a medical third party to provide facts that allow the coach to make an informed decision instead of relying on an athlete's communication about his or her health status. De Lench (n.d.) notes that athletes underreport serious health issues such as concussion because they do not want to be removed from a game. In essence, the thrill of a game is overpowering and more alluring than the danger posed by concussion. Bellos (2002) reports on a mysterious story that surrounded the then world number-one soccer player, Ronaldo, who prior to the final of the 1998 FIFA World Cup final game was rushed to the hospital in an ambulance following a seizure in his hotel room. Bellos reports that "Forty minutes before the kick off he showed up with the all-clear, insisting he should play" (para. 16). Though there are many conspiracy theories, it is plausible that the seduction of the biggest game in the world was irresistible to Ronaldo, and the fact that he had just emerged from an emergency health treatment did not dissuade him.

Furthermore, athletes believe that they **communicate toughness** by playing through injuries. This is a problem reported by stakeholders and the media. Murray (2014) quotes one athlete as follows: " 'The only thought in my mind was getting in the game,' she told TODAY's Sheinelle Jones. And despite her injury, the field-hockey player kept playing. 'I thought I had to be tough. I thought I had to go back in because we were losing and I needed to support my team' " (para. 2). The athlete ended up suffering permanent brain injuries, but her story is not unique. The feeling by athletes that playing through injuries or poor health demonstrates toughness is widely reported and communicated through interpersonal, team-group, and mass media channels. This widely communicated culture forces other athletes to think along similar lines and it ends up, frequently, in adverse outcomes for the athlete.

> **REFLECTION**
>
> Recall a sport story on an athlete's health issue that you recently read. Think about how the health issue affected the team and its performance. Think about how it may have affected you and then its effects on the team's fans. Then think whether those effects may have impacted how the athlete and team managed the injury. Would you manage the injury the same way after reflecting on how others managed the injury and the story about it?

However, there are times where athletes **refuse to participate** in sport by faking or exaggerating injuries or ill health. This is also a goal-oriented decision by the athlete. In international soccer, incidents where players fake injuries to avoid playing are plentiful. For instance, it was widely reported that Brazil's Marcelo wrote to Brazilian football authorities, including his coach, claiming that he was injured and unavailable for selection against Scotland. Marcelo made the false claim in order to play for his Spanish club. In another case, Infante (2013) reports that "An Italian derby match was called off yesterday after players for visiting side Nocerina, claimed they had received death threats and faked injuries to get off the pitch. After just 21 minutes the third division side (was) reduced to six men causing the match to be abandoned" (para. 1 & 2).

COMMUNICATING CONCUSSIONS IN SPORT

As identified earlier, there are multiple health issues related to sport. While these issues affect athletes, some cases go beyond athletes to affect other sport stakeholders. This section focuses on such health issues (i.e. concussions in sport).

Concussions are "a type of traumatic brain injury (TBI) caused by a bump, blow, or jolt to the head that disrupts the way the cells in the brain normally work" (Samiento, Mitchko, Klein, & Wong, 2010, p. 112). When one experiences concussion, he or she feels woozy, disoriented, and confused. Relief from concussion may take a few weeks or much longer. Dotson-Pierson (2017) points out that repeated blows to the head leads to chronic traumatic encephalopathy (CTE), which is a neurodegenerative disorder that adversely impacts the brain and leads to shortened attention spans and irrational behavior. Concussions occur in contact sport that include, but are not limited to, American gridiron football, rugby, hockey, soccer, boxing, ultimate fighting, and basketball, among several sports.

The dangers of concussions are large given various factors that impact the organization and athlete's motivations for communicating health issues discussed in previous sections. Recall the organization's quest to win and sometimes doing so at

Photo 15.1 A youth athlete winces with pain following an injury and is comforted by his coach.
Source: Dreamstime.com, reprinted with permission

all costs and its promotion of heroism culture and the athlete's motivation to play in games and feeling of toughness. Moreover, the mass media celebrate the heroism or "toughness" of an athlete who plays through an injury. All factors mentioned above mean that athletes who become concussed are encouraged to continue playing with dire consequences. In fact, a study by Samiento, Mitchko, Klein, and Wong (2010) shows that efforts by the Centers for Disease Control and Prevention (CDC) in the United States to stem the occurrence of concussion in high school sport faced barriers from factors identified earlier.

Changing the culture

Sport health communication has become a notable solution to the adverse impact of concussions in sport. It is very difficult to change the prevailing culture surrounding health issues in sport. Medical and academic scholars acknowledge the culture. Just like any other culture, it will take time to change widely adopted and maintained beliefs, values, and practices regarding concussion as well as other health issues in sport.

The CDC has created a toolkit communicating best and safe practices pertaining to concussions. These toolkits, which are free, are sent to coaches, sport administrators, parents, and athletes involved in youth and schools sport. The kit includes posters, clipboards, fact sheets, videos, and DVDs. The posters are placed in high-traffic areas for athletes so that they learn about concussions and what practices should take place when one feels concussed. Adler and Herring (2011) report that legislative action is necessary to support these communication efforts, and they note successful efforts to get state legislators to make enforceable regulations concerning concussion across the United States.

Communicating health information

Adler and Herring (2011) point to the importance of communication and legislation in helping to deal with problems that arise from concussion. They believe that communication is important if effective change is to occur. Beyond activities of the CDC in the United States, other institutions promote awareness of concussion and how best to deal with it. For instance, Asia rugby uses the World Rugby Concussion guidelines as the standard for its management of concussions in its sport. The guidelines include creating awareness that a player, who becomes concussed, must be removed from play and not return. Return of such athlete requires the athlete becoming symptom-free and a written note from a qualified healthcare professional.

The CDC concussion pack has also become available online, with an online education course for coaches and health care providers. Beyond the CDC and similar institutions all over the world, media reports on concussion issues, lectures, and public service announcements are used to communicate to athletes and others. Late in 2015, a movie on concussion was also released. All of those communicate sport health to consumers and participants.

McGeady (2015) points to the sharp increase in media communication about concussion in sport. He cites the "role of the media in helping shape public behavior and attitudes, drawing parallels with reporting on disease outbreaks" (para. 14). McGeady reports that media are the third-most important source of information about concussion for Irish school rugby players. The first two major sources are peers and school authorities. This recognizes the great importance of mass media in communicating sport health information that has a chance to positively influence action by affected athletes. That importance is further reflected in media articles about concussion that increased in February 2015 when "In those 28 days there were 444 articles with concussion references across all sports, with 266 of those having a rugby association" (McGeady, para. 4). In the past, the media focused concussion reports not on health dangers but on availability to the team of the concussed athlete. That has slowly changed as media have assumed the role of educator in creating awareness and helping locate information for those who may need it.

Obstacles to implementation

Unfortunately, despite increasing communication about the dangers of concussion, there remain obstacles. Some of those obstacles are identified in previous sections and traced back to sporting organizations, athletes, and mass media attitudes and actions. Some of those still remain. Webb (2014) argues that quicker diagnoses of concussion help in removing remaining obstacles that continue to put athletes in danger. At least, such diagnoses will remove the athlete's opinion from the decision to continue or not to continue playing after occurrence of what appears to be concussion. As pointed out already, an athlete's credibility and reliability in communicating his or her own true condition are doubtful because of interests in remaining in the game. Webb mentions:

> Among new proposals is a breath test, which successfully detects key chemicals in early laboratory trials. Produced by the damaged brain, these chemicals are known to indicate a brain injury when found in the blood stream. Further trials will establish whether the same markers can also be detected in athlete's breath, and whether such a breath test would pick up the kind of brain injuries commonly seen in sports like rugby, football and American football.
>
> (para. 3–5)

A quick diagnosis could help convince sport teams and athletes that a concussion diagnosis is accurate and prevent reliance on verbal responses from athletes and others on their own health status. Webb (2014) argues that the current psychological tests used for concussion tests in rugby are not reliable because athletes purposely underperform in the baseline test, allowing them to meet the baseline when actually concussed because one test is compared to the other in examining the presence of concussion. According to Webb (2014), recent concussion controversies linked to association football could be prevented using quicker and more scientific tests. One of those controversies occurred "during the World Cup (2014) in the summer, Alvaro Pereira of Uruguay was left unconscious following a collision with England's Raheem Sterling, but was able to carry on playing after remonstrating with doctors" (para. 17).

AMERICAN GRIDIRON FOOTBALL AND THE CASE OF CONCUSSION

Dr. Bennet Omalu, a pathologist, is well known to those who associate with American gridiron football based on his research. He found that gridiron footballers are dying of a new brain injury diagnosed as *Chronic Traumatic Encephalopathy* (CTE), which results from repeated blows to the head or concussions. Blows to the head occur in several sports, including gridiron football, boxing, wrestling, association football, ice hockey, and even baseball, which is usually considered a non-contact sport. Omalu says about his discovery of the disease: "When I read Mike Webster's (gridiron athlete) file before I began his autopsy, I knew he was more than a 50-year old heart attack victim. His file and the television reports of the death of the former Pittsburgh Steelers' center described a long, steep fall into bizarre behavior. I suspected he suffered from some sort of brain disorder."

Omalu examined Webster's brain and found something that is unique and unusual, and other doctors that he consulted confirmed his finding, prompting him to name the new disease CTE. There had been no previous findings of CTE, yet several athletes had possibly died of the disease. Certainly, concussions were known, and many athletes who died young exhibited similar bizarre behavior exhibited by Webster prior to his death. Furthermore, Omalu tested the brains of other athletes who died young and discovered injuries in their brain that are similar to those found in Webster's brain.

Yet, doctors associated with the American National Football League (NFL) resisted the findings. According to Omalu in an interview with CNN: "Some detractors, just like NFL doctors in the past, continue to deny that I discovered and named CTE. . . . If you continue to deny my work, people will continue to die." The NFL Commissioner, Roger Goodell, reacted to a movie on Dr. Omalu's findings by stating to the media: "We are not focused on a movie (film), we're focused on continuing to make progress. We have incredible progress that has been made, not only in rule changes, but also in what we saw today with materials and protection that will prevent these injuries from happening."

But Omalu's work, despite detractors, continues to spread forcing changes to many sports, including gridiron football where representatives of players force the League to change guidelines to practice routines and also amend rules of the game to reduce blows to the head area. The NFL agreed to pay $765 million to settle a lawsuit brought by thousands of players alleging that the league concealed information about head injuries that could protect players.

Concussion report in the league has risen, but experts are unsure whether it is because there are more concussions occurring or because athletes are more willing to report its occurrence. The traditional idea of the brave and heroic athlete who plays through injuries and concussion is experiencing a decline in both media commentary and athlete narratives. In fact, just before the start of the 2016/17 season, several players in the prime of their careers suddenly retired from the game, and observers associate the surprising decisions with concerns about concussion and CTE. It is believed that parents will increasingly prevent their children from participating in the sport at the youth level.

Though the professional league (NFL) has made changes to how gridiron football is played, there remain questions on whether it is willing to go all the way in making changes. For instance, Los Angeles Rams quarterback Case Keenum stayed in the game after being dazed from hitting his head on the turf late in a 2015 game. Then the league vetoed a plan to use part of its $30 million research grant for a study to diagnose CTE in the living human. Presently, diagnoses only occur after death. Yet, the grant was supposedly unrestricted when the NFL made the grant to the National Institutes of Health (NIH). The question is what does the NFL communicate by restricting actions to protect the health of its athletes?

Discussion questions

1. Why do you think the American gridiron football league (NFL) resisted adequate changes to protect the health of the league's athletes?
2. What may have been the motivation for athletes to underreport concussions in the past?
3. Are there ways to create more awareness of concussion in the future? Provide examples.
4. Do you believe the NFL runs a risk of consumers losing interest in the sport if the NFL supports concussion prevention or research? Would it discourage people from participating in the sport? If such a risk exists, are there ways that the NFL may ameliorate such risk?
5. What should be the media's role in sport communication? Consider that gridiron football generates massive revenue for the media via advertising opportunities.

MEDIA AND DRUG ABUSE IN SPORT

Drug and substance abuse are health areas where sport communication, particularly at the mass media level, has been prevalent. It is not easy to understand what constitutes drug abuse in sport, at least from the viewpoint of the larger public. There are many drugs that the general public uses but are not permitted for use by athletes. Some of these are drugs that the public may use for relief from a common cold, but they contain banned substances and athletes are banned from using them when participating in sport. A case in point is Canada's rower Silken Laumann, who failed a drug test in 1995 at the Pan American Games. Laumann had a cold and called her doctor for advice on what medication to take. The doctor recommended Benadryl, noting that it does not contain banned substances such as pseudoephedrine, which stimulates the body in much the same way as adrenaline and, thus, is a performance enhancement drug. Laumann trusted the doctor but inadvertently bought Benadryl Decongestant Allergy, which is different from regular Benadryl. The decongestant contains the banned ephedrine. Shortly after, Laumann failed the drug test and was stripped of her medal. Though Laumann was eventually exonerated for the mistake, careful communication with the doctor is advised. An athlete who is not careful checking with a team doctor before using a drug that is widely consumed by the public may find him or herself suspended from sport participation, and the story would be in the mass media reporting that the athlete failed a drug test.

Drugs usually prohibited in sport are in two categories. The first category contains drugs that enhance an athlete's performance. Those are banned in order to ensure that there is fairness during competition and that no one has an unfair advantage over the other. The second category contains illegal and prohibited drugs that are also prohibited in the general society. These drugs include cocaine, marijuana, heroin, and other recreational drugs. Most of the recreational drugs inhibit motor performance and disadvantage the athlete.

Communicating prevention

Communication is central to attempts to educate athletes about drug use and to prevent drug use among athletes. This communication takes place at interpersonal levels between sport officials and athletes and at the mass media level through distribution of information via fact sheets, other literature, and other means.

Anshel (1991) points to low success in change after attempts to educate athletes. In fact, Anshel notes that change occurred only among 5% of athletes who went through widely organized educational group sessions. Anshel notes that despite education and an increase in awareness and knowledge about drug use, the athletes' attitude or behavior is rarely affected. In a sense, athletes become more informed about drug use and its consequences but rarely act on that information.

What is clear, as it turns out, is that communication about drug use in sport requires acknowledgment of best practices. These practices include that communication on drug use should take place at an interpersonal level rather than in group or mass contexts. The coach-athlete communication or parent-athlete communication mentioned in a previous chapter are examples of interpersonal contexts that are effective. The athlete perceives the coach or parent as credible or a person who has interest in the athlete's well-being. Anshel notes that at the cognitive level, the coach, parent, or retired athlete should communicate personal concern for the athlete, build the athlete's self-esteem, discuss ethical issues, develop coping strategies, and provide a trusted communication outlet for the athlete. At the behavioral level, he cites structuring of free time to avoid boredom, jointly developing and implementing a plan of action, and implementing unannounced drug testing.

EPIDEMICS AND SPORT COMMUNICATION

Health issues such as concussion and drug abuse affect individual athletes, but they rarely reach epidemic proportions except when there is no regulation to curtail them. However, contagious diseases that break out in certain geographic areas around the world may spread in epidemic proportions and threaten entire populations that include athletes and sporting teams. These outbreaks affect competitions and become a topic for sport communication. In recent times, two such outbreaks created panic in several countries and the world of sport. One was the Ebola epidemic that began in 2013 in Guinea and lasted for a few years. The second was the Zika virus, which began in Brazil in 2016 and lasted for a shorter time period. On each occasion, the sport world was affected, and those epidemics became major topics for sport communication all over the world. In this section, the focus is on the Ebola epidemic. The section describes the epidemic and decisions made by sporting authorities and the communication that ensured.

Ebola is a deadly virus that kills more than 80% of people who contract it. It causes high fever, nausea, and pain before killing the carrier. It is believed that the disease only affected animals in the forest, killing several species such as rodents, bats, birds, and primates for centuries. However, the first human case occurred in 1976 in the Democratic Republic of the Congo when the victim came into contact with fluid deposited by an infected animal. It spread to other humans before it was curtailed. In 2013, the disease broke out in Guinea near the border with both Sierra Leone and Liberia. It spread quickly, killing hundreds of people who came into contact with the disease before medical help from all parts of the world arrived to stop its spread. Cases that appeared in other countries such as Nigeria were quickly curtailed. It was the largest Ebola outbreak, among human populations, ever.

Decisions by sport administrators and issues of health safety

Sport administrators participated in communicating about Ebola and advising on measures. In affected countries, for instance, sporting competition was temporarily suspended along with schooling. This reduced human contact and slowed the spread of Ebola among the population. At the continental level, an organization like the Confederation for African Football (CAF) banned travel to and from its member states into affected countries for competition and ordered affected countries to host home games in unaffected countries. Morocco took a unilateral action by withdrawing from hosting the important Cup for African Nations citing fear of Ebola-carrying fans traveling into Morocco. Morocco's decision was baffling considering that it allowed the Guinean team (from an affected country) to train and play games in Morocco. The CAF promptly suspended Morocco for such action (Baxter, 2014; Longman, 2014).

FIFA helped in several other ways as well. It dispatched a team of 11 of the world's best soccer players to communicate health messages with the slogan "Together, we can beat Ebola" recommended by medical specialists from Africa, the World Bank, and the World Health Organization. These athletes are globally known and include Cristiano Ronaldo of Real Madrid, Neymar of Brazil and Barcelona, Mikel Obi of Nigeria and Chelsea, and Didier Drogba of the Ivory Coast and Chelsea. These are familiar faces known even in remote areas of Africa and are likeable and credible.

Mindful communication and culture

While organizations like the CAF and FIFA were focused on positive communication around creating awareness, prevention, and safety, other types of communication were negative. Longman (2014), points out that rumors and fears surrounding Ebola led to negative reactions to teams and athletes from countries affected by Ebola. Some teams like the Seychelles Islands forfeited a match rather than play against Sierra Leone. European clubs were hesitant about releasing African players for national team competitions in Africa because of fear that they may contract the disease and spread it upon return. Longman (2014) wrote about the Sierra Leone team that was in Cameroon for a competition:

> Fans taunt them with chants of 'Ebola.' Some opponents have hesitated to shake their hands or engage in the traditional swapping of jerseys. Humiliating medical screenings have become routine. And in Cameroon, when the players on Sierra Leone's exiled national soccer team checked into their hotel . . . some guests grew alarmed. . . . The Leone Stars (the team's nickname) then moved to a newly built hotel where they remain the only occupants.
>
> (para. 1–3)

Sonke and Pesata (2014) studied communication strategies that worked in helping stem the spread of Ebola in West Africa and note that the most important aspect is that the communication message must be multimedia, culturally appropriate, and memorable in order to create change in beliefs and behavior. The culturally appropriate media included folk music, drama, and storytelling. There was also the use of short films to demonstrate effective behavior in countering Ebola.

CHAPTER SUMMARY

There are numerous health issues related to sport, and this chapter discusses health communication in the field of sport. Athletes, coaches, teams, media, and the public are involved in communicating about those health issues. The chapter not only deals with illness or injury-related issues, but it also addresses drug and substance abuse in sport.

One of the issues is the balancing required in maintaining health confidentiality versus the public's right to know since athletes are considered public figures. This balancing requirement is part of complex processes that affect sport organizations in making decisions on how best to manage communication of an athlete's health status. A section of the chapter investigates how an organization attempts to communicate an athlete's heroism, using health to disguise performance or other decisions on a player's playing status, assuaging health concerns surrounding a particular player, and other related decisions. It also describes an athlete's motivation for disclosing or not disclosing his or her health status. That motivation includes a desire to play, communication of toughness, or refusing participation for a myriad of reasons.

The chapter also dedicates a section on concussion in sport, which is one of the increasingly important sport health issues. The chapter defines concussion and describes the changing culture around concussion. It points to increasing availability of information pertaining to concussion and media creating awareness of health concerns. However, it notes drawbacks to preventing concussion, which include athletes devising methods to beat concussion tests and teams attempting to keep top players on the athletic field despite the health consequences of playing with concussion.

The section on media and drug abuse in sport explains two types of drug abuses in sport. One is the use of drugs to enhance an athlete's performance, creating unfair advantage in competition. The second is concern over the use of socially illegal and prohibited drugs. Interpersonal communication such as athlete-coach or athlete-parent is more effective, compared to small group or team communication, in preventing these types of drug and substance abuse.

The final section in the chapter is on health epidemics and sport communication. Two examples of recent global sport health epidemics – Zika virus and Ebola – are cited as examples. The section elaborates on an Ebola outbreak in West Africa in 2014, demonstrating actions taken by international football organizations and states in combatting Ebola. It also points to misunderstanding within sporting organizations, countries, and sport fans regarding the epidemics and shows how mindful and culturally appropriate communication is effective in curbing the spread of a health epidemic.

DISCUSSION QUESTIONS

1 How are motivations of athletes and sporting organizations related in terms of managing athlete injuries?
2 What does it mean when one claims that an athlete's motivation to underreport injury is because of a need to communicate toughness?
3 Is concussion a health issue that cuts across all sports? If not, in which ones does the health concern occur and why? If yes, then explain how and why.
4 Why is culture changing in communicating concussions in sport?
5 Are athletic organizations concerned about types of drug abuses in sport? Why?
6 Why is interpersonal communication more effective in preventing drug abuse in sport compared to use of small group communication?
7 What makes communication about a health epidemic in sport become culturally appropriate? Why is it important that it is culturally appropriate?

ACTIVITIES

1. Russia faced the prospects of sanctions prior to the 2016 Olympic Games because of an institutionally abetted drug abuse system in sport. Examine what really happened with Russian sport that led to possibilities of Olympic sanctions and what eventually occurred. Write a report and present it in class.
2. Review how Western media reported the Zika virus epidemic in Brazil and athlete responses to the reported Zika outbreak. How were athletes persuaded to participate at the 2016 Olympic Games? Write a report based on your findings.
3. Research a recent injury sustained by a major player in an elite sport team in your city or a close-by city. What type of injury was it? Was it disclosed by the club and on a timely basis? Why? What may be motivations that affected the injury's management? Write a report.
4. Review reports of drug test failures among athletes at a recent Olympic Games. Which of these tests are based on drugs that enhance performance and which are based on illegal and prohibited drugs? Consider how they are each communicated and the punishments. Write a report.

VIDEO RESOURCES

11 Against Ebola Video (YouTube/FIFATV 2.28 mins.) This is a brief video of a public service from 11 selected top association football players who speak on Ebola.

Concussion (Film/2h 3min.). Film on how a pathologist, Dr. Bennet Omalu, discovers CTE occurring after repeated concussions in American gridiron football.

Storytelling and Health Communication. (YouTube/29.46mins.). Storytelling in Africa regarding health communication.

Concussion Research at UBC: Sports and Head Trauma (YouTube/7.09 mins.). This is a video about a professional American hockey player who ended his career after repeated head trauma.

RECOMMENDED WEB RESOURCES

National Institute of Arthritis and Musculoskeletal and Skin Diseases (NIH). Sport injuries. www.niams.nih.gov/Health_Info/Sports_Injuries/default.asp

Prybicien, M. (2013, July 26). Communication, common sense key to preventing youth sports injuries. *Sport Safety International.* www.sportsafetyinternational.org/ communication-common-sense-key-to-preventing-youth-sports-injuries/

UNICEF. (2015, December 28). Ebola and Communication for Development (C4D). www.unicef.org/cbsc/index_73157.html

REFERENCES

Adler, R., & Herring, S. (2011). Changing the culture of concussion: Education meets legislation. *The American Academy of Physical Medicine and Rehabilitation*, 3: 468–470.

Anshel, M. (1991). Cognitive-behavioral strategies for combating drug abuse in sport: Implications for coaches and sport psychology consultants. *The Sport Psychologist*, 5: 152–166.

Baxter, K. (2014, November 22). Ebola also affects soccer's Africa Cup of Nations. *Los Angeles Times*. www.latimes.com/

Bellos, A. (2002, June 28). The mystery of Paris that refuses to go away. *The Guardian*. www.theguardian.com/

De Lench, B. (n.d.). Athletes' resistance to self-reporting of concussion continues despite increased education. *MomsTeam*. www.momsteam.com/

Dotson-Pierson, C. (2017). *'Do you know where you are?': Concussions, the emerging public health crisis and why media advocacy is needed*. Dissertation for the degree of doctor of philosophy at Howard University, Washington, DC.

Florio, M. (2016, January 15). Are Patriots deliberately overstating Gronkowski's injuries? *Profootballtalk*. http://profootballtalk.nbcsports.com/

Goldman, J. (2016, August 16). Germany's Olympic canoe coach dies following fatal car crash in Rio. http://metro.co.uk/

Infante, F. (2013, November 11). Italian football team 'fakes' injuries to halt match after receiving death threats from own fans. *Daily Mail*. www.dailymail.co.uk/

Jacobs, T. (2015, April 23). Athletes report pressure to keep playing after a head injury. https://psmag.com/

Longman, J. (2014, October 13). Sierra Leone's soccer team struggles with stigma over Ebola outbreak. *International New York Times*. www.nytimes.com/

McGeady, A. (2015, June 23). Andy McGeady: Concussion debate needs media to generate awareness. *The Irish Times*. www.irishtimes.com/

Mullen, B. (2014, May 30). Hero or sissy? Study explores perception of injured athletes. *The Newsstand*. http://newsstand.clemson.edu/

Murray, E. (2014, November 8). Teens playing through pain, not taking sports injuries seriously, says study. *TODAY*. www.today.com/

Opara, C. (2015, November 15). We now know players fit for Eagles, says Oliseh. *The Guardian*. http://guardian.ng/sport/

Samiento, K., Mitchko, J., Klein, C., & Wong, S. (2010). Evaluation of the Centers for Disease Control and Prevention's concussion initiative for high school coaches: 'Heads Up: Concussion in High School Sports.' *Journal of School Health*, 80(3): 112–118.

Sonke, J., & Pesata, V. (2014). The arts and health messaging: Exploring the evidence and lessons from the 20–14 Ebola Outbreak. http://oucomes.bmj.com/

Webb, J. (2014, September 11). Sports concussion 'breathalyser' proposed. *BBC News*. www.bbc.com/news/

CHAPTER 16

SPORT FICTION, FANTASY, AND VIDEO GAMES

> **LEARNING OBJECTIVES**
>
> After reading this chapter, you should be able to do the following:
>
> - Know the differences between fantasy sport and sport video games (SVGs).
> - Understand what fantasy sport is and how it demonstrates fandom.
> - Be aware of motivations to participate in fantasy sport.
> - Describe fantasy sport communities.
> - Identify SVGs and their impact on sport today and prospects for the future.
> - Be aware of motivations to participate in SVGs.
> - Describe SVG communities.
> - Understand the social impact of both fantasy sport and SVGs.

INTRODUCTION

Statistics demonstrate the importance of both fantasy sport and sport video games (SVGs). Gillies (2016) claims that $26 billion changed hands in the fantasy sport industry in the United States within one year (para. 3). Casselman (2015) reports that eSport worldwide, or sport video games (SVGs), were played by 205 million people in 2014 and are growing by 21% annually. Growth in the two areas threatens to outstrip growth in real sport within a few years. This development means that neither fantasy sport nor SVGs can be ignored in a discussion of sport communication. Therefore, this chapter focuses attention on both.

FANTASY SPORT

Fantasy sport is largely played online in today's world. In the United States, the Unlawful Internet Gambling Enforcement Act of 2006 defines fantasy sport as a game of skill, differentiating it from gambling. It requires analysis of information and statistics that take into account various factors before making decisions. Fantasy sport is a make-believe game where participants assemble and manage imaginary sport teams of real professional athletes and compete against each other based on points allocated for performances of real-world athletes. This competition takes place during professional sport when the real athletes are in action and their performances can be tracked.

Montague (2010) points to the rapid growth of fantasy sport by noting that the English Premier League fantasy game is played in more than 200 different territories in the world. Sites like Oulala.com advertise to attract participants who play English Premier League fantasy for money. Heitner (2015) reports that the sport has grown at a 25% rate since 2011 with more than 50 million people playing fantasy sport in Canada and America. DraftKings, a fantasy sport company, has "spent more on television commercials than any other company in the U.S. in one week in September of 2015" (Heitner, 2015, para. 1). Along with venture capitalist contributions, media organizations pump in millions of dollars to support the industry because of its rapid growth. According to Heitner (2015), media companies such as Comcast, NBC Sports, Time Warner, and Fox Sports invest heavily in fantasy sport, which has increased revenue by about 10% annually. Furthermore, Gillies (2016) reports that: "Professional sports leagues, including the NFL, NBA, and Major League Baseball (all in America), have all invested in fantasy sports companies to some degree" (para. 15).

Fantasy sport began because of intrinsic human interest in fantasizing and/or playing in a world of make-believe. This is an interest that develops at a young age. For instance, children even before they walk are introduced to a world of make-believe with dolls and different types of toys. Beyond this, Disney theme parks, which make a huge amount of revenue on a daily basis, is built on a world of make-believe, offering people what they crave (i.e. to imagine and act on that imagination). Sport is no different. In sport, individuals adore sport stars and imagine themselves as those stars. Those are precursors for the start of fantasy sport. However, formal knowledge of the beginning of fantasy sport goes back to the early 1960s when friends in Oakland, California, United States developed a paper-based competition among themselves using results and statistics from professional American gridiron football.

However, the current development of fantasy sport as a major revenue-earning activity is made possible with the technological development of the Internet connecting people who live far from each other in real time. This overcomes geographic limitations that existed previously for participants in fantasy sport.

FANTASY SPORT AS COMPETITIVE FANDOM

Martin (2013) equates fantasy sport with competitive fandom, and the analogy is accurate. Fans are no longer restricted to merely attending a sporting event as observers. Instead, they are active participants in the sport that they love. One way of becoming an active participant is through fantasy sport. Playing sport video games is another way, but SVGs are discussed in other sections of this chapter. Fantasy sport not only offers active participation; it offers competitive participation. By competitive participation, one refers to an environment where fans compete against each other and there are winners and losers. In certain leagues, only those who rank high in their fantasy leagues continue participation during the playoffs. In essence, fantasy sport mirrors real professional sport leagues with a regular as well as playoff schedule.

How new media help growth

New technologies and their platforms, such as Twitter, blogs, Facebook, and mobile devices, provide context for the rapid growth of this competitive form of fandom. The media platforms provide opportunities for the competitive fan in several ways, including social interaction, meeting locations, context for demonstrable skill, individually searchable information, and access to experts.

Friends form a large number of fantasy sport leagues. The leagues, therefore, serve to maintain and extend relationships among friends through **social interaction** on a technological platform and outside of such platforms. The topics of discussion are not restricted to fantasy sport competition but extend to other topics that friends are likely to discuss. However, there are also much larger leagues that span a large number of people located in geographically diverse places. In such cases, most of the social interaction is on league activities.

Furthermore, electronic platforms provide a **meeting location** for competing fans who organize themselves into a fantasy sport league. Prior to the arrival of new technologies, a meeting place to calculate scores for the week was a physical location, perhaps a family home. With new media, the meeting location is now virtual and league activities also take place virtually. A virtual meeting does not have to be synchronous where all participants are connected at the same time. Instead, there are asynchronous meetings where each participant arrives at the virtual location when it is suitable for that individual.

Importantly, the virtual technological platform provides context for participants to **demonstrate their skill**. As mentioned earlier, fantasy sport is a skill-based activity and different from gambling, even though both activities share things in common. However, while gambling is based on the luck of a draw, fantasy sport requires analysis of information and statistics in order to make informed choices that change from week to week depending on real-world athletic changes that include injuries to athletes, suspension of athletes, weather information, and much more. Participants in fantasy sport, therefore, use the new media to demonstrate to other competitors the skill that they have in playing a make-believe managerial sport.

Individuals take advantage of new media platforms to search for **appropriate information** that helps them become successful playing fantasy sport. This information includes records of athletic performance, news about a team or athlete, and injury reports, among other types of relevant information. There is ample data on any sporting information needed to be successful in fantasy sport competition. Frequently, it is the ability to search and use relevant information that differentiates one fantasy sport participant from the next.

Finally, there are numerous fantasy **sport experts and analysts** online. Fantasy sport organizations and websites employ the services of experts who analyze a sport and provide solicited and unsolicited advice to participants regarding which players to own and which ones to line up on a particular match day. These experts consume media communication on the sport and apply the information in ways that are helpful to fantasy sport participants. Beyond experts, websites provide interactive polling and detailed statistical analysis. Increasingly, media organizations also participate in fantasy sport by providing information on fantasy sport leagues, interviewing experts, and hosting panel discussions on fantasy sport drafts.

MOTIVATION TO PARTICIPATE

Scholars study the motivations of participants in fantasy sport. In other words, what makes someone decide to be part of this world of make-believe instead of remaining in the role of a match day fan who goes to the stadium, pays a gate fee, and occupies a stadium seat to watch a sporting event? This section briefly discusses what scholars find about these individuals' motivations. The motivations include a search for entertainment, autonomy, relationship building and maintenance, addiction to the sport, excitement of sport imagination without huge emotional backlash, and self-esteem.

Billings, Butterworth, and Turman (2012) capture all of these motivations in their book titled *Communication and Sport: Surveying the Field*. In addition, other scholars confirm the existence of those motivations. Names of the motivations may change, but they are relatively similar motivations found by different scholars in the field.

Entertainment is, perhaps, a motivation that stands out. Individuals are not satisfied by the entertainment obtained from watching live sport, and they enhance this by not only supporting their real-world sport team but also by supporting players who are in their fantasy team. Billings, Butterworth, and Turman (2012) describe this enhanced enjoyment as consisting of arousal, entertainment, and amusement. They argue that fantasy sport "provides another reason to watch games with a much greater focus" (p. 279).

A strong motivation is also **autonomy** to control and manage a team even though such a team is only imaginary. Fans who seek autonomy in decision making feel that there is power in the imaginary establishment of their own team and managing it in competition against other persons. It increases excitement for them. Not only do they believe that they have the skill for selecting good players who can win, but they test that belief in competition against others.

A third motivator is that fantasy sport offers participants opportunities to build on established **relationships** with friends, establish new ones, and maintain old relationships. Certainly, fantasy sport provides additional topics of conversation and friendly banter. Of course, some play fantasy sport for money and in competition against people who are not friends. Thus, this motivator is not always applicable to all participants in fantasy sport.

Billings, Butterworth, and Turman (2012) also list **addiction** as a motivator by noting the following: "Obviously, (addiction) . . . is a motive for continued play rather than for initially deciding to become part of the fantasy sport community, but it is a growing phenomenon" (p. 279). It is unusual to mention addiction as motivation, but the authors make it clear that it is only a motivator after one is already involved in fantasy sport. That explanation is compelling and confirms why some people and municipalities claim that fantasy sport is gambling and that people become addicted to it.

Imagination in sport is exciting, and this chapter has shown how humans act out roles and imagine from childhood to adulthood. Sport has major stars who become constant in the national media, and people imagine being in those positions. Fantasy sport presents fans with the opportunity to imagine self-involvement in top-level athletics even when one is not an athlete. Moreover, managing an imagined team and participating in fantasy sport has less emotional cost compared to supporting real professional teams because fans realize that fantasy sport is not real.

Additionally, **self-esteem** is a motivation for people to get involved in fantasy sport. Those who participate are confident in their ability to select a winning sport team. Thus, they have a high esteem about themselves and their ability. Of course, this internal belief about oneself is further affirmed when participants become successful during the league season. Ultimately, fantasy sport makes participants feel good about themselves.

FANTASY SPORT COMMUNITIES

Several scholars break down fantasy sport communities into personality characteristics or by roles in fantasy sport leagues. Such methods of characterizing fantasy sport communities are helpful because they indicate categories in fantasy leagues that are not different from categories of other types of communities elsewhere in society. However, this section on fantasy sport communities focuses on analysis of fantasy wrestling, as described by Crystle Martin (2013), who investigated the phenomenon in a recent conference paper.

Martin describes fantasy wrestling as consisting of a mixture between text-based role-playing and fan-developed fiction surrounding the sport of professional wrestling. Martin focuses attention on a fantasy wrestling federation (FWF) that goes by the name *Over the Ropes* with memberships from all over the world, including North America, Europe, South America, and Asia. Participants are aged between 16 and 25.

Over the Ropes involves character creation, and extensive text is written describing wrestler character/personality and moves. Text is written on play cards coordinated by a booker. Some participants add videos, audio, and design the wrestler, to help in presenting the wrestler to the community. Martin adds:

> Players use a variety of source for images for their wrestlers, some use images of actual professional wrestlers as they are, others Photoshop images of actual wrestlers, and others yet use their WWE (World Wrestling Entertainment) videogame character creator to create their own unique image. Players can also design managers, interviewers, and referees who often play into storylines in WWE shows.
>
> (p. 3)

These fantasy wrestlers represent real-life professional wrestlers in both name and character. At the beginning of the season, the booker calls for entries and selects about 20 fantasy wrestlers who compete against each other during the season.

Contests are scheduled between various wrestlers on days of fantasy competition. Martin notes that creators with "the highest quality of conversation win matches and get booked for more prestigious matches going forward" (p. 3). Other members of *Over the Ropes* participate as the audience and interact with others on the wrestling discussion board.

As you can see with the example of fantasy wrestling, sport communication is central to fantasy competition that takes place. Written communication is central to character narrative created for each fantasy wrestler. Then the fantasy wrestling contests are based on the quality of conversation during the contest.

FANTASY, FANDOM, AND SPORT COMPETITION

Fantasy football (gridiron) is popular among Eric White's friends in his neighborhood. Most of his friends play fantasy football, and they are excited when the National Football League (NFL) comes around in America. Eric calls it "exciting times," and he loves to play in the fantasy league created by ESPN. He is in the same league with his closest friend, Byron Muster, and six other people that he does not know, nor has he ever met any of them. They all use pseudonyms to participate in the league run by ESPN.

These ten participants go through a draft as the NFL season begins. The draft involves each person picking a player from a list of real players who will participate in the NFL league of that season. They pick sequentially based on a random queue number assigned by the ESPN website. This year, Eric is picking number two and Byron picking eight. Each participant selects an NFL player that they believe will bring them the most points during each week of NFL games. They do this through 16 rounds of the draft. Each participant also picks an NFL team's defense and special team. After the draft, they each monitor what their selected player does during actual NFL game week when a participant must pick his or her best eight players to start for his or her team of that week.

On each game week, a participant is scheduled to play against another participant, and each team will complete 14 games (playing each other twice) in 14 weeks by the end of the season. A participant is declared to be the weekly winner if his or her selected set of players accrues more points (based on their real game performance) compared to the other participant's selected set of players.

On game week six, Eric finally is scheduled to play against Byron. He has done better than Byron in the league, winning four of his games, whereas Byron has only won two games. However, Byron tells Eric: "Man, you are only doing better because you were ahead of me in the draft and chose better players." Eric disagrees: "You forgot that I still did better last year when I was selecting last. Man, I just have better skills in picking players that produce." Byron shakes his head and states: "Well, we will find out how good you are this week without Aaron Rogers who is out injured." Aaron Rogers, the prolific quarterback of the Green Bay Packers, is out injured but Eric has replaced him in the lineup with a middling quarterback, Jay Cutler of the Chicago Bears. This type of banter by Eric and Byron can take place between participants in a text box created by ESPN for smack talk. ESPN provides a lot of information, including analysis of players, rankings, and projections. They also provide extra information for those who subscribe to more informed data.

Eric and Byron make it a habit to watch NFL games each week, cheering on their selected players who play for several teams, and they hope that each of them racks up a large number of points by their performance. For instance, if Cutler throws a touchdown this week, Eric gets four points, and if he throws a pass at least 25 yards, that is another point for Eric. Defensively, if his team gets an interception and a fumble recovery, each of those would be two points. There are numerous other ways that each participant gets points. This week, Eric is having a torrid time because his players are not producing, and he watches each of them in several games. "They are just messing up. . . . I wish

Rogers was available today. Byron, I see that you are surprisingly doing well with your guys," Eric added. Byron smiled, "I told you . . . chalk up the win this week for me. We've got the heart of champions, Boyyyy." Eric took it in stride. After all, he is still doing better and headed for the playoffs.

Discussion questions

1. What do you think motivates Eric and Byron to participate in fantasy football? Provide support for each motivation that you identify.
2. What role or roles do you think Eric and Byron assume in their fantasizing related to NFL football?
3. What does the host – ESPN – provide that helps participants improve their ability to participate effectively in the game?
4. Going by information from this case and the chapter information, in which ways does fantasy sport communication impact sport fans and the media? Provide examples to support your position.
5. Do you think that participating in fantasy NFL football has led Eric and Byron to focus on individual players instead of teams in the league? Support your position with case and chapter analysis.

SPORT VIDEO GAMES (SVGS)

A sport video game (SVG) is digitally based, simulates sport, and allows people to participate in the game using a controller. The game mimics real action in a particular sport, and names and characteristics of actual professional athletes are used. The videos include artistic impressions of the athletes. The game player is allowed to create his or her own digital character athlete and may also create his or her own team if needed. A player can control one character at a time and can play a remotely located competitor online. Furthermore, there can be as many as four game players in a two-team competition with two on each team. Professional athlete characters are also rated on various skills based on perception of their real-world performances.

The SVGs involve physical and tactical challenges that test the human player's ability. They come in different modes to compensate for the player's experience with the game, with the most experienced players more likely to use more advanced playing modes. Today's games feature artistic impressions that sometimes make it difficult to differentiate characters in the game from athletes participating in real live televised games.

SVGs evolved from tabletop games that include ice hockey and soccer, where athletic objects are fixed on a board with a ball and people played with the objects

Photo 16.1 Two friends, wearing American baseball team uniforms, go at it playing an SVG on a television monitor.

Source: Dreamstime.com, reprinted with permission

simulating a sport of interest. Today, such games have become SVGs played on electronic video platforms that include telephone screens or television monitors.

Importantly, SVGs are popular and form "more than 30% of all video game sales," according to Leonard (2003). Casselman (2015) shows that 74% of video gamers are 21 years or older. This is a surprising statistic that debunks the myth that gamers are children. The 74% includes females (38%) and parents (44%). Casselman also shows that 292 million people watched or played eSport in 2014, with most of them in Asia. ESport revenue rose to $463 million, according to Young (2016), who notes that "In South Korea, stadiums once used to host football matches at the 2002 FIFA World Cup are now frequently packed to capacity with eSport fans, looking on as a new generation of heroes wields keyboard and mouse (controllers)" (para. 6).

Differentiating SVGs from fantasy sport

SVGs differ from fantasy sport in various ways. There are at least six major differences between the two, discussed as follows.

SVGs allow the game player to become **directly involved in the digital playing** of the sport via simulation. The game player operates a game stick to remotely control action of his or her character on the digital monitor. Fantasy sport does not. Instead, the fantasy sport participant or player relies on the performance of real-world professional athletes in order to earn points that he or she uses to compete against other fantasy sport players.

In SVGs, an individual is able to **compete against** the computer if needed. In fantasy sport, at least two persons are required for competition to take place. In fact, it is preferred, in fantasy sport, to have multiple competitors who compete against each other in a league.

There is no **time or day restriction** for playing an SVG. On the other hand, fantasy sport is restricted to the season of an actual professional sport league because scores needed for competition are derived from the sport league competition.

Revenue sources are slightly different for both SVGs and fantasy sport. SVG revenue goes to sport video game makers who sell game consoles and the sticks needed to play the game. Also, the actual game DVDs bring in revenue. Additionally, advertisement inserted into the games or embedded in signages within the game bring in revenue to the game maker. For fantasy sport, revenue comes from multiple sources, including advertisements, league entry fees, and sponsorships.

The video game designer controls the rules of the game and the simulation. In fantasy sport, the individual creates the league and determines the rules for competition.

What do SVGs communicate?

SVGs not only allow people to play the role of an athlete, but they communicate various messages while doing so. Various communication scholars, like Leonard (2003), who study those messages mention statistics communicated through video game characters: "Indeed, over 80% of black characters appear as competitors within sport-oriented games. In addition, African-American characters are more likely to display aggressive behaviors in sports games (i.e., trash talking and pushing) than whites" (p. 2).

Though Leonard's work focuses on race/sport relations in America, it has implications for the rest of the world. Essentially, such statistics on SVGs reveal social stereotyping transferred to virtual reality. His work shows also the silencing of women conveyed in SVGs, where there are few female athletes. Leonard claims that "sports games legitimize stereotypical ideas about black athletic superiority and white intellectual abilities" (p. 6). Leonard goes on to state:

> Television commercials and print ads romanticize the crumbling urban spaces in which African-Americans play, creating demand for the sneakers that they wear. . . . Video game players become tourists in the virtual ghetto. On one level, they enjoy what they experience. On another level, they come to believe that social problems are the result of community or individual failure. . . . The relationship between the black community and the video game industry is one

of exploitation. Companies and players benefit through the consumption of inner-city communities, while poverty, unemployment, and police brutality run rampant.

(p. 7)

Though Leonard focuses on issues of race, SVGs communicate other messages to consumers, too. Among these is the ability of gamers to construct narratives through the characters that they create or use in the game that they play. Moreover, as Crawford and Rutter (2007) claim, "knowledge and information from digital gaming can be used to inform conversations or social interactions based around other subject matter" (p. 12). They give examples of how their interviewees point to the SVG *Championship Manager*, which provides them sport management information that they use in conversation about real management in sport.

Other types of sport communication appear in messages advertising products and services. Cianfrone, Zhang, Trail, and Lutz (2008) note that advertising in SVGs are popular because of SVGs' "authenticity and similarity to televised sporting events, made possible by licensing contracts with sport leagues. Sponsorships of SVGs, fulfilled as in-game advertisements, also enhance the authenticity of the video game because televised sporting events are generally littered with sponsors' logos and advertisements" (p. 196).

Sponsorship in SVGs takes many forms beyond in-game advertisements that pop up as the game is played. Other types of sponsorships include athlete or sport icon endorsement (e.g. *Brian Lara's Cricket* and *Madden NFL*) on screen signages around the video-designed stadium (logos of companies), product placements, transition advertisements (displayed for brief seconds transitioning from one level of the game to another), and then mention by voice of the video sport commentator. SVGs provide an advantage for sponsors because the advertisements repeatedly appear as long as the SVG is played, and a player cannot avoid them. These sponsorships help create awareness of products among video players.

Video companies derive sponsorship revenues in millions of dollars. Cianfrone, Zhang, Trail, and Lutz (2008), citing sources three to four years prior, report that "Electronic Arts (EA) Sports, which owns 70% of the market for SVGs, generally charges 10 cents per in-game sign, multiplied by the number of games sold. For EA Sports' *NASCAR 2005: Chase for the Cup*, five sponsors (Levi's, Mr. Clean, Old Spice, Wal-Mart, and Dodge) purchased a collective $1.5 million of in-game advertising" (p. 196).

MOTIVATION TO PLAY SVGS

Study of motivations for playing video games stretches back to 1984 when Selnow discovered motivators that include diversion, arousal, competition, challenge, social interaction, and fantasy (Sherry, Lucas, Greenberg, and Lachlan, 2006).

Scholars find that SVGs are used to **divert attention** from other issues that may be impacting the gamer's life. In essence, playing an SVG helps the gamer to cool off, relax, take a break, or escape from a stressful situation. This is an effective diversion because playing requires the gamer to focus on the game.

Arousal refers to an SVG's ability to stimulate emotions because of the fast action and the win-lose possibilities and, thus, players experience sudden highs and lows due to stimulation that takes place. Often, it appears gamers are on edge using sudden and quick movement of the game stick to drive the fast action and maintain control simultaneously.

As Sherry, Lucas, Greenberg, and Lachlan (2006) mention, **competition** is frequently a motivation to play the game, and it is not surprising. They state as follows: "Typically, competition response came from male respondents who spoke of competing for pride or money. Hence, video game competition served the function of dominance among males most often seen in sports" (p. 217).

Ordinarily, there is temptation to view challenge and competition to be one and the same. However, there is a difference. **Challenge** as a motivation is not necessarily to test oneself against the other. Instead, it is about testing one's skill in playing the game even when doing so alone. The gamer seeks advanced game level challenges in order to improve, to move to a higher level, and to overcome game-based difficulties.

Social interaction is another motivation that most gamers mention. This interaction may involve a friend who participates with the gamer or competes against and interacts with others. Playing games together helps develop relationships between friends.

Finally, **fantasy** is also a motivation to play SVGs. Here, gamers fantasize about being a prominent athlete and play the athlete's video character, or they may fantasize about being in a game against prominent athletes, and they achieve this by creating their own character and use this character in the game.

REFLECTION

Maybe you have participated in a sport video game (SVG) or you know someone who has. If you have, then recall the excitement that builds up when you are involved and, perhaps, your concentration as you compete against someone else or against several others. Those are things that motivate so many others to participate. If you have not been involved in playing an SVG before, ask a friend who has. Listen to how they feel about the excitement surrounding the game and ask them if that is what motivates them to play or if there are other motivators. Reflect on the answers and compare them to what you learned reading the chapter.

VIDEO GAME COMMUNITY: FIFA

One of the most popular SVGs is FIFA, which is a simulated association football video game that uses characters of true elite football players, major clubs, and top national teams. FIFA is produced by EA Sports, which has a new release each year. The most current release is FIFA 17, and it comes with several improvements. Apart from new technical improvements, new teams are added. In FIFA 17, for example, teams from the Japanese elite league have been added for the first time, and some elite African national teams are also newly added. Other interesting new features include a scuba-diving goal-scoring celebration and a narrative of a fictitious youngster, Alex Hunter, who attempts to make an English Premier League team. Essentially, this SVG creates a virtual version of real-world sport communication where the SVG includes not only the commentaries of the game but also a "televised" story of a young player.

Of course, apart from media communication aspects of the game, it provides the gamer with the ability to participate virtually in a professional game. Not only does it allow play in individual mode, where the individual can play against the electronic system, but it also allows a multiplayer mode where individuals can play against friends, in-person or via remote connections.

The game's popularity means that major media carry stories about the game. Professional athletes, whose look-alikes appear in SVGs, are also gamers, and they comment in the regular media about the game. Dowd (2016) reports Chelsea's Michy Batshuayi not being pleased with his rating for passing. Batshuayi had tweeted that he thought he deserved at least a 69 rating out of 100. The top-rated player in FIFA 17 is Real Madrid's Ronaldo at 94. Also, McKeegan (2016) reports that Manchester United's Fosu-Mensah tweeted complaining about his character avatar on FIFA 17. These reactions affirm the popularity of the SVG, even among elite athletes. Obviously, the SVG is a major topic of interpersonal and small group sport communication among both athletes and fans all over the world.

The future for SVGs is big, and increasingly it is competing with real elite sport. This competition can be assessed in terms of SVGs increasing revenue from different sources but also from their fan attraction. An earlier section of this chapter points to SVG competitions watched by fans that fill to capacity stadiums in Asia. This popularity also exists in locations outside of Asia. Ojinmah (2016) reports a nationwide SVG competition in Nigeria. Ojinmah writes as follows: "There are well over a hundred thousand gamers in Nigeria. . . . ProGamesHub will then launch an immense selection process worthy of Nigeria to identify the best players that in turn will face the best from other countries" (para. 5 & 9). Essentially, in a not-too-distant time in the future, there could be an SVG World Cup watched by millions of fans and covered by global media.

FANTASY SPORT AND SVGS: SOCIAL IMPACT

There are, of course, social impacts on fans and media from fantasy sport and SVGs. Additionally, they may also affect social attitudes and interactions and, in certain cases, teach stereotypes.

The role of sport fans is deeply affected. Traditionally, fans attend sporting events and restrict their role to supporting favorite teams. However, increased participation in fantasy sport and SVGs has expanded the role of sport fans to include vicarious participation in sport. In the case of fantasy sport, that role is reflected in responsibility for managing a fantasy team. In SVGs, fans can play the role of professional athlete and participate in games. This role was not previously possible for a sport fan.

The media's role is also affected by fantasy sport and SVGs. The media maintain the role of communicating sport, but how they do so is changed. In fantasy sport, for example, rather than merely covering and reporting a sporting event, the media may provide analysis and information pertaining to fantasy sport activities and hosting leagues. There are television shows, radio programming topics, websites, newspapers, and magazines dedicated to fantasy sport. Traditionally, the media retain the role of advertising goods and services within fantasy sport activities. In SVGs, media cover SVG competitions the way they cover traditional sporting events.

Social attitudes and interactions are also impacted by both SVGs and fantasy sport. For instance, sporting results were valued in the past, but that is changing as fantasy sport players turn attention to performances of individual players, which has become the most valued outcomes from a sporting contest. Furthermore, fantasy sport is increasingly significant in sport discussions and interactions.

As Leonard (2003) claims, SVGs can teach or reinforce social stereotypes. A previous section points to several stereotypes that SVGs teach, which include racial relationships and power, gender inequality, and other stereotypes.

CHAPTER SUMMARY

Fantasy sport and SVGs are increasingly popular, demonstrated in the large number of people participating globally and the number increasing significantly on a yearly basis. The chapter points to the differences between both fantasy sport and SVGs, noting critical factors that differentiate one from the other.

It first addresses fantasy sport as competitive fandom. A particular mention is how social media assist the growth of fantasy sport by providing virtual meeting locations, access to interaction, individually searchable information, and access to experts, among others. It also points to different factors motivating people to participate in fantasy sport. One notable mention is addiction, which is counter-intuitive. However, the mention of addiction is based on the fact that as soon as a person participates, he or she finds it difficult to leave participation and, thus, addiction becomes a motivator. The sections on fantasy sport end with a description of a fantasy wrestling community.

The sections on SVGs begin with a definition of what an SVG is and how SVGs grew out of traditional tabletop sport. It then mentions surprising statistics associated with SVGs, which include that more than 70% of the participants are 21 years and older and almost 40% of them are females. Additionally, SVGs or eSport is increasingly watched by thousands of people who crowd regular sport stadiums to watch eSport competitions. There are also motivations for participating in SVGs, including diverting attention from other things, seeking arousal and excitement, needing challenges, providing social interaction, and allowing participants to fantasize the role of athletes or sport managers. An example of a sport video game community is demonstrated through description of FIFA 17, which is an association football video game. The description shows that professional athletes participate in eSport and are sensitive to how their images are presented in digital form.

The final section of the chapter reviews the social impact of both SVGs and fantasy sport. It shows that these emerging sport types are expanding the role of fans from spectating to managing virtual teams and playing the role of athletes. They also expand the role of media coverage from covering real sport to covering eSport and fantasy sport, as well as providing information on both. Finally, this section notes that the fan focus on individual players is increasingly valued over teams.

DISCUSSION QUESTIONS

1 Why is it important to discuss fantasy sport and sport video games (SVGs) as critical aspects of sport communication?
2 What are differences between fantasy sport and SVGs? What do they share and what differentiates them from real sport?
3 What are motivations for participating in fantasy sport?
4 What are motivations for participating in SVGs?
5 What do you think is the reason that more than 70% of participants in eSport are 21 years and older?
6 What types of social stereotypes are communicated by eSport?
7 What are the social impacts of both fantasy sport and SVGs? Please discuss these impacts in the areas of sport fans and the media.

ACTIVITIES

1 Identify various advertisements of fantasy sport and sport video games (SVGs) in the media. What messages are provided by those advertisements? Categorize the messages into themes and present a PowerPoint report of your findings.
2 Working within a group, arrange an interview of five to ten friends who participate in either fantasy sport or SVGs. Find out why they participate and what

benefits they derive in doing so and how long they spend on each one on a weekly basis. Collate the results and write a report.
3   Carry out research on either fantasy sport or an SVG. The research should focus on history and revenue generation by fantasy sport or SVG industry and the future of either one. Write a three- to four-page report on your finding.

VIDEO RESOURCES

The Fantasy Sports Gamble (Frontline PBS film/54.11 mins.). This is a story about the industry and betting.
Perfect Line Up (Documentary/93 mins.). This is an insider view of the fantasy sport industry that includes history, perspectives from participants, and more.
E:60 – Evolution of Sports Video Games (YouTube/123.28 mins.).
FM17 Features of Football Manager 2017 (YouTube/31.42 mins.). Provides information of additions to the football manager video game for 2017.

RECOMMENDED WEB RESOURCES

Fantasy Sports Trade Association (FSTA). *Industry demographics.* http://fsta.org/research/industry-demographics/
Kang, J. (2016, January 6). How the daily fantasy sports industry turns fans into suckers. *The New York Times Magazine.* www.nytimes.com/2016/01/06/magazine/how-the-daily-fantasy-sports-industry-turns-fans-into-suckers.html
Campbell, C. (2013, July 12). *Competitive gaming recognized in U.S. as a pro sport.* www.polygon.com/2013/7/12/4518936/competitive-gaming-recognized-in-u-s-as-a-pro-sport
Paresh, D. (2016, August 18). Video games in the Olympics? E-sports industry will have to get past some hurdles. *Los Angeles Times.* www.latimes.com/business/technology/la-fi-tn-olympics-esports-20160811-snap-story.html

REFERENCES

Billings, A., Butterworth, M., & Turman, P. (2012). *Communication and sport: Surveying the field.* Los Angeles, CA: Sage Publications, Inc.
Casselman, B. (2015, May 22). Resistance is futile: eSports is massive . . . and growing. *ESPN.* www.espn.com/espn/story
Cianfrone, B., Zhang, J., Trail, G., & Lutz, R. (2008). Effectiveness of in-game advertisements in sport video games: An experimental inquiry on current gamers. *International Journal of Sport Communication*, 1: 195–218.
Crawford, G., & Rutter, J. (2007). Playing the game: Performance in digital game audiences. In Gray, J., Sandvoss, C., & Harrington, C. (Eds.), *Fandom: Identities and communities in a mediated world* (pp. 271–281). New York: New York University Press.
Dowd, A. (2016, Sep. 14). Chelsea's Michy Batshuayi can't believe his FIFA 17 rating, says it's 'so weak.' *Foxsports.com.* www.foxsports.com/soccer/
Gillies, T. (2016, Feb 7). Fantasy sports: The lucrative market that may be legal. *CNBC.* www.cnbc.com/
Heitner, D. (2015, September 16). The hyper growth of daily fantasy sports is going to change our culture and our laws. *Forbes.* www.forbes.com/

Leonard, D. (2003). 'Live in your world, play in ours': Race, video games, and consuming the other. *Studies in Media & Information Literacy Education*, 3(4): 1–9.

Martin, C. (2013). *Fantasy wrestling: A text-based RPG as a competitive fandom and place for learning*. Proceedings of DiGRA 2013 Conference: DeFragging Game studies.

McKeegan, A. (2016, September 16). Fifa 17 image 'angers' Manchester United player Timothy Fosu-Mensah. *Msn.com*. www.msn.com/

Montague, J. (2010, January 20). The rise and rise of fantasy sports. *CNN*. www.cnn.com/

Ojinmah, I. (2016, Sep. 30). ProGamesHub to make eSports football official. *Supersport.com*. Http://www. supersport.com/

Selnow, G. (1984). Playing videogames: The electronic friend. *Journal of Communication*, 34(2): 148–156.

Sherry, J., Lucas, K., Greenberg, B., & Lachlan, K. (2006). Video game uses and gratifications as predictors of use and game preference. In Bryant, J., & Vorderer, P. (Eds.), *Playing video games: Motives, responses, and consequences* (pp. 213–224). Mahwah, NJ: Lawrence Erlbaum.

Young, H. (2016, May 31). Seven-figure salaries, sold-out stadiums: Is pro video gaming a sport? *CNN*. http://edition.cnn.com/

CHAPTER 17

LEGAL AND ETHICAL ISSUES IN SPORT COMMUNICATION

> **LEARNING OBJECTIVES**
>
> After reading this chapter, you should be able to do the following:
>
> - Know definitions for legal and ethical issues in sport communication.
> - Understand rights and limits of media in sport.
> - Understand athletes' publicity rights.
> - Recognize differences between public and private figures.
> - Understand copyright and trademark issues in sport.
> - Understand different types of ethics.
> - Be aware of ethical issues in sport communication.

There are numerous activities in sport and communication that intersect with legal and ethical issues. **Legal** refers to actions related to or permitted by law or rules. **Ethics** refer to behaviors that are accepted as morally right or correct by a majority of those within the interested group. The two are distinctively different. While legal refers to actions that are stipulated in law and statute and are actionable in court, ethical issues are not. Ethics refer to opinions or perceptions of the community following an act. Thus, while a particular act or behavior may be deemed unethical, that same act or behavior may not be illegal.

From this definition, it should be clear that there are differences in what is legal and/or ethical in various countries of the world. As mentioned in previous chapters, cultures differ across the world. Those differences mean, for instance, that what is ethical in one place may not be ethical elsewhere. After all, ethics depend on values and practices of a certain locality, and those same values, ethics, and beliefs define culture. The same applies to laws, because localities make laws and, thus, there is expectation that they differ depending on locality.

The object of this chapter is to focus attention on legal matters pertaining to media rights in sport, the differentiation between public and private figures, the rights of sport organizers, rights of athletes, and trademark issues in sport. Additionally, the chapter investigates ethical issues in sport communication.

THE RIGHTS OF MEDIA IN SPORT

Previous chapters discuss media rights and the costs of those rights to cover different sporting events. The main focus in those chapters was how such rights impact sport revenue and how they provide access to a large number of consumers. In this chapter, the focus is different. This chapter looks at why media rights make legal sense and what those rights achieve.

Legal rights given to media to cover sport are based on the following considerations:

1. That media incur sunk costs in covering a sporting event.
2. That, in certain cases, public interest may trump the interest of a mass medium on issues of coverage rights.
3. That piracy may devalue the rights of media to cover a sporting event.

The public does not understand or grasp the cost that goes into media preparation to cover elite sporting events. These costs cover equipment, travel, accommodation, wages, and others. The cost is enormous. This explains the need for a legal basis to protect media rights from infringements and to give the media company or companies opportunities for profit making. The International Convention for the Protection of Performers, Producers of Phonograms and Broadcasting Organizations of 1961 grants broadcasters 20 years of exclusive rights that cover rebroadcasting, reproducing, recording, and communicating the product to consumers. The 1961 Convention makes exceptions that allow access to short excerpts of those products if used as part of reporting current events (e.g. news) and for educational and scientific uses.

In several countries, a single media organization is not allowed to secure exclusive rights for a major sporting event that is of public interest. Such events, for instance, include the FIFA World Cup and the Olympic Games. In essence, national laws can be used to determine, also, the extent of media rights in special circumstances. The European Commission applies public interest across Europe, but it is also important to note that countries such as France and the United Kingdom already had this restriction or limitation to exclusive rights. Chetcuti (2008) states that, in the case of the Commission: "These (major) events must be broadcast unencrypted even if exclusive rights are bought by pay-television stations" (p. 6).

As noted previously, the key issue regarding media rights revolves around a balance between allowing the media opportunity to make profit and the public's right to information on a significant sporting event. Where, for instance, it is judged that a sporting event does not have an overriding public interest, there remains a possibility that media rights may be devalued by unauthorized infringement on those rights. This occurs when competitors or persons pirate signals of a media company. Increasingly, this has become a problem, particularly on the Internet where persons or organizations stream sporting events without authorization.

THE LIMITS OF MEDIA

Besides issues that surround media rights, particularly in Europe, media content is another area with legal concerns. In the United States, for instance, there are limits to free speech in the media. In America, the media are granted the right of freedom of speech but not to the extent that they can use it to tarnish the image of persons. Similar laws exist in Europe, but the chance of legal success is different. In the UK, for instance, Shapiro (2015) points out that: "Britain does not have the same free speech protections as the United States. . . . English laws are much more favorable for someone looking to protect their reputation" (para. 4 & 10). These limits are in the area of defamatory comments in the media. Defamatory comments are those that are harmful and have the likelihood of tarnishing an individual's image. As you can image, such comments when consumed by third parties are likely to impact the party's view of the defamed individual to the extent that the individual's image becomes difficult to repair, let alone restore.

Defamation comes in two forms. One is *slander*, which is defamation that occurs from oral communication, and the other is *libel*, which is defamation that occurs through written communication.

Elements of defamation

Pederson, Miloch, and Laucella (2007) affirm that there are six elements that must be established in order to have a successful case in court. These elements are as follows: (a) that the comments or narrative are indeed defamatory; (b) that the defamatory statement clearly identifies the plaintiff; (c) that the statement is published and then accessible to third parties; (d) that the defamatory statements are published recklessly and negligently without recourse to checking the facts; (e) that the defamatory statements are indeed false; and (f) an establishment that personal harm occurs from such publication.

As you can see, winning a case of defamation is not easy, even in a case where a plaintiff establishes that the media content is defamatory or damaging to his or her image. If the statements are true, then the plaintiff is unlikely to win. In the case where the media make attempts to confirm the veracity of the story, the plaintiff is also unlikely to win.

However, as noted in previous parts of this section, these laws differ from country to country in terms of standards required to prove defamation. The elements identified are strictly elements within the United States. Chu (2015) reports a defamation case filed by the Hong Kong FA Vice-Chairman, Pui Kwan-kay, against a Chinese-language newspaper, *Ming Pao*. Pui argued that *Ming Pao* defamed him by claiming that Pui acted suspiciously by giving conflicting information regarding an allegedly fixed soccer match in 2009. Pui claimed that he lost HK $6 million in business opportunities because of *Ming Pao*'s editorial that doubted his administrative competency and his truthfulness. In the trial, a jury had found *Ming Pao* defamed Pui and ordered *Ming Pao* to pay Pui HK$500,000 in compensation. However, that judgment was overturned on appeal because the court found that *Ming Pao*'s report was in the public's interest. Chu (2015) reports that the Appeal Court concluded that: "*Ming Pao* has established a defence of public interest in the present case and the choice of wording and presentation of material was within [the bounds of] editorial judgment" (para. 3).

PUBLIC VS. PRIVATE FIGURES

Athletes have a harder time winning defamation cases in comparison to ordinary citizens of a country. The difference is that athletes are considered public figures and, thus, do not have the same privacy rights as other citizens. To be sure, not only athletes are considered public figures. The designation includes politicians, government officials, and other persons perceived as well known or prominent in their community.

Pederson, Miloch, and Laucella (2007) argue that: "to win a defamation claim, a public official must prove 'that the statement was made with actual malice.' Actual malice means reckless disregard for the truth, indicating that the information was published with no attempt to verify its truth" (p. 345). Thus, for public figures, like athletes, it is difficult to prove defamation in courts. Pederson, Miloch, and Laucella point out that athletes and top sport officials are public figures based on several factors, which include that they seek and consent to publicity and that they are perceived by consumers as inherently public. Additionally, they also claim that the label "public figure" is based on public interest in matters concerning athletes and top sporting officials. That public interest, therefore, justifies the right of the media to focus on them and their lives. This designation as public figures significantly narrows the privacy rights of athletes and top sport administrators.

RIGHTS OF SPORT ORGANIZERS

Sport organizers have legal rights to protect their interest in hosting sporting events. The rights, like media rights, are of great importance to ensure the viability of hosting sporting events. Those rights enable organizers to retain grounds for awarding media rights to their (organizer's) sporting event. Three key rights are important for organizers of sporting events: (a) property rights, (b) intellectual property rights, and (c) unfair competition laws.

Property rights, which also refer to "house rights," cover a dedicated venue or venues where the sporting event takes place. The sport organizer has ownership of those venues or, in most cases, exclusive rights to use those venues or locations. This legal coverage allows the sport organizer to determine who can have access to those locations and who to exclude. Ultimately, property rights allow the organizer to earn revenue during the hosting of a sporting event. This occurs because media or sponsors, who are allowed to access the location, are those who pay a fee. Those who do not are excluded. Furthermore, it allows the organizer to prohibit "unauthorized video and/or recording through mobile phones or other recording devices, and sometimes even flash photography, are explicitly forbidden" (Asser Institute, 2014, p. 27). But even with property rights, sport organizers find it difficult to control or secure a location for an event. There are sports, for instance, held outside a secured building and, therefore, it is difficult to control public access. These sports include marathon races, bicycle races, and automobile races that cover miles of territory and, therefore, provide ample opportunities for illegal coverage by people who illegally record the event. In such a case, property rights offer the sport organizer a legal remedy only after the fact.

The second category of rights is the **intellectual property rights** that exist in many countries to protect creative productions pertaining to sport. In Europe, for instance, the courts hold that broadcast production and recordings constitute intellectual property that is protected. However, the courts also make it clear that the sporting event cannot be classified as an intellectual property. This was the judgment of the Court of Justice of the European Union (CJEU) in a case that the Football Association Premier League (FAPL) of England brought to the court against broadcasters that provided decoder cards to pubs to access FAPL games that they were not meant to access. The CJEU (2011) wrote as follows:

> the Court observes that the FAPL cannot claim copyright in the Premier League matches themselves, as those sporting events cannot be considered to be an author's own intellectual creation and, therefore, to be "works" for the purpose of copyright in the European Union.
>
> (para. 6)

In essence, a sporting event is not a creative work.

Intellectual property, ordinarily, covers items such as copyright, trademarks, trade secrets, patents, and the like. The World Intellectual Property Organization (WIPO) provides the following reasons for existence of intellectual property rights:

> One is to give statutory expression to the moral and economic rights of creators in their creations and the rights of the public in access to those creations. The

second is to promote, as a deliberate act of government policy, creativity, and the dissemination and application of its results and to encourage fair trading which would contribute to economic and social development.

(WIPO, 2008, p. 3)

These intellectual property rights were already available in certain European countries, such as in France and Italy, but with the European Union those rights largely apply across Europe.

The third category of sport organizers' rights fall under **unfair competition laws**, which ensure equal grounds for competition in a free market. A major concern in this area is the misappropriation of the work of others in an unfair manner. Misappropriation occurs through taking advantage of other's trade value or goodwill by copying or counterfeiting products, goods, or ideas of others, which leads consumers to believe that those are owned by the wrong party. The Asser Institute (2014) provides an example of an organizer of amateur football games in Germany (WFV) suing a German website (Hartplatzhhelden) for posting video of its games on the latter's website. The Asser Institute (2014) notes that a German Court ruled that

> the videos cannot be considered an imitation of the live games since these are two different concepts and the public will not be confused as to the source of these services; . . . Interestingly, the Court also considered that football matches as such have no commercial value. The value lies in the ticket sale and the exploitation of audio-visual broadcasting rights. Both of these can be protected under the "house right" of the organisers.
>
> (p. 35)

ATHLETES AND RIGHTS

Athletes have also sought to establish value and protect that value through image rights or right to publicity. According to Pederson, Miloch, and Laucella (2007), **right of publicity** is defined as "the right of 'the public figure or the celebrity to control commercial value and exploitation of his (her) name or likeness'" (p. 349). Athletes seek the right to publicity because they realize the value of their image to the consumer from the athlete's sport performance and popularity that comes from that performance. To claim unlawful use of name and likeness, there are usually important elements that must be established. These include (a) that there is use of a **protected attribute**. This attribute is one protected by law, such as the person's name or likeness. (b) The use is for an **exploitative or commercial purpose**. The use of the person's likeness for scientific, educational, and or news reporting purpose does not meet this standard. (c) The use takes place **without the consent** or permission of the plaintiff.

The right of publicity provides athletes leverage to negotiate lucrative and exclusive contracts for the use of their image in communicating to the public. In many cases, this right provides extra remuneration and income for professional athletes. To protect this right, athletes may file cases against unauthorized use of their image through two types of claims: (a) invasion of privacy by misappropriating the athlete's image or likeness without authorization; and (b) violation of the athlete's right of publicity or essentially the athlete's right to make money from their own likeness or image.

However, it is important to note that there are limitations to athletes' claims to the right of publicity or right to privacy, and there are examples in both America and Europe as well as elsewhere. In America, for example, Pederson, Miloch, and Laucella (2007) cite a case between American gridiron football player Joe Montana and the *San Jose Mercury*, where the latter used photographs of the Super Bowl–winning San Francisco 49ers (Montana's team) in posters to commemorate the team's Super Bowl wins in a decade. Montana sued the newspaper claiming that his likeness had been used, without his consent, for commercial appropriation. According to Pederson, Miloch, and Laucella (2007), the court ruled in favor of the newspaper, noting that the paper's action was in the public interest and the newspaper had "a constitutional right to promote itself by reproducing news stories" (p. 350). The Asser Institute (2014) notes that in Europe, recent case law "in Germany and the Netherlands suggests, players or athletes can, however, not invoke their image rights to prohibit, or require remuneration for, audiovisual coverage of sport events in which they participate" (p. 2).

In essence, while athletes have secured rights to negotiate contracts of how their image and likeness can be communicated to the public, those rights are not absolute. In general, whether the case is in Europe, America, or elsewhere, the courts balance the public interest to know against the athlete's claims to privacy or claims to rights of publicity.

REFLECTION

Do you recall any legal cases involving a sport team or an athlete that were communicated in the media? If you do not recall any, it is time to ask a friend or family member. Was the case won by the sporting organization or by the athlete? What may have explained the outcome? Is there anything from your chapter reading that may help with explanation of the outcome?

COPYRIGHT AND TRADEMARK ISSUES

Pederson, Miloch, and Laucella (2007) define **trademark** as "any work, name, symbol, or device or combination thereof adopted and used by a manufacturer or merchant to identify goods and distinguish them from those manufactured or sold by others"

(p. 348). Invariably, sporting organizations and athletes use copyright and trademarks to protect their merchandise and logos. This has proven to be a valuable and generally effective way of protecting their brand identity from being stolen or diluted by others who seek to associate themselves illegally with the brand or create identity confusion in the minds of consumers. Pederson, Miloch, and Laucella (2007) point out, however, that a Fair Use Doctrine allows use of trademarked items by others as long as the use is for commenting on the item, or for educational or scientific purposes.

McKelvey and Moorman (2007) outline the course of action that are possible if there is a trademark violation. These courses of action are trademark infringement claim, trademark dilution claim, false designation of origin and/or false descriptions, and the misappropriation of goodwill claim.

The **infringement** of a registered trademark occurs when a non-owner decides to reproduce a trademark of another for the purposes of commerce or distribution in ways in which the use of the trademark is likely to cause confusion, deception, or mistakes on the part of consumers. McKelvey and Moorman (2007) point to eight factors critical in the illegal use of a trademark. These factors, according to McKelvey and Moorman, are "strength of plaintiff's mark, similarity of uses, proximity of the products, likelihood that the prior owner will bridge the gap (this refers to one of the manufacturers' expanding into the domain of the other), actual confusion, defendant's good or bad faith in using plaintiff's mark, quality of the junior user's product, and sophistication of consumers" (p. 85). These factors demonstrate the difficulty of proving trademark infringement in court. It is not simply a matter of a competitor copying another's trademark, but there has to be proof that such copying caused confusion among users of the product.

Trademark dilution is a claim indicating that a competitor's use of another's trademark adversely affects the quality of the trademark in the eyes of consumers. This could occur in two major ways. The first is *blurring*, where the competitor's use appears to extend the trademark beyond the scope of the product represented by the current trademark and in such a way that consumers are confused as to the scope of products represented by the trademark. The second is *tarnishment*, where the infringer's use denigrates the value of the trademark. McKelvey and Moorman provide an example of trademark dilution that uses tarnishment. They cite the United States Olympic Committee (USOC) filing a case against a Jamaican-based online sport betting company that used the trademarked word "Olympic" in advertising its sport betting services. Dilution is alleged because betting is considered unwholesome, and the sport betting company's use of "Olympic" creates the impression that its services are associated with the Olympic Games.

The **false designation of origin and false descriptions** provides legal force supporting litigation of trademark violation, involving the use of advertising and/or promotion to present false or misleading information associating a product with another product produced by the legal owner of a trademark. For instance, it is illegal and a trademark violation for a clothing merchandiser, who had not been permitted by Puma (an athletic manufacturer of athletic equipment and apparel), to promote his or her merchandise with the logo of Puma in order to drive sales.

Finally, McKelvey and Moorman (2007) cite **misappropriation of goodwill** as another course of action against a trademark violation. They note that use of this claim is grounded in state laws within the United States. This claim assumes that a trademark accumulates a measure of goodwill for the owner. This goodwill, as is usually the case, is built over a long period of time and, thus, has value. Therefore, if unauthorized persons or an organization uses the trademark, there is a tendency that they will unduly benefit from this accumulated goodwill and value without having paid the owner of the trademark a compensation. Thus, litigation is a way of ensuring fair compensation to the owner.

The special case of the Olympics

The Olympics, along with a couple of hundred organizations, have super trademark protection. This means that these organizations are allowed to trademark several words related to their interests, and none of these words may be used without compensating the organization. According to Mazumdar (2016), the Olympics has "more than 200 U.S. trademark registrations or pending registration applications. . . . The super-trademark rights extended to the USOC by the Ted Stevens Olympic and Amateur Sports Act of 1998, 36 U.S.C. §220501, give it leverage to seek higher sponsorship fees than it otherwise could" (para. 27 & 29).

The Olympics, in 2016, trademarked words that appear mundane such as "Road to Rio." Additionally, the Olympics Committee is aggressive in pursuing potential trademark violations, no matter how small they may be. Usually, a warning letter from the committee is enough to dissuade potential violators. For those who persist in violation, they may find themselves in court. In court, the Committee also has tremendous leverage because "unlike run-of-the-mill trademark owners, the USOC, under the Act (36 U.S.C.), isn't required to show that another entity's use of its trademark creates a likelihood of confusion on the part of consumers as to goods or services' sources, sponsorships or affiliations" (para. 31).

Trademark violations across international borders

Abel (1998) claims that the first trademark case on domain names involving organizations and courts in two different countries may have occurred when Prince Sports Group in the United States charged another company with a similar name, Prince PLC, over the use of prince.com as a domain name. The U.S. company is a manufacturer of tennis rackets and sporting goods, and the UK company (Prince PLC) is a computer service company. The U.S. company discovered that the domain name prince.com was already taken when it attempted to register it. The American company has several trademarks associated with its name in both the United States and the United Kingdom. Prince PLC, at the time, was not trademarked in the United Kingdom.

The U.S. company wrote to Prince PLC threatening litigation if it did not surrender the domain name and agree not to use the name "Prince" in any other domain registration in the future. According to Abel (1998), Prince PLC refused to comply and instead filed a civil action in a UK court. In response, Prince Sports Group filed a case in the United States. The United Kingdom was the first to rule on the case and stated that the threat of the U.S. company was not justified. Both parties "subsequently settled with Prince Sports Group dropping its U.S. lawsuit and Prince PLC retaining ownership of the domain (name)," according to Abel (p. 22).

ETHICAL ISSUES

Ethics was defined earlier in the chapter. This section focuses attention on broad types of ethics before providing examples of ethical issues in sport communication. The examples are drawn from cases that occur within sport communication.

Types of ethics

There are two broad types of ethics. All other types of ethics can be categorized under one or the other, as we shall see. The two are consequential ethics and non-consequential ethics.

NADAL AND DEFAMATION

There was a major newsbreak in April 2016 when leading tennis star Rafael Nadal of Spain filed a defamation lawsuit in a French court against former French Sports Minister Roselyne Bachelot. The case is scheduled for 2017. Nadal said: "I am tired about these things. I let it go a few times in the past. No more."

Bachelot had told French television Channel D8: "It is known that Rafael Nadal's injury, which forced him to convalesce for seven months, was really a positive doping control." Nadal claims that Bachelot's statement defamed him, and it was time to file a lawsuit. Nadal responded that he has not failed a drug test and asked the International Tennis Federation (ITF) to make public all his drug test records.

However, suspicions had long swirled around Nadal for various reasons. Bachelot's comment was part of an avalanche of responses after another tennis star, Maria Sharapova, announced in a press conference that she tested positive for use of performance-enhancing drugs (PEDs). Nadal was one of the athletes to denounce Maria, even though there had been rumors of his involvement in PEDs. The accusations against Nadal stem from his sudden departure from the 2012 Wimbledon. At the time, Nadal claimed that he was injured, but then he also opted out, surprisingly, from carrying his country's flag at that year's London Olympics. Opting out of the Olympics was suspicious because it occurred after the head of London Olympics declared that all athletes at the Games would face a drug test. Then Nadal did not request a protected ranking, which is available to athletes who are not competing because of long-term injury of at least six months, but the request requires verification of medical records to ascertain seriousness of the injury.

The reality, however, is that despite rumors and circumstantial support for such rumors, Nadal never failed a drug test, and Bachelot's claims are possibly based on rumors swirling around Nadal's seven months away from the sport. Did Nadal fail a drug test that the ATP was not willing to tell the public? Possibly, but there is no hard evidence. Rumors are that the ATP, in the past, hid positive test results to protect the sport's image. An example is methamphetamine use by Andre Agassi that later became public knowledge even though the ATP was mute about it.

Nadal has always responded to drug use accusations with statements like "comedy show that I do not take seriously" until Bachelot's accusation and, perhaps, because Bachelot was "Minister of a big country and a great country like France," according to Nadal. That much seems clear as Nadal reiterated: "I also wish to avoid any public figure from making insulting or false allegations against an athlete using the media, without any evidence or foundation and to go unpunished." Nadal has said that if he wins the case, he will donate the money to a nongovernmental organization or foundation in France.

Fortunately for Nadal, his case will be heard in a French court, where Bachelot has the burden of establishing her statements as facts. Nadal is not burdened with high thresholds required in an American court, where a defamed public figure must prove that the defamer's statement is made out of malice.

Discussion questions

1 What is meant by defamation and why is Rafael Nadal claiming that Bachelot's statements are defaming?
2 Is this a case of slander or libel? Why?
3 Usually, proving malice in a case of defamation requires that Rafael Nadal prove what about Bachelot's statement?
4 Why was Rafael Nadal concerned that the statement came from a public figure and not a private citizen? Provide support for your answer.
5 Why is Nadal fortunate that this case is before a French court instead of a court in America, for example? Please explain.

Consequential ethics are socially determined right and wrong based or dependent on outcomes of the action. In essence, an action is determined as ethical based on consequences of taking such an action. If the action, for example, results in what most people in that society consider good, then it is ethical. An example is telling a lie. Society may consider lying to save a life to be good. In such a situation, the person who tells such a lie to save a life is ethical.

On the other hand, a higher authority determines **non-consequential ethics**. This higher authority may come from religious teaching or a sense of duty. Thus, it is not determined by what most people within the community perceive as good. Instead, the ethical individual is bound by religious principles of what is right or wrong and not by what the public may consider right. Thus, if lying is considered a sin, then the individual cannot be ethical if they lie no matter the context for that lie.

Ethical issues in sport communication

This section provides two examples of ethical issues in sport. One example is from match-fixing incidences pertaining to South African football and the other pertains to a fake injury in a rugby game in Asia.

The *Southern African News* (2014) commented on a scourge of match-fixing incidences and corruption involving both match officials and players of South Africa that led to global investigation of the sport. The question is whether it is unethical practice when top sport officials are involved in fixing games marketed to people as authentic matches. In such a case, the public paid money and was deceived by some officials and players who are involved in fixing the results of those games. The article concludes that: "even the sponsors will also abandon the various sports codes as nobody (wants) to be associated with fake and tainted sports competitions whose results are predetermined by some underworld crime bosses" (para. 15).

A question of ethics also arose in a bizarre incidence in the quarterfinal of the European Rugby Heineken Cup in the United Kingdom in 2010 between Harlequins and Leinster. A substituted player cannot return to play except to replace a teammate who has a bleeding injury. In this case, however, Harlequins were down 5–6 and wanted to send in a specialist who was previously replaced. The specialist could only replace an injured player. A Harlequin player, Tom Williams, then faked injury and was seen to have removed a blood capsule from his sock, chewed on it, and as he left the field the blood oozed and opposing players knew it was faked and screamed about it. In the locker room, the team doctor met with Williams for treatment. Williams was, however, agitated that his deception was exposed. He persuaded the doctor to cut the inside of his lip, which the doctor proceeded to do. It was unethical for the team doctor to cut the player's lips as part of an elaborate deception scheme. Carter (2010) writes about the doctor: "She (doctor) admits actions likely to bring the medical profession into disrepute and dishonest conduct" (para. 4). The doctor was suspended, Williams was banned for a lengthy period, and the club's director of rugby, Dean Richards, resigned. It had been an elaborate and unethical scheme to deceive match officials and was unacceptable practice in the game.

CHAPTER SUMMARY

This chapter demonstrates the differences between legal and ethical issues. It also points out that each of these issues is different from one country to the other and from one culture to the next.

On legal matters, it begins with a discussion of media rights in sport and notes reasons why media rights are strongly protected. Among the reasons are sunk costs of media in covering sport and the need to allow room for media to make financial recovery of such costs. Nevertheless, it also notes that there are times when the public interest, particularly in significant sporting events, overrides media exclusivity rights. Furthermore, media communication has limitations, which come in the area of defamation laws. The chapter explains the difference between two types of defamation (i.e. slander and libel). An example of a sport defamation case is drawn from Hong Kong. An important issue in defamation cases is the difference between a private and public figure. For a public figure, like athletes, winning a defamation case is difficult because it requires proof of malice.

Besides the rights of media are the rights of the sport organizer. Again, these rights are protected for good reasons. In this case, the rights cover property (venue or house rights), intellectual property, and against unfair competition. Property rights allow the organizer to determine who can and who cannot access a defined area of the event. This enables advertising protection among others. In the case of intellectual property, protection comes in the areas of trademarks and copyrights, among other areas. However, the chapter makes it clear that these rights differ from one location or country to the other.

There are also rights of athletes covered in the chapter. These rights focus on image and right to publicity. Like other rights discussed in the chapter, athletes' rights are not absolute, and there is an example of an American gridiron athlete who lost an image protection case against a newspaper.

A section on copyright and trademark issues includes infringement, dilution, false designation of origin, and others. Furthermore, it provides an example of the Olympic Games, which has super-trademark protection for various reasons, including significant expenditure by those who sponsor such a mega event. This protection allows protection of words, however mundane, associated with the event. It also points out how Olympic officials are active enforcers of protection. Finally, on legal matters, the chapter provides an example of a trademark violation across international borders.

The section on ethical issues describes two general types of ethics, which are consequential and non-consequential ethics. Then it brings up issues of ethics in sport, with examples from South Africa and from the United Kingdom.

DISCUSSION QUESTIONS

1. What are major differences between ethical and legal issues in sport?
2. What are overriding reasons for granting rights to the mass media to cover sporting events? Why should those rights, in certain cases, supersede the rights of the public to access the sporting event through media of their choice?
3. What is the major difference between slander and libel? How do slander and libel balance media rights of free speech and rights of others not to be defamed?
4. How does one prove malice in a case of sport defamation? Why is it difficult to prove?
5. What is meant by unfair competition when one speaks of the rights of a sport organizer?
6. What is meant by a super-trademark protection? Is this type of protection granted only to the Olympic Games? Why is it necessary to grant such rights? Provide examples of what is covered in super-trademark rights?
7. How may an athlete's rights to image protection be limited? Provide examples and possible reasons for it.
8. What does ethical issue in sport mean? What is the difference between consequential and non-consequential ethics? Please provide examples of each type of ethics.

ACTIVITIES

1. Identify a recent sport defamation case reported in the media. Review the case as deeply as you can, bearing in mind what you have read in this chapter. Then write a paper that explains your understanding of the defamation case.
2. Examine a recent media sport rights contract detailed in the media. Identify key areas of the contract and analyze them. Write an analytical report of your findings in three to four pages.
3. There are numerous ethical issues across the sport world. Identify a recent case that occurred in your country. Write a report on the issue, making sure that you clarify why it should be considered an ethical issue, what was violated, and whether or not it was sanctioned.
4. As a group, explore recent violations of the Olympic Games' trademark reported in the media. Examine details of the case, including why it occurred and its eventual outcome. Analyze key elements and then write a report of no more than five pages.

VIDEO RESOURCES

Legal Autonomy of Sports Governing Bodies (Video/136.57 mins.). This video comes from the video conference of the Sports Law Conference 2016. www.lawinsport.com/features/videos/item/the-future-of-the-legal-autonomy-of-sport-session-3-legal-autonomy

Commercial Issues That National Governing Bodies of Sport Have to Consider (YouTube/13.21 mins.). The solicitor for Rugby Union speaks on commercial and legal issues.

Ethical Issues in Horse Racing (Episode 24/YouTube/58.48 mins.) This video is from the *Sports Ethicist*, and here it discusses ethical issues in horse racing.

Sports Rights and Broadcasting: Legal Analysis (YouTube/17.42 mins.). Provides history of media rights in sport in the United Kingdom.

RECOMMENDED WEB RESOURCES

Hanson, K., & Savage, M. What role does ethics play in sports? *Markkula Center for Applied Ethics*. www.scu.edu/ethics/focus-areas/more/resources/what-role-does-ethics-play-in-sports/

Website of the Sports Ethicist. https://sportsethicist.com/2012/08/19/sports-ethics-five-years-running/

Antitrust labor law issues in sports. *USLegal.com*. https://sportslaw.uslegal.com/antitrust-and-labor-law-issues-in-sports/

REFERENCES

Abel, S. (1998). *Trademark issues in cyberspace: The brave new frontier*. Mountain View, CA: Fenwick & West LLP.

Asser Institute Centre for International & European Law (2014). *Study on sports organisers' rights in the European Union: Final report*. Luxembourg: Publications Office of the European Union.

Carter, H. (2010, August 23). Bloodgate scandal doctor 'pressured into cutting rugby player's lip.' *The Guardian*. www.theguardian.com/uk/

Chetcuti, A. (2008). *The exploitation of football media rights in the EU: A competition law analysis*. Paper presented at the Institute of Computer and Communications Law Centre for Commercial Law Studies, Queens Mary University of London, UK.

Chu, J. (2015, November 15). Defamation ruling for Hong Kong Football Association against Ming Pao overturned. *South China Morning Post*. www.scmp.com/

Court of Justice of the European Union (CJEU). (2011, October 4). *Press release: Football Association Premier League and Others v QC Leisure and Others*. http://curia.europa.eu/jcms/

Mazumdar, A. (2016, July 25). For Olympics, much at stake in trademark enforcement. *Bloomberg BNA*. www.bna.com/

McKelvey, S., & Moorman, A. (2007). Bush-whacked: A legal analysis of the unauthorized use of sports organizations' intellectual property in political campaign advertising. *Journal of Sport Management*, 21: 79–102.

Pederson, P., Miloch, K., & Laucella, P. (2007). *Strategic sport communication*. Champaign, IL: Human Kinetics.

Shapiro, A. (2015, March 21). On libel and the law, U.S. and U.K. go separate ways. *NPR*. www.npr.org/

Southern African News. (2014, April 25). Ethics and integrity in sport. *The Southern Times*. http://southernafrican.news/

WIPO. (2008). (2nd ed.). *WIPO intellectual property handbook: Policy, law and use*. Geneva, Switzerland: WIPO.

PART V

MEASUREMENT AND RESEARCH IN SPORT

Source: Roxane Coche, reprinted with permission

CHAPTER 18

SPORT ANALYTICS

LEARNING OBJECTIVES

After reading this chapter, you should be able to do the following:

- Define analytics.
- Describe attributes of organizations focused on the use of analytics.
- Enumerate and describe benefits of analytics.
- Be aware of three areas of sport analytics used by sport managers.
- Understand how analytics help in media communications of sport.
- Describe the importance of sport analytics in secondary industries related to sport.

INTRODUCTION

Sport analytics emerged in recent years as a major interest area for improving sport business and performance operations. What is it? What does it refer to? Sport analytics is the use of statistical models on huge data to inform managers and decision makers on how to improve their products or services for competitive advantage. However, it is important to acknowledge that statistics have always been available and used in sport to seek improvement and, thus, the question becomes what is unique about sport analytics? There is a big difference between sport analytics and how statistics were used in sport. First, in sport analytics, there is a huge amount of data produced for analysis that was not available previously. Without such a huge amount of data, there will not be any meaningful sport analytics. Second, access to big data provides opportunities to develop statistical models that describe sporting situations and predict the future with a high level of accuracy.

The success of organizations that use sport analytics motivates others to follow despite some resistance in the sporting field. This creates employment opportunities for those interested in sport statistics and also encourages technological innovations. Importantly, as demand for human resources increases in the area, universities are offering courses and degrees in sport analytics. Reimer (2016) reports that Syracuse University in the United States became the first university to offer an undergraduate degree in sport analytics beginning August 2017. Students combine studies in the fields of mathematics, statistics, computer programming, sport, and communication. Reimer mentions that "the program will stress the importance of communication. . . . It's vital for students to be able to articulate these abstract concepts in a clear and concise manner" (para. 8).

ATTRIBUTES OF ORGANIZATIONS FOCUSED ON ANALYTICS

Sporting organizations that rely on analytics to improve their operations are increasing, and they are successful in what they do. For instance, teams like Athletic Club (AC) Milan in Italy is reputed for its Milan Laboratory, which analyzes a huge amount of data focusing on player health. Fawkes (2008), who critiqued the Milan Lab, acknowledged the following:

> the lab aims to reduce injuries by intricate analysis of each player, from the way they jump to the type of shoes and clothes they wear. Every detail makes a difference and according to an interview made in the *Financial Times* there has been a reduction of traumatic injuries by 90%.
>
> (para. 5)

Sporting organizations such as AC Milan have developed certain attributes that have made them effective in the use of analytics and communicating it for effectiveness. These attributes include accumulation of large data, formulation of organizational strategies based on the data, widespread use of modeling and optimization of data, investment in technology, having senior advocates for analytics, creating an analytic culture (HR), embracing an enterprise approach, and importantly, developing the ability to communicate analytics.

An organization committed to analytics must have access to **huge databases**. These databases come from internal and external sources. Analytics is now widely used by top association football clubs in Europe and by other elite sport organizations in the United States. Data are obtained from various surveys of consumers and then from cameras and data recordings of player performances. Ecker (2015) reports that three companies: "Stats, Zebra Technologies and Sportvision – collectively have motion-tracking agreements with the top professional sports leagues: the NFL,

NBA, MLB, NHL and Nascar (in America). . . . (Analytics for Stats company) is one of the fastest-growing pieces of the estimated $100 million in revenue the company will pull in this year" (para. 1 & 4).

Organizations that are successful do not only accumulate large amounts of data but they make data a fulcrum of their **strategic business planning**. Soper (2016) pointedly states that: "Utilizing data to win games and make more money is now a requirement – not an option – for franchises around the globe" (para. 2). Thus, data must become embedded in the organization's strategies to achieve the fundamental goals of every elite sporting organization, which involves winning and making profit while doing so.

Another attribute of such organizations is widespread use of **modeling and optimization**. Davenport (2006) notes that

> analytics competitors look well beyond basic statistics. These companies use predictive modeling to identify the most profitable customers – plus those with the greatest profit potential and the ones most likely to cancel their accounts. They pool data generated in-house and data acquired from outside sources.
>
> (p. 3)

This is a major difference between organizations that use analytics and those that do not. Those companies that do not use analytics develop statistical analysis that are descriptive, explaining past performance, but that is all they do. For organizations that are focused on analytics, they not only have mundane descriptive statistics of past performance but they have more. They use their huge databases to develop

Photo 18.1 Today's sport analytics use a variety of measurements and graphs to explore efficiency and effectiveness in various areas.

Source: Dreamstime.com, reprinted with permission

predictive models, allowing them to optimize resources in order to acquire additional revenue through savings and maximization of profits. For instance, they are able to establish real-time prices by adjusting consumer fees because they accurately predict consumer demand in real time, they do segmentation ticket pricing because they know who can afford to pay more and who cannot, and they can use simulation technologies to hypothesize the financial implications of real-time changes.

Above all, these types of organizations **invest in technologies** that help in data storage, data collection, and data analysis. Alamar and Mehrotra (2011) report that factors contributing to competition on the technological front include (a) innovations in sport science; (b) Internet communications significantly increasing the amount of data generated, stored, and distributed by scouts, coaches, and even fans; and (c) increasing computing power, reducing storage costs and raising data analysis capabilities. For instance, "the advent of motion capture technology has expanded the data collected from each game. This technology tracks everything that moves on a field every 100th of a second" (para. 16). Companies are willing to compete on the basis of appropriate technologies because they realize that technology will pay for itself by reducing organizational waste and improving efficiency and effectiveness through analytics. In certain cases, organizations build their own technology if market-based technologies are not effective in providing the kind of information required to move forward.

The key to making a sporting organization focus on analytics is leadership. A major change of strategic direction for an organization requires buy-in from the organization's top executives. The executives become **advocates for analytics** in order to encourage members of the organization to participate. Essentially, executives who advocate for adoption and use of analytics become cheerleaders and change agents. An example is the owner of the Dallas Mavericks of the National Basketball Association (NBA) in America, Mark Cuban, who is a staunch advocate for use of analytics in basketball and has invested in DFS, an analytics company.

The top executives involved in introducing analytics to their organization also lead **cultural change** in those organizations. Cultural change requires a new thinking about how things are done. If an organization adopts the use of analytics as part of its cultural change, then the organization's process and operations must reflect this. Some of this is becoming apparent as an attribute of organizations that adopt analytics. Davenport (2006) states that these organizations "instill a company-wide respect for measuring, testing, and evaluating quantitative evidence. Employees are urged to base decisions on hard facts" (p. 6). These organizations move quicker towards cultural change by their hiring practices and putting right people in the right jobs. In essence, the companies employ people who enjoy analytics and are comfortable working with numbers.

Davenport (2006, 2014) found that **embracing an enterprise approach** is common among sporting organizations that adopt analytics. Davenport points out that an enterprise approach does not require the use of analytics in one business process of the organization but in using it in multiple processes to gain advantages of integrated use. Such a use provides insights to patterns while examining different points in the organization's processes. The patterns are those that affect the business plan and outcomes and, thus, their appropriate modifications yield positive outcomes in areas such as revenue, consumer satisfaction, and others.

Finally, **communication** is important in sport analytics. Gorski (2013) points out the reason for this: "Whether you're analyzing optical tracking data from a basketball game or attempting to reconstruct the history of the climate from tree rings, one of the most significant challenges is communicating the new information effectively" (para. 4). Gorski informs that communicating analytics requires knowledge of consumers and other stakeholders like coaches, administrators, athletes, and sponsors, among others. Visualization techniques, brief descriptive analysis of data, and short text messages of key actions are options available in communicating a piece of analytics information. Gorski gives an example of effective communication by noting that a few maps and pictures can effectively describe a complicated analytical project.

BENEFITS OF ANALYTICS

Organizations that adopt analytics see benefits to the use of analytics, particularly if they are able to maximize such use. Benefits that commonly emerge from the use of analytics include value creation, the ability to manage the future efficiently, creating new product opportunities, and communication insights to unique data sets.

Value creation means the process of increasing the worth of a product, service, or an idea. In essence, it represents ways to maximize revenue. Analytics, in that sense, is an essential practice in an organization's value creation process. Analytics creates efficiency in decision making across the organization. For instance, analytics help the organization with performance information on its athletes, allowing coaches to easily and quickly identify weak areas that need rectification. A similar process for value creation takes place in the area of sport marketing, using analytics to identify what consumers need, what the optimal product pricing would be, and how many consumers would be willing to consume a product.

REFLECTION

Think of a recent sport tactical analysis that you read. If you have not read any, perhaps a family member or friend did. Find that person and ask him or her a few questions about their recollections of what they read. The focus should be on recalling a bunch of numbers, a model or models, and perhaps graph(s) provided in an analytical report. Recall what it was for. For instance, did it help you compare the performance of certain athletes, and in which ways did it assist? As you reflect on these recollections, think about how useful they are based on what you read in this chapter.

Furthermore, analytics help organizations build unique models for identifying characteristics of athletes that an organization should acquire for **future productivity**. Models are essential, but they require substantive data and tests to confirm their effectiveness. Previously, organizations did not have access to the amount of data required for effective modeling and testing. That has changed over the years. Presently, organizations have access to large amounts of relevant data and the ability to build testable models from the data.

Davenport (n.d.) argues that analytics provide benefits in **building new product or service opportunities** for the organization. A new service or product may be created by an organization based on insights identified through analytics. Davenport states that:

> For the Phoenix Suns, an (American) NBA basketball team, Verizon's Precision Market Insights offered information on where people attending the team's games live, what percentage of game attendees are from out of town, and how often game attendees combine a basketball game with a baseball spring training game or a visit to a fast food chain. Such insights are obviously valuable to the Suns in targeting advertising and promotions.
>
> (para. 14)

However, there are difficulties associated with analytics. Analytics are based on quantification and number crunching. Sometimes, they also use complex statistical analysis and mathematical modeling. This means that it limits the number of persons who are comfortable with the information and able to understand it. Thus, a critical aspect is how does one communicate the information with clarity to a large number of persons? This is where organizations employ persons with the ability to break down complex numbers and models in such a way that others can easily comprehend the overall picture. The great communicators may use analogies, visualization, and other **communication techniques to generate insights** to the data sets. It is at this point that analytics provide great benefits to the organization.

IMPORTANCE OF ANALYTICS IN SPORT MANAGEMENT COMMUNICATIONS

Sport management functions include value creation, which is mentioned in the previous section. Sport managers are charged with developing ways to create value for sporting organizations and ensure that the means for creating such value are communicated to stakeholders who are helpful in accomplishing organizational goals.

Analytics have become very important to sport managers in several ways. One of such ways is that they provide managers with access to objective data for measuring management processes and for making decisions about future actions. For instance, Morgan writes that:

McLaren's cars (at a Grand Prix race) send a torrent of data back to the pit teams; the information is analyzed in real time using SAP's HANA in-memory technology. HANA employs data compression technology, which enables McLaren to store the data in random-access memory, ensuring that it can be analyzed in the blink of an eye – and as result, the team can act on the incoming data in time to make race-changing adjustments.

(para. 11)

SAP is a German software company that produces High Performance Analytic Appliance (HANA). SAP's HANA in-memory technology involves integration of relational databases and quick processing of data through advanced analytics that include predictive analytics, spatial data processing, streaming analytics, and graph data processing.

Sport managers and top executives find that analytics can be very helpful in various work domains that include direct management of athletic assets, marketing, among other areas. Sport managers take advantage of analytics in multiple areas in order to improve the organization's output. These areas, which were previously identified, include player and team performance on the sport field, injury prevention, organizational market performance, and community relationship building (Davenport, 2014).

One area that sport managers have made significant progress in is fan engagement. According to Davenport (2014), several American professional sport leagues are using both statistics and video in websites to increase engagement with sport fans. In fact, Davenport points to an innovative engagement strategy by American professional basketball team the Orlando Magic, which is developing a way "to personalize web content for each person who visits their website. . . . The goal is to not treat all fans as if they were alike, and to develop increasingly targeted approaches to marketing based on a fan's history and past purchases" (p. 19). Analytic data have helped American gridiron football team the New England Patriots to a record 97% season ticket renewal for the 2010 season, according to Davenport. Analytic data are obtained on sport fans through installation of wifi systems in a sporting arena to track what fans do while at the arena and to help sporting managers strategize how best to meet fans' needs. For instance, American professional basketball team the Phoenix Suns was able to track the number of its fans that frequented a fast-food chain based on a team promotion within 24 hours after a game.

PREPARING FOR THE CHAMPIONSHIP

"The football championship game next week is going to be a big challenge," Jose Lopez of Alpha City FC reminds his assistants, Kwesi Boateng and Kevin Brown. In front of them and on the computer monitor are various open windows that include Opta Analysis data and a Zonal Marking website. These windows contain information about City's upcoming opponent, United. Kwesi points to recent Zonal Marking's tactical analyses of United, which gives Alpha City a clue on how United prefers to play and the key athletes on United. The three men agree on the tactical preference of United, and they now move on to study individual players.

Kwesi prefers to use Opta Statistics for analysis of United's individual players. He says: "I have taken a preliminary look, Coach, and I am concerned." Jose takes a look at the data on several of United's players, and numerous statistics are provided for each player. Jose, Kwesi, and Kevin focus on players whom they consider the key athletes based on previous statistical reports from a variety of sources including Opta. Jose nods his head: "Wow, this tells us why they've won this championship for the past two years. We have a challenge ahead of us, to put it mildly."

They find out that United has scored quite a number of goals from two types of plays. One is from set pieces close to the box and the other is from crosses made by two players who seek out a tall striker. The striker, Thomas, leads United in scoring with 60% of his goals from headers. This is of particular concern. Jose reminds everyone: "As you guys know, we really do not have tall center backs to challenge this guy in the air." Kevin responds: "Well, maybe instead of letting them get to the zones where they make these dangerous crosses, we should force their wide players to the middle where we will have more support." They argue about this proposed solution for a few minutes but eventually agree that Kevin's solution may work. Then Jose asks: "What do we do about set pieces?" There are no easy solutions, except to find tactical alternatives that reduce United's access to dangerous spots where they have had success with set pieces. They decide to find ways to do this at a later time, because the championship is still a week away.

They now turn to data on their own players. For this, they turn on the team's Prozone software. Prozone is very helpful in performance analysis. It is not restricted to analyzing a match. Instead, it is very helpful in analyzing players for recruitment, evaluating player performance, analyzing training, trends, and much more. With Prozone, there is a section called *Matchviewer* that provides data for passing, heading, shooting, tackling, and other plays. Prozone uses GPS to collect an athlete's motion for analysis of player's geo-positioning, distance covered in a game, and intensity of activity.

Prozone provides the coaches with heat maps on all Alpha City players. They discover that one of their key backs, Joel, is successful at preventing opponents from making crosses. The heat map shows that Joel's most intense activity (in red) is higher up the field where he makes most of his tackling, and the heat maps of his opponents also show that he had restricted their activities up the field and away from optimal crossing zones. The heat map activity goes from blue (no activity), green, yellow, and to red as a player's activity increases. Jose is excited: "Guys, Joel appears to be our solution to United's crosses. He has to play! Kevin, you must prepare him with all the information we have." Kevin agrees, "No problem, boss. We've got a good chance against those United guys." The coaches also work on various other statistical data related to the team.

Later on, and closer to game day, the coaches meet with players to discuss analytical data and work on tactics for the game. During the tactical session, each player is informed about what is expected of him. The session involves clarifying issues, answering player questions, and demonstrating action with simulated visuals and use of graphical data. Afterwards, each player simulates the tactics during on-field training, which is also recorded and uploaded to Prozone in order to determine how effective each player is at working on team tactics and individual roles.

On game day, the team beats United to win the championship. The media report the outcome as an upset. Jose and his coaches are elated. The data from the game show that Alpha City is successful at preventing United's crosses into the box, and they limit United's set pieces on spots close to the box. The coaches celebrate, knowing that their hard work, using analytics, is successful. There are hugs, screams of joy, and champagne everywhere. The fans cheer and enjoy the moment.

Discussion questions

1. Was City's success due to technology available to coaches? Provide support for your perspective.
2. Reading this case, how do you think sport analytics has changed preparation of sport teams?
3. What communication strategies did the coaches use to ensure that players understand the data and how to apply the data for team and individual effectiveness and success?
4. Based on information from the case, how else can the coaches use analytics data? Please cite case incidents to support your recommendation.
5. Suggest ways that Alpha City may use sport analytics to engage fans.

IMPORTANCE IN MEDIA COMMUNICATIONS

So far this chapter has focused on how analytics is used within sporting organizations and how such organizations use analytics to communicate with both internal and external publics. However, sport analytics is not only important to sporting organizations. In fact, a large amount of sport analytics is used outside of the sporting organization, and one of those types of organizations that find such analytics useful are media organizations.

Media organizations have at least two ways that they apply analytics to their work pertaining to sport. One involves providing and engaging sport consumers with deep analysis of games and the other is creating unique views of the sport for consumers.

The first instance involves media organizations increasingly providing huge data and analytics to sporting consumers. The Profootballfocus.com website is an example of a sport medium that makes sport analytics accessible to consumers. It provides access for a fee as much as $249 monthly for fans and at premium costs for media and sport organizations. Sport fans not only use the data for daily conversations with friends but use the unique data for participation in fantasy sport competitions and for gambling. The data is extensive, covering all conceivable areas at the athlete, team, field, and organizational levels with the ability to build own models.

Sport media increasingly use analytics to provide consumers with unique data of the game in recent years. Burns (2015) writes that: "Sports fans have likely noticed something new during broadcasts and media coverage of games in the last couple of years: Numbers are everywhere" (para. 4). Essentially, more and more data are used to better inform consumers about why teams take certain actions on the field, significant accomplishment in sport, and other narratives needing empirical support. In Europe, several sport media use heat maps developed by the likes of Optasports and Viz Libero to assist data visualization of athlete and team performances.

IMPORTANCE IN SECONDARY INDUSTRIES

Analytics, as alluded to in the previous section, also provide opportunities in several secondary sport industries. Secondary sport industries refer to sport industries that do not involve live sport competition among athletes. In this category is fantasy sport and gambling. Each of those industries uses sport analytics as mentioned previously and elaborated as follows.

Gambling and fantasy sport are increasingly dependent on the use of sport analytics. The sport analytics are not created by fans but are derived from organizations whose service is precisely providing sport analytics for gambling and fantasy sport. Juergen (2013) writes about an organization, *numberFire*, that develops unique analytics for bettors and fantasy sport players. At the time of Juergen's writing, *numberFire* had about 40,000 users and an amazing reputation for predicting sport results accurately using mathematical models based on sport data. According to Juergen (2013), *numberFire* outpredicts "experts at ESPN and Yahoo 70 percent of the time . . . [and] continues to consistently beat the projections of CBS, NFL and Yahoo" (para. 4).

Organizations like *numberFire* are growing in revenue, demonstrating their success in using analytics to make sporting predictions. Juergen (2013) notes that *numberFire*, a new company at the time, had grown from $10,000 in 2011 to $250,000 by the next year with huge room for further revenue growth. Though mathematical modeling can never guarantee a correct forecast of sporting outcomes, it has demonstrated that it increases the odds of being correct in a significant way. Its consistent outprediction of sport analysts shows that sport analytics is indeed effective.

ANALYTICS IN ACTION

This section looks at two different sport analytics reports in two sports. This introduces specific sport analytics and how it improves particular sport. The examples come from the National Hockey League (NHL) and elite tennis.

Sport analytics in the NHL

Though American sports are in the vanguard of sport analytics usage, not all American sports have benefitted from widespread popularity of and usage of analytics. Thus, while sports like baseball and basketball are way ahead of other sports in America in the use of analytics, several other sports are just now catching up. One of those sports seeking to catch up is the NHL, which features some of the world's elite hockey players.

Macdonald (2011) recently studied the use of statistics in the NHL and developed a model for improving measurement of player performance in the league. The NHL remains a sport league that continues to provide mundane statistics in its media communication to fans. However, with accessibility to huge amounts of data, much improved statistical measures with deeper insight to both athlete and team performance are possible. Macdonald explores this possibility by applying a statistical measure – the adjusted plus-minus (APM) statistic – already in use by the elite basketball league (NBA) in America. The APM was developed to reduce the effect of team performance on an individual player's PM statistic.

However, Macdonald notes that differences between hockey and basketball mean that the APM could not be used in hockey without a meaningful adjustment to the model. Differences between both sports include the fact that hockey does not always have teams with an equal number of athletes in-game because of power plays and shorthanded rules that send players to the penalty box for short periods in the game. Thus, Macdonald had to develop a unique APM to account for those special situations.

Macdonald evaluated the model against widely held perceptions of a player's offensive and defensive contributions in order to test the model's validity. This is an important aspect in any test of models as a model must make logical sense and provide consistency in its output for it to be considered valid.

Macdonald's work produced insights that are not available in the legacy statistics used by the NHL. In its measure of offensive plus-minus (OPM) statistic, his measures correlate with top offensive players regularly promoted among stars of the NHL, including two players – Sidney Crosby and Alex Ovechkin – who are believed to be the superstars of the league. However, the APM accounting for both offensive and defensive contributions did not rank those two among the league's top 10. More insightful is the measure of a player's defensive contribution during shorthanded situations in terms of goals per 60 minutes of playing time. This statistic was not previously provided by the NHL. The shock result is that the Vancouver Canucks' Alex Burrows led the list by a huge margin and ahead of his line mate, Ryan Kesler. Yet, the NHL does not appear to recognize this performance and, instead, the NHL recognizes Burrows' line mate, Kesler, as the finalist for the best defensive forward award in two consecutive years before Macdonald's study.

Essentially, work like this study by Macdonald brings insight to athletic performance that was not previously communicated by legacy statistics. For instance, statistics like the one regarding Burrows' performance indicate a need for rethinking methods for sporting awards in the NHL.

Sport analytics in tennis

Tennis is another sport that can profit from sport analytics. Presently, the sport uses statistics that record basic serves, winners, and number of shots and volleys, but it is possible, as demonstrated by Wei, Lucey, Morgan, and Sridharan (2013), to track more inferential statistics of player performance in-game that may help predict with some accuracy a winning shot or an error.

Wei, Lucey, Morgan, and Sridharan (2013) studied data from the play of Djokovic, Nadal, and Federer at the 2012 Australian Tennis Open. The data are derived from "Hawk-Eye" technology, and they help predict a live in-point winner, continuation, or error during rallies. The scholars used a graphical model to predict the chance of a winning shot based on analysis of variables such as player leg placement, speed, and angle of the shot.

They found that impact location of an incoming shot is the single best predictor of a winner while feet location is the next best predictor. In combination, the best predictor is speed plus impact location and feet location. Other findings are also insightful. For instance, Federer is more likely to hit winning shots to the boundaries of the width of the court and also to produce winners with volleys compared to Nadal and Djokovic. For Nadal, his winners come when his opponent is forced to play from his left side (backhand side), whereas Djokovic hits more winners when his opponent is on the forehand side.

This detailed in-game analysis provides sources of communication topics for media coverage of the sport and also for coaches working with these athletes or their opponents. Importantly, these types of analysis are only possible because of large amounts of data from emerging tracking technologies, in this case the "Hawk-Eye." Of course, the work of Wei, Lucey, Morgan, and Sridharan (2013), which uses a probabilistic graphical model from the Bayesian Network (BN) framework, allows modeling that is complex and requires the use of visualization techniques and a good statistics interpreter to make findings accessible to a large number of people.

CHAPTER SUMMARY

Sport analytics is important in improving sport business and performance operations. Additionally, interest in the study of analytics has gone up, with universities introducing courses and degrees in sport analytics.

This chapter discusses the key attributes of organizations focused on analytics, using the example of Athletic Club (AC) Milan in Italy, which is an association football team that built a reputation in the use of sport analytics. AC Milan has a widely reputed lab and claims that its use of analytics directly led to a 90% reduction of athlete injuries. In any case, attributes of analytic-using organizations include access to a huge database, investment in technology, embracing an enterprise approach, and the use of modeling and optimization, among other key factors.

There are several benefits of analytics, which include creating value for the organization, building new product or service opportunities, allowing for future productivity in athletics by providing vital data for planning, and helping organizations generate great insights into their activities. These benefits are demonstrated in key areas of sport management communication, media communications, and in secondary industries. In sport management communications, they help increase fan engagement and are applicable in several management domains. In media communications, they can be offered to highly interested fans for a fee and can also inform fans about the game. Finally, they are essential for prediction in the secondary industries such as fantasy sport and gambling.

The last section demonstrates use of analytics in two sports – hockey and tennis. In the NHL, analytics provide surprising insights on a valuable player who was not previously considered a star but analytics data show otherwise. In tennis, analytics of shot-making data find that impact location of an incoming shot is the best single predictor of a winner while feet location is the next best predictor.

DISCUSSION QUESTIONS

1. Why have sport analytics become important and popular? Provide support for your position.
2. Why would a huge database, cultural change, and technological investment be important to effective use of sport analytics?
3. Why is value creation a benefit of sport analytics? How is value created with sport analytics?

4 Demonstrate how fan engagement is accomplished with sport analytics.
5 Why would fans be interested in paying a fee to access sport analytics? What value do they have for some sport fans?
6 Do you think analytics is a good predictor of athletic results compared to experience and intuition? Please provide support for your argument.

ACTIVITIES

1 Research published activities of AC Milan's Laboratory related to sport analytics. Identify the type of data produced by the Lab and how the club tends to use data and what outcomes the club generates. Then write a report for presentation.
2 Visit a major sport club in your city or a nearby city. Find out whether the club uses sport analytics. If it uses analytics, why and how does it use analytics? If it does not use sport analytics, find out why and whether it will consider using it in the future and for what reasons.
3 As a group, research universities that currently offer a degree in sport analytics or plan to offer one. Which courses are offered as part of a sport analytics degree and why have those courses become part of the degree? Write a five-page report detailing your finding.

VIDEO RESOURCES

Moneyball (Drama/2h 13min.). This is the story of an American baseball manager who builds his team based on computer-generated sport analytics.

SSAC15: Basketball Analytics: Push the Tempo (YouTube/1h 1 min.). This is a panel discussion at the ninth MIT Sloan Sports Analytics Conference held in February 2015 in Boston, USA.

Sports Analytics: The Good, the Bad, the . . . (YouTube/56.15 mins.). This is a video to talk about what is learned from sport analytics in recent years.

RECOMMENDED WEB RESOURCES

Steinberg, L. (2015, August 18). Changing the game: The rise of sports analytics. *Forbes*. www.forbes.com/sites/leighsteinberg/2015/08/18/changing-the-game-the-rise-of-sports-analytics/#6d48937331b2

Dizikes, P. (2015, March 2). Six keys to sports analytics. *MIT News*. http://news.mit.edu/2015/mit-sloan-sports-analytics-conference-0302

Journal of Sports Analytics via http://journalofsportsanalytics.com

REFERENCES

Alamar, B., & Mehrotra, V. (2011, September/October). Beyond 'Moneyball': Rapidly evolving world of sports analytics, Part I. *Analytics Magazine*.

Burns, E. (2015). Use of analytics in sports media becomes contentious. http://searchbusinessanalytics.techtarget.com/

Davenport, T. (2006, January). Competing on analytics. *Harvard Business Review*. Available at: https://hbr.org/2006/01/

Davenport, T. (2014). *Analytics in sports: The new science of winning*. SAS: International Institute for Analytics.

Davenport, T. (n.d.). Three big benefits of big data analytics. *SAS*. www.sas com/

Ecker, D. (2015, July 24). This is why Chicago is the epicenter for sports tech. *Crain's Chicago Business*.

Fawkes, B. (2008, March 26). Milan Lab – is it really the source of Milan's success? *Soccerlens*. http://soccerlens.com/

Gorski, C. (2013, March 5). Where sports analytics and science communication collide. *Inside Science*. Http://www.insidescience.org/

Juergen, M. (2013, June). An analytics platform that has mastered sports predictions. *Entrepreneur*. www.entrepreneur.com/

Macdonald, B. (2011, March 4–5). *An improved Adjusted Plus-Minus statistic for NHL players*. Paper presented at the MIT Sloan Sports Analytics Conference in Boston, MA.

Reimer, A. (2016, May 11). Syracuse University will launch first sports analytics degree in the U.S. *Forbes*. www.forbes.com/

Soper, T. (2016, March 18). Secrets of sports analytics: Top athletes, coaches, execs explain importance of analyzing data. *Geekwire.com*. Http://www.geekwire.com/

Wei, X., Lucey, P., Morgan, S., & Sridharan, S. (2013, March 1–3) *'Sweet-spot': Using spatiotemporal data to discover and predict shots in tennis*. Paper presented at the MIT Sloan Sports Analytics Conference in Boston, MA.

CHAPTER 19

THEORIZING IN COMMUNICATION AND SPORT

> **LEARNING OBJECTIVES**
>
> After reading this chapter, you should be able to do the following:
>
> - Demonstrate an understanding of what a theory is.
> - Explain the functions of communication theories.
> - Identify ways in which theory is useful to research study in sport communication.
> - Demonstrate a knowledge of various theories applicable to sport communication and the tenets of each theory.
> - Apply theory to an understanding of various aspects of sport communication.

INTRODUCTION TO THEORY

Theories serve as a framework that guides our knowledge of particular phenomenon. Thus, students of sport communication require knowledge of appropriate theories to have a better understanding of particular occurrences on the field. This chapter focuses on a discussion of communication theories that is relevant for a study of sport communication.

Communication theory is a systematic description and/or explanation of communication phenomenon based on informed ideas about that phenomenon. A communication theory starts from careful observation of a particular communication phenomenon. For instance, one may observe several activities of how people greet each other when they first meet. These observations may include whether the context of the meetings affect how they greet each other. The observations or ideas about the communication phenomenon are analyzed to determine causes, relationships, and other processes of the action. The analyses lead to a systematic description and/or explanation of the phenomenon or what becomes a theory of the phenomenon.

Of course, the focus of this chapter is to identify theories that are relevant to sport communication. As you will notice, theories included in this chapter are relevant to topics discussed throughout this textbook. Selected theories are far from exhaustive. Instead, they represent a small sample of communication theories applicable to the field of sport communication.

Functions of theories

Theories have various functions (i.e. they provide a certain set of services). For instance, theories help us describe and/or explain phenomenon, understand phenomenon, and make predictions. Each function, as you shall note, introduces us to the importance of theory in the field.

If you recall the definition of theory presented in the previous section, it notes that theories describe and/or explain phenomenon. Those two criteria of a theory also specify the function of describing what happens in a very systematic way. For instance, a theory about the effect of mass media coverage on popularity of a sport would **describe** various types of the effect. The function of **explanation** involves the theory providing reasons for each type of effect. It helps with explanation, as Griffin, Ledbetter, and Sparks (2015) note, because an effective theory "should bring clarity to an otherwise jumbled state of affairs; it should draw order out of chaos" (p. 25).

By focusing attention on things that are important, a theory greatly helps our **understanding** of a phenomenon. Good theories focus our attention on important aspects of a phenomenon, and they make those aspects simple to understand by clarifying complex concepts and relationships.

Finally, theories go beyond merely describing, explaining, and helping our understanding of a phenomenon. By carrying out those functions effectively, they enable us to **predict** an occurrence in the future when encountering a similar phenomenon. This prediction is possible because patterns are established relative to an activity or phenomenon.

Relationship to research

Theory is essential to effective research in sport communication. It provides a framework for understanding a research project and is used for deducting what is important to study. It lays out the scope of what the research investigates. In essence, research hypotheses are derived from a theoretical framework for a particular study. In such a case, the test of hypotheses helps to either confirm or disconfirm theoretical propositions. However, there are cases where a theory is not used to deduct what the research investigates. Instead, the goal is to arrive at results from which a theory is inductively developed.

Whether the relationship between theory and sport communication research is deductive or inductive, theory is always significant in sport communication research. Therefore, students need a strong background in theoretical knowledge and an ability to apply theory to the real world.

In the section that follows, several communication theories are examined with the goal of identifying why they are important in the field of sport communication.

COMMUNICATION THEORIES THAT APPLY TO SPORT COMMUNICATION

Chapter topics covered in this textbook serve as a guide for selecting theories discussed in this section. Of course, not every chapter topic is used as a guide because of limited space. Selected theories are examined to determine how each helps us understand aspects of sport communication.

Sport and interpersonal communication

Communication Privacy Management (CPM) theory by Sandra Petronio (2013) is a widely tested theory on how people disclose private information and how that impacts their relationships with others. The theory is applicable to interpersonal sport communication, as we shall see in the analysis in this section.

The CPM theory involves three critical phases in disclosure of private information. The first phase is *privacy ownership*, which describes information that a person may have and chooses to keep protected within a boundary that is kept tight or may be held loosely depending on the individual. The important thing is that the person has the ability to control this information in most cases, and he or she uses privacy rules for such protection. These rules depend on various factors, including the person's culture, gender, motivation, the context of the information, and the person's calculation of the risk/benefit from disclosure of the information. Ultimately, the person's decision to disclose information may be due to a desire to relieve a burden, create an impression, or prevent a wrong, among other personal considerations.

There may come a time when the person decides to disclose information to another person in an interpersonal communication setting. This phase is identified as *privacy control*. Sharing private information with another person changes the boundaries of privacy ownership by expanding ownership because the receiver of the private information is now included as co-owner of the information. This is a complex phase where the co-owners have to "negotiate" how best to control the information. Petronio (2013) points out that this "negotiation" is complex, with several variables determining security of the private information in terms of whether it is highly protected or easily disclosed to others. For instance, a receiver who is eager to act as confidant is more likely to protect the information, whereas a reluctant confidant is not. Furthermore, the relationship between the source and the receiver of the information is critical. If it is close and trusting, then the information is protected, but if it isn't, then the information may be disclosed.

The third phase, identified as *privacy turbulence*, occurs when "negotiation fails" and there is no mutually agreed-upon way to manage private information, so it leaks out to third parties that the initial owner of the information does not expect to have the information. Petronio points to three factors that may lead to a leakage and, thus, creation of privacy turbulence: (1) existence of fuzzy boundaries when both receiver and source have no agreed-upon or agreeable boundary determined for information protection, (2) an intentional revelation of the private information based on private interest, and (3) a mistake made because of forgetfulness.

In sport communication, for example, a track star may be privately considering retirement from the sport, but she does not want to reveal it to the team because she feels that revelation of her plan may adversely affect the team's performance in a season in which she wants to win the championship to highlight her final season. Nevertheless, she decides to reveal her plan to her closest teammate and friend. Her friend feels the information should be made known to the coach because she believes the coach would want a celebration in-season and would not be happy if told after the season. However, the friend agrees to keep the information confidential despite her personal wish to let the coach know. Eventually, the information leaks to both the coach and some members of the media as a rumor item. A situation such as this would be a context in which the CPM is used as a framework to study how the retirement information leaked to the media.

REFLECTION

Think about situations in sport when a rumor emerges about an athlete's activities that you think should be private. Put yourself in the role of that athlete and having to keep the particular information private. You may have taken certain measures to achieve that goal of maintaining privacy, but you may also have chosen to share the information with those close to you. So when the story appears in the media, what comes immediately to mind? (Remember, you are playing the role of the athlete.) Do you understand how the CPM theory may help you determine why private information leaks to the media?

Sport and leadership communication

Peters and Waterman (1982) carried out an extensive study of 62 successful American companies and discovered that they share significant leadership characteristics. These characteristics form the framework for what is known as the theory of **transformational leadership**. The theory is significantly a theory of leadership communication applicable to sport communication. Importantly, Bennis and Nanus (1997) extended the understanding of the theory after studying leaders from 90 organizations that included sporting organizations.

The theory of transformational leaders points to five characteristics of leaders that are important to achieving leadership vision. These characteristics are passion, vision, interactivity, creativity, and empowerment.

Passion refers to an unbridled demonstration of interest in the task and work relationships that indicates knowledge, joy, and love. This involves exuberant enthusiasm that includes emotional commitment to a task. Passion is exhibited, for instance, in the way a coach carries out his or her engagement with athletes.

Bennis and Nanus (1997) note that transformational leaders also have a *vision* of what they want the organization to achieve, and they use this vision to energize followers such as athletes. Sport managers or coaches, who are transformational leaders, create compelling messages about a vision, and athletes buy into the vision believing it to be achievable.

As mentioned above, a key factor is the leader's ability to communicate the message to followers. This involves creating a highly effective strategy or strategies for *interacting* with followers. Effective leaders know what motivates their followers and use different strategies to appeal to those motivators. Among messaging strategies are the use of imagery, humor, and metaphors. Above all, leaders create open communication channels that encourage sharing of information across the organization to advance the organization towards the collective vision.

Creativity describes foresight and innovativeness of transformational leaders. However, creativity comes with a risk of failure. Thus, a transformational leader is willing to take risks and is not afraid of failure. He or she is willing to try new ways of doing things, to experiment, to ask questions, and to dream of new possibilities.

Another factor in transformational leadership is willingness to *empower* followers. A transformational leader realizes that he or she cannot solely achieve the vision and that success requires everyone in the organization to work collectively for the greater good. That means that the leader actively empowers followers to take initiative in planning and decision making.

The theory of transformational leadership applies to leadership within sporting organizations and sport teams. It requires extensive but effective ongoing communication between the transformational leader and followers. This theory may inform a study of effective leadership among championship winning teams in a particular sport to identify whether they exhibit factors of transformational leadership. Investigations may also involve leadership of sporting organizations that achieve major changes in their sport.

Sport and strategic communications

Relationship Management Theory is an important theory in strategic communications and public relations. John Ledingham (2003) reviewed literature related to relationship management and used the information to articulate a theory of relationship management. Ledingham's work concludes that public *relationships* are much more encompassing than public communication. The building of public relationships requires communication flowing between the organization and its publics but, in addition, time is spent cultivating relationships.

The theory specifies that the goal of relationship management is accomplishment of mutual benefits for both the organization and its publics. This mutual benefit is achieved through satisfaction of five key dimensions of relationship, which are trust, openness, involvement, investment, and commitment. In essence, the theory suggests that organizations, including sporting organizations, pay close attention to each dimension in order to build strong and sustained positive relationships with their publics. Notably, accomplishments in those dimensions are linked with public awareness of the organization and positive attitude towards the organization.

Ledingham prescribes a process model for building relationship, which is referred to as SMARTS. The first **S** refers to scanning the environment. In essence, it requires the organization to continually scan the environment because relationships with the public are dynamic and involve change over time. **M** refers to mapping or the process of setting goals for building, sustaining, or repairing relationships with the relevant public. **A** is acting on goals that are set. The organization develops strategies to meet goals and objectives for the relationship. **R** refers to rolling out strategies and implementing them, most likely in a campaign. **T** refers to tracking implementation of strategies through evaluations that determine whether goals for the relationships are met successfully or not. The final **S** refers to stewardship, where the organization sustains good relationships by continual monitoring. The organization quickly responds to monitoring results by acting to maintain high-quality relationships.

Applying relationship management theory to sport communication is seen in public relations activities that sporting organizations implement in their communities. In many of those cases, the sporting organization involves its top athletes who are widely known to the public. These relationship management activities by sporting organizations present opportunities for research that apply this theory. The research goal, for example, might be to determine which teams closely implement what the theory recommends and whether such implementation is associated with public awareness, positive attitude towards the organization, and satisfaction.

Sport media communication

Arthur Raney expanded **affective disposition theory** (ADT) to sport communication in 2006, but the initial theory was proposed in 1977 by Zillman and Cantor. The ADT claims that media consumers become emotionally attached to entertainment and media characters. Some of these attachments are positive, which allows consumers to see particular characters as heroes and others as villains. Emotional affiliations to characters are formed in a continuum that ranges from extremely positive through indifference to some characters and to the opposite extreme of negativity towards others. Based on these dispositions towards a variety of characters, consumers experience tension that surrounds both anticipation and apprehension while watching an entertainment show, and conflict between characters on extreme ends of the scales elicit very high emotions from consumers. Consumers seek justice for characters based on where they may fall on their scale of disposition.

The media create high levels of arousal and emotions in sport consumers by creating particular narratives surrounding certain sport teams. These are created with storylines identifying heroes and villains and recounting historical incidences characterizing certain athletes in ways to make them likeable or unlikeable. These media characterizations communicate to consumers about whom to become positively attached and who should be at the negative end of their dispositional scale. Thus, the meeting of a hero team and a villain team heightens tension within the consumer, and the consumer develops apprehension that the hero may lose while anticipating victory for the hero. This conflicting thinking creates a high level of tension but also excitement.

Raney's application of the ADT to sport became a version of the theory identified as **disposition theory of sport spectatorship**. Raney's version of the ADT may be used to examine sport media coverage of certain sport rivalries such as Jamaican Usain Bolt versus American Tyson Gay in track, Australia versus England in cricket, or India versus Pakistan in field hockey. In such coverage, the media narrative is examined to identify how narratives correlate with consumer emotional attachment to an athlete or theme.

Sport fan

An interesting and exciting theory for the study of sport fans is the general systems theory. This theory has been in existence for more than half a century, but it remains effective in helping us understand social and networked activities. Ludwig von Bertalanffy is credited with proposing the **general systems theory** back in 1968, when he proposed that systems are made up of interrelated elements that work for the goal of a unified whole. He focused on open systems (i.e. systems that sustain themselves with constant activities) that involve communicating with their environment and making changes in order to meet demands of the environment.

The structure of general systems includes objects, internal relationships, attributes, and the environment. *Objects* are components of a system. For instance, each individual supporter is an object of a sport team's supporters system. The characteristics of these supporters are *attributes* of the system. Each object, based on its attributes, develops *relationships* and interacts or communicates with other objects in the system with the goal of achieving collective goals that sustain the system. The *environment* refers to activities that occur outside of or are external to the system.

For instance, the environment may include new rules made by the sporting team on how supporters should behave when attending games or rules made by enforcement officers of the community. All those constitute the environment that impacts activities of the system's objects.

Furthermore, the system's objects perform a variety of tasks that include inputs, throughput (processing), output, and feedback. *Input* tasks, for instance, include obtaining information from the environment and presenting that information to objects to act on. The information is acted on during the process of *throughput*. At this stage, the information may be modified or the group or groups make a determination on how to respond to the information. The *output* occurs when the objects implement or produce a response, which goes back to the environment and encounters the environment. The *feedback* loop is dynamic and ongoing as the various actions of the system's objects lead to responses, which are classified as feedback to the system.

The general systems theory can be applied to diverse areas of sport communication. However, the theory is listed under the area of sport fans because it provides answers to questions such as: how connected are fans of certain sport teams? What kind of information do certain groups of fans obtain? How does that information become disseminated through a fan network? Who are key figures or nodes in the fan system that help reach others to form a critical mass? A general systems theory could help frame these kinds of questions.

Sport and critical communication

Critical theories of communication focus on disparate issues, including social class struggle, cultural oppression, feminism, and patriarchy, among others. Generally, each critical theory is denoted critical because it critiques current structure and relations in society. The goal of the critique is to expose relationships that are uneven or unequal and recommend change.

Sport, being an important social activity, is not immune to social issues of inequality and oppression. Previous chapters already identified some of those inequalities. This section presents one of several critical theories to demonstrate what it says about relationships and how those apply to sport communication. The selected theory is Michel Foucault's **governmentality**, which appears in several of his writings, particularly in the early 1970s.

By governmentality, Foucault (2011) refers to "mentality" that results from persistent and sustained governing where governing does not necessarily refer to the use of state apparatuses. Instead, governing refers to the practice of command and control of behavior in daily living. Governmentality creates, in those impacted by it, certain effects, which include "docile bodies" resulting from imposition of the concept of *disciplinary* where the subject is normalized, both socially and culturally, through command and control rules. The state of disciplinary is imposed through a variety of social institutions, and the body comes to accept and internalize social teachings as "common sense." Other instruments used in creating governmentality are sanctions, violence, and force, which are used when the subject resists social and institutional teachings.

Littlejohn (1999) argues that a class of powerful people creates a dominant discursive structure, which is used to regulate and govern the actions of others. The governing discourse contains communication elements such as "written texts, but it also includes spoken language, and nonverbal forms such as architecture, institutional practices, even charts and graphs" (p. 237). That is what Foucault meant by governmentality.

Michel Foucault's governmentality is applicable to sport communication in various ways. One way is to use the framework in analyzing communication between sport administrators and athletes, exposing elements of power and inequality embedded in their communication texts. In doing so, the framework unpacks for public view hidden texts that explain true relationships between administrators and athletes. According to Littlejohn, this type of analysis "centers on analyzing discourse in a way that reveals its rules and structure. This he (Foucault) calls *archaeology*. Archaeology seeks to uncover, through careful description, the regularities of discourse. . . . We look to what the discourse says about knowledge, power, and ethics" (p. 239).

Sport and identity

Tajfel and Turner's (1986) **social identity theory** (SIT) is a widely used theory in the study of identity, and it is useful for understanding fan identity with athletic teams. The theory was initially proposed in 1979 as a descriptive theory that does not go into elaborate explanations of why people identify with certain groups and not others.

The SIT notes that an individual may belong to multiple groups simultaneously. An example of this is a female who identifies with Indian nationality, loves her badminton team, and is a devout Hindu. Each of those represents social identities for that individual. The SIT describes cognitive processes that persons follow in order to identify with a social group. These processes include social categorization, social identification, and social comparison.

Social categorization represents a process that involves a person categorizing him or herself as a member of a group. Categorization does not mean that the individual solely decides on membership in a group. In certain cases, a person becomes a member of a group due to biological makeup, incidence of birth, and others. In other cases, the person makes a choice of which group to belong to.

Social identification is the next phase and an important one as the individual is actively involved in the identity process. The individual self-identifies with the group and accepts norms and attitudes of the group as compatible with his or her own. Furthermore, the person shows preference for group members as in-group and sees others as out-group members and is able to identify what he or she shares in common with in-group members and what differentiates him or herself from those considered as out-group members.

The last cognitive process is called *social comparison*. Here, the person does not simply identify with his or her group but actively compares the group with other groups. The person compares his or her own group favorably in order to maintain positive self-esteem. In cases where the individual's comparison leads to favoring the out-group, then it is an indication of dissatisfaction with his or her social identity.

The SIT may be applied to an understanding of fan identification with sport teams. In such identification, fans express similarity with fellow fans of the same team while fans of other teams are members of the out-group. Importantly, such fans, even when their favorite team is performing poorly, remain steadfast in support of their team and find positive things about their team in order to maintain self-esteem. Furthermore, athletic teams provide narratives to their fans, helping them find positive discourse around their favorite teams. The above suggests one way in which SIT may be used as a framework to understand sport communication in the area of fan behavior.

Sport and image communication

In 1997, William Benoit introduced **image restoration theory** (IRT), describing rhetorical strategies that individuals and organizations use when responding to a crisis that adversely impacts their image. A later critique of the theory led to a change in the title of the theory from image restoration to image repair. The essence of the critique is that an image, when damaged, can hardly ever be restored to its original state and, instead, a repair of the image is more likely an accurate description of what may occur.

Since the introduction of the IRT, it has been used in several studies of sport communication, particularly in the United States. Most of the studies focus on an attempt by athletes to restore their image after a crisis. The theory's wide use in sport communication is denoted by inclusion as a chapter dedicated to sport and entertainment in Benoit's later book titled *Accounts, Excuses, and Apologies* (2015).

IRT argues that a rhetorical response occurs when someone or an organization is held responsible for an action that is considered offensive. The response occurs because there is a possibility that the accused will suffer damage to public image. Thus, the response mitigates damage.

IRT identifies, in its original iteration, five strategies the accused may use in response (see Table 19.1). The strategies are further broken down into tactics. The five strategies are denial, evasion of responsibility, reducing of offensiveness of the act, corrective action, and mortification.

Denial occurs in two ways. One is a simple denial where the accused denies performing the act. Alternatively, the individual may shift blame. In that case, the accused does not directly deny the act but, instead, blames the performance on another person or organization.

Evading responsibility has four options. One is to claim that the performed act is a response to another's act and, thus, the accused cannot be held directly responsible.

Second, the accused may apply defeasibility, which refers to a plea that they should not be held responsible because they did not have full information, ability, or control over the matter. Or they may claim the act was an accident. Finally, the accused may claim that the act is intended in good faith and, therefore, cannot be held responsible for a bad outcome considering the intention.

Reducing offensiveness of the act has six tactical options. The first is bolstering, where the accused mentions previous good acts to divert attention from the offensiveness of the current act. Second, the accused may attempt to minimize the act's offensiveness by reducing its significance, or the accused may use differentiation by claiming that it was less offensive in comparison to other similar acts. Transcendence is used to claim that the act is justified because there are other important considerations for evaluating the act. The accused may also choose to attack the accuser by challenging the accuser's credibility. Finally, by offering compensation to the victim, the accused may reduce the offensiveness of the act.

Table 19.1 Adapted from William Benoit's description of Image Repair Theory (IRT). These strategies are used in responding to an image-damaging crisis.

CRISIS OCCURS	WHO IS RESPONSIBLE?	RESPONSE	STRATEGY OPTIONS
It is offensive (image-damaging capability)	Not held responsible		
	Held responsible	Deny	Direct denial or shift blame
		Evade responsibility	Act in response to the other/defeasibility/accident/act in good faith
		Accept responsibility	Minimize offensiveness/bolster/transcendence/attack accuser/offer compensation
			Mortification
			Corrective action

Source: Adapted from Benoit (2015)

A fourth strategy is to offer *corrective action* to prevent a future occurrence of the act. This may involve outlining new practices that the accused has or will put in place that prevents re-occurrence.

The final strategy is *mortification*. This strategy includes acceptance of responsibility for the act and a plea for forgiveness. This is an apology where the accused demonstrate contriteness.

Benoit's IRT is applicable to sport communication as indicated earlier. Scholars use it when an athlete or a sporting organization encounters a crisis with the potential to damage the organization or athlete's image. An example is a sporting organization accused of persistent violation of competitive rules in an elite league. This information has the potential to damage the organization's image and attract negative media coverage. In such a case, the organization may use the IRT to frame its public response. Studies using IRT have identified use of multiple strategies for achieving image repair.

CHAPTER SUMMARY

This chapter introduces communication theories applicable to an understanding of sport communication. Of course, because numerous theories are applicable, only a few can be discussed in the space available in this chapter. In any case, the chapter begins by discussing the importance of theory and then defines what a theory means. Additionally, it outlines four important functions of theory, which are description, explanation, understanding, and prediction.

The chapter also points to relationship between theory and research. It notes two important ways that this relationship exists. One is an inductive relationship, where research studies are conducted in order to induct a theory from results obtained from those research studies. The second is a deductive relationship, which recognizes that a theory may already exist to frame a particular research study. This theory is then deduced for use in planning and investigating a particular phenomenon.

The final section of the chapter identifies particular areas of sport communication and then provides an applicable theory for study in that area along with real-world examples. There are eight areas identified, including interpersonal communication, leadership, media, image, identity, and so on. The theories discussed include affective disposition theory (ADT), governmentality, social identity theory (SIT), and image repair theory (IRT).

DISCUSSION QUESTIONS

1. Explain two functions of communication theories using sport communication examples.
2. What types of relationships exist between communication theories and research in sport communication?

3 Going by information in this chapter, does one always require a communication theory to conduct research study in sport communication?
4 Point to two recent occurrences in the world of sport that are amenable to study using Michel Foucault's governmentality as a framework.
5 Tajfel and Turner's social identity theory (SIT) is widely used in the communication field. In which way may you apply SIT to an understanding of sport fans' behavior?

ACTIVITIES

1 The media often identify great sport leaders. Research media archives and select a sport person identified as a great leader. What are attributes of that person? Which leadership theory would be applicable to understanding the person's leadership style? Write a report on your findings.
2 Research additional communication theories not mentioned in the chapter. Identify at least one that applies to a sport communication activity. Why and how does it apply? Write a three- to four-page report that identifies both theory and theorist. Describe the theory and show why it is a communication theory and how it applies to sport communication.
3 Identify a recent crisis situation experienced by a major athlete in your country. What did the athlete do to protect her or his image? Use the IRT theory to evaluate whether the athlete was successful in image repair. Write a report on your findings.

VIDEO RESOURCES

Sandra Petronio on Communication Privacy Management Theory (YouTube/8.27 mins.). This is an interview with the theorist of CPM.
Cheris Kramarae on Muted Group Theory (YouTube/8.08 mins.). This is an interview with the theorist of Muted Group Theory.
Stan Deetz on Critical Theory of Communication in Organizations (YouTube/7.58 mins.). This is an interview with the theorist of Critical Theory in Organizations.

RECOMMENDED WEB RESOURCES

Communication studies: Communication theories. www.communicationstudies.com/communication-theories
Brugger, N. (2003). Theories of media and communication: Histories and relevance. Aarhus, Denmark. www.medieteori.dk/publikationer/001_bruegger.pdf
Encyclopedia.com. Communication theory. www.encyclopedia.com/science-and-technology/computers-and-electrical-engineering/computers-and-computing/communication

REFERENCES

Bennis, W., & Nanus, B. (1997). (2nd ed.). *Leaders: The strategies for taking charge*. New York: Harper & Row.

Benoit, W. (2015). (2nd ed.). *Accounts, excuses, and apologies: Image repair theory and research*. New York: State University of New York Press.

Foucault, M. (2011). *The government of self and others: Lectures at the College de France, 1982–1983*. Basingstoke: Palgrave Macmillan.

Griffin, E., Ledbetter, A., & Sparks, G. (2015). (9th ed.). *A first look at communication theory*. New York: McGraw-Hill Education.

Ledingham, J. (2003). Explicating relationship management as a general theory of public relations. *Journal of Public Relations Research*, 15(2): 181–198.

Littlejohn, S. (1999). (6th ed.). *Theories of human communication*. Belmont, CA: Wadsworth Publishing.

Peters, T., & Waterman, R. (1982). *In search of excellence*. New York: Harper & Row.

Petronio, S. (2013). Brief status report on communication privacy management theory. *Journal of Family Communication*, 13: 6–14.

Raney, A. (2006). The psychology of disposition-based theories of media enjoyment. In Bryant, J., & Vorderer, P. (Eds.), *Psychology of entertainment* (pp. 137–150). Mahwah, NJ: Lawrence Erlbaum.

Tajfel, H., & Turner, J. (1986). The social identity theory of intergroup behavior. In Worchen, S., & Austin, W. (Eds.), *Psychology of intergroup relations* (pp. 7–24). Chicago, IL: Nelson Hall.

Von Bertalanffy, L. (1968). *General systems theory*. New York: Braziller.

Zillman, D., & Cantor, J. (1977). Affective responses to the emotions of a protagonist. *Journal of Experimental Social Psychology*, 13(2): 155–165.

CHAPTER 20

SCHOLARLY RESEARCH

> **LEARNING OBJECTIVES**
>
> After reading this chapter, you should be able to do the following:
>
> - Demonstrate an awareness of the importance of scholarly research in sport communication.
> - Understand the difference between qualitative and quantitative research methods.
> - Understand types of qualitative research methods used in sport communication research.
> - Understand types of quantitative research methods used in sport communication.
> - Demonstrate a knowledge of how scholars in the field apply research methods to different sport communication problems.
> - Demonstrate an ability to apply a type of research method to a sport communication problem of interest.

INTRODUCTION

Previous chapters of this textbook demonstrate that scholarly research is central to knowledge that we have about sport communication. We depend on research to know about several things in the field, from consumer reactions to sport communication, to media strategies, and many other interesting issues. In many cases, theory (see previous chapter) informs scholarly research. Beyond theory informing research or serving as a framework for research in the field, there are other important facets of research. One of those is determining methods used in researching sport communication. These methods are numerous, and not all of them are discussed in this chapter. What this chapter does is pick and describe (along with an application) a few methods used in the field. To do that, the chapter breaks the selected methods into two categories of methods: qualitative and quantitative.

QUALITATIVE AND QUANTITATIVE RESEARCH METHODS IN SPORT

Research methods fall under one of two general categories of methods for investigating phenomena, including those that pertain to sport communication. Qualitative research methods differ from quantitative methods in several ways but three of the most important ways, according to Chambliss and Schutt (2013), are that (1) results from qualitative methods seek attention to a specified context of study while quantitative measures seek universal generalizations using statistical projection; (2) qualitative methods seek to achieve rich descriptions of what they measure while quantitative measurements seek statistical measurement of specific variables; and (3) qualitative methods rely on a large amount of descriptive data from few cases while quantitative methods depend on a smaller amount of quantifiable data from large number of cases.

Qualitative methods

Qualitative methods in sport communication are numerous, but this chapter has selected six of them: interviews, textual analysis, thematic analysis, rhetorical analysis, critical analysis, and case study. Each is described in subsequent paragraphs and supported with one or two examples of research study on sport communication using the method.

The **interview** is a popular research method involving conversation with research participants through in-person meetings, telephone, Skype, and other ways for collecting data. Interviews are broken down into three types: structured, semi-structured, and unstructured. *A structured* interview involves the interviewer using a written guide where all questions are determined prior to the start of the interview and the guide is strictly followed to collect data in predetermined areas of interest. It is also referred to as a fixed-response interview. The same standardized questions are asked of each participant. *A semi-structured* interview has more flexibility compared to the structured type. In a semi-structured interview, there is a guide with questions that the interviewer uses. The interviewer also has the freedom to ad lib and probe to further investigate responses that the interviewee may give. An *unstructured* interview has a simple guide that informs the interviewer on a scope for the questioning, but the interviewer then develops his or her questions based entirely on responses from the interviewee. In essence, the interviewees are allowed to create their own stories. Collected data are then examined for similarity across participants so that conclusions may be drawn.

Gibbs and Haynes (2013) used semi-structured interviews to explore lived experiences of 18 Canadian and American sport media professionals. The study focused on their use of Twitter and its impact on their lives. The researchers contacted each interviewee by email to schedule an hour of telephone interview. Gibbs and Haynes (2013) note that: "During the interviews, the researcher would frequently follow up with more questions or ask for further explanation to probe deeper into the phenomenon" (p. 399). The study confirmed that Twitter had a significant impact on the work of media professionals by changing the structure of their work in profound ways. Among the changes were increased speed in dissemination of sport news, increased media competition, forcing media professionals to frequently monitor Twitter to check on fan, media, and player activities, reliance on using Twitter to put out news before issuing press releases, and the fact that Twitter has broken down sport organization hierarchies.

There is confusion on differences among several research methods because a number of them involve analyzing textual material. However, it is important to note differences among methods used for analyzing text. For instance, **textual analysis** refers to all qualitative analysis of text. Text refers to meaning derived from an object or subject. Textual analysis is different from a quantitative analysis of text, which is known more commonly as Content Analysis. Textual analysis exposes meanings within the text through the educated interpretation of the researcher. In a textual analysis, focus is on the structure of the content, interactions among elements in the content, and also the context of the text. The interpretation can be unique to the reader of the text because the goal of this type of study is to present a deep and insightful interpretation.

Pamela Laucella (2010) used textual analysis to study media coverage of Michael Vick's dogfighting charges. Vick was a popular quarterback playing with the Atlanta Falcons of the American gridiron professional football league. Laucella sought, among other issues, to uncover the master myths used by newspaper journalists in narrating the Vick story. She selected 243 stories from four American newspapers: *The New York Times*, *USA Today*, *Atlanta Journal-Constitution*, and the *Richmond Times-Dispatch*. Laucella sought to discover five predetermined myths in the coverage of the Vick story. She did this by examining the underlying structure used to produce the story contents. Laucella points out: "Throughout the coverage, master myths repeatedly appeared in journalists' stories. They included scapegoat, victim, trickster, hero (or fallen hero), and other world" (p. 50).

Thematic analysis is another qualitative method widely used by researchers. Thematic analysis is based on seeking recurrent patterns in the data to arrive at largely independent themes that give meanings to study findings. A theme consists of data that cluster around a similar meaning and emerge from an inductive analysis of the data. The process of thematic analysis is somewhat systematic, but it is important to note that in thematic analysis, the themes are usually not predetermined. Data for thematic analysis are obtained from interviews and, thus, the data are thick. The researcher goes through several iterations of reviewing and analyzing the data to discover patterns and group them into preliminary themes. The preliminary themes are examined and re-examined to ensure that they are not redundant or overlapping. If redundancy and overlapping occurs, then the themes are re-organized with the goal of arriving at independent themes. The process is only stopped when the researcher no longer discovers redundancy and overlaps and, thus, the iteration is judged to be exhaustive. At this point, the researcher has the final themes, which are then examined in an integrated form to expose the story that they tell collectively. The themes and the collective story are then reported as findings from the study.

An example of thematic analysis emerges in Lauren Smith's study of media broadcasts of Oscar Pistorius's participation in both the Olympic and Paralympic Games. Smith sought to discover how sport broadcasters frame Pistorius at both mega events. As pointed out earlier, textual analysis includes various types of methods used in analyzing the content of texts. In this case, thematic analysis is a type of textual analysis. Smith describes the process for the study as follows:

> The individual researchers derived themes by looking for multiple repetitions of the same topics of conversations, similar phrases and words, examining synonyms of frequently found words. Each researcher generated initial codes for the commentary and then worked to identify themes. Once separate examinations were finalized, the two researchers met to compare themes.
>
> (p. 396)

Eventually, the researchers arrived at ten themes from three different broadcasts they examined. Smith concluded from the themes that broadcasters use stereotypical descriptors and that this could be seen in different descriptors given to the same athlete in the two Olympic Games.

Another method that involves analysis of textual material is **rhetorical analysis**. This analysis focuses on breaking down into parts the verbal or written communication made to persuade an audience. Frey, Botan, and Kreps (2000) define the method as "a systematic method for describing, analyzing, interpreting, and evaluating the persuasive force of messages embedded within texts" (p. 229). They also point to a process for conducting a study using rhetorical analysis. There are four general steps for such a study, beginning with identifying the text to be analyzed. Usually, this is a text that is considered important or significant about an issue worthy of study. The next step is choosing an appropriate rhetorical analysis for the text. This is important as there are several different types of models for rhetorical analysis, as we shall see in the sport communication example that follows. The third step is the application of the rhetorical analysis model to the text to expose meanings from the text. The final step is to write the research report using discovered findings from the analysis.

Frandsen and Johansen (2007), for instance, use rhetorical analysis to evaluate the effectiveness of a public apology by celebrated Danish handball coach, Anja Andersen, made on television to the public. Handball is a popular sport in Denmark, and Coach Andersen is internationally known for her accomplishments in the sport. In this case, she is coaching Slagelse, unbeaten at the time, and she is angered by a series of calls and makes physical contact with an official. She is sent off for the contact. Andersen orders her players to leave the court with her, but the team returns later to complete the televised game, losing to Aalborg DH. The next day, as the media savage her behavior, she holds a press conference and issues an apology. However, the apology appears not to be effective because the media continue with negative reports about Andersen's behavior. So why didn't the apology work? That was what Frandsen and Johansen decided to study using a rhetorical analysis model recommended by Keith Hearit. They find that Andersen fails to adhere to several expectations of an effective apology. For instance, Frandsen and Johansen note that

> she (Andersen) shifts the focus away from herself as a human being who seeks reconciliation and apologizes from the very bottom of her heart to 'all persons who are in need of an apology' (Andersen's words). . . . Anja Andersen does not explicitly accept full responsibility, but she expresses regret thereby acknowledging that she acted in a wrongful way. . . . She does not offer to perform an appropriate corrective action neither, like saying that in future she intends to behave differently during handball matches.
>
> (pp. 101–102)

Holdener and Kauffman (2014) also conducted a rhetorical analysis but use a different model – Benoit's image repair theory (IRT). They examine image repair strategies employed by Michael Vick in responding to charges of maltreatment of dogs. Michael Vick's encounter with the law was a major story in American sport at the time. Vick faced a barrage of negative media reports and attacks by animal rights and other groups. This chapter already briefly described another research study using a non-rhetorical textual analysis on the Michael Vick case. In the Holdener and Kauffman study, they sought to measure the effectiveness of Vick's press conference following federal charges, and IRT is used as an evaluative tool. They find that Vick accepts full responsibility for his actions, is contrite, and appears sincere in his apology. Particularly effective is his statement that he has "turned his life over to Jesus" (p. 95). Holdener and Kauffman conclude that Vick's apology is effective, noting that

> Vick received mostly positive reviews for his apology from the general media . . . on the field, Vick received a second chance from the Philadelphia Eagles. . . . In a unique twist, Humane Society CEO Wayne Pacelle offered Vick a second chance off the field.
>
> (p. 96)

Scholars seeking to critique sport communication use the method of **critical analysis** to help expose power, inequality, and oppression that impact sport communication. Guba and Lincoln (1994) argue that: "The term critical theory is (for us) a blanket term denoting a set of several alternative paradigms, including additionally (but not limited to) neo-Marxism, feminism, materialism, and participatory inquiry" (p. 109). Lichtman (2014) argues that critical analysis fosters a political and social agenda through examining issues of power and resistance with the goal of changing society. This perspective is affirmed by Creswell (2007), who claims that it is "concerned with empowering human beings to transcend the constraints placed on them by race, class, and gender" (p. 27). Guba and Lincoln (1994) go on to argue that the method for applying a critical methodology requires "a dialogue between the investigator and the subjects of the inquiry; that dialogue must be dialectical in nature to transform ignorance and misapprehensions . . . into more informed consciousness" (p. 110). Similar to rhetorical analysis, there is not a single method for critical analysis. Instead, a variety of methods can be used.

For instance, Kristiansen, Broch, and Pedersen's (2014) study of female professional soccer in America uses critical analysis from the perspective of Connell's critical gender studies, which is largely informed by the work of Antonio Gramsci. In an interesting choice of methods, rather than using historical literature and then applying critical analysis to expose power relations in the content of the literature, the researchers choose to conduct in-person interviews of four female elite soccer players in America and then use critical analysis to understand the interview data. The interview data consist of three interview themes of role models/socialization, media images/invisibility of female soccer players, and sexualization of the bodies of elite female athletes. The researchers conclude from their data:

> The interviewees saw themselves as proper role models for a sport that, in their opinion, struggles to overcome gendered barriers . . . their reasoning and devaluing of selves, female coaches and their coaching style symbolically reproduce the very same gender binary and order they are struggling against. In light of Connell's theory, this is the gender order in the sport field where a specific kind of hegemonic masculinity is considered to bare the symbolic characteristics of success. . . . Stereotypical notions of gender color their presentation.
>
> (p. 21)

Onwumechili (2014) also uses critical analysis to expose power imbalances in the administration of football in Nigeria and the struggle of football labor. He does this by using several models of critical analysis, including Marx, Horkheimer, and Gramsci. For instance, he argues:

> Though Gramsci wrote about the state in his home country Italy, his work today is applicable to differential power distributions in other nations, societies, and

organizations. In Nigerian football, management is able to control football and impose hegemony through 'capture' of certain critical aspects of football in the country . . . domination of seats in the nation's football association boardroom, accumulation of capital . . . collusion with football regulators, and taking advantage of cultural practices of power distance.

(p. 148)

Onwumechili's work leads to exposition of several problematic relationships between football labor and those who administer the game. He supports these relationships with practical examples. He concludes by showing how Jurgen Habermas's communicative action provides an opening to address inequalities through free expression and discussion among various classes – player labor and administration – in a "public sphere."

Lichtman (2014) describes **case study** as an "in-depth examination of a particular case (e.g. individual, program, project, work unit) or several cases" (p. 118). A selected case or cases involves collection of data through various sources, which help illuminate the case as it pertains to the variables of interest. However, some researchers wonder whether a case study is a method or if it simply reflects the subject of a study. While there are truths to this criticism, many scholars continue to regard case study as a distinct method.

The fact that case study refers to the subject of study and not the method makes it difficult to identify a guide for studying a case. In fact, Lichtman (2014) notes that:

I find that details of how to conduct a case study are not spelled out. . . . So, when you read that a particular piece of research is a case study or uses a case-study methodology, you might find a variety of ways of going about gathering data, analyzing data, and writing up the data.

(p. 1243)

However, despite those misgivings, others such as Creswell (2007) believe that credible procedures are available for conducting a case study. Creswell advises that a case study requires bounded subjects and a clear interest in results that focus on those selected cases. The next step is determining sources of data on selected cases before analyzing each data set to generate themes or other types of integrated findings about the case or cases. The final stage is interpreting the analysis in ways to provide insight on the cases.

Fujak and Frawley (2016) use a multiple case approach in their study of television ratings for a sample of fixtures for two Australian sport leagues over a five-year period. The goal is to determine if broadcast coverage of sport leagues is evenly distributed since "Australian sporting landscape is characterized by centralized broadcasting agreements that leave individual clubs at the mercy of league and broadcaster objectives in determining the nature and degree of their broadcast exposure" (p. 187). Fujak and Frawley select two cases of the Australian Football League (AFL) and the National Rugby League (NRL) for study. Data come from two providers of broadcast ratings in Australia for the period under coverage. Data show "significant variance was evident in the cumulative audiences recorded by each club within both the AFL and NRL" (p. 197). The results are at odds with the goals of both leagues that vow to be egalitarian, and there is surprisingly little correlation between team performances and broadcast exposure. Instead, broadcast exposure correlates with average broadcast audiences but in a skewed way, where Western Sydney receives 22% more exposure than non-Western Sydney, even though it had just 1.6% greater average broadcast audience.

Quantitative methods

For quantitative research methods, this chapter focuses attention on three types: experimental, content analysis, and survey research. These methods focus on analyzing data and generalizing results to a larger population compared to the sample from which the data are drawn.

Wrench, Thomas-Maddox, Richmond, and McCroskey (2013) point to **experiments** occurring "when a researcher purposefully manipulates one or more variables in the hope of seeing how this manipulation affects other variables of interest" (p. 290). Invariably, the experimental method helps establish a cause-and-effect relationship among studied variables. Generally, an independent variable is identified. This variable is manipulated through what is called a treatment with the hope that it produces an effect on a dependent variable. For instance, assume a hypothesis that persons who watch a lot of broadcast coverage of a particular sport team (A) are more likely to support that team (A) in a future encounter against another team (B) that receives little or no broadcast coverage. An experiment may be set up where a group of persons are fed several broadcast coverages of a high school team (Team A) while another group does not receive any coverage of a high school team. After a specified time, when an effect is expected to have taken place, both groups are shown two teams preparing to play against each other. One of the teams is Team A and the other is Team B. The expected result will be that most people in the group that watched lots of broadcasts will indicate a preference for Team A to win, whereas in the other group that did not watch any broadcast, there will not be a difference between those choosing Team A or B. If the actual result matches the prediction, then one concludes that the broadcasts caused the preference for Team A. This simple explanation is how experiments work. In reality there are additional controls to prevent the effects of spurious variables, among other mechanisms to ensure precision of the results.

As you can imagine, an experiment requires effective controls to ensure that the results are reliable. These controls start from selection of sample participants, where it is important to select the sample randomly when possible and to ensure that prior knowledge of the phenomenon being tested does not contaminate the test results. Because of these requirements, it is difficult to conduct experiments in sport communication, and it is not the most used method. However, if one is to test causality or the cause of a certain outcome, then experiment should be the choice. Furthermore, several types of experimental designs are available to researchers.

Northup and Carpentier (2015) use a 2x2x2 between-subjects experimental method to assess how racial stereotypes could be activated with a media story that has variables of image distinctiveness and positive/negative valence of an image and text. The study is tangential to sport communication but provides an example of how a significantly focused sport communication experiment may be conducted. In their work, Northup and Carpentier introduce sport communication with use of Michael Jordan and Michael Vick's images to denote image distinctiveness (i.e. images that participants in the experiment are familiar with). Jordan is a well-known basketball player and Vick a well-known American gridiron football player. Both men are Black. The researchers recruited 287 participants in the study but use 229 of them who are Caucasians. They are shown a media site with a negative crime story, which does not identify the race or name of the criminal. On the side of the story is an unrelated image of a distinctive Black man who is either smiling or frowning. After viewing the page, participants are asked to click to the next page that has the profile of a fictitious Black man without an image. Participants are then asked their first impressions of the profiled man and "how 'fun' of a friend they think he would be" (p. 142). The study finds that the Caucasian participants demonstrate activated stereotypes of a Black man after viewing the story with an image of a Black man placed next to the story in an unrelated issue. It did not matter whether the image of the Black man was distinctive (a known personality) or not.

A quantitative type of textual analysis is the **content analysis** method, which is sometimes referred to as quantitative content analysis. Content analysis involves examination of text in a systematic way, where the content of the text is made quantifiable. Neuendorf (2002) also demonstrates that "content analysis may be conducted on written text, transcribed speech, verbal interactions, visual images, characterizations, nonverbal behaviors, sound events, or any other type of message" (p. 24). In essence, there is a wide range of context where content analysis may be used. The key consideration is the measurement of content in a way that such content is amenable to quantification.

The process of content analysis requires clearly conceptualizing what the researcher intends to measure and defining the unit of analysis. The unit of analysis refers to what units should be selected as data for collection. For instance, a researcher may measure whether *El Comercio*, a leading Peruvian newspaper, is favorable in its coverage of female sport in the country. The unit of analysis may be an entire article, which is coded favorable, neutral, or negative depending on the significant presence of positive or negative comments in the article. Of course, the variables positive, neutral, and negative are defined in detail with attributes for easy identification by coders. Those variables are coded 3, 2, and 1 denoting positive, neutral, and negative, respectively. Importantly, coders, usually two or more, are trained to easily recognize the variables in each article and to code each one appropriately. After data are collected, researchers use statistical methods to analyze the data and draw conclusions.

Denham (2014) employed content analysis in studying how investigative reports in the *New York Times* about doping and other malpractices in the horse racing industry in America set the agenda for similar reports in American national and regional media. Denham noted that the *New York Times* began publishing a series of reports on doping and other malpractices in American horse racing in March 2012. He then hypothesizes that such an investigative series is likely to influence how other media report on horse racing. He proceeded to set up a content analysis study of American national media including radio, television, and newspapers. He was also particularly interested in the local New Mexico newspaper – the *Albuquerque Journal* – since New Mexico is directly cited in the *New York Times* investigation. To identify agenda setting by the *New York Times*, Denham's study involves media contents from January 1, 2011, until the first date of the *New York Times* report (Period 1). Additionally, he looks at reports after the investigation reports began. This is Period 2, stretching till November 2012. The goal is to compare the two periods in order to find out whether media contents changed after the first investigative reports in the *New York Times*.

Denham ran several statistical tests, such as bivariate analysis and regression analysis, on the quantitative data generated from the content analysis. He finds that the media more frequently mention deceased horses, drug use, and disciplinary actions in their reports during Period 2 compared to Period 1. Remarkably, Denham finds that "at the national level, intermedia agenda-setting effects appeared most pronounced in broadcast news, which revealed almost no attribute observations (i.e. malpractices) prior to the *Times* coverage" (p. 30). Importantly, Denham also finds that several reports on radio, newspapers, and magazines actually cite the *New York Times* investigation in their reports. Also important is that the *Albuquerque Journal* reacted quickly by citing malpractices after the first *Times* report.

Chambliss and Schutt (2013) write that **survey research** is a popular research method because it has "three advantages: (1) versatility, (2) efficiency, and (3) generalizability" (p. 129). Researchers use survey research for collection of all types of data and are able to do so quickly on so many issues and covering a large number of research participants. Finally, because it is used to collect data from a representative sample, it can be generalized to a larger population. Ultimately, survey research comes in handy when a researcher seeks to study a large population of people. In such a case, the researcher collects data from a sample that is systematically or randomly drawn from that population. The purpose is to "ask questions about the beliefs, attitudes, and behaviors of respondents for the purpose of describing both the characteristics of those respondents and the population(s) they were chosen to represent" (Frey, Botan, & Kreps, 2000, p. 198).

The process for survey research begins by designing the data collection instrument, which is often a questionnaire. This questionnaire is carefully designed to collect data that helps the researcher answer the research question that he or she has set out to investigate. The questionnaire is closed-ended, which means that possible answers to each question are provided to the participant in a multiple-choice format. This is critical because it eases the coding of data in a quantifiable format. However, there are times when a questionnaire includes open-ended questions, and this occurs when alternative answers to the question may be unknown or too numerous to place in a few categories. The next stage is to determine the number of participants to sample and then what sampling method to use in selecting the sample. There are a number of sampling methods to choose from, but it is more appropriate to choose a probability sampling method because that allows generalizability of research results to a larger population. After designing the instrument and selecting the sample, the next phase is to collect the data using the instrument. Data can be collected in-person, online, through regular postal mail, or through the telephone. After data collection, a statistical analysis package is used to analyze collected data before reporting the result.

Wang, Cheng, Purwanto, and Erimurti (2011) use the survey research method to investigate "determinants of a sports team sponsor's brand equity and whether the proposed structural relationships vary across countries" (p. 1). Taiwan and Indonesia are two countries used for this research, and a sport team is selected from each of the two countries. The researchers use Sinon Bulls, a baseball team, and its major sponsor (Acer computer) to represent Taiwan. For Indonesia, they use PSIM, a soccer team, and its major sponsor (Djarum/a tobacco producer). A total of 474 persons participated in the study, with roughly even participation in both countries. The questionnaire was modified from four scales previously used to collect similar data. A further modification was translation of original scales, which were in the English language, to appropriate local languages in both Taiwan and Indonesia. Despite these modifications, the questionnaire tested highly in a reliability test used to determine the robustness of the research instrument. After the data were collected, various statistical tests were then applied to the data and results were reported. In both countries, the results show that higher sponsor credibility lead to higher sponsor brand equity, which refers to high positive recognition of the brand name. However, there are differences across countries. In Indonesia, high identification with the team is associated with perceived sponsor credibility, whereas in Taiwan, high perceived congruence between the sponsor and the sponsored team lead to high sponsor credibility.

Miloch and Lambrecht (2006) surveyed 492 people attending a grassroots sporting event hosted by a state association in the Midwest in America. The survey is intended to measure level of recall of sponsors and intention to purchase a sponsor's product. The researchers developed an in-person completed questionnaire that they gave to every fifth person exiting the grassroots event. They then used various statistical tests to analyze collected data, which they published in an academic journal. They find that recall rates are similar but somewhat lower than rates found in studies completed at mega events. Only 2% of the sample could name five or more sponsors while 11% could name three or more. Among the most recognized names are four, of which one is not an event sponsor but apparently gained by the fact that it had a huge signage as a sponsor of the venue. Two of the other three not only had multiple and visible signages but also passed out souvenirs while the third also had multiple and visible signage and sponsored the same event for three years running. The researchers also find that volunteers at the event have better recall than the athletes. Purchase intention measurements indicate that those who expressed deep interest in the events and those younger than 55 years intend to purchase sponsors' products. Importantly, the researchers also find that having signage in a visible and high-traffic location increases recall.

REFLECTION

Maybe you are already familiar with a research study on a communication topic or on a sport topic. Maybe not. Maybe you are not familiar with research on sport communication. Perhaps, if you are not familiar with any of those, you know someone who is. If not, then think of some sport communication issue that you may want to study. Think in terms of whether a qualitative or quantitative method is appropriate for such a study. What makes you think that one of those methods is appropriate?

CHAPTER SUMMARY

The chapter points to the importance of research in sport communication because it informs new knowledge in the field and builds on existing ones. Importantly, because the field is relatively new, there is a major need for research in various areas in the field.

The chapter breaks down the research methods used in the field into two general categories of quantitative and qualitative. It describes differences between the two categories of research methods, noting that quantitative methods seek universal generalizations from a study, statistical measurements, and collecting data from a large number of cases. On the other hand, qualitative methods focus on detailed descriptions of a studied phenomenon and collecting data from fewer cases.

The chapter provides examples of various research methods that are qualitative in nature. Each of them meets the description of qualitative method mentioned in the earlier paragraph. Qualitative methods discussed in this section include interviews, textual analysis, thematic analysis, rhetorical analysis, critical analysis, and case study. An example of a research study is presented to support each method. For instance, Laucella (2010) uses textual analysis to study media coverage of Michael Vick's dogfighting case, and Onwumechili (2014) completes a critical analysis of the administration of football in Nigeria.

Three methods are provided as examples of quantitative methods. These are experimental, content analysis, and survey research, with an example of a research study presented as an application of each of the three methods. Northup and Carpentier's (2015) 2x2x2 between-subjects study of racial stereotype activation is an example of an experimental study, and Wang, Cheng, Purwanto, and Erimurti's (2011) investigation of two teams in Taiwan and Indonesia is presented as a survey research example.

DISCUSSION QUESTIONS

1. In which ways does research inform the field of sport communication? Provide examples to support your views.
2. What differentiates qualitative from quantitative research methods?
3. Must a researcher choose one of those two methods to study a sport communication issue? Is it possible to use both methods simultaneously to study a single issue?
4. How does the critical analysis method differ from a rhetorical analysis method?
5. In which ways does textual analysis differ or is similar to content analysis?
6. Of the methods presented in this chapter, which one is most appropriate for a study of cause and effect in sport communication? Why?
7. Please describe survey research. How does survey research differ from critical analysis or textual analysis?

ACTIVITIES

1. Visit the library or browse through a journal database with a focus on locating journals in the field of sport communication. Identify two academic articles from the journals. One of the articles must use a qualitative research method and the other a quantitative method. Review each article and report on what was studied, the method used, and what was found. Then write a report to present in class.
2. As a group, identify a sport communication topic that is amenable to study using a quantitative method. Select a sample for study, collect data, and analyze the data. Write a report of your study and present it.
3. Identify a sport communication issue covered recently in the media. Use a qualitative research method to obtain data on the issue and analyze it. Present a research report specifying the issue studied, method, and what was found.

VIDEO RESOURCES

Research Minute with Jimmy Sanderson, Clemson University. (YouTube/1.14 mins.). This video is a brief interview with Professor Sanderson on his research agenda in sport communication.

Do High Fives Help Sports Teams Win? (YouTube/1.53 mins.). Research study on how high fives correlate with wins in American basketball.

What Is.. ? Textual Analysis (YouTube/44.31 mins.). This video discusses how to do textual analysis.

A Survey in 10 Steps (YouTube/4.22 mins.). This is a quick introduction to survey research.

Scarlett Cornelisen (YouTube/7.29 mins.). Describes a study on how African states can cultivate sport development. It discusses communication aspects of this issue.

RECOMMENDED WEB RESOURCES

Human Kinetics. Explore four methods for collecting qualitative research. www.humankinetics.com/excerpts/excerpts/explore-four-methods-for-collecting-qualitative-research

Gashaw, A., O'Reilly, N., Dottori, M., Seguin, B., & Nzindukiyimana, O. (2015). Mixed methods research in sport marketing. *International Journal of Multiple Research Approaches*, 9: 40–56. www.tandfonline.com/doi/full/10.1080/18340806.2015.1076758?scroll=top&needAccess=true

Hunger, I., & Thiele, J. (2000). Qualitative research in sport science. *Forum Qualitative Sozialforschung/Forum: Qualitative Social Research*, 1(1): Art. 8. http://nbn-resolving.de/urn:nbn:de:0114-fqs000185.

REFERENCES

Chambliss, D., & Schutt, R. (2013). (4th ed.). *Making sense of the social world: Methods of investigation*. Los Angeles, CA: Sage Publications.

Creswell, J. (2007). (2nd ed.). *Qualitative inquiry & research design: Choosing among five approaches*. Thousand Oaks, CA: Sage Publications.

Denham, B. (2014). Intermedia attribute agenda setting in the *New York Times*: The case of animal abuse in U.S. horse racing. *Journalism & Mass Communication Quarterly*, 91(1): 17–37.

Frandsen, F., & Johansen, W. (2007). The apology of a sports icon: Crisis communication and apologetic ethics. *Hermes, Journal of Linguistics*, 38: 85–104.

Frey, L., Botan, K., & Kreps, G. (2000). (2nd ed.). *Investigating communication: An introduction to research methods*. Boston, MA: Allyn & Bacon.

Fujak, H., & Frawley, S. (2016). Broadcast inequality in Australian football. *Communication & Sport*, 4(2): 187–211.

Gibbs, C., & Haynes, R. (2013). A phenomenological investigation into how Twitter has changed the nature of sport media relations. *International Journal of Sport Communication*, 6: 394–408.

Guba, E., & Lincoln, Y. (1994). Competing paradigms in qualitative research. In Denzin, N., & Lincoln, Y. (Eds.), *Handbook of qualitative research* (pp. 105–117). Thousand Oaks, CA: Sage Publications.

Holdener, M., & Kauffman, J. (2014). Getting out of the doghouse: The image repair strategies of Michael Vick. *Public Relations Review*, 40: 92–99.

Kristiansen, E., Broch, T., & Pedersen, P. (2014). Negotiating gender in professional soccer: An analysis of female footballers in the United States. *Choregia: International Journal of Sport Management*, 10(1): 5–27.

Laucella, P. (2010). Michael Vick: An analysis of press coverage on federal dogfighting charges. *Journal of Sports Media*, 5(2): 35–76.

Lichtman, M. (2014). *Qualitative research for the social sciences*. Los Angeles, CA: Sage Publications.

Miloch, K., & Lambrecht, K. (2006). Consumer awareness of sponsorship at grassroots sports events. *Sport Marketing Quarterly*, 15: 147–154.

Neuendorf, K. (2002). *The content analysis guidebook*. Thousand Oaks, CA: Sage Publications.

Northup, T., & Carpentier, F. (2015). Michael Jordan, Michael Vick, or Michael Who?: Activating stereotypes in a complex media environment. *Howard Journal of Communications*, 26(2): 132–152.

Onwumechili, C. (2014). Nigerian football: Interests, marginalization, and struggle. *Critical African Studies*, 6(2–3): 144–156.

Wang, M., Cheng, J., Purwanto, B., & Erimurti, K. (2011). The determinants of the sports team sponsor's brand equity: A cross-country comparison in Asia. *International Journal of Market Research*, 53(6): 1–19.

Wrench, J., Thomas-Maddox, C., Richmond, V., & McCroskey, J. (2013). *Quantitative research methods for communication: A hands-on approach*. New York: Oxford University Press.

GLOSSARY

Ableism defines sporting thought and practices designed to cater solely to the abilities of able-bodied athletes.

Apologia is a speech of self-defense following an accusation.

Commodification is the process of valuing and commercializing an activity in a way that it becomes a commodity for purchase.

Defamation is a widely communicated message capable of tarnishing a person's image.

Emotional intelligence is the ability to control one's emotion in a way to solve communication problems.

Ethnie is a group of people who share common ancestry.

Evoked set is a group of products or ideas that consumers or an audience have in mind that is quickly recollected following a cue.

Fanzine is a fan-produced unofficial publication on a favorite sport team.

Fundamental attribution error occurs when one attributes another's actions to internal rather than external causes.

Gatekeeper refers to a person, usually in the media, who makes professional decisions on the news that eventually get to the public.

Gender marking occurs when the reported performance of an athlete, of a particular gender, is restricted within the perceived scope of the gender's abilities.

Globalization describes the increasing integration of peoples, cultures, and systems of the world.

Glocalization is the adaptation of a global phenomenon to local needs and culture.

Hegemony is the idea of a dominant class manipulating societal values so that their own worldview becomes that of the society.

Heroism culture refers to values, beliefs, and practices within sport that celebrate athletes who play while injured.

Image repair is action taken by an athlete or organization to positively sway public perception of its image following a crisis where the athlete or organization was held responsible.

Image rights grant an athlete legal rights to control the commercial value and exploitative use of his or her name or likeness.

Intellectual property rights provide legal protection of creative sport products.

Language descriptor refers to language used in describing athletic activity that frames how the public understands the activity.

Libel is a distributed written statement capable of tarnishing a person's image.

Media kit is a glossy organizational publication designed for the media that includes a media release, fact sheet, and other materials that help the media to write a story.

Media release is news disseminated by an organization in an official and formal manner to the media.

Media rights refer to legal rights awarded to the media to cover a particular sporting event or events. These rights often come in exchange for cash or other compensation.

Masculinity refers to enduring activities and images that are considered valuable to the achievement of male adulthood.

Market segmentation is the categorization of an audience into groups for marketing purposes.

Multidimensional communication involves delivery of information via a platform that allows various contexts of communication to take place.

Naming rights are awarded to an entity, usually a corporation, to name a sporting facility in exchange for cash.

Organizational climate describes the emotional and social atmosphere in an organization that are created by a leader.

Organizational culture is the assumptions, values, and symbols shared by an organization and its members over a period.

Programmed decision is a routine decision that consumers learn to make purchasing a product.

Property rights are awarded to a sport organizer allowing legal control of a sporting venue for a specified period.

Q-rating is a formula for determining the ability of a sport celebrity to effectively reach a particular audience.

Qualitative research seeks to make informed, rich descriptions of a studied phenomenon.

Quantitative research seeks to use statistical analysis of quantified data to generalize phenomenon.

Signage is a sign – usually a name, logo, or other graphic – identifying a sponsor that is placed in highly visible spaces in a sporting arena.

Slander is a widely communicated oral statement capable of tarnishing a person's image.

Sport analytics refer to the use of statistical models to analyze big data and inform sporting decisions.

Sport ritual refers to widespread regular cultural practices by a particular group or groups of sport fans.

Supercrip is a problematic media story focusing on an athlete's disability and his or her overcoming odds instead of on the athletic feat.

Super trademark is a special trademark right granted to unique sport organizers that include protection of multiple words, including mundane words, associated with the sport event.

Tailgate involves groups of fans in a pre-game party, usually outside the sporting venue, that includes drinking, eating, and playing games.

Talk show is a broadcast program that involves ongoing discussion that allows interaction between the host and listeners who call in.

Trademark is a device adopted and used by a manufacturer or merchant to identify goods and distinguish them from those manufactured and sold by others.

Transnational media refers to media that disseminates its content across national borders.

Troll is a person on the Internet who sows discord by upsetting others.

INDEX

ableism 131–2
Abrahamson, Michael 82
A.C. Milan 304
advertising 134, 184, 187, 188–9; advertising spots 188; athlete endorsers 239–40; challenges 190–1; sport video games 278; *see also* NBC; revenue
Africa: African athlete 150; merchandising in 185
amputee athletes 133; *see also* disability
analyst *see* color analyst
analytics 303–4; analytic attributes of organizations 304–7; benefits of 307–9; media organizations use of 312; sport gambling use of 312
Andersen, Anja 336
apologia 226–7
Armstrong, Lance 190
athlete rights 290–1; limits to rights 291; publicity 290
Athletic Bilbao 154
Australia 29; aboriginal 151; Canterbury Bulldogs 222; Rules football 151; television ratings study 338–9

Barcelona FC 164–5
Belch, G. 239, 241; Belch, M. 239, 241
Belichick, Bill 253
Benoit, W. 219, 221–3
Billings, A. 112, 113–14, 271–2; Butterworth, M. 112, 113–14, 271–2; Turman, P. 112, 113–14, 271–2

Black magic 151, 173
blogs 98; blogger 13
branding 62, 195–6; brand awareness 62; brand equity 62–3; brand loyalty 63; celebrity athletes 240; product image 62
Brazil: advertising revenue 184; Marcelo 256; Olympics at 218; Ronaldo 255; Zika virus 263
Britain *see* United Kingdom
BSkyB 183
BT Group 83

cable television 83
Canada 28
Canal Horizon 85
Caucasian 150, 151
celebrity 236; categories of 238–9; endorsement risks of 241–2; factors in 238; financial returns of 240; as product endorsers 239–40; selecting endorser 242
Chabal, Sebastien 89
Chad 192–3
Chadwick, Henry 6
Chaffey, D. 93–4, 102
Chelladurai, P. 45–6; Reimer, H. 45–6
China: sponsorship 185
climate 49; organizational climate 49
coach *see* interpersonal communication
color analyst 12
columnist 12

commentator *see* play-by-play announcer
commodification 181
communication 3, 194, 307
communication theory 318; affective disposition theory 323–4; communication privacy management 320–1; critical theory 325–6; functions of 319; general systems theory 324–5; image repair theory 327–9, 336; relationship management theory 322–3; relationship to research 319–20; social identity theory 326–7; transformational leadership 321–2
community relations 67, 123
competition laws 290
concussion 256–7; Centers for Disease Control and Prevention (CDC) toolkit of 257–8; changing culture of 257–8; Chronic Traumatic Encephalopathy (CTE) 256; obstacles 258–9; World Rugby concussion guideline 258
Connor, Clare 52
Coombs, T. 217
crisis 216; communication of 217; confronting 222–3; image repair after 224–5; preparation for 220–2; types of 217
crisis communication *see* crisis
culture 5, 171; concussion culture 257; cultural change 306; individualism/collectivism 172; indulgence/restraint 174; masculinity/femininity 172; organizational culture 49; power distance 171–2; short-term/long-term orientation 173; uncertainty dimension of 172; women participation 174

Deaflympics 130 *see also* disability
defamation 287; elements of 287–8; libel 287; slander 287
Director of Information 10
disability 129–30; elite athletes 139; media coverage of 132–4; new media 137; power soccer 138; quad rugby 138
drug abuse 261–2; categories of prohibited drugs 262; horse racing industry 341; prevention communication 262
Dueck, Josh 138
Dumaresq, Michele 170

Ebola 263; communication strategy for 264; Confederation for African Football (CAF) 263; Congo DR 263; Morocco 263; negative communication 264
El Salvador 167–8
emotion 60; passion 322
endorsement 189–90; behavior clause 190; risks of 241–2
Entertainment Sports Programming Network (ESPN) 83, 84, 85
E-Sport *see* Sport Video Games (SVGs)
ethics 285; types of 294, 296
ethnic 145, 161; rivalry 154
evoked set 185
exclusive rights 183, 286

fact sheet 67; *see also* media kit
fan 111–12; cultivation of 122–3; dysfunctional 125; identity of 117–18; identity theory of 326–7; methods of sport consumption 116; motivations of 113–16; myth creation 123–4; rituals of 118–20; system theory of 324–5; types of 112; ultras 113
fantasy sport 269, 270; analytics of 312–13; fantasy wrestling 272–3; growth of 269; impact of 281; motivations to participate 271; revenue source 277; role of new media 270–1
fanzine 13
females banned from 146
FIFA 225–6; Ebola 263
film maker 13
Finland 212–13
France 89
freelance 14
fundamental attribution error 25

game 2; *see also* sport
gender 144, 146; media gendering 147–8; stigmatization of 148; unequal treatment of 148
Germany 254; unfair competition 290
Gestalt effect 25
Gilbert, Dan 60
globalization *see* mega sporting event
Graen, G. 43–4; Uhl-Bien, M. 43–4
Gretzky, Wayne 45
Grusky, O. 45

Hall, S. 168
halo effect 25
health communication 253; athlete motivation and 255–6; confidentiality of 253; heroism culture and 254; motivation of organization 253–5
hegemony 148
Henderson, Crazy George 119
Henze, Stefan 254
hero 235–6; development of 236–7
Hofstede, G. 171–4
Honduras 167–8
Hong Kong 288
Horne, J. 202; Manzenreiter, W. 202
horn effect 25
horse racing 341

identity 168; theory of 326–7
image 216; celebrity athlete and 240; repair of 327–9
intellectual property rights 289–90
International Association of Athletics Federations (IAAF) 212–13
International Cricket Council (ICC) 156; anti-racism policy of 156
International Olympic Committee (IOC) *see* Olympic Games
International Paralympic Committee (IPC) *see* Paralympics
interpersonal communication 3, 19–20; coach/athlete in 26–8; coach/parent in 28–9; emotion and 20; emotional intelligence and 20–1; goals of 21; parent/athlete in 29–30; self in 22–4; theory of 320–1
intrapersonal communication 3

Japan 78–9; newspapers in 78–9; Yomiuri Giants 78; *Yomiuri Shinbum* 78
Johari Window 23–4
Johnson, Magic 253
Johnson, Martin 51–2
Jordan, Michael 190, 240

Kanu, Nwankwo 164
Kenya 119; fan songs 119
Keshi, Stephen 52
Kournikova, Anna 236

Landis, Floyd 224
Lara, Brian 245
Larson, C. 58, 59
Laumann, Silken 261
leadership 38; functional 42; leaders 39, 40; leadership communication 37, 39; leadership communication theory 321–2; relationship leadership 43–4; situational leadership 42–3; styles of 41; trait in 41; transformational leadership 44
legal issues *see* defamation
Lennon, Neil 154
liberalization 85
Liberty Media Group 184–5
Lin, Jeremy 241; celebrity extinction of 241
Lindemann, K. 137–8; Cherney, J. 137–8
Littlejohn, S. 326
Lochte, Ryan 218
Lombardi, Vince 51

McChesney, R. 6
McQuail, D. 131
magazine 80–1; decline 81; sport magazines 80–1
management 40; manager 40
Mandela, Nelson 39
Maradona, Diego 246
marketing 186–7; complex decisions in 186; programmed decision in 187; segmentation in 187; strategy of 186
masculinity 145, 148; naming and 146
Maslow, A. 21, 59
Maslow's Hierarchy of Needs 21, 59–60
mass communication 4; sport media theory 323–4
media conference 64–5
media interviews 65
media kit 65
media organization 11, 83; informing consumers 312
media relations 63
media relations officer 10
media releases 64
media rights 182–3, 286–7; freedom of speech 287; revenue from 77; rights of organizers 288–9; *see also* revenue
mega sporting event 201–2; employment opportunities 204; globalization and 206–10; growth of 202–3; physical

facility development of 203; promotional opportunities of 203; public support for 204; resistance to 205–6; tax revenue from 204; tourism 204
merchandise 123, 185
Montana, Joe 291
multidimensional communication 4
Murdoch, Rupert 183
Muslim countries 5; women participation in 5
myths *see* fan

Na, Li 245–6
nation 161
National Broadcasting Company (NBC) 132–3
National Broadcasting Company Universal (NBCUniversal) *see* NBC
National Hockey League (NHL) 313–14
nationalism 161; expression of 161–4; politics of 167; rituals of 163
new media 93, 138; characteristics of 95; Facebook 94, 98; functions of 100–2; growth of 102–3; trolls in 106; types of 97–100
newspaper 78; decline of 80; ownership of teams 78; sport facility building 78–9
news values 88–9
Nigeria 24–5; endorsement risk in 242; Enugu Rangers of 166–7; football administration of 337–8; Igbo nationalism 166; myth of Thunder 124; naming women teams in 146–7; newspapers 79; uncertainty dimension in 172–3; *West African Pilot* 79; ZAC clubs 79
Nike 193; Air Jordan 240
Norway 140–1
novelty games 145

Odemwingie, Peter 218–19
Oliseh, Sunday 254–5
Olympic Games 184; International Olympic Committee (IOC) 130; public interest broadcasting and 184; super trademark 293
online news media *see* new media
Oramedia 76
organizational communication 3–4

Paralympics 131, 139–40; International Paralympics Committee (IPC) 131, 139–40; Paralympicsport.tv of 140
parent 29; types of 29–30
Park, Chan-ho 167; *see also* South Korea
Pederson, P. 188–9, 191, 194; Laucella, P. 188–9, 191, 194; Miloch, K. 188–9, 191, 194
Pekerman, Jose 51
Performance Enhancement Drugs (PEDs) *see* drug abuse
personal selling 187
persuasion 58; appeals in 58–9; evidence of 61; premises of 59–61
Pienaar, Francois 38–9; *see also* South Africa
Pistorius, Oscar 138, 140, 335
play-by-play announcer 12
power 50; sources of 50–1
print media *see* traditional media
promotion 182–5, 187, 188
public figure 288
public interest 286, 288, 291; *see also* Olympic Games; World Cup
publicity 187; publicist 13
public relations 187; public relations officer 10

Q rating 242–3
qualitative research 333; case study 338–9; critical analysis 337–8; interview 333–4; rhetorical analysis 335–6; textual analysis 334; thematic analysis 334–5
quantitative research 333; content analysis 340–1; experimental 339–40; survey research 341–2

race 144–5, 149–50; portrayal of 150; stereotypes of 150; taunting 151; underrepresentation of 150
racism *see* race
radio 81–2; sport talk in 82
Real Madrid FC 49
reporter 11
reputation 216–17
research *see* qualitative research; quantitative research
revenue 182; advertising 184; gate receipts 182; media rights 182; subscription television 183–4

ritual *see* fan; nationalism
rivalry 124–5
Roche, M. 206–10
Rodman, Dennis 247–8
Rome, Jim 84
Rome Convention 183
Rooney, Wayne 190

satellite television 202
Scahill, Des 82
Semenya, Caster 170–1; *see also* South Africa
sideline reporter 11
Sidhu, Heena 106
small group communication 3
social media specialist 10
South Africa 38; identity 118; short term orientation in 173; Springboks of 38, 39; Supersport TV of 85; vuvuzela 119
South Korea 167; *Dokdo* 167
Spain 80; Catalan nationalism in 164; *Marca* 80
Special Olympics 139; *see also* disability
spectator 112; *see also* fan
sponsorship 185–6, 191–5; challenges of 194–5; impact of signages 343; naming rights in 191–2; placement rights in 192; relationship marketing 194; sponsor credibility 342
sport 2; *see also* game
sport analyst 12
sport economics 182
sport editor 12
sport marketer 10
sport organization 122, 185; communicating athlete health 253–5; image of 219; international sport organization 225–6
sport producer 12
sport researcher 13
sport show anchor 12
sport talk show host 13
sport video games (SVG) 275; different from fantasy sport 276–7; FIFA 17 280; growth of 268; impact of 281; motivation to play 278–9; revenue source of 277; social stereotyping of 277–8
state 161; *see also* nation
stereotype 25–6; activated racial stereotypes 340

Stodgill, R. 41
strategic communication 57–8, 70–2; theory of 322–3
subscription television *see* revenue
substance abuse *see* drug abuse
summarizer *see* color analyst
supercrip 134

Tajfel, H. 117, 236–7; Turner, J. 117, 236–7
television 83; rights in 83; sport talk in 84; transnational 84–6
tennis 314–15
theory *see* communication theory
trademark 291–3; courses of action 292–3; fair use doctrine 292; international violations of 293–4; super trademark protection 293
traditional media 75; types of 76, 138
Trail, G. 115; James, J. 115
transgender 169–70; female-to-male transsexual 170; identity in 169–70; intersex 170; male-to-female 170; sex reassignment surgery 170; transsexual 170
transnational media 85–6; *see also* liberalization
Twitter 99, 169; hashtag identity in 169

Ugboajah, F. 76
ultra *see* fan
Under Armour 190; branding of 195–6
United Kingdom: ethics in rugby 296–7
United States: culture 172; fan engagement 309; limits to publicity rights in 291; National Basketball League (NBA) heroism culture 254; National Basketball League (NBA) media rights 183; National Football League (NFL) myths 124; sport advertising 77; Title IX 155–6
Unlawful Internet Gambling Enforcement Act 269

vertical integration 184
Vick, Michael 225, 334; image repair of 336
video game designer 14

Wakefield, K. 125; Wann, D. 125
Ward, Hines 247; *see also* South Korea
Weaver, W. 3, 22; Shannon, C. 3, 22
WeChat 100

wheelchair athlete 133, 134–5; media consumption of 135; media coverage of 134–5; see also disability
Whiteness 151
Wiio, O. 3
Winmar, Nicky 151
Woods, Tiger 240

World Cup 184; public interest broadcasting of 184
writer *see* reporter

Youtube 99–100

Zika virus *see* Brazil